John H. Elliott

Suggestive Outline Bible studies and Bible readings

John H. Elliott

Suggestive Outline Bible studies and Bible readings

ISBN/EAN: 9783337171599

Printed in Europe, USA, Canada, Australia, Japan

Cover: Foto ©Lupo / pixelio.de

More available books at **www.hansebooks.com**

OUTLINE BIBLE STUDIES

AND

BIBLE READINGS.

EDITED BY

JOHN H. ELLIOTT.

———⋆•⋆———

ALBANY, N. Y.:
D. R. NIVER, PUBLISHER.
46 North Pearl St.
1883.

G. H. REYNOLDS, Printer,
395 Broadway, Albany, N. Y.

PREFACE.

The work of the present volume was undertaken by the editor in response to the earnestly expressed desire of many with whom he has had sweet fellowship in the truth, who wished to have access to many of the readings in his possession. Furthermore, the desire seemed to be general for a book which should take in a larger scope of truth than a former volume of similar character, touching at least on all of the principal points that should be used in testimony for the Master.

The careful topical arrangement and analytical index, which are features of this work, will commend the book to Bible students, and will, we trust, meet a long and widely felt want. If it results in a fuller and deeper study of those precious portions of the Word which are too often neglected, it will have met the purpose and desire of the one who has been greatly blessed and instructed in its collection and arrangement.

Thanks are due for the special favors so kindly and readily granted by many honored teachers of the Word of God, to whom we are indebted for the larger part of the valuable matter which appears in these pages.

JOHN H. ELLIOTT.

MINNEAPOLIS, MINN.

ADVANTAGES OF BIBLE READINGS.

BY REV. GEORGE F. PENTECOST, D.D.

"Bible readings" is a term of very wide application. It may apply to the old-fashioned — and it ought to be an ever new and current fashion — expository service, or to a topical reading and explanation of the Scriptures, to the simple reading of Scriptures from different portions of the Word that are germane, without note or comment, or, it may be a homiletical reading of a whole chapter or book. Any or all of these kinds of Bible reading are profitable and legitimate.

It is a term now used in contradistinction from mere textual preaching, in which a single text is brought to the attention of the people, and that text opened, developed, and applied. A Bible reading, on the other hand, leads the people over a wide tract of Scriptures, and gives a many-sided view of a subject from a Biblical, rather than from a pulpit, standpoint. In the one case, it is as though an ardent admirer and lover of flowers should pluck a fair and beautiful rose from his green-house, bring it into his parlor, show it to his guests, and descant on its beauties, give them a whiff of its fragrance, and then pick it to pieces, showing them in turn leaf, petal, corona, and stamen. In the other case, it is as if the same man should carry his guests into his rose-house and walk with them through that wilderness of beauty and floral wealth, pointing out, in general terms, the difference in variety, or some striking feature of a particular flower, leaving them to pluck, here and there, as they went through, to carry away with them. Both methods are useful and desirable — neither should be neglected. Upon the whole, I think the Bible reading the more important and productive of the most good ; helping the people more than the modern and almost exclusive method of textual and essay style of preaching. As to the advantages of Bible-readings, I would suggest the following: —

1. You get a more compresensive knowledge of the mind of the Spirit. Take, for instance, a case like this: The Epistle to the Romans abounds in striking *texts*, from each of which an isolated truth may be strikingly illustrated. But the whole book deals with a grand thought; viz.: The righteousness of God, and how He can be so, and yet the justifier of the ungodly. Now, there would be great

advantage in so reading the thread of this argument out of the book, and pointing out the illustrations and exhortations of the apostle in the course of his argument. Or, take the Epistle to the Hebrews, which is, in the main, an earnest entreaty to the Hebrew converts not to depart from the faith of Christ and go back to Judaism. It becomes, in its development, a magnificent setting forth of sin and unbelief as the great enemies of the believer, and the atonement and Word of God (for faith to rest on) as the great cure and defense for this double disease and two-headed enemy. No mere text, or a dozen of them, could in anywise give a congregation any adequate idea of that sublime book, containing, as it does, such a wealth of instruction and comfort. And yet a reading, or two or three, would put a congregation of Christians in possession of the hidden treasures of grace therein. Here, for instance, is a little analysis of the book which would afford twelve readings from it — one based on each chapter: 1. The Sin-Purger. 2. The Captain of our salvation. 3. Christ the Head of His house. 4. His people's rest. 5. The Great High Priest. 6. The Forerunner. 7. The Surety of the better covenant. 8. The Minister of the sanctuary. 9. The perfect Offering. 10. The obedient One. 11. Object and Pattern of faith. 12. The Prince and Pattern of faith. 13. The great Shepherd of the sheep. Around these leading thoughts, in these chapters, all the chapter may be grouped and embraced. Or, take "the better things of Hebrews," and you have a rich mine. Or the key-word "*once*," as it appears in the same book, and you may unlock a mine of riches with it. And so, indeed, every book in the Bible may be treated, with untold advantage, and in a way that preaching from a single text could never afford.

2. This method awakens an astonishing interest among the people in the Bible itself, and helps and inspires them in their own personal study of the precious volume. Any method that sets the people to reading and searching the Scriptures for themselves is *a* best method.

3. It greatly enriches the life and mind of the preacher himself. The minister who studies texts alone, or, indeed, who studies texts so largely as most ministers do, can never be a *full* Biblical preacher. Besides, it gives to the minister such a wealth of material, that his embarrassment will be for opportunities to preach, and not where his next sermon is to come from. My Wednesday evening Bible reading service always supplies me with more "texts" to preach from than I can possibly use up for "sermons." After a course of Bible readings in a New England city, a distinguished clergyman and doctor of divinity came to me and said: "These Bible readings are a revelation to me." "In what way?" I queried. "Why, in this: *I never dreamed there was so much material for sermons in the Bible.*"

He had fallen into the pernicious habit of using the Bible to supply him with suggestive texts, and then weaving the sermon from his own brain or from books. What the Church needs to-day, and what sinners need too, is to be flooded and saturated with God's thoughts. and not with our thoughts *about* God's thoughts.

4. Bible readings tend to promote a much better *style* or *manner*, in preaching. That is, it encourages the preacher in the use of the easy, conversational (not necessarily colloquial) style of address, which does not weary the people as the modern, bad, semi-oratorical manner does. There are but few orators in or out of the pulpit; and it is the worst of folly for a man who is not an orator by the gift of God, to attempt to be one by the aid of the master of elocution. Any man who is called to preach can talk or discourse ($\lambda\alpha\lambda\epsilon\omega$) the Gospel. Even a man of ordinary talent can be a man of extraordinary interest, if he only be the bearer of rich and precious gifts. The Church has too long depended on great *human* abilities in her ministers; she will be far richer when she demands of her ministry more of God's words and less human thinking poised on oratorical wing, and flashing with rhetorical light. Many a good minister who has failed as a pulpit orator may be a successful and sought-after man, if he will abandon that role, and be the simple bearer of good news and the teacher of God's thoughts. I know a man, and all the world knows him, who utterly failed as a preacher, but who, with his heart burning to communicate the Gospel of Christ, said to himself, I can, at least, read God's Word to the people; and now no building in any city can contain the people who are always anxious to hear him read God's Word and offer his homely, but heart-burning comments upon it as he goes rushing along, Bible in hand, from Genesis to Revelation, gathering and scattering honey from every book in his bee-like flight through the garden of the Lord. Men wonder at the secret of his power, and don't understand why many a great preacher has empty benches for an audience, while this unlettered man has crowds of the common people — yes, and the uncommon too — to hear him gladly. "Why and what?" Answer: "They come to hear the Word of God, not the thoughts of men."

5. It was the Master's method, and also that of the great apostle. "And He preached ($\epsilon\lambda\alpha\lambda\epsilon\iota$) the word unto them" (Mark ii, 2). He talked to them of the Scriptures. No oratory here. No preaching in the modern sense here — simple discourse, in which he repeated and commented on the Word of God as to his disciples (Luke xxiv): "And beginning at Moses and *all* the prophets, He expounded unto them in all the Scriptures the things concerning Himself." What a Bible reading that must have been! Some modern preaching critic, doubtless, would call it a "grasshopper exegesis"

(with a sneer at the Bible reading method), because, forsooth, instead of expatiating on one text the Master jumped from one passage to another to give a whole idea of Himself. Paul did likewise: "And when they had appointed to him a day, there came many unto his lodging, to whom he expounded and testified the Kingdom of God, persuading them concerning Jesus, both out of the law of Moses and out of the prophets, from morning until evening" (Acts. xxviii, 23). This was Bible reading. I do not wonder that he felt the need of the parchment he left at Troas, and longed for it, and charged Timothy to bring it to him. These were no well written sermons that he wanted to preach over, but the Scriptures out of which he wanted to give Bible readings.

BIBLE READINGS.

BY A. J. GORDON, D.D.

BIBLE readings have come to be one of the most interesting features in the religious service of many of our churches. The interest that has grown up in connection with these exercises should be the occasion of sincere gratitude on the part of all lovers of the truth. The time is very recent when it was the problem to know how to win the attention of the church-goers to scripture exposition. Now the most attractive service which can be offered to many congregations, is the Bible reading. We are acquainted with a pastor who holds one service on the Lord's Day, in which he simply reads the Word, without note or comment, letting one passage interpret another, and one text light up another; and so great is the interest in the service that the church is always crowded when it occurs.

We have sometimes heard severe criticisms passed upon the method, now much employed, of expounding the Scripture by the concordance, taking some word-phrase in a given text, and tracing it through the whole Bible, and so unfolding the meaning of a passage by tracing out all the threads of thought running from it and woven up with it. It is charged that it is an indolent method, making little demand for severe thought and rigid meditation. But we are inclined to think that it is the simplest and most natural plan of Scripture exposition. The anatomist, when he would study the structure of the human body, picks up a nerve or a vein or an artery, and follows it out in all its branchings. Every doctrine has its nerves running through the whole body of Scripture; every text has its veins through which the life blood of its thought courses; and the true anatomical method is to dissect and trace out these nerves and veins.

The tracing of a word throughout the Scripture is not a fanciful or trivial method of study. For words are inspired when found in the pages of the Bible. They are the shining way-marks which the Holy Ghost has fixed for us, to guide us throughout the mysteries of Scripture. They are often the illumined footprints by which we can trace the way of Him "whose goings-forth have been of old, from everlasting." Hence the word-study of the Bible is by no means to be despised. And we believe that it is not too much to say, that of the commentaries which have been written on the Scriptures, the concordance is the best. Hear the weighty testimony of Bishop Horsely on this point. He says: "It is incredible to any one who had not made the experiment, what a proficiency may be made in the knowledge that maketh wise unto salvation by studying the Scriptures with reference to the parallel passages, without any other commentary or expositor than that the different parts of the sacred volume mutually furnish for each other." Let the most illiterate Christian study them in this manner, and let him never cease to pray for the illumination of the spirit by which these books were dictated, and the whole compass of abstruse philosophy and recondite history shall furnish no argument with which the perverse will of man shall be able to shake this learned Christian's faith.

Of course we do not imply that Scripture study should end with the concordance. After the threads have been traced out and unraveled from the web of Scripture, then comes the reweaving them into such patterns of beauty as shall delight the eye, and into such garments of grace as shall fit the various forms of human need. We need despise nothing that can make the gospel plain and attractive; illustration, argument, experience and parable; anything that may help man to discern the meaning of the word. But all is to be woven into and upon the strong warp of literal Scripture truth.

WHY WRITTEN.

BY A. J. GORDON, D.D.

NOTHING is more important for us than the discovery that the Word of God is the absolute resting place for our faith. Christ is, indeed, the supreme object of faith; but, since we know him only through the Scriptures, we must believe the Word in order to believe on Christ. There are many ways through which the temptation comes to us to take our eyes off from the written testimony of Scripture, and to fasten them on something else — upon tradition, or religious experience, or the testimony of conscience; but a glance at the matter will show us how absolutely God shuts us up to his Word for all that we need to know for our salvation and life.

Let us consider four passages from the Gospel and Epistles of John, as showing the purpose of his writing: "But these are written that ye might believe that Jesus is the Christ, the Son of God, and that, believing, ye might have life through His name (John xx, 31).

Here is the evidential purpose of the Word. Christ proved Himself the Son of God by many signs and wonders before his crucifixion; and "He showed Himself alive after His passion by many infallible proofs." Record was made of these things that we might have the strongest possible evidence of the Sonship of Jesus Christ. Many other signs truly did Jesus in the presence of His disciples which are not written in this book; but these are written that ye might believe that Jesus is the Christ, the Son of God." This is the first thing we are required to believe. "Whosoever believeth that Jesus is the Christ, is born of God" (1 John v, 1). "But how may I know that He is the Christ?" it may be asked. Not from tradition, not by some extraordinary revelation of the spirit to the heart, but by the record of facts which God has caused to be written. The first look of faith is fastened to evidence. There are things which we are required to believe without evidence, as we shall see later. But this truth of the Sonship of Jesus rests solely on the record of the miraculous facts by which he proved himself the Christ.

Believing, on the testimony of what is written, that Jesus is the Christ, we "have life through His name." But how do we know that we have life when we have believed? These things have I written unto you that believe on the Son of God, that ye may *know* that ye *have* Eternal Life, and that ye may believe on the name of the Son of God" (1 John v, 13). Here the thought is taken up exactly where the previous text dropped it. Believing the record, know that Jesus is the Christ; believing that Jesus is the Christ, we have life. And now these things are written that we may *know* that we *have* life.

The constant tendency is for believers to search in their own hearts for the evidence of their renewal and sonship. No doubt there are such evidences to be found, if they are truly born of God. But God does not send us these chiefly or first of all. The testimony of the word is first. The testimony of the consciousness is secondary. The inward witness we would not deny; but this can be trustworthy only as the transcript and fac simile of the written witness of Scripture.

From what is written we know Jesus Christ to be the Son of God; from what is written we know ourselves to be the sons of God through faith in Jesus Christ. And to every temptation to doubt and distrust, we should oppose with the same weapon that Christ thrice used against the Tempter. "It is written" (John i, 12, 13; iii, 30; v, 24; vi, 47; 1 John v, 11, 12), "and these things write we unto you, that your joy may be full" (1 John i, 4). What things? These: that the life was manifested; and through this life we have not only sonship, but fellowship, one with another, and pre-eminently "with the Father, and with his Son, Jesus Christ." Even our joy must have its spring in the record. We rejoice because from God's Word we know that we are sons. We do not know that we are sons because of the joy which we have in our own hearts. Joy comes from the great and wonderful truth which God tells us in his writings, but which we could never have found out ourselves alone, that we have fellowship, actual birth-kindredship, with Christ and the Father.

This joy will be perennial and full, because, instead of being pumped up from the shallow reservoir of our own feelings, it flows down from God himself through the channel of his Word. "These things write we unto you that your joy may be full;" full because the fountain is in God and Christ, and not in self. "We also joy in God through our Lord Jesus Christ, by whom we have now received the reconciliation" (Phil. i, 26; iv, 4; John xvi, 22; xvii, 13). "My little children, these things write I unto you that ye sin not" (1 John ii, 1).

Does it give license to sin, to know that by the atonement of our Savior, our sins have all been taken away and freely forgiven? So it has often been said; but not so does it seem to the Holy Ghost and to us. One sight or remembrance of the blood that was shed for the remission of our sins is mightier than all other arguments combined for dissuading us from sin. To be told that Jesus Christ has so settled the whole question of sin between us and God that now not the mercy only, but the very justice of God, demands that we should be forgiven when we confess our transgressions; what motive against continuing in sin is more powerful? We have fellowship with the Father and the Son," indeed, and, through them, "with one another" (i, 7). That is for our joy. But instantly occurs the thought of sin, the sense of which may well mar our joy, and check our rejoicings. Yes; but "the blood of Jesus Christ His Son cleanseth us from all sin" (i, 7); "and, if we confess our sins he is faithful and just to forgive us our sins, and to cleanse us from all unrighteousness." "My little children, these things write I unto you that ye sin not." Where can we find such dissuasions against sin as in the record of what Christ has suffered and accomplished to put away sin" (Rom. vi, 1, 2, 6, 15; Heb. vi, 6).

PRINCIPLES OF INTERPRETATION.

FIRST, the Bible is a plain book, addressed to men without reference to the distinctions in human society that are made by rank, wealth, and culture. It was to the people at large, and not to a learned few, Jesus gave the command, "Search the Scriptures" (John v, 39). Of the Bereans it is said, "These were more noble than those in Thessalonica, in that they received the word in all readiness of mind, and searched the Scriptures daily whether those things were so" (Acts xvii, 11). The stamp of nobility, therefore, which God recognizes is a searching, not a casual reading merely, but a devout and diligent searching of the Scriptures, not only on the part of the educated, but of those esteemed by the world as ignorant; "For after that in the wisdom of God, the world by wisdom knew not God, it pleased God by the foolishness of preaching to save them that believe" (1 Cor. i, 21). "Eye hath not seen, nor ear heard, neither hath entered into the heart of man, the things which God hath prepared for them that love him. But God hath revealed them unto us by his Spirit; for the Spirit searcheth all things, yea, the deep things of God. * * * Which things also we speak, not in the words which man's wisdom teacheth, but which the Holy Ghost teacheth; comparing Spiritual things with Spiritual" (1 Cor. ix, 12). Hence the uncultivated who know nothing but the words which the Holy Ghost teacheth, may have far greater wisdom than eminent scholars admired for their literary attainments; and the former may meet the opinions and theories and expositions of the latter with the solemn summons: "To the law and to the testimony; if they speak not according to these words, it is because there is no light in them" (Isa. viii, 20). The prophets were directed to speak to all the people (Ex. xix, 8; Lev. ix, 23; Num. xi, 29; Deu. xxvii, 15; Ps. lxvii, 3; Jer. xxvi, 8); and the Epistles are addressed to "all that in every place call upon the name of Jesus Christ our Lord" (1 Cor. 1, 2). There is not the slightest doubt, then, that God's Word is adapted to all, and intended for all, and consequently it is both the duty and the privilege of all His people, without exception, to make it their daily and delightful companion, and to search its sacred pages "as for hid treasures" (Prov. ii, 4).

Second, as the Bible is a plain book designed for people of common understanding, its deepest teachings may be learned with the aid of the Holy Spirit, who has been given without measure to all real believers; and we have no right to put upon its statements any other meaning than that which the simple and accepted sense of its words implies. For example, when we read the opening verse of Isaiah: "The vision of Isaiah the son of Amoz, which he saw concerning Judah and Jerusalem, in the days of Uzziah, Jotham, Ahaz, and Hezekiah, kings of Judah," we must take it for granted that the vision is really concerning Judah and Jerusalem, and not concerning ourselves of the present dispensation, whatever profitable lessons we may gather from it for the Christian Church. If Judah does not mean Judah, and Jerusalem does not mean Jerusalem, all through the prophecy, then, as Dean Alford well says to those who deny the clear assertion of the Holy Ghost about the two resurrections, separated from each other by the interval of a thousand years: "There is an end of all significance in language, and Scripture is wiped out as a definite testimony to anything." So when we find in the New Testament that one verse out of twenty-five refers directly or indirectly to the second coming of Christ, it is fatal to all correct principles of interpretation, and to any hope of understanding the Bible, to suppose that nothing more is meant than death, or the destruction of Jerusalem, or some other important event in the history of individuals and nations. If the Lord Jesus, and the Holy Ghost who dictated the words used by the Apostles, had meant death, they would have said death; and if we are at liberty to imagine that when they constantly spoke of His coming, they had in view something that has no more resemblance to His coming than midnight has to noon day, it will be apparent that their teachings become as vague and indefinite as the ambiguous utterances of the ancient heathen oracles. Long ago the Psalmist could say: "Thy word is a lamp unto my feet, and a light unto my path," and "the entrance of thy words giveth light" (Ps. cxix, 105, 130); but unless we take the words of Scripture in their plain, obvious, commonly accepted, and historical sense, they can only shed darkness along our way, and the need of an infallible Church to interpret will be at once perceived.

Third, "All Scripture is given by inspiration of God, and is profitable for doctrine, for reproof, for correction, for instruction in righteousness; that the man of God [whether learned or unlearned, ordained or unordained] may be perfect, throughly furnished unto all good works" (2 Tim. iii, 16, 17). The Scripture means writing, and a writing is made up of words, and words are composed of the letters of the alphabet; so that the words and letters of the sacred Scripture are given by inspiration of God. In hundreds of instances in the Old and New Testaments, we are told that "the word of the Lord came" to the prophets and people, and that "God said," and

"God spake." It is not enough, therefore, to hold that the thoughts are inspired, nor is there the slightest ground for the assertion, often made by those who ought to know better, that there are different degrees of inspiration, as superintendance, elevation, and suggestion, but the child of God should dismiss such fancies with contempt. All Scripture is inspired, and hence every little word is worthy of close attention, as we often find Christ and the Apostles establishing a great doctrine upon a single expression in the Old Testament, and upon the difference between the singular and plural number. "We have also a more sure word of prophecy; whereunto ye do well that ye take heed, as unto a light that shineth in a dark place, until the day dawn, and the day star arise in your hearts, knowing this first, that no prophecy of the Scripture is of any private interpretation. For the prophecy came not in old time [at any time] by the will of man. But holy men of God spake as they were moved by the Holy Ghost" (2 Peter i, 19-21). There are many who tell us it is well to avoid prophecy; but the Bible declares it is well to pay heed to it. There are many who tell us it is a dark place; but the Bible declares it is a light that shineth in a dark place. Moreover, no prophecy is limited to the range of the prophet's vision at the time it was uttered, nor to the fulfillment in the mere letter of the event predicted; but it reaches on to the grand climax in the world's strange history, even to the second coming of Christ. For the prophecy never came by the will of man, but holy men of God spake [as well as thought,] as they were moved by the Holy Ghost. "The Spirit of the Lord spake by me, and his word was in my tongue" (2 Samuel xxiii, 2). "This Scripture must needs have been fulfilled, which the Holy Ghost, by the mouth of David, spake before concerning Judas" (Acts i, 16).

Fourth, all Scripture is about Jesus Christ. "Search the Scriptures, for in them ye think ye have eternal life; and they are they which testify of me. * * * Had ye believed Moses, ye would have believed me; for he wrote of me"(John v, 39, 46). "And beginning at Moses, and all the prophets, he expounded unto them in all the Scriptures the things concerning himself. * * * These are the words which I spake unto you while I was yet with you, that all things must be fulfilled which were written in the law of Moses, and in the prophets, and in the Psalms concerning me" (Luke xxiv, 27, 44). For three Sabbath days Paul reasoned with the Jews out of the Old Testament Scriptures, opening and alleging that Jesus is the Christ (Acts xviii, 28). Paul persuaded them concerning Jesus, both out of the law of Moses, and out of the prophets, from morning till evening (Acts xxviii, 23).

If any one were to read Isaiah vii, 11-16, alone, he would not dream that Christ was there; but turning over to Matthew i, 22, 23, he learns that the complete fulfillment of the prophecy terminates in the person of our Lord. So, in the Old Testament, we read, "When Israel was a child, then I loved him, and called my son out of Egypt" (Hosea xi, 1). Is Christ in such a simple statement of an event that had occurred long before? Let the answer be found in Matthew ii, 15. Another prophet describes the grief of the mothers of Israel weeping over their children slaughtered and carried into captivity (Jer. xxxi, 15–17); but we learn that the real fulfillment of the woe extended to the infancy of Jesus (Matt. ii, 17, 18). Again, all the prophets, in type or prediction, testified beforehand His sufferings, and the glory that should follow (Num. vi; Ps. xxii; Isa. iii; Mic. v, 1, 2; Matt. ii, 23; Acts iii, 21; x, 43; 1 Pet. i, 11), showing conclusively that Christ is the great object of the Holy Ghost in Scripture, and that He not only took the place of His people in all ages, but went through their history in His own person, illustrating the precious and remarkable text, "We have not a high priest which cannot be touched with the feeling of our infirmities, but was in all points tempted like as we are, yet without sin" (Heb. iv, 15).

Fifth, all Scripture has a direct bearing upon our personal privileges and responsibilities. "Whatsoever things were written aforetime were written for our learning, that we through patience and comfort of the Scriptures might have hope" (Rom. xv, 4). The inspired apostle, mentioning a number of incidents that transpired during the journey of Israel from Egypt to Canaan, adds the important testimony: "Now all these things happened unto them for ensamples [or types, as it is in the margin], and they are written for our admonition, upon whom the ends of the world are come" (1 Cor. x, 2). If, then, we will keep in mind the two facts, so easily remembered, that every part of the Old Testament has Christ in it, and that every part was written for our learning, a new interest and power will be imparted to our study of God's Word. Leviticus, Numbers, Deuteronomy, and the books of Chronicles, will no longer be the dry and barren field, which so many Christians now find them to be in their perfunctory and profitless reading, but will become full of beauty and fragrance, even as the garden of the Lord; and they will be ready to exclaim of each particular portion, as Isaac said of Jacob's raiment: "See, the smell of my son is as the smell of a field which the Lord hath blessed" (Gen. xxvii, 27).

Sixth, all Scripture must be studied in the light which the Holy Ghost throws upon the inspired page. "Now we have received, not the spirit of the world, but the spirit which is of God, that we might know the things that are freely given to us of God. * * * But the natural man receiveth not the things of the Spirit of God, for they are foolishness unto him, neither can he know them, because they are spiritually discerned" (1 Cor. ii, 12, 14). The natural man is in a Christian no less than in an unbeliever, and if he brings nothing but his own intellect to the examination of the Bible, he will utterly fail to grasp its meaning, because it is discerned only by the Spirit. But it is comforting for the humble believer to read the precious assurance, "The anointing which ye have received of Him abideth in you, and ye need not that any man teach you" (1 John ii, 27). The spirit of truth has been sent as our abiding comforter, teacher, helper; and never does He take His departure from the child of God even for one moment. "The comforter, which is the Holy Ghost, whom the Father will send in my name, he shall teach you all things and shall bring all things to your remembrance whatsoever I have said unto you" (John xiv, 26). "When He, the spirit of truth, is come, He will guide you into all truth, for He shall not speak of Himself, but whatsoever He shall bear, that shall He speak, and He will show you things to come" (John xvi, 13). It is comforting, too, to know that the spirit in the Word does not direct our attention to our feelings, or to His own work in us, as the ground of assurance, but wholly to the work of Christ for us. "When the comforter is come, whom I will send unto you from the Father even the spirit of truth, which proceedeth from the Father, he shall testify of me" (John xv, 26).

Seventh, all Scripture must be studied in communion with Jesus Himself. Then will we say, as the two disciples on the way to Emmaus said: "Did not our heart burn within us while He talked with us by the way, and while He opened to us the Scriptures?" Still later, on the day of resurrection, He appeared to the assembled disciples, and, after showing that He was everywhere in the Old Testament, "Then opened He their understanding, that they might understand the Scriptures" (Luke xxiv, 32, 45). This is what we need, to have Him open to us the Scriptures, and to have Him open our understanding, that we may understand the Scriptures; and this need will always be met when we are walking in the enjoyment of unclouded fellowship with Himself. But how can this fellowship be maintained? "If ye keep my commandments, ye shall abide in my love; even as I have kept my Father's commandments, and abide in his love" (John xv, 10). "He that saith he abideth in Him, ought himself also so to walk, even as He walked" (1 John ii, 6). "If we walk in the light, as he is in the light, we have fellowship with one another, and the blood of Jesus Christ His Son cleanseth us from all sin" (1 John i, 7).

THE STUDY OF THE BIBLE.

BY REV. HORATIUS BONAR, D.D.

Do not skim it or read it, but *study* it, every word of it; study the whole Bible, Old Testament and New; not your favorite chapters merely, but the complete Word of God from beginning to end. Don't trouble yourself with commentators; they may be of use if kept in their place, but they are not your guide. Your guide is "the Interpreter," the one among a thousand (Job xxxiii, 23) who will lead you into all truth (John xvi, 13), and keep you from all error. Not that you are to read no book but the Bible. All that is true and good is worth the reading, *if you have time for it;* and all, if properly used, will help you in the study of the Scriptures. A Christian does not shut his eyes to the natural scenes of beauty spread around him. He does not cease to admire the hills, or plains, or rivers, or forests of the earth because he has learned to love the God that made them; nor does he turn away from books of science or true poetry, because he has discovered one book truer, more precious and more poetical than all the rest together. Besides, the soul can no more continue in one posture than the body. The eye must be relieved by variety of objects, and the limbs by motion, so must the soul by change of subject and position. Let the Bible be to us the book of books, the one book in all the world, whose every word is truth, and whose every verse is wisdom. In studying it, be sure to take it for what it really is, the revelation of the *thoughts* of God given us in the *words* of God. Were it only the book of *divine* thoughts and *human* words, it would profit little, for we never could be sure whether the words really represented the thoughts; nay, we might be sure that man would fail in his *words* when attempting to embody divine *thoughts;* and that, therefore, if we have only man's words, that is man's translation of the divine thoughts. But, knowing that we have *divine thoughts* embodied in *divine words* through the inspiration of an unerring translator, we sit down to the study of the heavenly volume, assured that we shall find in all its teachings the perfection of wisdom, and in its language the *most accurate expression of that wisdom* that the finite speech of man could utter. Every word of God is as perfect as it is pure (Psa. xix, 7; xii, 6). Let us read and re-read the Scriptures, meditating on them day and night; they never grow old, they never lose their sap, they never run dry. Don't let man's book thrust God's book into a corner; don't let commentaries smother the text; don't let the true and the good smother the truer and the better. Beware of light reading. *Shun novels,* they are the literary curse of the age; they are to the soul what ardent spirits are to the body. See that your relish for the Bible be above every other enjoyment, and the moment you begin to feel greater relish for any other book, lay it down till you have sought deliverance from such a snare, and obtained from the Holy Spirit an intenser relish, a keener appetite for the Word of God (Jer. xv, 16; Psa. xix, 7–10).

IS IT SAFE FOR ALL PERSONS TO STUDY ALL THE BIBLE?

BY A. J. GORDON, D.D.

IN the discussions between the early English Reformers and the Papists, in regard to giving the Bible to the common people, we remember this passage: "The Reformers, having claimed that the Bible, being written in plain language, could be read and understood by plain people, and that every man ought, therefore, to have it in his mother tongue, to study at will." The Papists answered that the common people, being uninstructed, might use it to their own hurt, and cited this illustration: "If thine eye offend thee pluck it out." "A plain man," said the Romanist, "might understand this text literally, and so consider it his duty to gouge out his offending eye with a sharp instrument, to the detriment of his sight, and even of his life; therefore, the Bible should be only in the hands of the priests and bishops, who are alone competent to interpret it for themselves and for their flock." This argument, with multiplied illustrations, was very vehemently urged against the attempt of the Reformers to translate the Scriptures and circulate them among the people. The common sense of Protestants, it is needless to say, rejects such reasoning as trivial and preposterous; yet, we have heard it repeated, substantially, of late, in several Protestant papers. And the manner in which it is used furnishes a singular instance of prejudice outwitting sound judgment, and the desire to carry a point logically, carrying away a most vital principle. We refer to the objections which have been urged against the study of unfulfilled prophecy. The *Advance* and *Watchman*, and several other papers, have recently put forth very serious, though guarded, cautions in this direction. They have pointed out the peril of fanaticism attending such study, and put in what, in plain terms, must be called a plea for ignorance, touching the prophetic Scriptures. We have known pastors, in one or two instances, to quarantine their churches against such publications as give attention to prophecy, lest their flocks might become infected with the dangerous desire to search into the unfulfilled predictions of God's Word. All of this we believe to be utterly in the face, both of God's plain requirements and of apostolic injunction and example. We plead for the study of unfulfilled prophecy as a duty most solemnly enjoined by Christ, and most sadly neglected by His church to-day. We plead for such a study as dares to note signs, and consider dates, even, since Christ has given dates by the score in the Apocalypse, and since He has distinctly required us to "discern the signs of the times." The example of God's early saints is certainly safe for us; and this is given in the words of Peter: "Searching what, or what manner of time the spirit of Christ which was in them did signify, when it testified beforehand the sufferings of Christ, and the glory that should follow." A text which has done wide service in these dissuasions from the study of unfulfilled prophecy, is the following from an eminent theologian. We quote it, that we may give the subjoined admirable reply to it from the pages of Faith's Record:—

"A late religious paper holds the following language:"—

'We once heard the venerable Dr. Archibald Alexander remark that an absorbing study of the unfulfilled prophecies was somewhat dangerous ground for unsteady people to tread; that it had unsettled some minds and wrecked others. This remark was made to the students of the Theological Seminary, at a time when the gifted but erratic Prof. George Bush was lecturing in Princeton, and ventilating some of his peculiar views on the prophetic Scriptures. His remarkable career, so brilliant in the opening, and so sad in the ending, well illustrates the danger of going beyond what is written as it regards the things of the future.' "In this statement of Dr. Alexander — if he ever made it — there is but one truth, and that is, there is some ground dangerous for unsteady people to tread; it would have been still truer if he had said that all ground is dangerous for unsteady people to tread, both of which the students probably knew before they went to Princeton. But again: it is the study of the 'unfulfilled prophecies' that is so dangerous; but how can one tell which are fulfilled and which are unfulfilled, until he studies them all? Put the Bible into the hands of a man who has just come to Christ, but who has never read the book, and caution him against reading the 'unfulfilled prophecies,' and what will he make of it? It may be objected to this, that the Doctor was talking to theological students. Well, is the matter so clear that all theological students can tell which are 'fulfilled and which unfulfilled?' It certainly is not so clear to all theological professors, for it is not long since one asserted that the predictions of Christ's second coming were all fulfilled at the siege of Jerusalem, though the last prediction of His second coming was made some years after that siege. History does not warrant the assertion of the Professor. Joseph, Moses and Daniel were clearly all students of the 'unfulfilled prophecies,' not to mention any others, and it did not seem either to 'unsettle' or 'wreck' them. But it may be objected that this is not quite fair, as the Doctor was speaking of 'unsteady people.' This is a vague expression, and we regret its use. It admits of an infinity of interpretations, for which we have no space; we will merely show who are not 'unsteady people,' and such may study even the 'unfulfilled prophecies.'

"1. Those are not unsteady who are anchored, as are all who trust in Christ" (Heb. vi, 19).

"2. Nor those who are taught of God" (John vi, 45).

"3. Nor those who study the Word with the purpose of doing what they are taught" (John vii, 17).

"The study of the 'unfulfilled prophecies' will not hurt those having these qualifications, and those who have them not will derive but little benefit from the study of any part of the Word.

"Furthermore, the Savior very sharply rebukes His disciples as 'fools and slow of heart to believe all that the prophets have spoken' (Luke xxiv, 25); whence we should conclude that 'the fools and slow of heart to believe' were just the ones that needed this very study of all the prophecies — fulfilled or unfulfilled. Finally, we are told (1 Tim. iii, 16), 'All Scripture is given by inspiration of God, and is profitable for doctrine, for reproof, for correction, for instruction in righteousness.' Who shall venture, then, to build a wall around any part of the Word of God, and put up over the gateway, 'Dangerous ground.' The closing sentence speaks of 'the danger of going beyond what is written as it regards the things of the future.' We heartily join in reprobating any study of any prophecies not 'written' in the Word of God, and as heartily join in reprobating the course of all — especially religious teachers — who say: 'Here is a part of the Word of God which I will neither study myself nor permit any one else to study, if I can help it.' This, truly, is 'dangerous ground' for unsteady people and all others; such would do well to study Revelations xxii, 19. It is just such assertions as these that have brought so many unbelievers into the Church, and not a few into the pulpits, even — that have given infidelity such a vantage ground. Were the Church true to its trust, did it study the whole Bible and live up to its teachings, the world would be presented with evidences of Christianity which no one would dare to gainsay."

MARK YOUR BIBLES.

BY REV. GEORGE F. PENTECOST.

I KNOW that Bible marking can be very meaningless and very mechanical, and that many silly people have begun to mark their Bibles, not for personal profit, but just to have a marked Bible. I saw a Bible, not long ago, that a man had hired a Bible student to mark for him. I thought, "Why did you not hire somebody to thumb it for you?" The thumbing would have done him as much good as the marking did. The Bible I mostly use is a wide margin Bagster, the gift of a friend. When it was first given to me it was so beautiful and clean that I felt very badly to discover one of its fair, white margins soiled by someone's dirty finger; but now its worn edges, with its margins covered with notes, its pages lined, and its lines underscored, are far more beautiful to me. I have put the practical results of three blessed years of study into that Bible with pen and ink, here a little and there a little. A thousand precious things are stored up in that book; with it in my hand I am never at a loss for a sermon, or word of illustration and help. The best thoughts of many Bible students are tucked away on half blank pages, the outline of scores of sermons, the indicated analysis of many books, the testimony and comments of saints upon certain passages. Now the help of all this is that you fix things in your mind and heart that you would not otherwise fix. On opening your Bible your mind is at once pricked with a thought or a memory; indeed, every one's own Bible should carry the student's own spiritual history in notes—not necessarily intelligent to anyone else. When I returned from a delightful pedestrian trip through Germany, Switzerland and northern Italy, I took a little map and marked the roads I had passed over, the mountains I had climbed, the towns and villages I had stopped in, and, with my note book and map, I can retrace many happy days. So I have noted in my Bible the sweet wells of salvation I have drunk from, the paths I have walked over, the cities I have been in, the mountains I have climbed, the valleys I have passed through, the people I have met and whose characters I have studied; and I love to take up the precious book and turn page after page, and refresh my mind and heart with many, many precious things, and so drink over again the waters of other days, and rest again at the many Elims I have found on the way. I have heard of a Christian lady whose Bible showed the following marks on the margin, over against some of the promises and truths of the Word: "T.," "P.," and "T." When asked what those letters meant, she said: "'T.' means, I have tried that promise, and

'T.' and 'P.' means, that having tried it, I have also proved it. There are many that I have only as yet tried, but when the answer comes, or the experimental knowledge of the truth comes, I make the completed note 'T.' and 'P.' How precious to keep account of God's promises by this system of " double entry!" Indeed, I often say to my friends, I have two Bibles: one the whole book, "from back to back," from Genesis to Revelations; that Bible I accept as God's word, on what to me is sufficient evidence. But then, I have another Bible that is peculiarly my own — a Bible within a Bible — consisting of those certain Scriptures of whose truth I have experimental and personal knowledge, and those truths not as yet tested by experience, such as resurrection and heaven, with all that is therein implied, but which are so confirmed to me and in me by faith, that it is all one as if God had revealed those things to me directly by His spirit, and not immediately through His Word. Of these, we can say our eye hath not seen, our ear hath not heard, neither hath it entered into our heart, the things that God hath prepared for us; but He hath revealed them to us by His Word and Spirit (1 Cor. ii, 9, 10).

These things comprise my Bible within the Bible, and daily this inner Bible is growing. This Bible I have marked out on the printed page of my study Bible. Let me say, that I think it well, also, to keep a Bible free from marks of any kind, to read in, that you may not be limited, or have the Word limited, by old thoughts. Our marking, important and helpful as I think Bible marking is, should not be allowed to "bind the Word of God." You must adopt your own system of marking. Do not take somebody else's method. And yet you may find many suggestions that will be helpful to you from the experience and work of others. For example, I have taken a camel's hair brush, and, dipping it into blue ink, I have passed it lightly over all those passages in the Word of God that speak of His love to man; such, for example, as John iii, 16 : "God so loved the world," etc.; and with red ink and the brush I have covered those passages that speak of the blood of Jesus Christ, in the New Testament; for example, 1 Peter i, 19; 1 John i, 7, and the blood of atonement in the Old. It is surprising how blue and red your Bible will be, thus marked. And then, suppose you were to take some purple ink, and cover all those passages that are closely related to, and are based on love and atonement ; you would still further have your Bible interpreted to your eye at a glance. And then, for contrast, take your pen and run a deep line of black around those passages that expose and lay bare the depravity and sinfulness of the human heart, and the fact of the righteous judgment of God to come, and the perdition of ungodly men; such, for example, as Gen. vi, 5; Isa. i, 5; Matt. xv, 19; Rom. ii, 6–9. But I forbear any further suggestion in this line, being assured that a hint to the wise is sufficient.

A SAFE DOCTRINAL BELIEF.

BY J. H. BROOKS, D.D.

I.

WE believe "that all Scripture is given by inspiration of God," by which we understand the whole of the book called The Bible; nor do we take the statement in the sense in which it is sometimes foolishly said that works of human genius are inspired, but in the sense that the Holy Ghost gave the very words of the sacred writings to holy men of old; and that His divine inspiration is not in different degrees, but extends equally and fully to all parts of these writings, historical, poetical, doctrinal, and prophetical, and to the smallest word, and inflection of a word, provided such a word is found in the original manuscripts (2 Tim. iii, 16, 17; 2 Peter i, 21; 1 Cor. ii, 13; Mark xii, 26, 36; xiii, ii; Acts, i, 16; ii, 4).

II.

We believe that the Godhead eternally exists in three persons, the Father, the Son, and the Holy Spirit; and that these are one God, having precisely the same nature, attributes, and perfections, and worthy of precisely the same homage, confidence, and obedience (Mark xii, 29; John i, 1–4; Matt. xxviii, 19, 20; Acts v, 3, 4; 2 Cor. xiii, 14; Heb. i, 1–3; Rev. i, 4–6).

III.

We believe that man, originally created in the image and after the likeness of God, fell from his high and holy estate by eating the forbidden fruit, and as the consequence of his disobedience the threatened penalty of death was then and there inflicted, so that his moral nature was not only grievously injured by the fall, but he totally lost all spiritual life, becoming dead in trespasses and sins, and subject to the power of the devil (Gen. i, 26; ii, 17; John v, 40; vi, 53; Eph. ii, 1–3; 1 Tim. v, 6; 1 John iii, 8).

IV.

We believe that this spiritual death, or total corruption of human nature, has been transmitted to the entire race of man, the man Christ Jesus only excepted; and hence that every child of Adam is born into the world with a nature which not only possesses no spark of divine life, but is essentially and unchangeably bad, being enmity against God, and incapable by any educational process whatever of subjection to His law (Gen. vi, 5; Ps. xiv, 1–3; li, 5; Jer. xvii, 9; John iii, 6; Rom. v, 12–19; viii, 6, 7).

V.

We believe that, owing to this universal depravity and death in sin, no one can enter the kingdom of God unless born again; and that no degree of reformation however great, no attainment in morality however high, no culture however attractive, no humanitarian and philanthropic schemes and societies however useful, no baptism or other ordinance however administered, can help the sinner to take even one step toward heaven; but a new nature imparted from above, a new life implanted by the Holy Ghost through the word, is absolutely essential to salvation (Isa. lxiv, 6; John iii, 5, 18; Gal. vi, 15; Phil. iii, 4–9; Tit. iii, 5; James i, 18; 1 Peter i, 23).

VI.

We believe that our redemption has been accomplished solely by the blood of our Lord Jesus Christ, who was made to be sin, and made a curse for us, dying in our room and stead; and that no repentance, no feeling, no faith, no good resolutions, no sincere efforts, no submission to the rules and regulations of any church, or of all the churches that have existed since the days of the Apostles, can add in the very least to the value of that precious blood, or to the merit of that finished work, wrought for us by Him who united in His person true and proper divinity with perfect and sinless humanity (Lev. xvi, 11; Matt. xxvi, 28; Rom. v, 6–9; 2 Cor. v, 21; Gal. iii, 13; Eph. i, 7; 1 Peter i, 18, 19.)

VII.

We believe that Christ, in the fulness of the blessings He has secured by His obedience unto death, is received by faith alone, and that the moment we trust in Him as our Savior, we pass out of death into everlasting life, being justified from all things, accepted before the Father according to the measure of his acceptance, loved as He is loved, and having his place and portion, as linked to Him, and one with Him forever (John v, 24; xvii, 23; Acts xiii, 39; Rom. v, 1; Eph. ii, 4–6, 13; 1 John iv, 17; v, 11, 12).

VIII.

We believe that it is the privilege not only of some, but of all, who are born again by the spirit through faith in Christ, as revealed in the Scriptures, to be assured of their salvation from the very day they take him to be their Savior; and that this assurance is not founded upon any fancied discovery of their own worthiness, but wholly upon the testimony of God in His written Word, exciting within His children filial love, gratitude and obedience (Luke x, 20;

xii, 32; John vi, 47; Rom. viii, 33-39; 2 Cor. v, 1, 6-8; 2 Tim. i, 12; 1 John v, 13).

IX.

We believe that all the Scriptures, from first to last, centre about our Lord Jesus Christ, in His person and work, in His first and second coming; and hence that no chapter, even of the Old Testament, is properly read or understood until it leads to Him; and moreover, that all the Scriptures, from first to last, including every chapter, even of the Old Testament, were designed for our practical instruction (Luke xxiv, 27, 44; John v, 39; Acts xvii, 2, 3; xviii, 28; xxvi, 22, 23; xxviii, 23; Rom. xv, 4; 1 Cor. x, 11).

X.

We believe that the church is composed of all who are united by the Holy Spirit to the risen and ascended Son of God; that by the same we are all baptized into one body, whether we be Jews or Gentiles; and thus, being members of one another, we are responsible to keep the unity of the spirit in the bond of peace, rising above all sectarian prejudices and denominational bigotry, and loving one another with a pure heart fervently (Matt. xvi, 16-18; Acts xi, 32-47; Rom. xii, 5; 1 Cor. xii, 12-27; Eph. i. 20-23; iv, 3-10; Col. iii, 14, 15).

XI.

We believe that the Holy Spirit, not as an influence, but as a divine person, the source and power of all acceptable worship and service, is our abiding comforter and helper; that He never takes His departure from the church, nor from the feeblest of the saints, but is ever present to testify of Christ, seeking to occupy us with Him, and not with ourselves, nor with our experiences (John vii, 38, 39 ; xiv, 16, 17 ; xv, 26 ; xvi, 13, 14 ; Acts i, 8 ; Rom. viii, 9 ; Phil. iii, 3).

XII.

We believe that we are called with a holy calling to walk, not after the flesh, but after the spirit, and so as to live in the spirit, that we shall not fulfill the lusts of the flesh; but the flesh, being still in us, to the end of our earthly pilgrimage, needs to be kept constantly in subjection to Christ, or it will surely manifest its presence to the dishonor of His name (Rom. viii, 12, 13; xiii, 14; Gal. v, 16-25; Eph. iv, 22-24; Col. iii, 1-10; 1 Peter i, 14-16; 1 John iii, 5-9).

XIII.

We believe that the souls of those who have trusted in the Lord Jesus Christ for salvation do, at death, immediately pass into His presence, and there remain in conscious bliss until the resurrection of the body at His coming, when soul and body, reunited, shall be associated with him for ever in glory. But the souls of unbelievers remain after death in conscious misery until the final judgment of the great white throne at the close of the millennium, when soul and body, reunited, shall be cast into the lake of fire, not to be annihilated, but to be punished with everlasting destruction from the presence of the Lord, and from the glory of His power (Luke xvi, 19–26; xxiii, 43; 2 Cor. v, 8; Phil. i, 2, 3; 2 Thess. i, 7–9; Jude 6, 7; Rev. xx, 11–15).

XIV.

We believe that the world will not be converted during the present dispensation, but is fast ripening for judgment, while there will be a fearful apostacy in the professing Christian body; and hence that the Lord Jesus will come in person to introduce the millenial age, when Israel shall be restored to their own land, and the earth shall be full of the knowledge of the Lord, and that this personal and pre-millennial advent is the blessed hope set before us in the Gospel for which we should be constantly looking (Luke xii, 35–40; xvii, 26–30; xviii 8; Acts xv, 14–17; 2 Thess. ii, 3–8; 2 Tim. iii, 1–5; Tit. ii, 11–15.

PERSONAL BIBLE STUDY FOR GOSPEL WORK.

BY J. H. ELLIOTT.

HE who most honors God's Word in his work will be most honored in his work by God. We fear that many who engage in Gospel work, and are sincerely desirous of accomplishing much in the name of Christ, fail of results because they rely on something other than "the Word of God" simply, to secure attention and interest, or to produce conviction of sin. They try to lead the unsaved sinner to the Rock of Salvation by any and every means save the very one God has promised to bless (2 Tim. iv, 2; 1 Cor. ii, 1–5; Jer. xxiii, 28; Matt. vii, 20). Mere religious activity can never take the place of that consecrated zeal which is first made intelligent by the study of the Word, and then used of God in proclaiming His testimony, and not some man's original (?) ideas. Neither can "the gift of speech" take the place of a clear, loving, earnest presentation of Christ in the very words of Scripture. It is astounding how few persons know their Bibles well enough to even be at liberty in the practical use of the sword of the Spirit in the simplest service either of offensive or defensive warfare. The fact is plain; there must be far more personal Bible study, if there is to be more intelligent Gospel work done. There are few who make any attempt at all to do Gospel work who do not, in some sort of fashion, habitually read the Bible; but that cannot be considered study such as is here referred to. Many Christians, it is to be feared, read the book merely as a perfunctory duty, with little or no real enjoyment or profit. It is almost a task. They feel quite relieved when the morning or evening chapter is over, and turn with evident relish to the daily newspaper or to the interesting business or pleasure of the hour. Two hours after reading they could not for their lives tell anything of what was read out of the precious volume. Mr. Moody tells how, when a boy at home on the farm, he was put at hoeing corn, he did it so poorly he was obliged to put up a stick in order to tell where to begin in the morning. Just so with many who read their Bibles; they do it so poorly, and the truth read makes so little impression on them, it is necessary to use a book mark to tell where to begin again. Surely this is not "searching the Scriptures," as the noble Bereans did (Acts xvii, 11). Delighting to meditate in the law of the Lord (Psa. i, 1, 2), or studying to show ourselves approved unto God, rightly dividing the Word of Truth (2 Tim. ii, 15). When one undertakes to get a knowledge of medicine, such as will fit him to minister to the physical wants of men, he does not expect to get such a knowledge by a hasty reading of one or two chapters daily of the books put into his hand. It requires study; and he will put in practice, at the first opportunity, all that he has learned, if he be wise, for nothing so fastens in the memory facts and truths as a practical every day use of them. Cannot he who would minister to the wants of "sin sick souls" learn a lesson here? God's Word is his medical library, in which he may learn not only of the disease but of its cure, and if he would be a follower of the great Physician Himself, he must try to fit himself for the work by constant study and practice. Just here many make a mistake; they are kept from studying the Word because they fear it will take up so much time. Now, while it is true that much time may be profitably consumed in Bible study, a practical knowledge of the Word may be gained by simply using time that would otherwise be wasted, as for instance, while waiting for breakfast or at the depot for a train, or the odd moments at place of business. Twenty or thirty minutes of earnest, faithful Bible study daily will accomplish wonders in a year's time or less, for one who with no greater library than a good Reference Bible, a Concordance or Text Book, and the help of the great Teacher, the Holy Spirit, is content to wait thus on the Lord.

Personal Bible study in the Gospel worker is all important

1st. For individual growth. When Paul was about to leave the young converts and Christians in the church at Ephesus, speaking in the Spirit, he said: "And now, brethren, I commend you to God and *the Word* of His grace, which is able to build you up, etc." (Acts xx, 32); and the Holy Spirit, by the mouth of Peter, also said to the elect throughout Pontius, Galatia, Cappadocia, Asia and Bithynia: "As new born babes desire the sincere milk of the Word that ye may grow thereby" (1 Peter ii, 2). The fact must be clear that there can be no growth in spiritual things without proper food, and that food is "the Word of God," and nothing short of it can supply the need of the soul. The fact that so many apparently stand still in the Christian life may easily be accounted for when it is known that they habitually neglect to take the nourishment that God has provided, or they take it in such small quantities and so irregularly as to produce mere starvelings or sorrowful dyspeptics in the church. Many Christians expect to grow spiritually on about one or two good meals per week, which they get from the sacred desk on the Lord's Day. No wonder they have so little relish for the weekly prayer meeting, or for Christian service in the Sunday school or elsewhere.

2nd. To furnish for work. The clear and unequivocal testimony of the Holy Spirit is that "All Scripture is given by inspiration of God, and is profitable for doctrine, for reproof, for correction, for instruction in righteousness, that the man of God may be perfect, throughly furnished unto all good works" (2 Tim. iii, 16, 17). If all Scripture be given for this purpose, it must follow that no other sort of furnishing can take the place of that which God has provided and designs should be used. A worker "throughly furnished" with a stock of interesting and affecting anecdotes, upon which he can, by a little ingenious twisting, fasten a moral, may move an audience to tears, but unless his confidence be upon the truth as revealed in the Word of God, we have little confidence in the final results. While he who attempts to reason out that which was clear as the light of Heaven in the mind of God before the world began, and to so present it with profound logic and endless rhetoric as to convince men, has not learned the first lesson toward success in the ministry of the Word, which is, after all, the old-fashioned plan of proclaiming "the testimony of God," "not with the enticing words of man's wisdom, but in demonstration of the Spirit and of power," that men's "faith should not stand in the wisdom of men, but in the power of God" (1 Cor. ii, 1, 4, 5; Jer. xxiii, 28). The power of the use of the Bible in Gospel work is manifest.

1st. In personal work. The secret of power in personal work is the wise use of "the sword of the Spirit, which is the Word of God" (Eph. vi, 17), because this is God's chosen way under the Holy Spirit to convince and convert men. Mere eloquence or wise argument will not always convince men; what is needed is the convincing power of the Holy Ghost accompanying the use of the Word (Acts xix, 24, 28). This was the instrument that our Lord used to prove His divinity, even with those who were ignorant of the Scriptures (Luke xxiv, 25, 32).

Phillip used the same agency when he preached Christ so successfully to the eunuch (Acts viii, 35); indeed this is the Scriptural plan, and experience has shown that this is the only wise method to use in dealing with inquirers, because they are thus brought face to face with God in His Word, and the responsibility placed upon them personally to accept or reject what He says (1 John v, 9, 12).

Our own experience, be it never so clear or interesting, will not fit every other man's case, and if we try to make it fit every one we deal with, we shall be more than likely to put a stumbling block in the way of some one. The writer once met an inquirer who for many years had stumbled over the fact that a companion had been led to Christ after great agony of soul for weeks, and had taught them that such an experience was necessary to a genuine conversion. The Bible contains in itself the best of all answers to the arguments of the skeptic or the excuses of the inquirer. A young man who had shown interest in a Gospel meeting, was asked if he was saved, and answered that he didn't know; he hoped he was; he was a member of the church; but that he didn't believe anybody could know they were saved in this world. The worker who conversed with him suggested kindly that "God's Word indicated very clearly that the Christian could know he was saved now," but, said the young man, "the Bible teaches that 'we don't yet know what we shall be.'" He was asked where such teaching was to be found, and replied that he "didn't just remember, but was sure it was somewhere in the Bible." Imagine his surprise and the added force given to the truth when the worker quietly turned in his Bible to 1 John iii, 2, and read the identical passage he has so wrested (2 Peter iii, 16), as follows: "Beloved, *now* are we the sons of God, and it doth not yet appear what we shall be," etc.

2d. *In public work.* The worker who is "throughly furnished for work" by familiarity with Gospel truth as presented in the Word, is not afraid at any time or any place to speak God's testimony, and that is all that the Gospel worker is called upon to do (Eze. xxxiii, 7-11; Psa. cxix, 27, 171). God's word in the heart is not only a safeguard against sin, but a burning fire (Psa. cxix, 11; Jer. xx, 9). Every worker ought to be at least so well acquainted with the work as to be ready at all times to give a Scriptural reason for the hope that is in him, and to have a well defined knowledge of the fundamental doctrines of the Word concerning man's lost condition, God's remedy for sin, and how it may be secured to the lost sinner. This alone will give the greatest liberty in all kinds of Gospel work.

MISAPPLIED SCRIPTURE.
1 John i, 9.

A FAMOUS evangelist, conducting an immense meeting, was urging Christians to speak to the unconverted, and to those who remained after the preaching for conversation. He remarked that there were many who were willing to speak and to work in the inquiry room, but they did not know what to say. Then raising his voice, he exclaimed very earnestly: "Say this to them: 'If we confess our sins, he is faithful and just to forgive us our sins and to cleanse us from all unrighteousness.'"

It is difficult to imagine a more dangerous perversion of Scripture than the advice he thus gave to Christian workers. Probably there is not a Unitarian in the world, however strenuously he may deny the divinity of the Lord Jesus, regeneration by the Holy Ghost, and the blood of atonement, who would be unwilling to confess that he is a sinner. Probably there is not a Deist who is not ready to make the same confession. If all that the unbeliever needs to do is to confess his sins in order to be assured of the justice and righteousness of God in forgiving and cleansing him, it is obvious that it is not necessary to tell him of the death upon the cross, and of faith in the crucified and risen Redeemer.

But a glance at the text is sufficient to show that it does not have the slightest reference to unbelievers. The Apostle says: "If we confess our sins, he is faithful and just to forgive us our sins, and to cleanse us from all unrighteousness." He is not writing to unbelievers, nor about unbelievers, but he is showing those who are already saved how they may be restored to fellowship, if they have lost the light of God's face by falling into sin. They are to come "as dear children," not simply saying: "Forgive us our sins," but confessing their faults and failures, and then knowing, upon the sure testimony of God's Word, that He has taken them back into communion.

It seems to be forgotten that the inspired epistles were addressed to none but the saints; and it has come to pass that believers and unbelievers, the justified and the unjustified, the regenerate and the unregenerate, are thrown together in public prayers and discourses, as if they were not separated "as far as hell's depths from heaven." Let us suppose that a letter is sent by mail or by the hands of a chosen messenger to such and such a church, in such and such a city;

would any who did not belong to that church imagine that its instructions, exhortations, or admonitions, were intended for them? Could the minister or reader of the letter imagine that it was written to persons who had "neither part nor lot in this matter?"

When the believers, to whom the Holy Ghost sent an epistle by the Apostle John, heard the words read in their meetings: "If we confess our sins, he is faithful and just to forgive us our sins, and to cleanse us from all unrighteousness," could they be in a moment's doubt concerning those who were meant by the word *we?* Could they think that the message was designed for the heathen who, like Gallio, "Cared for none of those things?" But the soul of the most cultivated man in Christendom, that has not yet been made alive by the Holy Ghost through faith in the Lord Jesus Christ, is not less dead in trespasses and sins than the soul of the most degraded heathen.

There is not one single promise to the unbeliever, so long as he refuses to receive the Savior; and apart from that Savior, the faithfulness and justice of God would consign him to everlasting punishment upon the confession of his sins. But if in Christ, and betrayed into sin, the same faithfulness and justice will surely forgive and cleanse him from all unrighteousness.

THE TRUTH.

HOW CAN I GET THE MOST GOOD FROM READING AND STUDYING THE BIBLE?

BY CHAS. M. WHITTELSEY.

Brief Summary.—2 Tim. iii, 14-17. Compare at home: 2 Peter i, 1-4; 1 Peter ii, 2; John xvii, 17; Acts xx, 32; John xv, 7; Eph. vi, 16, 17.

I. IN OUR MINDS AND HEARTS.

1. Realizing the authority of the Bible, as the Word of God, over our opinions and conduct: 1 Thess. ii, 13; 1 Cor. ii, 11-16. Reverently: Hab. ii, 20; Ps. cxix, 89; 2 Peter i, 21. In faith to submit to its utterances: Acts xxiv, 14. Compare Titus ii, 9; 1 Peter ii, 1; 1 Cor. i, 19-22; 2 Cor. x, 5.

2. Recognizing the Holy Spirit as a present teacher: John xiv, 16, 17, 26; xvi. 13-15; 1 Cor. ii, 5, 9, 10; iii, 16, 18-23; John vi, 45; 1 John ii, 27.

3. As a child of God: Rom. i. 7; and other greetings in Epistles. The family personal pronouns: Rom. v, 1-5; viii, 16, 17, 26, 3-39, etc.

4. As an inquirer: Rom. iv, 3. "It shall grately helpe ye to understand Scripture yf thou marke not onely what is spoken or wrytten, but of whom, unto whom, with what wordes, at what tyme, where, to what intent, with what circomstance, consyderynge what goeth before and what followeth after."—*Coverdale.*

5. Not to prove your point; as *e.g.*, a lawyer studies precedents, but to yield your mind to God: Isa. lv, 7-13.

6. Searching into Scripture, expecting discoveries, as scientists study nature: John v. 39; Acts vii, 11; Prov. ii, 4; Ps. cxix, 162.

7. Applying the truth to your own heart and life: Rom. xv, 4; 1 Cor. xvi, 11; ix, 10, 11; Ps. cxix, 11, 105; Josh. i, 7, 8.

8. Prayerfully: Psalms cxix, 18; 1 John v, 14, 15.

9. Thoughtfully: Prov. iv, 8.

10. With meditation: Ps. cxix, 97-100, 148.

11. Patiently: John xvi, 12.

12. As an interview with Christ: John i, 1, 14; v, 46; Luke xxiv, 25-27, 44-47; John xiv, 21-28.

II. HELPS.

Large print Bible, with references.
Concordance, unabridged.
Bible Text Book.
Bible Dictionary.
"Gospel Truth,"—American Tract Society.
How to Study the Bible—Moody.
How to Use the Bible—Brookes.
Mrs. Menzie's Bible Marking.
New Translations by Trustworthy Scholars.

III. METHODS.

1. Of Reading.

A. By course from Genesis to Revelation: 2 Tim. iii, 16 (Deut. xxx, 11, 49; xxxiv, 1-4).

B. Old and New Testament books together; *e.g.*, Exodus with Romans; Leviticus with Hebrews; Numbers with Acts; Deuteronomy with the practical injunctions in the latter part of the Epistles; Joshua with Ephesians; the Prophets with Revelation.

C. The types and narratives with the teaching they suggest; *e.g.*,

Gen. iv, 1-7, with sacrifice; 16-24, with the progress of the world (Jude 2) as ignoring God; Gen. xxii, with God's gift of His Son; Gen. xxiv, with God's purpose that Christ should have a bride, etc.

D. One of the Gospels as a portrait of Christ as King, as Servant, as Man, as God — or one of the letters of the Holy Spirit — through at a sitting.

2. Of Study.

Looking up the same or similar incidents elsewhere in the Bible.

Analyzing the argument — the process of the thought. Note the force of the context. Define the words or phrases from an English dictionary, and by turning with a Concordance to the other places where they are used in the Bible.

Learn all that is said in the Bible and Bible Dictionary about a person or a place.

Look at places and follow journeys on a map.

Seek the teaching of each passage in regard to human nature; the character of God; the offices of the Father, the Son, and the Holy Spirit; the way of salvation, the privileges, relations and hopes of believers; the life and duties of believers toward God, themselves and other Christians and the world.

Distinguish things that differ as with a microscope: 2 Tim. ii, 15; 1 Cor. x, 32.

IV. TOPICS.

Bible Doctrines. — The person of Christ; Redemption; Regeneration; Sonship; the Hope set before us.

Dispensations. — John v, 17; Eph. iii, 1-6.

Subject and object and analysis of each book in the Bible, with its history.

Differences of the four Gospels.

Phrases, such as "At Jesus' feet," "In Christ," "Fear not," "Be not deceived."

Words, such as "Bread," "Hath," "Now," "Peace," "Therefore."

The volume of the book about Christ; the experience of believers in New Testament, etc.

Things to come: John xvi, 13; 2 Peter i, 19.

The astronomy, stones, animals, flowers, colors, and metals of the Bible.

Occupations; *e.g.*, the farmer, mechanic, merchant, etc., wise use of money.

Family relations — how to be a good father, mother, husband, wife, son, etc.

According to present experience of joy or sorrow or temptation.

Sowing in Bible broadcast: Matt. xiii, 1-23; Luke viii, 11, for future need.

---

2 Tim. ii, 15.

HOW SHOULD I STUDY MY BIBLE?

I. WITH FAITH.

1. Able to make wise unto salvation through faith: 2 Tim. iii, 15.
2. Power of God unto salvation * * * for therein is the righteousness of God revealed from faith to faith: Rom. i, 16, 17.
3. Received as word of God * * * effectually worketh in you that believe: 1 Thes. ii, 13.
4. Will not profit without: Heb. iv, 2.

II. WITH PRAYER.

1. Open thou mine eyes, etc.: Ps. cxix, 18.
2. The Lord giveth wisdom, etc.: Prov. ii, 3-6.
3. If any of you lack wisdom, etc.: James i, 5.
4. Then opened he their understanding: Luke xxiv, 45.

III. WITH EARNEST HEED UNTO DOCTRINE.

1. God hath spoken through His Son: 1 Tim. iv, 16. Therefore we ought to give: Heb. i, 1-3; Heb. ii, 1-4.
2. Illustrated: Jas. i, 22-25.

IV. WITH STEADFAST PURPOSE.
1. All things else counted loss for excellency of knowledge of Christ of Jesus my Lord: Peter iii, 8.
2. Exportation: Phil. iii, 10–16.
3. Illustrated. There were none able, etc.: Acts xvii, 2.

V. CONSTANTLY — DAY AND NIGHT.
1. Sitting, walking (morning and evening), on retiring and rising: Deut. vi, 6–9.
2. Day and night: John i, 8.
3. God great promise: Psa. i, 1–3.
JOHN H. ELLIOTT.

BOOKS OF THE BIBLE.

The Bible is one book, not many. It has one subject — Redemption — and everything in the book is more or less related to this grand fundamental idea.

GEN. The beginning. The necessity arising from man's failure: iii, 23, 24; redemption is promised through blood: iii, 15, 21; iv, 4.

EXOD. A picture of redemption: xii, 13. It is the work of God: xiv, 13.

LEV. The method of redemption: xvi, 15–21.

NUM. The journey and warfare of the redeemed. God dealing with them as with sons (Conf. Gal.): i, 18. "Able to go forth to war."

DEUT. Remember your redemption: vii, 7, 8.

JOSH. The warfare and the victory of the redeemed secured by Jehovah: i, 2, 5, 9. Words of cheer.

JUDG. The failures of the redeemed and the Lord's continual interposition. "I will guide thee." "I will never leave thee:" ii, 11–16.

RUTH. A picture of a redeemed family. The social life of the redeemed: ii, 4, 5, 14–16, 18.

SAM., KINGS, CHRON. The type of the Kingdom. The throne of David: 2 Sam. vii, 13.

EZRA. The return of the redeemed from chastening bondage, and separation from the world: x, 11.

NEH. The necessity for constant activity and repairing of losses, on the part of the redeemed. "Let us rise up and build:" i, 3, 10; ii, 18; iii, 28–30; iv, 6. The use of the written word: viii, 3, 5, 7.

ESTHER. God's secret purposes toward the redeemed: iii, 13; viii, 8.

JOB. The experiences of a redeemed man: i, 21; ii, 10; xlii, 10, 12.

PS. Songs for the Redeemed. Prophetic praises for the final glory of the Redeemer and His Kingdom. The first psalm is a preface. The second is the contents: ii, 6.

PROV. Wisdom for the redeemed for life in this world: i, 5.

ECC. The experiences of a redeemed man who has served the world and finds that all that does not relate to redemption is vanity: xii, 13, 14.

SONGS. The mutual love of the Redeemer and the redeemed: ii, 16.

ISA. A prophetic view of the Redeemer in humiliation and glory, and the ultimate universality of His Kingdom: i, 2; ix, 6, 7; liii, 11.

JER. Judgment on the redeemed. A new covenant with them: xxxi, 31, 34.

LAM. An appendix to Jeremiah. The prophet's grief for the desolation of the city and the temple of the Redeemer. The Lord's chastenings of the redeemed: iii, 22, et seq.

EZEK. The old and the new dispensations, the dissolution of the old, the grandeur of the new: xxxvii, 11, 12.

DAN. The coming Redeemer, the King of Kings. The date of redemption: ix, 26.

HOSEA. Call to the back-slider to return: xiv, 1–4.

JOEL. The promise of redemption to all: ii, 32.

AMOS. Judgment and restoration: v, 4.

OBAD. Judgment on the enemies of the redeemed: i, 10.

JONAH. The redeemed among the Gentiles. God's grace: i, 2; ii, 10.
MICAH. Parallel with Isaiah: iv, 2.
NAHUM. Appendix to Jonah. Execution of judgments on the redeemed: i, 10.
HAB. Woes on the evil: ii, 12.
ZEPH. Chastisement, unsparing judgment and punishment: i, 12.
HAG. Encouragement to those waiting for the Redeemer: ii, 4, 7, 9.
ZECH. Preparation for the coming Redeemer. The beginning of the last days: xiv. 7; xiii, 1; xiv, 20.
MALACHI. The messenger of the Redeemer; iii, 1. God's last word to Israel before the Redeemer comes.
MATH., MARK, LUKE, JOHN. The Redeemer in person seen in four pictures as the fulfiller of prophecy, as the servant of Jehovah, as the Son of man, and is God manifest in the flesh. The Redeemer pays the price of redemption and completes the bargain: John xix, 30.
ACTS. The power of the story of redemption: ii, 36, 37.
ROMANS. The doctrines of redemption systematized: i, 16.
1 AND 2 COR. The redeemed associated in the church: i, 10.
GAL. The liberty of the redeemed as sons: iv, 1-7.
EPH. The redeemed walking together in heavenly places together with Christ: ii, 10.
PHIL. The perfecting of God's work in the redeemed: ii, 13.

COL. The union of the redeemed with the Redeemer. Christ in you: i, 27.
1 AND 2 THESS. The second coming of the Redeemer for the redeemed: 1 Thess. iii, 13.
1 AND 2 TIM. Pastoral instructions to the ministry of redemption: 2 Tim. ii, 1.
TITUS. Qualifications of, and advice to, the ministry: i, 7; ii, 15.
PHILEMON. Brotherly joy among the ministers of Christ: Verse 20.
HEB. The better things of the new covenant: xi, 40.
JAMES. The good works that accompany redemption: ii, 17.
1 AND 2 PETER. The precious things of redemption: i, 19.
1 JOHN. The assurance of redemption: v, 13.
2 JOHN. Warnings to be redeemed against false doctrine: Verse 7.
3 JOHN. Hospitality among the redeemed (Conf. Ruth): Verses 5 and 6.
JUDE. Warning of the apostacy in the last days: Verses 17 and 18.
REV. God's last written word to us through His Spirit, informing us of the great event that is to end this age, to which we are to look and for which we are to pray — the glorious appearing of the Redeemer to establish His kingdom on earth and consummate redemption: xxii, 20.

REV. JOHN C. HILL.

BOOKS OF THE NEW TESTAMENT. THEIR SEVERAL SUBJECTS, AND THE RELATION OF EACH ONE TO THE OTHER.

BY WILLIAM LINCOLN.

THE general relation of the Gospels to the Epistles is somewhat similar to that of the alabaster box of precious nard, with that same ointment poured forth when the box had been broken. In the Gospels there is He present who is full of grace and truth. Ever and anon His love overflows, until Calvary is reached. There we see him, slain for our transgressions, now from Him raised again, the streams of life and love commence to flow freely forth to us. The Epistles mark the currents in which those streams run. The Acts shows us the incipient defects of Divine love having quite reached us. There we read of God's love at the beginning of this dispensation. The Revelation unveils to us His work at the end. The former shows us His goodness unexpected; the latter, His judgment discriminating, searching and eternal. Now, as there is but one Christ, so there is, and can be, but one Gospel. But the Spirit reveals to us four divers views or aspects of that one Christ. The first two of these are the picture of the official glories of Christ; the remaining two, of His personal glories. In Matthew we behold the Royal Master; in Mark, the lowly Servant. But Luke tells us of the perfect Man; whilst John writes of God manifest in the flesh. Here, then, in the four together, is evidently completeness of design. Combined they afford us a full view of Christ. Hence there could not be either more or less than four, nor other than these very four. And whether you look at the beginning, or at the middle, or at the close of either one of the four accounts, you will, with attention, easily perceive that all that is written by any one only of the four, or what is written differently, or omitted by him, which is contained in any of the others, all is there according to the picture which the Spirit is portraying before your eye.

There is much design, too, in the fact that the book of the Acts is written by the same Evangelist as drew the picture of Christ, as Man. For it is hence implied that the church's union is with the new, the risen, the glorified man. Commencing, too, his account with the Lord's ascension, and with the consequent descent of the Holy Ghost, he thus teaches us that the church derives her existence from that Divine Man; is sustained in life ever by Him, and is united with Him there. Here, therefore, we behold the Holy Ghost at His work. This book is completed in four parts.

Part one, chapter i, 7, Christ glorified, preached unto the Jews, with the Holy Ghost sent down from heaven. Part two, chapter viii, 12, the testimony slowly receding from Israel. Part three, chapter xiii, 20, Christ preached to the Gentiles; and Part four, His Ambassador in chains. But, in each of these four parts, the references to the work of the Holy Ghost are remarkable. Thus, at the commencement of each of the first three parts, we read of the Holy Ghost at once. So, too, again at the very close of the book. And since the Lord is faithful, His Spirit still remains with us, even though the ship of the church, as to its outward manifestation, is wrecked and gone to pieces.

Coming now to the Epistles, we find that seven Gentile churches are addressed by Paul. The communication to each of these is on a distinct subject. For God never repeats Himself. If a reader of the Word apprehends that a given subject occupies each Epistle, and observes how that subject is opened out piece by piece by the Holy Ghost, he will rapidly grow in the knowledge of the Word, and of the thoughts of God; he will be able to perceive much better the point of any expression, and its bearing where it occurs in the treatment of the general subject. Besides which, it will be found, on examination, that at least in Paul's writings the subject is broached at the beginning of each letter.

Romans is found, on perusal, to be "The Gospel of God." This very expression occurs at verse 1, and observe how this Gospel is set forth by an inspired hand. First, to chapter iii, 19, the sinful condition of irreligious, and then next of religious man is sketched. Then to chapter v, 11, how God righteously forgives sins. Next, to end of chapter viii, how He delivers us from our evil nature, and gives us a new nature in Christ risen, and seals us with the Holy Ghost. Then in chapters ix–xi, we see how He has woven our salvation into the general plan of His vast designs. Then chapter xiii to end, directions follow to the saved, as to their walk.

First Corinthians comes next. Its subject is indicated in chapter i, 9. It looks at those professing to be saved, as in fellowship together, and instructs them as to that fellowship.

Galatians deports us from the admixture of Judaism with Christianity. For Judaism presupposes that the world is on trial, and is a religion for man in it. But Christ takes us clean out of the world, and at infinite cost to Himself. Hence the attempt to make man religious in the world is in direct opposition to His cross. So this Epistle has been defined to be the voice of Scripture by Paul as erst by Sarah, casting the bond woman out of Abraham's house. Part one is to chapter i, 5, and contains an epitome of the subject. Part two, to end of chapter ii, gives us the writer's warrant for his mandate, and shows us how he himself had opposed the bond woman in Peter. In part three, to chapter iii, 14, he cites the Galatians' experience and the Old Testament in further proof. In fourth part, to chapter iv, 7, he proves the time to have fully come for this expulsion. In fifth part, to chapter v, 12, he exhibits what the bond woman is. In sixth part, to chapter, v, 10, he demands the removal out of the house of all that belongs to her; her customs, works of flesh and boastings, and enjoins the practice of the opposite habits and ways; and then, lastly, he reminds us of the importance of this mandate: "Cast out, stand fast," etc., and closes as he began, by pointing to Christ's cross. Oh, when will men perceive that religiousness it was which murdered Christ?

Ephesians carries on the subject where Romans dropped it; or rather, as Romans begins at the bottom, so Ephesians commences at the very top. It shows the high counsels of God concerning us, ere the world began. Its entire teaching is briefly summed up in that one sentence: "God hath blessed us with all spiritual blessings in the heavenliness in Christ." Part one, chapter i, God's eternal love to us individually. Part two, chapter ii, our hopeless condition by nature. Part three, chapter iii, God's grace to us corporately. Here we have the unfolding of the great mystery of Christ and the church. Part four, to chapter iv, 16, traces our corporate walk in view of this grace. Part five, to chapter v, 21, our individual walk. Part six, bids us stand where God has placed us, and tells us of the armor provided by God in order that we may do so.

Philippians traces how we are to apprehend that for which we are apprehended of Christ Jesus. It regards us as pressing on toward the mark for the prize of God's calling up on high — throught God working in us day by day. Throughout this Epistle, therefore, salvation is regarded as the result of the race, and as our complete and future deliverance. Only it is here, as ever in the New Testament, regarded as our own to begin with. In the Old, the salvation is constantly termed God's. Also in Luke i, we have "Thy salvation," because that was uttered ere Christ had actually reached our case. But, now, after His cross, it is invariably declared to be "ours," "my," "your own," earned by Christ for us, He freely gives it to all who believe in Him. And then we are daily to live out that life imparted; and hence, as the entire path of the perfect One is marked out in chapter ii, so we are seen following Him in chapter iii. Hence, chapter i, 6, is an epitome of this Epistle. Colossians is about the Head, as Ephesians is about the Body. The latter characteristically says that we are Christ's fullness (i, 23); the former, that He is our fullness (see Greek of ii, 10). Each thus needs the other. Philippians presupposes an object, Christ before the soul, and everything set aside to win that object. Colossians testifies of worthiness of that object. Part one, to chapter i, 20, tells us of the what the Lord has done, and who He is. Part two, to chapter i, 29, adverts to what we were, and to the great mystery. Part three, to chapter ii, 7, expresses the desire that we may understand this mystery. Part four, to chapter ii, 23, teaches us how the fullness in Him is denied by rationalism and by ritualism. Part five, to chapter iii, 17, how Christ's claim as Lord is to be owned. Part six, to chapter iv, 1, relative duties. Here note that wives, husbands, children, etc., are all addressed as risen together with Christ, and all that is done by these is to be done to the Lord. In part seven, a few additional directions.

Lastly, the Epistle to the Thessalonians crowns all by instructing us about His coming. In chapter i, it is the coming of one who has already delivered us from impending wrath. In chapter ii, His coming is connected with our crown. In chapter iii, His coming is looked at in connection with brotherly love — a most obvious connection, surely; for if we are to spend an eternity together as God's children, it is a pity to fall out on the way thither. In chapter iv His coming is sketched in detail, and in chapter v the relation of our entire sanctification to His coming is suggested. Second Thessalonians treats, on the other hand, of His appearing and interposition in this world.

The Epistles to Timothy and Titus contain instructions for God's servants; second Timothy especially bearing on the last days, and if the singular use of the expression, "God our Savior," in first Timothy and in Titus, and if also the striking variation of its use in Titus from its use in Timothy, were reflected on, it would be perhaps acknowledged that the service in Timothy is rather of an evangelistic, and in Titus of a pastoral character. In fact that expression exhibits God's present attitude to man as preached by His servants according to His commandment, and the faithful sayings to be found only in these Epistles and in Revelation, exhibits the corresponding attitude that God would have us take toward Him. Most, pertinently, therefore, are they found just where they occur, and in the ordertoo, in which they stand. All is perfect and complete.

Philemon, as a closing word, takes up an extreme case, that even robbed and robber are, when in Christ, both one, in order to press home the truth that all saints stand on common ground. Hebrews is God's preservative against Judaism and religiousness. James is hortatory. Peter's Epistles are primarily addressed to believing Jews, and in the first, a contrast is drawn between God's deliverance from Egypt by Moses, and Christ's costly salvation. Second Peter, like all the second Epistles, bears specially on the last days.

John's Epistles exhibit the working of Divine life in us. As his Gospel is about the Son of God, so his Epistles are about the sons of God. In the first two chapters of the first Epistle, the family are regarded as with their Father; in the last three, the family are traced in their life as to this world.

Jude writes of the apostacy. The key to his Epistle is the word "common" in verse 3. The apostacy ignores God's "common salvation," and sets up a distinct clerisy. Hence, this same word "common" occurs with great appropriateness at the beginning of Titus.

The Revelation is the book of the unveiling of Christ.

DOUBLE TRUTHS OF SCRIPTURE.

BY WILLIAM LINCOLN.

1. CHRIST is God. He is also man. Avoid the peril of steering, in your view of the truth here, anywhere between the two extremes. He is God, being of the same substance as the Father, in one nature; He is man — perfect man — much more perfectly man than you or I; for we are fallen and imperfect men. We resemble a mirror smashed to atoms. He, as a man, is like the mirror whole. Or, rather, we by nature have been broken up by sin that was without, obtaining entrance into us. But He was bruised on the cross through the love that was erst pent up in Him, at length flowing out.

2. There are two advents of Christ; keep your eye on each. Each advent will be found to be comprised in two stages — the first at Bethlehem and Calvary, the second into the clouds for His saints, and then to the world, to judge and reign.

3. Christ crucified is both the burnt-offering in which God shall ever find exquisite delight, and the sin-offering from which he turned away his face (Lev. i and iv).

4. He that believes in Christ is clean every whit (John xiii). Yet is there need of a daily cleansing by Christ's priestly application unto us of the water of the Word (Eph. v, 12, and 1 John i, 8). Salvation is a present gift (John v, 24). It is also a process (Phill. ii, 12). Yet it is future (Rom. xiii, 11; Heb. ix, 28). Our sanctifica-

tion is complete, for Christ is it (1 Cor. i, 30). Yet it is progressive as to our apprehension (1 Thess. v, 23).

5. Scripture speaks not only of peace with God, but also of the peace of God. All Christians have the former; many have not the latter. The one is for my conscience; the other is for my heart. Having peace with God, I can look up to him boldly, and know that he has no anger toward me; yea, and that He beholds me in Christ with delight. In possession of the peace of God, I am then unmoved by any circumstances around me, however appalling.

6. In each believer the Holy Ghost intercedes with groanings which cannot be uttered; for each believer Christ intercedes with God. Each Christian has the Holy Ghost as his paraclete, comforter, or advocate; but Christ also is our advocate with the Father. Thus the Holy Ghost and Christ are both our intercessors as to God; both our advocates as to the Father.

7. Two attitudes as to us does the Lord Jesus take: he is both in the ship of the church with us here, and he is on yon mountain's brow, watching it as tossed with the waves and billows (Mark iv, 38, and vi, 48).

8. Two attitudes or characters does the Holy Ghost take: he is the seal, marking God's claim on us; he, as the earnest, marking our claims, through grace and blood.

9. And if we follow Christ, we will find that He has a second rest to which He can bring us. If we give Him the burden of our sin, He will give us rest. If we take His yoke and His burden on us, we shall enjoy a found rest. Thus there are two burdens and two rests in Matthew xi, 28–30.

10. There are two resurrections — the one of all the dead in Christ on the morning of the millennial reign, and called in Scripture "the resurrection of the just;" the other the ressurrection of the unjust, at the close of that reign.

DIVINE TITLES.

THERE are treasures of precious truth in the Titles of God and of Christ, which are more or less hidden or obscured in the Authorized Version. One object of the Englishman's Hebrew Bible is to present to the eye of the reader these various titles as they really exist in the Inspired Originals.

A name or title is expressive of nature and character. Each separate title of God may be regarded as one letter, complete indeed in itself, yet, when arranged and combined together, spelling out in full the one grand and wondrous name of the God of the Bible.

EL.

The title El (God, singular) occurs about 250 times.

The first occurrence is in Gen. xiv, 18, 19, 20, 22: "Most High God (El), possessor of heaven and earth."

El signifies "strong," "first." It is the title which shows God to be the Mighty One, the First Great Cause of all.

This title is generally connected with some one or more of the Divine attributes or perfections, as —

"Almighty God," Gen. xvii, 1.
"Everlasting God," Gen. xxi, 33.
"A jealous God," Ex. xx, 5.
"A God of truth and without iniquity, just and right is he," Deut. xxxii, 4.
"A great God, a mighty and a terrible," Deut. x, 19.
"The living God," Josh. iii, 10.
"A merciful God," Deut. iv, 31.
"A faithful God," Deut. vii, 9.
"A mighty and terrible God," Deut. vii, 21, etc.

The persons of the Godhead are three: Father, Son, and Spirit; but in nature and essence God is one.

Each attribute of God is infinite. One infinite, eternal love, one infinite almighty power, and so on; hence the attributes are connected generally with the singular name for God, El.

ELOAH.

Eloah (God, singular), from Ahlah, to worship, to adore, presents God as the one supreme object of worship, the adorable One.

It occurs about fifty-six times.

First, in Deut. xxxii, 15: "Then He forsook Eloah, which made him;" again, vs. 17: "They sacrificed to devils, not to Eloah." It is very frequently used in the Book of Job.

ELAH; OR, ELAHAH.

The corresponding title to Eloah, in the Chaldee language, is Elah (God, in the singular), or Elahah, emphatic. It is found in the Books of Ezra and Daniel seventy-seven times, and always in the singular.

The Chaldee portions of the Scriptures occur in Ezra and Daniel, with one verse in Jeremiah (chap. x, 11). Thus the record of Israel's captivity is inwrought in the sacred Word.

ELOHIM.

Elohim (God, plural of Eloah) occurs about 2,500 times; first, in Gen. i, 1: "In the beginning God created the heavens and the earth."

Here it is joined to a verb in the singular: "God (Elohim, plural) created" (singular). Showing Trinity acting in unity.

It also frequently occurs with adjectives, pronouns, and verbs in the plural. Gen. i, 26: "And God said, Let us make (plural) man in our image" (singular). Gen. iii, 22: "As one of us." Gen. xx, 13: "When God caused me to wander." Josh. xxiv, 19: "He is a holy God (plural). He is a jealous God" (singular). See also, Isa. vi, 3. The Chaldee form, Elahhayah, occurs in Jer. x, 11, applied to false gods.

JEHOVAH.

Jehovah (the Lord). The title Jehovah occurs about 6,000 times, but it is generally rendered "the Lord," and only occasionally "Jehovah," as Ex. vi, 3; Ps. lxxxiii, 18; Isa. xii, 2; xxvi, 4; and in combination, as Gen. xxii, 14; Ex. xvii, 15; Judg. vi, 24; in all seven times.

It first occurs, in connection with Elohim, in Gen. ii, 4: "The Lord God (Jehovah Elohim) made." And alone, Gen. iv, 1, 3, etc.

The signification is: He that always was, that always is, and that ever is to come. We have it thus translated and interpreted in Rev. i, 4: "From Him which is" (present participle, the ever-existing One), "and which was" (imperfect tense, expressing continuance in the past), "and which is to come" (present participle, the Coming One, ever to come).

It is a combination in marvellous perfection of the three periods of existence in one word, the future, the present, and the past.

First. Yehi, "He will be," long tense. Second. Hove, "being," participle. Third. Hahyah, "He was," short tense used in the past.

Taking the three first letters of Yehi, Yeh, the two middle letters of Hove, ov, and the two last letters of Hahyah, ah, we have Jehovah, or Jehovah, in full; Yeh–ov–ah.

I AM THAT I AM.

Ehyah Asher Ehyeh. Literally: "I will be that I will be," Ex. iii, 14. But as the so-called future or long tense expresses not simply the future, but also and especially continuance, the force is: "I continue to be, and will be." Ehyeh, "I Am," literally, "I will be," Ex. iii, 14. But in force and meaning: "I that ever will be;" "The Ever-existing One," or "He that is to come," or, "The Coming One."

JAH.

Jah (the Lord). This title occurs forty-nine times, and only in the books of Exodus, Psalms, and Isaiah.

Its first occurrence is in Ex. xv, 2: "The Lord (Jah) is my strength and song." It is often associated with the words: "Praise ye," in the word Hallelujah: "Praise ye Jah."

This title is expressive of eternal existence. It is the title of God, as inhabiting eternity, to whom past, present, and future is one eternal Now.

It is composed of the first and last letters of the name Jehovah, Yh, with the central vowel, ah, Jah, or Yah. It is a sublime title; see Ps. lxviii, 4: "Extol Him that rideth upon the heavens" (or the void spaces of infinitude), "by His name Jah" (the eternal One), "and rejoice before Him."

The word for heavens here is not the usual word, but a word expressive of desolateness — space untenanted and void. Infinitude and eternity are indwelt by Him.

The title Jah or Yah is at once one of the sublimest and yet simplest of the Divine names. "The simplest form of speech which infant lips can try," yet expressive of God's infinitude.

EL SHADDAY.

El Shadday (God Almighty, or God All-Sufficient). El, God, singular; Shadday, either from Shaddid, almighty, strong, or from Shadday, the breasts. This title combines the singular title, El, with the plural title, Shadday.

It occurs in combination: "God Almighty," or, "the Almighty God," seven times; and alone, "the Almighty," forty-one times. Chiefly in the Book of Job. Its first occurrence is in Gen. xvii, 1: "I am the Almighty God."

ADON.

Adon ("Lord, singular"), Lord, Master, Possessor, or Proprietor. Root either from Dun, to rule, govern, to judge; or from Aden, a base. Occurs about thirty times. First occurrence, Ex. xxiii, 17: "Three times in the year all the males shall appear before the Adon Jehovah."

ADONAHY.

Adonahy ("Lord," plural), Lord, or Master. In this form used only as a Divine title; different from Adonay, plural of Adon. The one is Adonahy; the other, Adonay.

Occurs about 290 times. First occurrence, Gen. xv, 2, 8: "And Abraham said, Adonahy Jehovah."

JEHOVAH TITLES.

Jehovah-Jireh, "Jehovah will see," or "provide," Gen. xxii, 14.
Jehovah-Ropheca, "Jehovah that healeth thee," Ex. xv, 26.
Jehovah-Nissi, "Jehovah my banner," Ex. xvii, 15.

Jehovah-Mekaddeshcem, "Jehovah that doth sanctify you," Ex. xxxi, 13; Lev. xx, 8; xxi, 8; xxii, 9, 16, 32; Ezek. xx, 12.
Jehovah-Shalom, "Jehovah send peace," Jud. vi, 24.
Jehovah-Tsebahoth, "Jehovah of hosts," 1 Sam. i, 3, etc.
Jehovah-Rohi, "Jehovah, my shepherd," Ps. xxiii, 1.
Jehovah-Heleyon, "Jehovah, most high," Ps. vii, 17; xlvii, 2; xcvii, 9.
Jehovah-Tsidkenu, "Jehovah, our righteousness," Jer. xxiii, 6; xxxiii, 17.
Jehovah-Shammah, "Jehovah is there," Ezek. xlviii, 35.

THE SACRIFICES OF THE OLD TESTAMENT.

BY D. W. WHITTLE.

Lev. i; Heb. ix, 22, 24.

THE Tabernacle was a type of heavenly things. Blood went in; blessing went out. The Holy Ghost was not given until Jesus was crucified and glorified. The Lord of glory spake of "The Tabernacle" (Lev. i, 1). We never find man seeking God. Man is always saved by heeding God's voice. This is seen in the lives of Noah, Abraham, Moses, and Joshua. In Leviticus five offerings are mentioned, viz.: the Burnt offering, Peace offering, Sin offering, and Trespass offering. The three first offerings were toward God, and the words "sin" or "forgiveness" are not mentioned. These offerings were a "sweet savor unto the Lord." In connection with the Sin and Trespass offering, "sin" is mentioned forty-seven times, and "It shall be forgiven him," seven times. These five offerings are united in the full presentation of the Lord Jesus Christ. The atonement was made for all the world, but redemption is enjoyed only by those who receive it. The fire was placed upon the altar (Lev. vi, 9-13; ix, 24; 2 Chron. vii, 1).

God kindled the fire, and Israel was commanded never to let it go out; but they failed, and let it go out again and again. After Jesus had fulfilled all things, and was laid in the tomb, God raised Him up, and the Holy Ghost was sent down on "the day of Pentecost" to "abide forever." God has thus kindled the fire, and we are commanded never to allow it to go out (Rom. xii, 1; John xiv, 15, 16).

Four things in regard to the Burnt offering:—

1. What kind of an offering (Lev. i, 3; Deut. xv, 19-21)? It must be the first born (Luke i, 35; ii, 7). It must also be "without blemish." The priests are commanded to take a cleaver and cut the

animal in twain; and if a blemish appear in the marrow, even, it was rejected (1 Peter i, 18, 19; ii, 22). The man Christ Jesus was born "without sin," and He was Holy and "without blemish."

2. How was this to be offered? "Of His own voluntary will" (Lev. i, 3). God places before us good and evil, and we must choose. If we choose the better par. then we must take it in God's appointed way (Rev. xxii, 17). If you can get a sinner to give up his will and go to God, then the work is done (Lev. i, 4). He must identify himself with his offering. "He shall put his hand upon the head of his offering" (John iii, 16; Eph. v, 25; Gal. ii, 20). "He loved me, and gave Himself for me" (Lev. i, 5). "He shall kill his offering" (1 Cor. xv, 3; 1 Peter iii, 18; Isaiah liii, 5).

3. Where was it to be offered (Lev. i, 3)? "At the door of the Tabernacle." God's claims must first be met, before we can have any dealings with Him whatever. This is the only way to come (Rom. ii, 26; Heb. x, 19). Think of an Israelite trying to crawl into the Tabernacle underneath the curtain!

4. What was it for (Lev. i, 4)? "To make atonement for him." The word is translated "ransomed," "sanctified," and "cleansed." It is translated sixty-seven times "to make atonement," seven times "to make reconciliation," nine times "to purge," twice "to make peace," three times "to forgive" (Rom. iv, 5–8; v, 9, 11; 2 Cor. v, 18–19; Eph. ii, 5–8, 20, 21). How nigh to God was an Israelite made by the blood? The blood was taken from the Holy Place and sprinkled on the mercy seat. We are made just as "nigh by the blood of Christ," because He has ascended into heaven. If we are built on this rock we are safe; for whoever heard of any one sinking through a rock?

THE TABERNACLE TYPES.

1. The Altar of Burnt Offering. — Ex. xxvii, 1, 2; Ex. xl, 6, 29; Ex. xxix, 36; Lev. ix, 24; Heb. xiii, 10.

2. The Laver. — Ex. xxx, 18; Ex. xxxi, 2–9; Ex. xxxviii, 8; Zech. xiii, 1; Rev. i, 5; Titus iii, 5; Eph. v, 26.

3. The Table of Shew Bread. — Lev. xxiv, 5; 1 Sam. xxi, 4; Ex. xxv, 30; Lev. xxiv, 8; John vi, 48–50; 1 Cor. v, 7.

4. The Golden Candlestick. — Ex. xxv, 31–36; 1 Sam. iii, 3; Zech. iv, 2; John viii, 12; John ix, 5; John xii, 35, 36; Mal. iv, 2; Rev. i, 20; Matt. v, 15.

5. The Altar of Incense. — Ex. xxx, 1–3; Ex. xxx, 7, 8; Rev. viii, 3; Rev. ix, 13.

6. *The Ark of the Covenant.* — Ex. xxv, 10, 11, 16-21; Ps. cxxxii, 8; Josh. iv, 7; Ps. xl, 8; Rev. xi, 19.

7. *The Mercy Seat.* — Ex. xxv, 17-20; Lev. xvi, 2; Num. vii, 89; Lev. xvi, 13-15; Rom. iii, 25; Heb. ix, 3; Heb. iv, 16.

THE JEWISH TABERNACLE.

1. *The growth of the altar idea.* The Jewish tabernacle was the expansion of the old altar. We see in the beautiful and complicated structure, and its service: a, the sacred place; b, the sacred priests; c, the sacred offerings; d, the sacred order.

2. *Object teaching.* God designed by all that pertained to the tabernacle to teach ignorant, sensuous minds deep and all important facts and principles of His kingdom and worship which they could not receive except through such appeal to the senses.

3. *Its lessons.* It revealed truths: a, concerning God's character; b, concerning man's character; c, concerning the approach of man to God; d, concerning the dwelling of God with man.

4. It was made after a divine pattern (Exod. xxv, 9; xxvi, 30; xxxix, 32, 42; Heb. viii, 5).

5. By divinely endowed architects (Ex. xxxi, 1-11; xxxv, 30-35; xxxvi, 1, 2, 5).

6. From divinely provided materials (Ex. xii, 35, 36; xxx, 12-16).

7. For divine uses (Ex. xxv, 20-22; xl, 34-38; xxix, 42, 43).

8. The names given to "the tabernacle" may be found in Ex. xxii, 19; xxv, 8, 9; xxix, 42-46; Lev. xii, 4; 1 Sam. i, 9; 1 Kings i, 39; Num. xvii, 7; xviii, 2.

9. Eight particulars pertaining to "the tabernacle" require notice here:

I. The court of "the Tabernacle is an image of the kingdom of God in Israel, a type of the Christian church. The court is the symbolical habitation of the people, while the sanctuary, or Tabernacle proper, is the habitation of God in their midst" (Dr. Hurtz). This court or inclosure, as to its shape, size, pillars, sockets, hooks, fillets, hangings, etc., may be studied in Ex. xxvii, 9-18. The following figures will indicate the size of certain parts, etc., in cubits (we estimate a cubit at eighteen inches): Commit to memory Psa. c, 4; xcii, 13. The court had one entrance or gate at the east end, only one gate to the court, only one door to "the Tabernacle;" only one vail by which to enter the holiest of all. There is but one way of approach to God. (See Acts iv, 12; John xiv, 6.)

II. *The tent.* For shape, size, sockets, pillars, boards, rings, bars, cords, curtains, coverings, material, etc., Ex. xxvi. The four coverings, beginning with the outside, were as follows: 1. Of badger's or seal skin; 2, of ram's skin dyed red; 3, of goat's hair; 4, of linen with embroidery of blue, purple and scarlet.

The tent Tabernacle, or sanctuary, was divided into two compartments, "the holy place," and the "Holy of Holies." The "vail" between the two was of blue, and purple and scarlet, and fine twined linen of cunning work. This "vail" typified the flesh of the Lord Jesus (Heb. x, 20). This "vail," like the body of the Lord Jesus, revealed in part His beauty, while it also concealed and separated from the fulness of Divine glory. The innermost sanctuary was very sacred.

III. *The altar of burnt offerings.* For size, shape, material location, objects, see Ex. xxvi, 1-8; xxix, 15-18; xxxvii, 1-7; Lev. vi, 13; viii, 15; Num. xxviii, 3-6. For names of the altar, see Exod. xxix, 37; xxx, 28; xxxix, 39; Mal. 1, 7, 12. There were horns on the altar, Exod. xxix, 12; xxi, 14; Psa. cxviii, 27; 1 Kings, 1-50. The utensils used at the altar: pans, shovels, basins, flesh-hooks, firepans, see Exod. xxvii, 3; xxxviii, 3. Read the words in Lev. viii, 15: "To make reconciliation." Compare with Col. 1, 20-22; John 1, 29-36; 1 Pet. i, 18, 19; 2 Cor. v, 21; Isa. liii. The first thing a Jew saw as he approached "the Tabernacle" court was the altar of sacrifice, the type of the crucified Christ. Let our first teaching in the school of the church be "Christ and Him crucified."

IV. *The laver of brass.* For a description of the laver see Exod. xxx, 18-21; xxxviii, 8; Lev. i, 9; xvi, 4. The "looking-glasses" used in those days were of brightly polished brass. "The Tabernacle" idea involved the Divine work of purification, and the human endeavor to keep one's self from sin as well as that of atonement. Consult Psa. xxvi, 6; John xiii, 8; Isa. i, 16; Psa. li, 2-7; Titus iii, 4-7. For suggestion concerning the "mirror" see James i, 23.

V. *The golden candlestick.* (See Exod. xxv, 31-39; xxxvii, 20, 21; Heb. ix, 2.) All gold, "pure gold, beaten gold;" of gold were the "tongs" and the "snuff dishes;" it was seven-branched, a light bearer; on each branch were "knobs" like seed-laden pomegranates, and flowers, the blossoms from the seeds, and bowls in which the light seemed like fruit. 1. For the truth concerning Christ which "the golden candlesticks taught, see John i, 9; viii, 12; xii, 46; Rev. i, 12, 13. 2. For the truth concerning Christians, which is taught, see Matt. v, 14-16; Luke xii, 35; Eph. v, 8, 9, 14. "The sevenfold light is the sanctifying efficacy of the spirit. Seven is the number of holiness" (Murphy). "Apply day by day to the great Aaron of your faith to remove the dross and cause the flame of your love and zeal to ascend" (White).

VI. "*The table of shew-bread.*" For material, size, shape, crown, staves, rings, platters, spoons, bowls, covers, see Exod. xxv, 23–30; xxxvii, 10–16. On the table was the bread called the shew-bread, because each tribe was represented on it by a loaf of unleavened bread. "Bread shown" or displayed before God. It was called the "bread of faces" or "presence;" that is, God's presence. (See Lev. xxi, 6, 8, 17, 21, 22; xxiv, 5–9.) "The table is the place of paternal and hospitable entertainment." "Bread and wine are the bloodless feast after the sacrifice." "This holy place is the type of the heavenly home." "The table contained the elements of the Lord's supper, bread, wine, and the incense of prayer" (Dr. Strong.)

VII. "*The altar of incense.*" For material, size, shape, uses, horns, rings, staves, etc., see Exod. xxx, 1–10; xxxvii, 25–28; Luke, i, 10; Psa. cxli, 2; Rev. v, 8; viii, 3, 4; Isa. lx, 6. For the incense burned on the altar, see Exod. xxx, 34–38. It was rare, precious, carefully compounded, of equal proportions, never to be imitated; none but the seed of Aaron dare to offer it; it was to be beaten very small and burned with fire, and was counted sweet and holy. A type it certainly was of prayer and of the precious merits of Immanuel. As "the altar of Burnt offerings" outside the sanctuary represented the atoning work of Christ on earth, the altar of incense represented His intercessory work in heaven.

VIII. "*The ark of the covenant.*" Toward this small and sacred center all things of the Tabernacle tended. It was the end of all. It gave value to all. It was the symbol of the Divine presence. For the shape, size, parts, crown, mercy seat, staves, rings, cherubim, etc., see Exod. xxv, 10–22; xxxvii, 1–9. For its names, see Exod. xl, 3; Num. xiv, 44; Josh. iii, 13; 1 Sam. iii, 3; 2 Chron. vi, 41; Psa. cxxxii, 8; 1 Sam. iv, 4; 1 Kings vi, 16. For the contents, see Deut. x, 5; xxxi, 24–26; Heb. ix, 4. For Christ, as set forth in the ark, see Heb. iv, 16; 2 Cor. iv, 6; Isa. xliii, 16; 1 Cor. xv, 25; Rev. xii, 10; Heb. ix, 11, 12, 24. "The symbol of the Divine majesty was the only light which the Holy of Holies contained" (1 Kings viii, 12; Psa. lxxx, 1; xcix, 1).

CHRIST'S WORK.

ATONEMENT.

A CAREFUL reading of the sixteenth chapter of Leviticus will supply a Divine and comprehensive answer to the oft repeated question, "What is atonement?" It is the two-fold aspect of the cross, or sacrificial work of Jesus; first toward *God*, and then toward *us*.

He "offered Himself without spot *to God;*" and besides, He "bore *our sins* upon His own body on the tree." These two parts of the atoning work of the Lord Jesus are fully developed and elaborated in the great atonement chapter of Leviticus (xvi), and, when combined, constitute a scriptural answer to the question, "What is atonement?" In Rom. vii, "atonement" should be "reconciliation;" the former being for *God*, while the latter addresses itself to *man*.

RECONCILIATION.

Reconciliation is the effect of the work of the cross applied to persons and things in bringing them back again to God. Believers are already reconciled (2 Cor. v, 18), and all things in heaven and on earth will be reconciled. This reconciliation of persons and things is presented as the fruit of atonement in Lev. xvi. Scripture gives no countenance to the thought common to many, either that God *has* to be reconciled, or that He *is* reconciled. God did not depart from man, hence needed not to be reconciled. To say that the death of Jesus turned the heart of God to man, is to deny the truth of that magnificent declaration contained in John iii, 16. God so loved the world *that* He *gave* His only begotten Son. He loved, therefore He gave—not gave in order to love. The reconciliation of man to *God* is the blessed character of God's present ministry toward the world (2 Cor. v, 18-20). It is important to distinguish between the reconciliation of persons and things; the former is a present blessing, the latter is millennial blessing. All *things* will be brought back to God but *not* all *persons* (Col. i, 20, 21). Universal subjection to Christ of all in heaven, earth and hell (Phil. ii, 10) is certainly more wide in its range and extent than all things in heaven and earth reconciled. The passage in Col. i, 20, 21, teaches the future reconciliation of things contained in heaven and earth; while the Philippian passage shows the future subjection of heaven, earth and hell's inhabitants to Christ.

PROPITIATION.

Atonement is the expression of the united aspect of the cross toward God and toward man. Thus, in the yearly return of that solemn and deeply impressive atonement day (Lev. xvi), two goats were presented before the Lord; the one was Jehovah's lot, while the other was for the people. One was killed and its blood carried within the vail and sprinkled *once* upon the mercy seat, and *seven* times before it. The other was presented alive before the Lord, and the sins of the people confessed over it by the high priest. Now these two parts of Christ work—glorifying God by the shed and sprinkled blood, and bearing away the sins of the people—when regarded as a whole, constitute atonement. If considered separately, however, propitiation would answer to that blessed work done within the vail and before the eye of God; while substitution would refer to the transference of the sins of the people to the head of the scapegoat, and its dismissal to a land not inhabited. Propitiation is for God, and for Him alone, although it vitally concerns us. It is the blessed answer of Jesus, meeting in death and before God, the holy and righteous claims of Jehovah's throne. God has been infinitely glorified, and His moral government gloriously vindicated in the blood shedding of Jesus. Christ is now God's propitiation or mercy seat (Rom. iii, 25; 1 John, ii, 2). In Heb. ii, 19, read propitiation, *not* reconciliation.

SUBSTITUTION.

Scripture nowhere speaks of Christ bearing the sins of the world. Dying for sins and bearing sins are believer's truths (1 Cor. xv, 3; 1 Pet. ii, 24). Universal bearing of sins by Christ necessarily involves universal salvation by Christ. Substitution is the actual bearing of the sins of all who believe, and is taught in such passages as Is. liii, 6; 1 Pet. ii, 24. The sins, iniquities and transgressions of the people (Israel) confessed over the head of the scapegoat, and the animal thus burdened sent away to return no more, fully illustrates the truth of substitution (Lev. xvi, 21, 22). We as believers on the Lord Jesus Christ can now say our sins were born by Him on the tree, and are remembered *no more;* and this on the sure testimony of the Holy Ghost (Heb. x, 17).

CHRIST IN THE OLD TESTAMENT.

SOME of God's dear people seem to regard the Old Testament Scriptures as more or less obsolete, uninteresting, and useless. It seems to them to be almost completely superseded by the New Testament. But only let us study these "Lively Oracles" more diligently, having our eyes anointed with the divine "Eye-salve" of the Holy Ghost, and we shall find:

That Christ, in His Divine person and redemption work, is the great and constant theme of the Old Testament Scriptures (John v, 39). Their testimony is chiefly of Christ (John v, 46). Moses' writings pertain chiefly to the person and work of Christ (Luke xxiv, 27–44). Christ, after His resurrection, began "At Moses and all the prophets," to expound the things concerning Himself, and declares that "All things must be fulfilled which are written in the law of Moses, and in the prophets, and in the Psalms," concerning Him (1

Peter i, 10-12). When the prophets sought more light upon their prophecies concerning "The sufferings of Christ, and the glory that should follow," it was told them that they were more especially speaking for us in the Holy Ghost (Acts xxvi, 22, 23). Paul declared that he preached "None other things than those which the prophets and Moses did say should come," etc. (John xvi, 14, 15). The Holy Ghost was sent to "Glorify Christ," and show us "The things concerning him" (John xv, 26). He testifies of Christ. Thus we see that Christ, in His Divine Person and Redemptive work, is the principal theme of all the Old Testament Scriptures. Genesis is the beginning and the seed-plot of all this Gospel truth and grace (Heb. i, 1). Christ is revealed progressively in many ways and many parts, by plain and literal prophecy; by a wonderful profusion of significant names; and by a charming picture gallery of types and similitudes.

The church, at times, has inclined to fanciful and fictitious typology, but since the Reformation this subject has been neglected. We should be cautious in this study, but not too cautious (Gal. iv, 24-25). Paul says that Sarah and Hagar typify two mountains (1 Cor. ix, 9). He proves, also, from the law of Moses about feeding oxen, that the people ought to pay their ministers. What apparently wild typology (1 Cor. x, 11). All the incidents in the history of Israel's deliverance from Egypt and in the wilderness journey happened "For types," and they were written "For our admonition." Prof. W. H. Green, of Princeton, declared that we may assume that Old Testament scenes and characters are types of spiritual truth, though we may not find all the anti-types.

The natural history of the Jews and their land is significant, indeed, in comparison with that of the four great inspired; but it towers above all other history in its spiritual import and typical teaching. This makes it "Sacred history."

No one can well understand either the Old Testament or the New without some knowledge of typology. What can we say of David's imprecatory and self-righteous Psalms, unless we understand him to be a theocratic king, speaking in the name of his greater Son, who is to sit on his throne? Without a knowledge of typology, what shall we say of Esther, Ruth, the Song of Solomon, and a multitude of Levitical ceremony? I do not wonder that the natural man scoffs at these things. How shall we understand Hebrews without studying Leviticus, or Revelation without studying Daniel? We should usually take our doctrine from the New Testament, and then go to the Old Testament for types, similitudes and illustrations. Thus, the Bible is "Illuminated," like some old books whose margins are covered with the most brilliant sketches and images. A type is a stroke or impress, or anything that makes a stroke or impress. It is a sketch or prefigurement. In nature, the seed may be a type of the plant, the leaf of the tree, and the fin of the fish. In Revelation, it is some person, action, place or thing divinely ordered, selected and recorded to teach spiritual truth.

It is usually prophetic, like "A shadow of good things to come." Let me point out, briefly, a few of the many types and similitudes of Christ in the Old Testament:

(Rom. v, 14.) The first Adam a figure of the last Adam (1 Cor. xv, 45–49). Fig-leaves to cover guilty nakedness — a type of the patched and filthy rage of self-righteousness. Blood was shed in type, and God made garments of the skins to cover them. Eve was "Builded" from Adam through his deep sleep, as the bride of Christ is procured through his death.

(Gen. iv, 8–10.) Abel's sacrifice (Heb. xii, 24). Cain and Abel represent the flesh and spirit (Gen. v, 24; Jude 14, 15). Enoch, the first millenarian on record, a type of the living church, to be translated when the Lord comes. Death triumphed for six generations; but man, in the seventh, triumphed over death. Just as when the gathering gloom of judgment hung heavy in the sky, and perhaps persecution sought the one who "Walked with God," and he was not, for God *took* him — so shall it be with the faithful and waiting church at the end of this age (Peter iii, 20, 21; Matt. xxiv, 37, 39; 2 Peter ii, 5–9). The times and scenes of Noah and of Lot will be repeated (Gen. xxii and xxiv). Isaac is a type of Christ. The similitude is easily traced; born out of the order of nature, his name meaning "Laughter," and his sacrifice in a figure on Mount Moriah. He had but one bride. Eleazer, like the Holy Spirit, is sent to call her the bride; presses his message before eating; tells of the riches of his master and of Isaac's heirship; presents an earnest of these riches; will not consent to let her remain for a dowry for Isaac; wanted her "Just as she was," and he was able to endow her; they met in the fields, and from the lowly condition of a shepherdess, she became a bride in the Royal line of the Messiah (Gen. xxviii, 12; John i, 51). Jacob's ladder, a type of Christ, and foreshadowing millenial communication between heaven and earth. Perhaps the history of Joseph presents the most full and beautiful type of Christ in all the Old Testament. We can scarcely believe that the Holy Ghost would have occupied one-third of the book of Genesis simply with the biography of a pious young man. Something more and higher than the moralities of this life must have been intended. The laws of probability stand as a thousand against one that these many coincidences should have been accidental. We believe they "Happened for types" of Gospel truth and grace. Trace them: Joseph, greatly beloved of his father; hated and envied by his brethren; sent on a mission to them; conspired against and placed in a pit, and lifted out, as in death and resurrection; sold by Judah (Judas) for twenty pieces of silver — the price of a minor slave; tempted, falsely accused, condemned and numbered with transgressors; began his public life at about the age of thirty; was exalted to a throne and called Savior of the land; took a bride from the Gentiles; every knee bowed before him; his brethren were restored to him, and he reigned in majesty. See, also, Gen. xlix, 22; John xv, 5.

We can trace the typology of Moses still more clearly, and with express divine warrant (Deut. xviii, 15; John v, 46). Moses' life was sought in infancy; he refused a throne, with its worldly emoluments, and chose "Affliction with the people of God;" chose twelve, then seventy; wrought miracles; overcame demonology; changed and controlled water; cured leprosy; fed the people miraculously; fasted forty days; reflected the glory of God's presence from his face; was meek; promised another comforter; prayed and interceded wonderfully, and instituted the passover, a forerunner of the Lord's Supper, In all these things and many more, he was like unto Christ. So we might trace in detail the typical life and character of the priests, Aaron and Melchisedec, David (Saul, as anti-christ), Solomon, Jerusalem, the Nazarite, Joshua, and the whole history of the deliverance of Israel from Egypt, the wilderness journey and the conquest of Canaan, with its multitude of typical Gospel incidents.

The tabernacle of the wilderness presents the most complete system of types in all the Old Testament, and the temple was modeled after it. We see, then, what pains God has taken in all the Scriptures to reveal Christ and His salvation in every possible form. All the lines of Gospel truth, all faith and all hope centre in Him. Let us, then, study, teach and preach Him constantly. — *The Watchword.*

THE BURNT OFFERING.

Lev. i; vi, 9–13; Num. xv, 3–12; 2 Chro. vii, 1–7.

THIS was the highest in character and the first in order of all the sacrifices. Jesus in death presenting Himself to accomplish the will and glory of God. It is the Godward aspect of the cross of Christ. How much more shall the blood of Christ, who through the Eternal Spirit offered Himself without spot to God, purge your conscience from dead works to serve the living God (Heb. ix, 14)?

The offering could be of the herd, flock, or birds. Thus the animals specified are bullocks, goats, sheep, rams, lambs, turtle doves, young pigeons. Here the offering is prominent; *he* offers the animal, lays his hand upon its head, kills it, flays it, cuts into pieces, and washes the inwards and legs in water.

When it was an offering of birds the priest killed it; but that was an exception, not being directly priestly work.

The priests sprinkled the blood and arranged the various parts on the altar.

The trumpets were to be blown over these offerings on special occasions, as a memorial before God (Num. x, 10). Also in the day of your gladness, and in your solemn days, and in the beginnings of months, ye shall blow with the trumpets over your Burnt offerings, and over the sacrifices of your Peace offerings; that they may to you for a memorial before your God; I am the Lord your God.

On the entrance of Israel into the land, no *Burnt* offering was complete without an accompanying *Meat* offering; God would have the death and life of His Son thus prefigured before Him.

THE PEACE OFFERING.

Lev. iii ; vii, 11–21; Num. xviii, 17, 18.

A SLAIN Christ the ground and material of communion, whether for God, the church, or any individual member of the priestly family.

This offering could be of the herd (male or female). Bullocks. lambs and goats are specified animals.

The fat and inwards burnt on the altar as a sweet savor.

The breast (*love*) and other parts eaten by the priestly family.

The shoulder (*strength*) heaved before the Lord, and eaten by the officiating priest.

The remainder of the animal (if any) was burnt on the third day, as communion with God could only be maintained in connection with the sacrifice.

The trumpets were to be blown over the sacrifices on all solemn occasions and seasons of gladness. Also in the day of your gladness, and in your solemn days, and in the beginnings of your months, ye shall blow with the trumpets over your Burnt offerings, and over the sacrifices of your Peace offerings; that they may be to you for a memorial before your God: I am the Lord your God (Num. x, 10).

Laid on the altar of Burnt offering, as was also the Meat offering, both of which derived their worth from the moral value expressed in the Burnt offering, when God found in the blessed and voluntary surrender of Jesus to accomplish the will of God.

THE TRESPASS OFFERING.

Lev. v, 14–19; vi, 1–7; vii, 1–7; Num. xviii, 9, 10.

SINS and transgressions against God or man divinely met by Christ's sacrifice, and restitution insisted upon.

This offering was of rams and lambs.

In these offerings the main thought is not what *I am*, but what *I have done*.

Having injured another, it can only be met by sacrifice, and the injury repaired by full and righteous restitution.

Most of the particulars bearing upon the Sin offering equally apply to these sacrifices. There was no laying on of hands on the victim's head (*identification*), as in the case of Sin offerings.

Sacrifice, restitution, with an additutional part added as compensation, accompanied with confession, are characteristics of these offerings.

The *guilt* of the person is more in view in the Sin offering; here it is the *injury* done, whether to God or man.

THE MEAT OFFERING.

Lev. ii; vi, 14–23; Num. xv, 4–9; Exod. xxix, 40–42.

JESUS as man presenting to God an unblemished life, with all its grace and moral perfectness; of Him who was "holy, harmless, undefiled, separate from sinners."

The offering consisted of "fine flour" or "green ears of corn." Its adjuncts were frankincense, oil, salt. The oil "*mingled*" with the flour sets forth the truth of the Divine conception of the human nature of our Lord (Matt. i, 20); while the flour, "*anointed*" with the oil, would as fittingly signify the weighty truth expressed in Acts x, 38. "God anointed Jesus of Nazareth with the Holy Ghost and with power; who went about doing good, and healing all that were oppressed of the devil; for God was with Him." God's part was a handful of the flour with the oil, and "all the frankincense."

This offering, as setting forth the holy humanity of our Lord, is not only a sweet savor offering, but is termed "*most holy*."

Salt was not to be omitted.

Honey was not to form an ingredient.

This offering was based upon and its value declared by that which God found in the Burnt offering.

The Meat offering for a priest was wholly consumed, none of it being eaten.

THE SIN OFFERING.

Lev. iv; v, 1–13; vi, 24–30; x, 16–20.

Jesus on the cross made sin for us. The judgment of God borne and sin condemned in the holy sacrifice of Christ.

This offering could be of the herd (male or female), of the flock (male or female), of birds, and in one case of a tenth part of an ephah of fine flour.

The goat was pre-eminently the Sin offering.

The Sin, Trespass, and Meat offerings were termed "most holy."

Here the offerings varied according to the position of the offender, sin being measured by the character of God, and the responsibility of the person by the position he was divinely set in. Thus the *value* of the animal and the *application* of its blood are important points in these Sin offerings.

Sins of ignorance were not passed over, but could only be met by sacrifice.

The very poorest were thought of by God; *they* could bring a pair of birds, or even the tenth part of an ephah of flour.

The fat (*excellency*) of this offering could *alone* be burned on the altar, and go up to God as a sweet savor.

THE DRINK OFFERING.

Exod. xxix, 40–42; Num. xv, 1–13; xxviii, 7.

The *joy* of God and man in the voluntary death and life obedience of Jesus.

This offering consisted of "strong wine," poured unto the Lord in the Holy Place (Num. xxviii, 7).

A Drink offering was to accompany the daily morning and evening burnt sacrifice.

This offering could only be offered in connection with that which set forth the death and life of Jesus, namely, the *Burnt* and *Meat* offerings.

The *fourth* part of wine and the *fourth* part of oil teach that our joy (wine) is proportionate to the power of the Holy Ghost (oil).

The wine and the oil always correspond in quantity.

Drink offerings will yet again be poured out before the Lord in expression of millenial gladness.

The touching expression of Paul in Phil. ii, 17, refers to this blessed character of offering: "Yea, and if I be *poured* out as a libation on the sacrifice and ministration of your faith."

SUGGESTIVE QUESTIONS CONCERNING THE WRITERS OF THE FOUR GOSPELS.

I. MATTHEW.

1. Who was Matthew, and what his business? Matt. ix, 9; Luke v, 27.
2. What do we know of his personal history? Matt. x, 1-3; Luke vi, 12-16; Acts i, 3-13.
3. What is the central idea of the Gospel? Matt. i, 1-21.
4. What is the leading object of all of Matthew's writings concerning Jesus? Matt. i, 22, 23; ii, 15, 17, 23; compare Luke xxiv, 25-27, 44-46.
5. To whom written? Matt. i, 1.
6. How does it differ from the other Gospels?
7. How is truth here presented in contrast with other Gospels? Matt. xiii, 38; Mark iv, 14; Luke viii, 11.

II. MARK.

1. What was Mark's full name? Acts xii, 12.
2. Name his first Gospel work? Acts xii, 25; Acts xiii, 2-5.
3. When did he leave this work, and what was the result? Acts xiii, 13; xv, 36.
4. What was Paul's later or final estimate of him? Philemon 24; 2 Tim. iv, 11.
5. How did Peter regard him? 1 Peter v, 13.
6. What is the leading thought of all of Mark's writings? Isa. xiii, 1-8.

(ILLUSTRATED OR SYMBOLIZED.)
Rev. iv, 7; Eze. i, 10.

7. To whom addressed? Acts x, 38. Compare whole chapter and notice explanations unnecessary to Jews: Mark iii, 17; v, 41; vii, 3; iv, 11; xv, 34-42.

III. LUKE.

1. What was Luke's profession? Col. iv, 14.
2. What other name was he also called? Philemon 24; Rom. xvi, 21.
3. What other book did he write? Note Luke i, 3; Acts i, 1.
4. What Gospel work did he do, and whose companion was he? Acts xvi, 10, 12; xx, 5, 6; xiii, 13-15; xxvii, 1-8; xxviii, 13-16; 2 Tim. iv, 11; 1 Thess. iii, 2.
5. In the narration of facts, how does Luke's writings differ from the other writers? Luke i, 1-4.
6. What is the leading thought of Luke's Gospel? Luke xix, 1-10 (especially note 10th verse, 1st clause).
7. How does Luke's Gospel differ from Matthew? Compare Matt. i, 1, with Luke iii, 38.

IV. JOHN.

1. What John was this? Matt. iv, 21.
2. What else do we know of his personal history? John i, 35; Matt. x, 2; xvii, 1; xxvi, 37; Mark v, 37; xiii, 3.
3. What was the highest honor Jesus ever bestowed on him? John xix, 26, 27.
4. What other writings is John author of?
5. In what respect does he appear like Luke? 1 John i, 1-3.
6. What is the central thought of the book? John i, 1-3, 14; compare Eph. ii, 4-7.
7. To whom addressed? 1 John v, 13; John xx, 31.

JOHN H. ELLIOTT.

WHAT THE SCRIPTURES ARE.

I. *The Word of God.* So then faith cometh by hearing, and hearing by THE WORD OF GOD: Rom. x, 17; Luke viii. 11; Acts xiii, 44.

II. *The oracles of God.* What advantage then hath the Jew? or what profit is there of circumcision? Much every way; chiefly because that unto them were committed THE ORACLES OF GOD: Rom. iii, 1, 2; Acts vii, 38.

III. *The Word of the Lord.* Finally, brethren, pray for us, that THE WORD OF THE LORD may have free course, and be glorified: 2 Thess. iii, 1; Acts xiii, 48.

IV. *The Word of Life.* Holding forth THE WORD OF LIFE; that I may rejoice in the day of Christ, that I have not run in vain, neither labored in vain: Phil. ii, 15, 16; Acts v, 20.

V. *The Word of Christ.* Let THE WORD OF CHRIST dwell in you richly in all wisdom: Col. iii, 16; John v, 40; 2 Tim. iii, 15.

VI. *The Word of Truth.* In whom ye also trusted, after that ye heard THE WORD OF TRUTH: Eph. i, 13. Rightly dividing the Word of truth: 2 Tim. ii, 15. Sanctify them through thy truth; thy Word is truth (John xvii, 17). In all things approving ourselves as the ministers of God *** by the Word of truth: 2 Cor. vi, 4–7.

VII. *The Word of Faith.* The Word is nigh thee, even in thy mouth, and in thy heart; that is, THE WORD OF FAITH, which we preach; that if thou shalt confess with thy mouth the Lord Jesus, and shalt believe in thine heart that God hath raised him from the dead, thou shalt be saved: Rom. x, 8, 9.

JAS. H. BROOKES, D.D.

WHAT THE SCRIPTURES DO.

I. *By them we are born again.* Being BORN AGAIN, not of corruptible seed, but of incorruptible, by the Word of God, which liveth and abideth for ever: 1 Peter i, 23; James i, 18.

II. *By them we are cleansed.* Now ye are CLEAN THROUGH THE WORD which I have spoken unto you: John xv, 3; Eph. v, 25, 26.

III. *By them we are built up.* And now, brethren, I commend you to God, and to the Word of His grace, which is able to BUILD YOU UP, and to give you an inheritance among all them which are sanctified: Acts xx, 32; 1 Peter ii, 2.

IV. *By them our hearts are made to burn.* Did not our heart BURN within us, while he talked with us by the way, and while he opened to us the Scriptures? Luke xxiv, 32, 45.

V. *By them God's will is accomplished.* So shall my Word be that goeth forth out of my mouth; it shall not return unto me void; but it shall ACCOMPLISH that which I please, and it shall prosper in the the thing whereto I sent it: Isa. lv, 10, 11; Jer. xxiii, 29.

VI. *By them the thoughts of the heart are exposed.* The Word of God is quick and powerful, and sharper than any two edged sword, piercing even to the dividing asunder of soul and spirit, and of the joints and marrow, and is a discerner of the THOUGHTS AND INTENTS of the heart: Heb. iv, 12; Ps. cxix, 11.

VII. *By them the sinner is to be judged.* The Word that I have spoken, the same shall JUDGE him in the last day: John xii, 48; Luke xvi, 29–31.

JAS. H. BROOKES, D.D.

ALL SCRIPTURE.

2 Tim. iii, 16.

Wonderful library of sixty-six distinct volumes. It took forty writers 1,500 years to write. They wrote in countries widely separated, and tongues often entirely different, but "all Scripture" is a unit; the sixty-six volumes are all one book. Two things are set forth in 2 Tim. iii, 16:

I. MAN THE WRITER, BUT GOD THE AUTHOR.

1. Plenary inspiration.

2. Not of men, but of God: 1 Thess. ii, 13; Heb. i, 1, 2.
3. Not man's wisdom: 1 Cor. ii, 13.
4. Not by will of man: 2 Peter i, 20, 21. The Holy Spirit is thus shown to be the author.
5. It is therefore called "the sword of the Spirit." Eph. vi, 17.

II. THE PROFITABLENESS OF "ALL SCRIPTURE."

1. For "Doctrine" (teaching). The simple principles of truth which the ignorant can only know through the dogmatic teaching of "all scripture."
2. For "Reproof" (correction of sin). The Holy Spirit wielding His Sword: John xvi, 7-11 (cf.); Eph. vi, 17.
3. For "Correction" of our errors concerning the truth; illustrate God's love, man's condition, the way of life, etc.: John iii, 1-16.
4. For "Instruction in Righteousness:" Matt. vi, 33 (cf.), with Rom. x, 1-10.

JOHN H. ELLIOTT.

WHAT GOD SAITH.

I. Concerning Himself, (1) Ex. xx, 3; (2) Ex. xxxiv, 6, 7; (3) Job xl, 9; (4) Jer. v, 22; (5) Jer. xvii, 10; (6) Isa. xlv, 21, 22; (7) 1 John v, 8-10.
II. Concerning ourselves, (1) Gen. vi, 5; (2) 1 Kings viii, 46; (3) Ps. xiv, 2, 3; (4) Isa. i, 5, 6; (5) Jer. xvii, 9; (6) John ii, 25, and Mark vii, 21; (7) Rom. iii, 10-19.
III. Concerning His feelings and purposes about sin, (1) Gen. ii, 17; (2) Jer. xliv, 4; (3) Ezekiel xviii, 20; (4) Rom. v, 12; (5) Rom. vi, 23; (6) Eph. ii, 1-3; (7) 1 Tim. v, 6.
IV. Concerning Jesus Christ His Son, (1) Matt. iii, 17; (2) John iii, 16; (3) John v, 22, 23; (4) Rom. viii, 3; (5) Gal. iv, 4; (6) 1 John i, 7; (7) 1 John v, 11, 12.
V Concerning the way of salvation. (1) John iii, 18: (2) John v, 24; (3) Acts x, 43; (4) Acts xiii, 39; (5) Acts xvi, 31; (6) Rom. iv, 5; (7) Rom. x, 1-10.

VI Concerning Heaven. The believer has there (1) a Father, Matt. v, 16; (2) Treasures, Matt. vi, 20; (3) A house. 2 Cor. v, 1, 2, (4) His citizenship. Phil. iii, 20; (5) A Hope, Col. i, 5; (6) A Friend, Heb. ix, 24, (7) An inheritance, 1 Peter i, 4.

VII. Concerning Hell. (1) Matt. x, 28; (2) Matt. xxv, 46; Luke xvi, 23, 26; (4) 2 Thess. i. 6-10; (5) 1 Tim v, 24; (6) Heb. x, 28, 29; (7) Rev. xxi, 8.

"THE MINISTERING OF THE WORD."

The necessity:
 Titus i, 3; 1 Cor. i, 21; Rom. x, 14.
The true Minister sent of God:
 Matt. ix, 37, 38; Rom. x, 15.
Who may minister?
 1 Cor. xii, 4-11; Rom. xii, 3-8; Eph. iv, 7, 8, 11, 13; 1 Peter iv, 10, 11.
Some cases in point:
 Num. xi, 26-29; Luke ix, 49-50; Acts ii, 1-4, 17, 18; viii, 1-4; xix, 1-6; Gal. i, 15-17; Acts ix, 20; 2 Cor. iv, 13.
The commission:
 Mark xvi, 15, 16; 1 Cor. xiv, 1-5, 31-39; Rev. xxii, 17.
What to preach:
 Jonah iii, 2; 2 Cor. iv, 5; 1 Cor. ii, 4, 5.
How to Preach:
 2 Tim. iv, 1-4; Gal. i, 10; Jer. xxiii, 28.
Some to remember:
 2 Cor. v, 20; Gal. i, 8, 9; 1 Cor. i, 26-29; Deut. xviii, 20; Prov. xxx, 5, 6; Jer. xxiii, 9-22.

L. W. MUIRHALL.

GOD'S WORD A MEANS OF REVIVAL.

IT CONVERTS.

The law of the Lord perfect converting the soul: Psa. xix, 7.
Of His own will begat He us with the Word of truth: James i, 18.
Born again, not of corruptible seed, but by the Word of God: 1 Peter i, 23.

IT PURIFIES.

That He might sanctify and cleanse * * * by the Word: Eph. v, 26.

Ye are clean through the Word which I have spoken: John xv, 3.

Sanctify them through Thy truth. Thy Word is truth: John xvii, 17.

TESTIMONY OF CHRIST.

Rich man and Lazarus: Luke xvi, 31.

Words that I speak * * * are life: John vi, 63.

Life through hearing and believing: John v, 24.

TESTIMONY OF GOD IN HISTORY.

Revival in time of Josiah: 2 Kings xxiii, 2, 3.

Revival in time of Nehemiah: Neh. ix, 3.

Revival in time of Apostles: Acts iv, 29–31.

H. E. BROWN.

JEHOVAH TITLES OF GOD.

I. Jehovah-Elohim. Gen. ii, 7; John i, 1–3: Col. i, 15–18; Heb. i, 1–3.

II. Jehovah-Jireh. Gen. xxii, 14; John iii. 16; 1 Cor. xv, 1–4; 1 Peter, ii, 24; iii, 18.

III. Jehovah-Rophi. Ex. xv, 26; Matt. ix. 12; Luke iv, 40; Acts x, 38; Heb. iv, 15, 16.

IV. Jehovah-Nissi. Ex. xvii, 15; Matt. xxviii, 18–20; Rom. viii, 31–39; Phil. iv, 13.

V. Jehovah-Shalon. Jud. vi, 24: Eph. ii, 14, 17; Col. i, 20; Rom. v, 1: John xiv, 27.

VI. Jehovah-Tsidkenu. Jer. xxiii, 6; xxxiii, 16; 1 Cor. i, 30; 2 Cor. v, 21.

VII. Jehovah-Shammah, Ezekiel xlviii, 35; John xiv, 1–3; 1 Thess. iv, 17; Rev. xxi, 1–6.

DIVINE RECONCILIATION.

2 Cor. v, 14–21.

God and man meet in Christ God glorified—sin put away—man reconciled.

Verse 21. No reconciliation until sin put away.

Ver. 17. No mending or patching—entirely new.

Inner life changed. New creation new man, new life. New views of God, Christ and the Holy Spirit. New views of soul, sin and salvation. New views of world, heaven and Bible.

Ver. 18. Reconciled first ourselves, then trying to reconcile others.

Ver. 19. As God was in Christ, so Holy Spirit in us. This and word of reconciliation all we need.

Ver. 20. In Christ's stead. He took our place; we take his.

God thinks of us as he does of Him.

God loves us as he loves Him.

Our sins laid on Him; His righteousness laid on us.

W. G. CARR.

THE RECONCILIATION OF GOD AND MAN.

I. The meaning of reconcile is to bring together again, to reunite, to restore to union and friendship after estrangement, Rom. v, 11 (margin). The Greek words used concerning reconciliation have peculiar meanings, as follows: (1) To be changed throughout or mutually, as in Matt. v, 24: 1 Sam. xxix, 4. (2) To change thoroughly a person to another; *i.e.* man toward God, from enmity to friendship, as in Rom. v, 10; xi. 15: 1 Cor. vii, 2; 2 Cor. v. 18–20. (3) To change thoroughly from; *i. e.*, fully, as in Eph. ii, 16: Col. i. 20–22. In all these words, as relating to God and man, is expressed the great change between a holy God and sinful man.

II. The case may be stated as follows: (1) Through the sin of man, the original relation of love and peace between God and man was broken; (2) through it man became both subject to the just displeasure and punishment of God, and also wholly estranged from God and at variance with God; (3) God through Christ crucified (himself the propitiation, 1 John ii, 2: iv, 10), expiates or cancels man's sin, removes man's guilt and so opens the way of man's return to God; accordingly, God in the gospel of His grace calls upon man to lay aside all enmity and distrust toward God, and to turn in faith and confidence and love to Him who first loved us. The call is, God is reconciled, be reconciled to Him; God is friendly, let us be friendly; God has come to us, let us go to Him, 2 Cor. v, 20. "In all natural religions. man is seeking God; in the Christian religion God is seeking man," Luke xix, 10.

III. The original and permanent type and illustration of the case is given in God's dealings with the first sinners of the race in the garden of Eden; in man's sin, fear and guilty hiding from God; in man's blaming (enmity) God; and in God's seeking the sinners, and in mysterious words and rites giving man hope of future deliverance, Gen. iii, 8–24. God from the beginning had the great end of reconciliation and salvation in view, and God also furnished the means. If His was the wrath, His was also the blood; if His the justice, His also the grace. It is God who in Christ propitiates God. Man becomes silent before God. Man must needs as a sinner be satisfied with what satisfies God.

IV. *The Scriptures concerning the reconciliation.* (1) It is God who reconciles the world unto Himself, 1 Cor. v, 16–20; (2) in such purpose and work, Christ as one with God is joined. God could not commend His love toward us in Christ's dying for us, if they are not one, Rom. v, 6–11; (3) it is through Christ crucified God reconciles, Rom. v, 5–11; 2 Cor. v, 13–21; Eph. ii, 14–18; Col. i, 18–22.

V. *The end and results of the reconciliation.* (1) The holiness of reconciled sinners, Eph. i, 4; Col. i, the 21, 22; 2 Cor. v, 20, 21; (2) the new creation, consisting of holy beings under the one head. Christ Jesus, Eph. i, 10; Col .i, 15–20; Phil. ii, 9–11; (3) the glory of God, and especially because of His grace to the church, the body of Christ, Eph. i, 5, 6, 22, 23; ii, 7; 1.i, 15–18.

W. J. ERDMAN.

THE LOVE OF GOD.
1 John iv, 7–16.

Shoreless, fathomless, boundless. Five things in this chapter: Life, peace, love, power, boldness.

Verse 7. Love not knowledge, the test of discipleship, John xxi, 15.

Ver. 8. Having the Divine life, we must love.

Ver. 9. Love *shown* by sending "only begotten" into the world, John iii, 16. Life *given* by raising "first begotten" from the dead, Col. i, 18; Rom. iv, 25.

Ver. 10. Love put Him on the cross to take my place; love puts me on the throne to take His place.

Ver. 13. *Knowing* is the secrect of power, 1 John v, 4.

Ver. 15. Men will be lost, not because they have done this or that, but because they reject the Lord Jesus Christ.

Ver. 17. "As He is" accepted, perfect, complete, so am I, Col. ii, 10.

Ver. 18. Such love never fears death, poverty nor the devil.

God cared for His Son. He wont forget His *child*.

We can't earn this love, but we may *apprehend it more.*

W. G. CARR.

GOD'S LOVE.

1. A part of His nature, 2 Cor. xiii, 11; 1 John iv, 8; Eph. ii, 4; Zeph. iii, 17; Isa. xlix, 15, 16; Rom. viii, 39; Hosea xi, 4; Jer. xxxi, 3.

2. Manifested through Christ, John iii, 16; Titus iii, 4; Luke xix, 10; Gal. ii, 2; John xv, 13; 1 John iii, 16.

3. Shown in gifts to His children,

1 John iii, 1; 2 Cor. ix, 15; James i, 5; Ps. xxix, 11; 2 Thess. i, 7; Rom. v, 6.

H. B. CHAMBERLAIN

GOD LOVES THEE.

1. God so loved the world that He gave His only begotten Son, * * * John iii, 16.
2. God commendeth His love toward us, in that while we were yet sinners, Christ died for us, Rom. v, 8.
3. God, who is rich in mercy, for his great love wherewith he loved us, even when we were dead in sins, hath quickened us together with Christ, Eph. ii, 4, 5.
4. Hereby perceive we the love of God, because He laid down His life for us, 1 John iii, 16.
5. In this was manifested the love of God toward us, because God sent His only begotten Son into the world that we might live through him, 1 John iv, 9.
6. Herein is love, not that we loved God, but that He loved us, and sent His Son to be the propitiation for our sins, 1 John iv, 10.
7. And we have known and believed the love that God hath to us, 1 John iv, 16.

JESUS HIMSELF.

I. EQUAL WITH GOD.

Equal with God, John v, 18.
Life in Himself, John v, 26.
Made Himself the Son of God, John xix, 7.

II. HIS HUMILITY.

Humbled Himself, Phil. ii, 6–8.
Glorified not Himself, Heb. v, 5.

III. HIS LIFE ON THE EARTH.

Knowing in Himself that virtue had gone out of him, Mark v, 30.
Himself cometh to the grave, John xi, 38.
Himself took our infirmities, Matt. viii, 17.
Girded Himself, John xiii, 4.
Christ pleased not Himself, Rom. xv, 3.
He Himself hath suffered, Heb. ii, 18.
Endured such contradiction of sinners against Himself, Heb. xii, 3.

IV. HIS DEATH.

He saved others; Himself He cannot save, Matt. xxvii, 42.
Who gave Himself for our sins, Gal. i, 4.
Christ also loved the church and gave himself for it, Eph. v, 25–27.
Who gave Himself a ransom for all, 1 Tim. ii, 6.
Who gave Himself for us, Titus ii, 14.
Who loved me, and gave Himself for me, Gal. ii, 20.
When He had by Himself purged our sins, sat down on the right hand of the Majesty on High, Heb. i, 3.
When He offered up himself, Heb. vii, 27.
Offered Himself to God, Heb. ix, 13, 14.
Nor yet that He should offer Himself often. But now, once in the end of the world, hath He appeared to put away sin by the sacrifice of Himself, Heb. ix, 25, 26.

V. HIS RESURRECTION.

Jesus Himself stood in the midst of them, Luke xxiv, 36.
After these things Jesus shewed Himself, John xxi, 1.
The third time that Jesus shewed Himself, John xxi, 14.
To whom also He shewed Himself alive, Acts i, 3.

VI. HIS ASCENSION.

God shall also glorify Him in Himself, John xiii, 31, 32.
Christ Himself being the chief corner stone, Eph. ii, 19, 20.

VII. HIS SECOND COMING.

The Lord Himself shall descend from heaven, 1 Thess. iv, 16, 17.
For our conversation [citizenship] is in heaven; from whence, also, we

look for the Savior, the Lord Jesus Christ, who shall change our vile body, according to the working whereby He is able even to subdue all things unto Himself, 1 Phil. iii, 20, 21. — *The Truth.*

WHAT CHRIST IS.

I am, John viii, 58.
I am He, John iv, 26.
I am the Door, John x, 9.
I am the True Vine, xv, 1.
I am the Bread of Life, vi, 35.
I am the Good Shepherd, John x, 11.
I am the Light of the World, John viii, 12.
I am the Resurrection and the Life, John xi, 25.
I am the Way, the Truth, and the Life, John xiv, 6.

THE NAME JESUS.

The peerless name Jesus, contains millions of ideas, millions of blessings, millions of wonders. Barnard has well said: "It is honey in the mouth, melody in the ear, and a jubilee in the heart." We often sing,

"How sweet the name of Jesus sounds
In a believer's ear,"

because we know, experimentally, somewhat of its preciousness. The very enunciation of that name should thrill our souls with holy delight, and fill our hearts with unspeakable gladness. Our Divine Lord wears many titles as well as many crowns. To Him, also, is given a multitude of names, all significant and expressive. In Isaiah ix, 6, are found a cluster of such goodly names, more precious than the grapes of Eschol — "Wonderful, Counselor, Mighty God, Everlasting Father, Prince of Peace." What child born, what son given, could win from heaven such appellations but He alone, who is God manifest in the flesh, and whose one name, Jesus, embraces all.

As an aid in our study, I will briefly outline one phase of this precious subject, the name Jesus.

1. It is personal, human name, Matt. i, 21.
2. What it expresses. "He shall save," Matt. i, 21.
3. Who Jesus is, Matt. i, 23; Isa. vii, 14. Name stands for character or quality. Vanderbilt or Rothschild means wealth: Washington, patriotism; Lincoln, goodness. This thought may be easily amplified and illustrated, Prov. xxii, i; Eccl. vii, 1; Prov. x, 7. Jesus means wealth and goodness and power and love; in a word, salvation.
4. Observe how wise men worshipped Him, Matt. ii. How angels announced Him, Luke ii. How Simeon proclaimed Him, Luke ii.
5. How His work of deliverance was typified by another Jesus. Joshua is the Hebrew, and Jesus the Greek forms of the same name. Joshua's victory, Acts vii, 45. Joshua's incomplete work, Heb. iv, 8. Compare Matt. xi, 28, 29. "I will give you rest;" "Ye shall find rest."
6. The name Jesus is power, Acts iv, 12.
7. It is life, John xx, 31.
8. It speaks forgiveness, Acts x, 43.
9. Devils are subject to it, Luke x, 17.
10. The perfume of the name, Songs of Sol. i, 3.
11. It means Lordship and universal dominion, Phil. ii, 10. (Here is a fine opportunity for profitable teaching.)
12. Prevailing prayer is offered in His name, John xiv, 13; xvi, 23, 24.
13. Thanksgiving arises as incense when offered in his name, Eph. v, 20; Heb. xiii, 12-15.
14. Every true act of Christian service to be performed in that name, Col. iii. 17.

Blessed be God, "His name shall endure forever."

GEO. C. NEEDHAM.

WHAT THERE IS IN JESUS' NAME.

Note the preciousness, Acts iv, 12; omnipotence. Isa. ix, 6; worthiness Rev. v. 11–13; excellence, Phil. ii; 9, 10; richness. Acts x, 43, of Jesus' name, Ps. xiv, 17; Mal. i, 11.

"All hail the power of Jesus' name."   J. HOWARD SEAL.

CHRIST IN OLD TESTAMENT.

I. Christ in His Divine person and work is the great and constant theme of the Old Testament, John v, 39, 46; Luke, xxiv, 27, 44; 1 Pet. i, 10–12; Acts xxvi, 22, 23; John xvi, 14, 15; John xv, 26; Rev. xix, 10.

II. Important to understand types and similitudes of Christ which "illuminate" the Scriptures. Be cautious but not too cautious, 1 Cor. x, 1; Gal. iv, 24, 25; 1 Cor. ix, 9. To the natural man, what "wild typology." Much of the Old Testament is almost meaningless without a knowledge of typology.

III. Christ and his work is foreshadowed in many persons, actions, places, things, divinely ordered and recorded. Adam, the fig leaves, Eve, Abel, Enoch and Noah, Rom. v, 14; 1 Cor. xv, 45–49; Heb. xii, 24; Jud. xiv, 15; 1 Pet. iii, 20, 21; 2 Pet. ii, 5–9; Matt. xxiv, 37–39.

Isaac, Joseph and David in about a score of important particulars each.

The whole history of Israel, from Egypt to Canaan, is typical. 1 Cor. x, 11. The tabernacle in its various parts — furniture, offerings — presents a complete set of types of Christ and redemption. These lineaments of the Redeemer and traces of redemption may seem dim at first, but in the progress of revelation and interpretation, they become more and more clear and luminous until —

> "Earth's sad story,
> Ends in glory,
> On yon shore."
>   E. P. M.

ADAM AND EVE.

Eve necessary to Adam. "Not good for man to be alone." "No helpmeet for him in creation." "I will make a helpmeet for him," Gen. iii, 18, 19, 20. "The woman for the man," 1 Cor. xi, 9. The man before God's mind, and the woman only as she ministers to the glory of the man. So God makes a "marriage for *His Son*." The Son is the centre of everything.

Eve seen in Adam before she had an actual existence apart from him, Gen. i, 26, 27. Shew the church in the Divine purpose, Ephesians i, 4. "Chosen in Him." Before the foundation of world. Blessed with all spiritual blessings in Him. "According to eternal purpose," Ch. iii, 11.

The formation of Eve, Gen. ii, 21, 22. The deep sleep fallen upon Adam. The death of Christ necessary to formation of the church, John xii, 24; Eph. v, 25, 26. The result, the builded woman. The process of building going on in the night of his sleep. In the morning of resurrection the church shall stand forth in beauty, and Christ will show his satisfaction in her. "She pleaseth me well" will be the answer, as it will be the admiration of all coming ages, Eph. ii, 7.

Adam fell through the woman, 1 Tim. i, 14. Christ came in grace into the place where we lay on account of our sin. Gave himself for us. Supported and sustained by His own love. See Ps. xxii. The results in blessing are ours, John v, 24.

The close union between Adam and Eve, Gen. i, 23; Eph. v, 30. Members of His body, flesh. A union of life. I am part of the Christ; necessary to the completeness of the man. Christ cannot lose a member, part of Himself, John x, 37, 38.

The separation of the church unto Christ. Rom. vii, 2; 1 Cor. vi, 16. 17; Eph. v, 28, 31, illustrate Gen. xxiv. 58, 59.

ADAM CREATED FOR DOMINION.
Gen. i, 26.

1. It was always God's intention to rule the world by man. All God's previous work with a view to this — previous work of creation; the process of fitting the earth for man.

2. Dominion lost by sin. God's purpose to rule world by man not thereby set aside. He brings in the second man, and invests all future dominion and blessing in his hand, Gen. iii, 15. Contains in promise to the second man. The Lord of the woman. The germ of all that God has developed, or ever will develop, in the way of blessing for man and the world. No promise to man as fallen, but to the woman's seed, or the second man.

3. Dominion will again be in the hands of man in the person of Christ, Ps. viii. Compare with Heb. ii, 6–9; 1 Cor. xv, 27, 28. Notice "All things put under Him." And all things subdued by Him. Christ's authority as man extends throughout the universe. And we shall see what "rule" is according to God.

4. The church as the Eve of the new creation, will share the dominion with Him, Eph. i, 23. Head over all things for the church. Adam did not rule over Eden but with her. Christ not King of the church, but of the Jews and the Head of the church. The church being "the fullness of Him who filled all things, with all." Eve owed everything to Adam. The church owes present blessing and future glory to Christ.

W. H. WALKER.

CHRIST OUR PASSOVER.
Exodus xii; 1 Cor. v, 7.

Israel was to begin a new existence from the time of their redemption out of Egypt, verse 2. John iii, 3–5; 1 Pet. iv, 3. Life until Christ is known a blank. Really death, Luke xv, 24. Eph. ii, 1–2. "Dead," "yet walking," activity in sin.

Every man a lamb. The lamb was every man's need, the lamb every man's provision camp, Rom. iii, 22. No difference, for all have sinned, Rom. ii, 1. No difference, for all who call upon the Lord shall be saved. Man's individuality before God.

The character of the lamb, verse 5. "Without blemish," 1 Pet. i, 19; Heb. vii, 26–28. "Examined," John viii, 46; xviii, 38; Matt. iv, etc.

The Lamb and the law. Ten days passed before the Lamb was taken. Ten, the measure of human responsibility, Rom. x, 4; Gal. iii, 22–25.

The Lamb to be slain, verse 6. Christ's death. Atonement. "Without shedding of blood no remission." Christ as an example merely, does not meet the need. Purity of character needed in order to the efficiency of the dead, Heb. ix, 14; 1 Pet. i, 19; ii, 22; 1 John iii, 5.

The sprinkled blood, verse 7. Appropriation, Gal. ii, 20. "Me," Rom. iii, 22. "Upon." No condemnation, Rom. viii, 1; John v, 24. Safety, Rom. v, 9, 10; Heb. vii, 25; Rom. viii, 32. Peace, Eph. ii. verse (15). "Made," (17). "Preached," (14). "Christ our."

Eating the flesh in the house, verses 8, 9. All the lamb must be eaten. A complete Christ presented in Gospel. Christ meeting divine and human requirements. Christ in His person. Offices, work, in past, present, future. Death the sustenance of Life. Illustrate Judges xiv, 9–14. Note the order, first, under shelter of the blood, then feeding on lamb.

"*Unleavened Bread,*" 1 Cor. v, 6–8; Gal. v, 9.

"*Bitter herbs,* Ex. i, 14; Num. ix, 11; Zech. xii, 10.

Loins girded, Matt. xxvi, 19, 20; Luke xii, 35; Eph. vi, 14; 1 Pet. i, 13.

Shoes on feet, Luke xv, 22; Eph. vi, 15.

Staff in hand, 1 Pet. ii, 11.

W. H. WALKER.

THE MERCY SEAT.
Exodus xxv, 17–22.

The mercy seat of pure gold. Divine mercy seat. Christ propitiation, Rom. iii, 25. The provision beyond human needs. It is Divine.

The graciousness of Divine mercy. The thought, pattern and provision all of God. The spontaneous outcome of grace to a sinful people, verse 17. "Grace first contrived a way."

The mercy seat covered the law, verse 16. Christ's obedience to law. Christ the end of the law. Came in between sinner and law. Mercy seat covered all the transgressions of the law. The law established in sinners justification, Rom. iii, 31. God's law honored in its precept and in its penalty.

The righteousness of Divine mercy, Lev. xvi, 14. Blood "upon" and before mercy seat. God not merely merciful but righteous, Isa. xlvi, 21; Rom. v, 21; Rom. iii, 26. God looks down and sees the blood and is satisfied. The sinner draws near and sees the blood and is justified. God and sinner both justified in the mercy seat.

The mercy seat the meeting place, verse 22, 2 Cor. v, 19. "God was in Christ," Rom. iii, 25. Whom God hath, Lev. xvi, 2. Divine glory on mercy seat, John i, 14; Deut. v, 26. God meeting not to destroy, but to save. John xiv, 6. No man cometh unto the Father but by Me. Acts iv, 12. Neither is salvation in any other.

The Titles of the Mercy. The sovereignty of Divine Mercy. Rom. ix, 15, 18. Rich Mercy. Eph. ii, 4. Abundant mercy. 1 Pet. i, 3. Come to "Throne of Grace" that we "may obtain Mercy." Heb. iv, 16.

The Mercy Seat and the Redeemed (Verse 18). One piece with mercy seat (18). Col. iii; Eph. v. Sustained by mercy seat (19). Ex. xxviii, 12. Faces toward mercy seat (20).

The rejection of the Mercy. 1 Sam. vi, 19. Mercy seat set aside. Ark looked into. Men of Beth-shemesh. Compare Heb. xii, 29.

W. H. WALKER.

"THE BRAZEN LAVER."
Exodus xxx, 17–22.

Its material and construction, Ex. xxxviii, 8. Made out of looking glasses. Brazen mirrors of the women. Looking glass to see myself. Water to wash. Word the glass. Jas. i, 23, 24. Word the water. Eph. v, 26. All the word manifest, Heb. iv, 12. The high priests meet, Heb. iv, 14.

Its purpose. For Aaron and his sons, verse 19. Once washed, ch. xxix, 4–9. Never repeated, Heb. x, 14. Daily defilement, John xii. Met in the advocacy, 1 John ii, 1, 2. Of Jesus Christ, the Righteous One. The Brazen Altar left, for the acceptance on the ground of atonement is complete, and the Brazen Laver is used to meet daily defilement. Laver, not *before* the alter but *after* it.

Its Teaching. 1. The Holy character of God. 2. Holiness required in those who would approach Him. 3. The blood the basis of true Holiness. 4. The Laver *behind* and not *before* the altar.

W. H. WALKER.

MANNA.
Exodus, xvi, John vi.

The gracious provision of God. The murmuring of people, verse 2. Grace triumphing instead of Judgment. Abundance of the provision, verse 4. I will rain. Christ the gracious provision of God for the Son of Man.

Christ the Manna. Its description. 1. Small. Is. liii. No beauty that we should desire him. 2. Round. Eternity of Christ. See Prov. viii, 22–31. Father of Eternity. Is. ix, 6. 3. White. Purity, Light. 4. Fell upon dew. Separation from earth, holy; harmless; undefiled; separate from sinners. No contact with earth. Christ nourished by Holy Ghost. John xvi.

Food for a Redeemed People. 1.

Earth cannot satisfy the Lord's Redeemed. 2. God redeemed them that He might feed them. 3. Children's food must come from the Father's Table. 4. The food *endures* unto everlasting life. 5. The manna ceased in wilderness, but Christ, who is our wilderness food, will also be our food in the land; hence the 'food' endures unto everlasting life. John vi, 27.

The Manna gathered. Christ appropriated. 1. They did not labor to procure it, but to appropriate it. John vi, 27. "Labor for." Comp. with "which the Son of Man shall *give* unto you." See, also, Prov. ii, 3, 4, 5, 6, especially noticing: "For the Lord *giveth* wisdom." 2. Daily provision for daily need. What is true Christian experience? The experience of Christ in me to-day. How much "sour" manna have we? Musty experience — living on past feelings, etc., instead of the Taste of the "fresh oil." Many of God's children feed on dried raisins instead of fresh grapes full of juice. 3. Gathered as much as they could appropriate. I can have as much of Christ as I can use.

The Manna a Testimony, verse 4 To prove them (the Israelites). 1. The grace of God proving the people. Christ the test now. The cross bringing out what man is. God in law and God in goodness. Heb. i, 13. God speaks *in* the Son. Heb. ii, 1. Therefore we ought to give heed, lest we neglect a salvation now.

The Manna a Memorial, 32, 33. 1. The Manna in the land same as in the wilderness. We are going to enjoy the same Christ in heaven we enjoyed in the wilderness. 2. Our wilderness experience of Christ will be better understoed and appreciated when we get Christ in the glory.

The Manna and the Sabbath. Rest. The appropriation of Christ secures rest of *soul.* Matt. xi, 28. Rest in *service.* Verse 29

W. H. WALKER.

BLOOD OF THE NEW TESTAMENT.

INTRODUCTORY.

The relation of the blood to Salvation.

Atonement through *penalty.* Lev. xvii, 12.

Without the *shedding* of blood, *no remissiou.* Heb. ix, 19–22.

"*Great,* through the blood of the everlasting covenant." "The *Good Shepherd* giveth his life for the sheep." Heb. xiii, 20, 21.

I. SACRAMENTAL IDEA.

Blood of the New Testament.

(a) Shed for *you*, addressed to His ministering disciples.

(b) *Shed for many.*

(c) *In all cases for the remission of sins.* Luke xxii, 20.

The blood is the life, typifying the Spirit which is life. John vi, 53–56. Where "*commununion*" is equivalent to *communication.* 1 Cor. x, 16.

II. SEVENFOLD WORK OF THE BLOOD.

1. *The Church is purchased with the blood.* Acts xx, 28.

2. *Sanctified by the blood.* Heb. xiii, 11, 12, the sin and burnt offerings.

The blood of the covenant. Heb. x, 28, 29.

The blood of sprinkling and its work. Lev. viii, 30.

3. *Made nigh by the blood of Christ.* Eph. ii, 13.

4. *Justified by the blood.* Rom. v, 8, 9. *Justified by His blood: saved by His life.*

5. *Redemption through His blood.* Redemption is the *forgiveness of sins.* Eph. i, 7.

Obtained by Christ entering the heavens with His blood. Heb. ix, 11, 12.

The *precious blood* of Christ is the *instrument* of our redemption. 1 Peter i, 17-19.

6. *Washed from our sins in His blood.* Rev. i, 5, 6. Because of Christ's love. 1 John i, 7; "IF we walk in the light."

7. *Purges the conscience from dead*

works. Heb. ix, 13, 14. Old Testament, *purifying of the flesh*, versus New Testament, *purging the conscience*.

REV. G. J. BROWN.

THE BLOOD OF CHRIST.
(Is. liii, 4 ; 1 Peter ii, 24.)

I. Justification by blood of Christ. Rev. v, 9.
II. Made nigh to God by blood of Christ. Eph. ii, 13, 14.
III. Have peace by blood of Christ. Col. i, 20.
IV. Redemption by blood of Christ. Col. i, 14 ; Heb. ix, 12 ; 1 Peter i, 18, 19.
V. Believers are purged by blood of Christ. Heb. ix, 22 ; Ps. viii, 7 ; 1 John i, 7.
VI. We enter into holiest by blood of Christ. Heb. x, 19.
VII. Enter heaven by the blood of Christ. Rev. vii, 9 ; xiv, 15.

GEO. A. WARBURTON.

THE BLOOD OF JESUS.

I. *The condition of the sinner as the blood finds and covers him.* Gen. iii, 7, 12. Verse 7 shows what man did for himself after he became a sinner. Verse 21 shows the first thing God did for him. Gen. iv, 3, 4 ; Is. lxi, 10.
II. *How the blood shelters him.* Exod. xii, 1–3, 6, 7, 13 ; John xii, 32 ; Exod. xii, 22, 23.
III. *Deliverance by the blood.* Heb. ix ch.; Heb. xii, 22–24.
IV. Definition and power of the blood. Lev. xvii, 11.
V. The body consecrated by the blood. Rom. xii, 1 ; Lev. viii, 22–24.
VI. The soul restored by the blood. Heb. ix, 13, 14 ; Num. xix, 17.
VII. Victory through the blood. Rev. i, 5, 6 ; xii, 10, 11 ; vii, 14.

A. P. GRAVES.

CHRIST DIED FOR THY SINS.

1. "He was ' wounded [margin, tormented] for our transgressions." Is. liii, 5.
2. "Behold the Lamb of God, which taketh away the sin of the world." John i, 29.
3. "Christ died for our sins according to the Scriptures." 1 Cor. xv, 3.
4. "God hath made Him to be sin for us, who knew no sin." 2 Cor. v, 21.
5. "Christ hath redeemed us from the curse of the law, being made a curse for us." Gal. iii, 13.
6. "Who His own self bare our sins in His own body on the tree." 1 Peter ii, 24.
7. "Christ also hath suffered for sins, the just for the unjust." 1 Pet. iii, 18.

FAITH IN CHRIST WILL SAVE THEE NOW.

1. "He that believeth on the Son *hath* everlasting life." John iii, 36.
2. "He that believeth on Me hath everlasting life." John vi, 47.
3. "By Him all that believe are justified from all things." Acts xiii, 39.
4. "Being justified by faith, we have peace with God, through our Lord Jesus Christ." Rom. v, 1.
5. "Ye are the children of God by faith in Christ Jesus." Gal. iii, 26.
6. "I know whom I have believed, and am persuaded that He is able to keep that which I have committed to Him against that day." 2 Tim. i, 12.
7. "These things have I written unto you that believe on the name of the Son of God, that ye may know that ye have eternal life." 1 John v, 13.

CHRIST GIVES THEE GREAT PROMISES.

1. "Lo, I am with you alway, even unto the end of the world." Matt. xxviii, 20.
2. "If I go and prepare a place for

you I will come again, and receive you unto Myself; that where I am, there ye may be also." John xiv, 3.

3. "I will pray the Father, and He shall give you another Comforter, that He may abide with you forever." John xiv, 16.

4. "He that loveth Me shall be loved of my Father, and I will love him, and will manifest Myself to him." John xiv, 21.

5. "Hitherto have ye asked nothing in My name: ask, and ye shall receive, that your joy may be full." John xvi, 24.

6. "I will never leave thee, nor forsake thee." Heb. xiii, 5.

7. "He that overcometh, the same shall be clothed in white raiment; and I will not blot out his name out of the book of life, but I will confess his name before My Father, and before His angels." Rev. iii, 5.

UNBELIEF WILL DAMN THEE.

1. "He that believeth not shall be damned." Mark xvi, 16.

2. "He that believeth not is condemned already, because he hath not believed in the name of the only begotten Son of God." John iii, 18.

3. "He that believeth not the Son shall not see life, but the wrath of God abideth on him." John iii, 36.

4. "If ye believe not that I am He, ye shall die in your sins." John viii, 24.

5. "Unto them that are contentious, and do not obey the truth, but obey unrighteousness, indignation and wrath, tribulation and anguish, upon every soul of man that doeth evil." Rom. ii, 8, 9.

6. "The Lord Jesus shall be revealed from heaven with His mighty angels, in flaming fire, taking vengeance on them that know not God, and that obey not the Gospel of our Lord Jesus Christ." 2 Thess. i, 7, 8.

7. "The fearful and unbelieving * * * shall have their part in the lake which burneth with fire and brimstone; which is the second death." Rev. xxi, 8.—*The Truth.*

"LAMB OF GOD."

Sacrifices—their character. Gen. iii, 21; iv, 3–7; viii, 20, 21; xx, 6–14.

Sacrificial lamb. Ex. xii, 3–7, 13; xxix, 38–42; Lev. xxiii, 9–12; 1 Sam. vii, 8–10.

Not the creatures, but the blood. Heb. ix, 19–22; Lev. xvii, 11.

Not the shadow, but the substance. Heb. x, 1–4.

Who then does it refer to? Prov. viii, 22–31; Heb. x, 2d clause of 5 to 7.

Who is it? John i, 29, 30, 35–37.

Application. 1 Peter i, 18–21; Heb. ix, 23–26, 11–14.

Jesus speaks. John xii, 27; Matt. xxvi, 24.

Agony (Prophecy, Isa. liii, 6). Matt. xxvi. 37, 38; Luke xxii, 41–48.

Taken and tried (Prophecy, Isa. liii, 7) John xii, 32, 33; Isa. i, 6. Matt. xxvi, 49, 50; Luke xxii, 54, 63, 65; Luke xxiii, 1; Matt. xxviii, latter part of 26–37, 45–53.

Burial (Prophecy, Isa. liii, 9). Matt. xxvii, 57–60.

Resurrection. (Prophecy, Matt. xx, 18, 19; Ps. xvi, 19;) Acts vii, 55, 56.

Lamb in heaven. Rev. iv, 1–5; v, 6–14; vii, 9–11; xxi, 9, 10, 22, 23; xxii, 3–5; vi, 15, 16; xxii, 16, 17, 20; John iii, 16–18; Acts iv, 12; Rev. xii, 11.

Exhortation. Heb. x, 19–25.

RUSSELL STURGIS, JR.

THE LAMB OF GOD.

BY HENRY MOORHOUSE.

BEHOLD THE LAMB OF GOD. — John i, 29.

WE will turn to a few passages of Scripture which, I trust, will fill all our hearts with joy, bearing, as they do, on a subject of which the Scripture speaks more than on any other — that is, the Lord Jesus Christ as the Lamb of God. The first passage is in Exodus xii, and that is the first place in the Bible where we read about the death of the lamb. In the fourth chapter of the book of Genesis, we read Abel brought of the firstlings of his flock, but the word "lamb" is not mentioned. And in Genesis xxi, we read that Isaac said to his father, as they were ascending Mount Moriah: "Where is the lamb for a burnt offering?" But we know that at the top of the mount it was not a lamb, but a ram, that was offered. Therefore the first place we read of the death of the lamb, as a sacrifice, is in our passage, Exodus, xii; and here there cannot be the slightest doubt that it represents the Lord Jesus Christ, for Paul tells us that "Christ our passover is sacrificed for us." Now this is a chapter that has been frequently expounded, and I do not mean to enter upon it, but merely to point out one or two beautiful facts; for there is always something fresh to be gathered from God's word. In the first place there must have been at least two hundred and fifty thousand lambs slain that night, and yet we never find the word lambs; the word is always in the singular, and never in the plural. And when God appoints the killing of these lambs, he does not say kill them, but "kill it in the evening." It is as though God would see in them all but one lamb.

One grand representation of His spotless lamb. All through it is the lamb which is spoken of, and it is the lamb of God that is pointed to. Again (verses 2-23) if you read that chapter very carefully you will find that it was not an angel who was sent to destroy the Egyptians; but that the Lord Himself, Jehovah, went round to smite the Egyptians and all the families where the blood was not found. At other times, when it was merely a question of destroying the enemy (as in the camp of the Assyrian), we read that God sent an angel; but here, when it was a question of the safety of his own people, it appears as if the Lord could not trust an angel, but must come Himself. Again and again in the chapter we read that it was the Lord, and not an angel at all. Then with what was the blood to be sprinkled upon the doorposts and lintels? It was with hyssop. I believe this has a meaning, though many may not agree with me here. The Bible tells us that Solomon "spake of trees from the cedar tree that is in Lebanon even unto the hyssop that springeth out of the wall." Everyone knows that the cedar signifies pride, magnificence; and so, on the same principle, the hyssop signifies humility and lowliness. Pride and the blood never go together. Wherever we see pride of heart, we may be sure that the blood is not there.

PICTURE OF SUBSTITUTION. — Exodus xiii, 13.

We at once notice what a wonderful picture we have here of substitution. Here is an unclean beast, an ass. As soon as it is born, it is sentenced to die; nothing can save it but substitution. Many tell us we do not need substitution. Well, you might develop the mind of that ass as much as you please, but no matter; unless redeemed, its neck must be broken. Man is in the same catalogue. You may educate him as much as you like; but unless he find a substitute, unless he is born again, he cannot see the kingdom of God.

THE GOSPEL PLAN. — Leviticus ix, 3, 4.

Here we have the whole plan of Christianity brought out with great clearness. First, the Israelites were to bring a Sin offering; then a Burnt offering; thirdly, a Peace offering; and lastly, a Meat offering. Here we have the Gospel plan. The first thing we have to do is to deal with Christ as the sin bearer. The Lord Jesus Christ has died for us, and there is our Sin offering. But when we have come to this we are not done with Christ or with Christianity. It is but the beginning, not the end. What is next? The Burnt offering. What is that? Something placed on the altar, given to God, and never to be taken back. Something which God had said should be given to him, and something burnt on the altar inside the Tabernacle, not, as was the case with the Sin offering, outside the gate. What does it mean? Consecration. What does God ask of me? Having put my sin away, He expects a consecrated life. Not saved because consecrated, but consecrated because saved. "I beseech you, therefore, brethren, by the mercies of God, that ye present your bodies a living sacrifice, holy, acceptable unto God; which is your reasonable service" (Rom. xiii, 1). It is not only our souls, but our bodies also. It is not "I have such a glow of feeling" here. That is not consecration. It is that every saved man and every saved woman should be wholly yielded to God, and ready to bear trials and troubles as the Master bore them. It is that our hands and feet should be consecrated and used for the Master. It is that our tongues should be used for Him. It is not enough to say that "we are consecrated in spirit." God says, "I want your bodies." But then that is not all. After the Burnt offering comes the Peace offering. The man or woman who has got the peace of God, is the man and the woman who are consecrated. It is only such who have God's peace, the peace of God. Then comes the Meat offering; and what does that imply? It is feasting on the Lamb of God. Why is it that a great many Christians prefer the newspaper to the Bible? Because they have not offered the Burnt offering, they are not consecrated; because they have not the Peace offering, and know not the peace of God; therefore they do not enjoy the Scriptures. Sin put away, the body consecrated, the peace of God realized, then they may feed on the Lamb of God, as revealed in His precious Word. The reason why many do not enjoy feeding on the Bread of Life, is they have a bad conscience. They are nursing some secret sin; they are not consecrated to God, and therefore they do not enjoy His Word of Truth.

THE GREAT ENEMY.—1 Samuel vii, 7–10.

The Israelites had learned one useful lesson, and that was to be afraid of the Philistines. One of the first lessons for an individual, or a church, is for that individual or church to learn to fear the enemy, Satan. There is terrible danger in the tendency of many to ignore Satan. A lady said to me the other day, "You are not so foolish as to believe in a personal devil?" "Oh, yes," I replied, "I am." "Why so?" "For the same reason that I believe in a personal Christ, because the Book tells me of both, and the Book cannot lie." What is written is enough for me; We have in these days songs about Satan, as if he were a myth; and we hear men shouting on the very streets about him. Nothing Satan likes so much as that; he just wants people to get familiar with him. The men who sing so lightly about him do not know much of his terrible power. Satan hates the church, just as he hated Christ; and he would fain do to the church just as he did to the Master. We must learn to dread him and avoid him. "Oh," said a man the other night, "I had a fight with the devil!" "Did he conquer you?" "No; I was a match for him?" I tell you the whole church of God is not a match for the old adversary. We want the power of Christ. We must trust a personal Christ to fight for us.

I once learned a lesson from a little boy. He was quarreling with a big boy, and the big boy hit him. The little boy said,

"Its no use my trying to fight thee; thou art too big for me. Just wait here until I fetch father, and he'll thrash thee." The big boy did not wait. But let us learn the lesson. It is no use our trying to fight Satan; let us get down on our knees and pray for help from God, and Satan will not wait for that.

THE LAMB OFFERED.

Now, these Israelites were afraid, and they sought help from God. They went to Samuel, and what did he do? He "took a sucking lamb, and offered it for a Burnt offering wholly unto the Lord." The whole lamb was there. The lesson for us is to take the whole lamb of God, Jesus, the Christ, the Son of God, the Son of man, as ours, with all his resources. The Philistines said: "We are not afraid of your sucking lamb. We will have you in captivity; we will destroy you." But God thundered on the Philistines, and discomfited them. There was more power in that lamb when offered to God than in all the mighty host of the Philistines put together. Many think we want some wonderful gift before we can serve God, but what we do want is faith to trust Him, and then go out and preach the simple Gospel, the story of the love of Christ. The man who preaches Christ will draw men to listen to him. The Christ of the Bible is still the mighty power. Men tell us we do not want the Bible now-a-days. If ever there was a time when we did want it, it is now. Honor the Bible in your preaching, and God will honor you. I have been about a good deal, but I have never known a man converted to God — I have known men converted to this or that religion, but never to God — apart from that blessed Book. So the Israelites sacificed a lamb, trusted in God and were saved, and that is still the only secret of our safety from the enemy. There is a great deal more about the Lamb in the Old Testament, and we might refer to very many interesting passages; but we must now pass on to the New Testament, and I will not touch upon the passages in the Gospel of John, the Acts of the Apostles, or the Epistle of Peter, but proceed to the closing book of the Bible (Rev. v, 1–8.)

There is something very wonderful about this scene in heaven, because it is the first time we read of the Lamb of God in the book of the Revelation. The last time we read of him was on the cross, in His sufferings and humiliation. That was where man put him, but now we look where God has put Him. Man nailed Him to the cross of shame; God set him on the throne of glory. Man had despised and rejected Him; but now everybody praises Him, because they know his value. Now, notice that when John got up there he began to weep. It is a strange thing, because it is the only place we read of tears of sorrow being shed in heaven. I believe that they were really tears of sorrow, although caused by a mistake which he made. The question is asked: "Who is worthy to take the book, and open the seal thereof?" There is at first no response. John looked around and saw no one come forward. People have right thoughts of themselves up yonder. There is not one in that shining throng, not one in the host of the redeemed, who thinks himself worthy. He looked round heaven — not one there; he looked on earth — not one there; he looked under the earth, and certainly saw none there who could open the book. John wept; but one of the elders said, "Weep not. This is not a place for sorrow; it is a place of rejoicing." There are no tears of sorrow in heaven. "God shall wipe away all tears from their eyes" (Rev. vii, 17).

Doubtless there are tears of joy. Those who have crossed the Atlantic have seen many such. Here are a young gentleman and his wife. They have been some years in America; they are coming over to see the old folks at home. As the steamer approaches the Mersey, they are talking much about the dear ones — wondering if mother will be altered much, and if father will be at the pier to meet them, and how their sisters are. By and by we enter the river; the tender comes puffing up alongside. They are getting nearer now, and you notice they have no eyes for the fine scenery, or the bustling passengers. They are absorbed watching for the pier. The young wife gets hold of the glass and looks through it earnestly. "No, I can't see any one yet," she says. They get nearer and nearer. Up with the glass again. "I think I see some one like mother." The tender reaches the landing stage; there is a great crowd, but soon she sees "mother," and as she flings herself in her arms there is a burst of tears, "mother, mother!" Are those tears of sorrow? Nay; but of wondrous joy. Is it not a little picture of what it may be when we get "home at last?" Do you not think that when we get to the pearly gates, and see the blessed Master waiting to receive us — see the wondrous Lamb of God, who took away our sins, ready to welcome us — there will be some such tears — weeping for fullness of joy? Such are the only tears that shall be shed "in that bright world above."

But John was weeping for sorrow, and so the elders say, "Why, you did not look in the right place, John." I have looked on the cherubim, I have looked among the twenty-four elders, I have looked amongst the multitude of angels and of saints, I have looked on the earth; but among them all there is no one worthy to take and to open the book!" "True, John, but you have not looked on the throne." He looks, and there are no more tears. The Lamb of God was worthy. On earth he was reckoned worthy of death, while there he is worthy of the throne, and the only one worthy to open the book.

So the first glimpse of the lamb in this book of the Revelation reveals him on the throne of glory.

FOLLOWING AND PRAISING. — Revelation vii, 13-17.

Now let us turn to Rev. vii, 13-17, where we get another glimpse at the Lamb of God. The Lamb of God in the midst of His redeemed host! And notice that He "shall feed them and lead them unto living fountains." He only does in heaven what He does for His own on earth. He satisfies us down here and leads us; and He will satisfy us and lead us in heaven, as well as on the earth (Rev. xii, 11).

The blood of the lamb is the secret of their conquering strength (Rev. xiv, 1-5). His "Father's name written in their foreheads." There is something very suggestive about this expression. We read in the thirteenth chapter that the mark of the beast might be placed on the brow, or on the right hand. It seems that some people might not like to have the mark blazoned on their foreheads, and so the beast permits them to put his mark on the palm of their right hand, where it might be hidden. But the Father's name must be blazoned on the forehead. It is not enough, then, to see that the mark of the beast is not on our brow, for it may be covered up in the hand. What we want is to see that the Father's name is stamped on the brow. He will not have any one ashamed of Him or His mark. If we have it at all, it must be displayed on the brow, where it can be seen of all. There is one thing more about a mark on the brow, and that is that the man who bears it is the only one who does not see it. So when a man is wholly consecrated to God, he is the last one to talk about it. His fellow disciples will see it; the world around will see it; but when a man himself finds it out, and begins to talk about it, very few other people can see it.

FIGHTING AND CONQUERING. — Revelation xv, 3, 4; xvii, 14.

I have read these passages because it is just the course of those who follow the lamb. First of all they are not ashamed of Him; and then they follow Him; and as they follow Him they sing "the song of the lamb." Nobody ever sings from the heart but those who follow the Lamb of God, and have been redeemed by his blood. Then, as they sing, they fight; and as they fight, they conquer. But how do they fight? The Lamb of God goes first and slays the enemy, and gives them the credit. Even as God thundered on the Philistines and smote them, and then gave Israel the credit of discomfiting them, so it is confessing, following, praising, fighting, conquering, and all with the Lamb of God and by the Lamb of God. In Rev. xix, 9, we find they finish up, as every one likes to finish their day's work, with a supper. Now this supper is the last meal of the day. After breakfast we go out to work; after dinner we have work again ; after tea we have, perhaps, a meeting to attend, or something else to do; but after supper we do not expect work; it is rest. So, after the marriage supper of the lamb, there lies before us God's grand, eternal rest. The weary pilgrimage is past, the hard fight is over, the victory is won, and the rest has come. Truly, they are blessed who shall sit down to that supper; and how thankful we should be that the Bible tells us of this supper !

(Rev. xxi, 22–27; xxii, 3.) This is the last place in the Bible that we read of the lamb. He is on the throne, and His servants serve Him, while their greatest delight is to see His face. We have seen where man put the Lamb of God, and we have seen where God, the Father, has put Him. Man put Him on the cross; God put Him on the throne. First there was suffering; then glory. And that is the rule for us, His people — first the cross, then the crown. But above all, there was for Him but one way to that grand mediatorial throne, and that way lay by the cross. Thus we see the Lamb of God suffering on the cross, and then crowned in glory. "Wherefore God also hath highly exalted Him, and given Him a name which is above every name, that at the name of Jesus every knee should bow, of things in heaven and things in earth, and things under the earth; and every tongue should confess that Jesus Christ is Lord, to the glory of God and the Father" (Phil. ii, 9–11).

THE GOOD SHEPHERD.

BY HENRY MOREHOUSE.

I AM THE GOOD SHEPHERD. — John x, ii.

I WANT to ask our friends to take their Bibles, and turn with me to a few passages of Scripture in connection with the subject of the Lord Jesus Christ as the Good Shepherd. You remember that in John x the Savior calls Himself "the Good Shepherd." And you know He told us His mission down here was to teach us about God, His Father. It was not very often He spoke about Himself, but when He did it was always something to cheer and encourage His people. Now the Lord Jesus tells us twice over in this wonderful chapter that He is "the Good Shepherd;" and knowing that there is not a single Christian in this place that doubts the Word of the Lord Jesus — and we all know that whatever the Savior said He meant — therefore, when He tells us He is the Good Shepherd, we know that He is so simply because He said it. But, my friends, we shall find it very profitable to take God's Word, and see for ourselves what the Good Shepherd has done for us, is doing for us, and will do for us. All these little details we find brought out so sweetly in God's blessed Word.

The first shepherd was Abel, though he was not called shepherd, that term being afterward used. God called him a "Keeper of sheep." Shepherd means simply a keeper of sheep. My friends, some Christians imagine that perhaps, after all, they may perish; but no, they cannot. A shepherd is not a loser, but a keeper of sheep. The Lord is the Good Shepherd, and will not lose us, but means to keep us.

The word "shepherd" is first used in Gen. xlvi, 32, in connection with Jacob and his family coming down to Joseph; and we read (verse 34) that "They went to dwell in the land of Goshen, for every shepherd is an abomination to the Egyptians;" so that the shepherd and the sheep were both detested by them. We are the sheep and Christ is the Shepherd, both being abominable to the world. If you want to go into the world as a sheep, the world will not have you; worldlings do not want the Master, and they do not want His sheep. Go to them as a worldly man, and you are all right; go as a child of God, and you are all wrong.

There is another noticeable thing in connection with the shepherd. The sheep were entrusted to him, and were required back from him. You remember what Jacob said to Laban concerning any that were missing from the flock: "I bear the loss; of my hand didst thou require it." But not a single sheep of the Lord Jesus can be lost, because He is the Good Shepherd, and has given His life for the sheep.

Now let us read together Ezek. xxxiv, 11–16: See what the shepherd had done for the sheep.

I want you to observe six things that the shepherd promised to do for the sheep; and mark, He says: "I will do them." He will do them himself, and not through another:

1. I will seek them. 2. I will deliver them. 3. I will separate them. 4. I will bring them to their own land. 5. I will satisfy them. 6. I will make them rest.

Eighteen hundred years ago, the Lord Jesus came to seek and to save that which was lost; and He is doing it now!

He found us in the house of bondage, in captivity, and He delivered us; He died not only to save us, but also to separate us, by His own precious blood, from a guilty world; then He will bring us to our own land, and there will He feed us.

It is striking that He never promises to feed the sheep until they get to their own land. God did not send the manna till the people had left Egypt; the prodigal son did not see his father till he left the far country. He will feed us, and you know feeding means satisfying. You cannot get a sheep to lie down until you have fed it — until it is satisfied; and the shepherd says: "I will feed and satisfy you, and cause you to lie down to rest."

Now turn to another passage, to which I am sure our minds will all go at once, Psalm xxiii.

I suppose nearly every one can repeat this Psalm from memory; but everyone cannot repeat it from the heart. I will tell you why. There is not a sheep in the fold of Christ that could say it from the heart, unless that sheep is satisfied; then he can lie down. Some are always seeking some one to satisfy them, but will not let the Master do it; yet none can satisfy, except the Good Shepherd Himself, and He will.

Until we come to Him, we can find nothing to satisfy. I want to call your attention to the three Psalms brought together here very sweetly: Psalms xxii, xxiii, and xxiv. They should never be read separately. You know in John, Jesus is called the Good Shepherd, because He has laid down His life for the sheep; in Hebrews, He is called the Great Shepherd, because He is risen from the dead; in Peter, He is called the Chief Shepherd, because He is coming back again. There is death, resurrection, and the second coming of Christ, in connection with His sheep. And if you will read this beautiful twenty-second Psalm, you find the Good Shepherd giving His life for them; in the twenty-third, you have the Great Shepherd in the resurrection blessing them; and in the twenty-fourth, you find the Chief Shepherd leading them through the pearly gates into the better land. There is the Good, Great, and Chief Shepherd. "The Lord is my Shepherd." He must be not only our shepherd, but my shepherd. And dismal and dark as are many places around us, there is not one poor wretched creature but can, if he believe on the Lord Jesus, say as much as David: "The Lord is my Shepherd." Yes, thank God, if we are in His fellowship, we can each say individually: "My Shepherd; I shall not want." Then He says: "He maketh me to lie down in green pastures," etc. You know we sometimes see sheep driven alone on the Whitechapel Road, and you see them wearied and tired; afterward they get a little grass, and the poor things are allowed to rest. That is not the way our Shepherd deals with us. He does not drive us till we are tired, and then feed us. It is not leading, and then resting; but rest first, and leading next.

But more, "He restoreth my soul." I wonder why the restoring came in there! But it is because the nearer we are to Him, the more Satan will tempt us. He will try to draw our hearts away;

but the shepherd puts out His right hand and restores us. Sheep must be near the shepherd to be restored, and they must be near Him to be tempted. Now I want you particularly to notice this fourth verse, because it is one of the sweetest in Scripture. "Yea, though I walk through the valley of the shadow of death, I will fear no evil; for thou art with me; thy rod and thy staff, they comfort me."

I believe the "valley of the shadow of death" means not only the shadow that is on everything around us here, but when passing through the valley, if the Lord tarries. And notice a beautiful change here. In the second and third verses it is "He;" but now, in the fourth, it is no longer "He." As soon as we get into the valley, there is something sweeter. You may talk of Him, but there is something better than that; in the valley we talk to Him, "For thou art with me." Is there not something very sweet and precious in that beautiful word "thou?" Have we not noticed, again and again, as we sat by the death-bed of some one that loved the Master, that after the eye is closed and they do not recognize you, when the ear is shut, and they cannot hear your voice, — have you not seen a beautiful glow steal across that face, and the lips moving as if conversing with some one? It was not you; it was not an angel. To whom were they speaking? Was it not the Good Shepherd? Yes, my brother; yes, my sister. If you have to enter that valley of the shadow of death, He will stand by you till you reach the other side.

He will stand by you in the dark night, and will never leave you, never forsake you. It is sweet to have Him to speak to; and though insensible of everything else around us, not insensible of his presence; He will make us to know Himself.

I used to wonder also why the rod and staff are there: "Thy rod and thy staff, they comfort me." I once heard it said that they were kept to beat the sheep with. Well, the crook at the end is used to draw the sheep out of ditches when in the wilderness; but here, in the valley of the shadow of death, they are with the Master, and talking to Him. The reason why they get into the ditches when in the wilderness is, that they are trying to get away from the shepherd; but the Lord Jesus does not need to beat them, or to pull his own out of ditches when near to Himself. His purpose is to protect and to defend us. The next verse tells us there are enemies there (verse 5); but we have not a defenceless shepherd; we have one with a rod and a staff in his hand, not to beat his sheep, but to put away his and their enemies — to make all for you and me, passing through the valley.

Notice further, it is a valley. You know it is hard work climbing a hill-side sometimes; but how very easy it is to go down a valley! and, thank God, it is down a valley we have to go. He had made it easy for us.

We must also notice that little word, "through." We walk through the valley of the shadow of death — right through it. We do not stay there. I do not need to care when, sometimes, in a train I enter a tunnel, because I know we shall soon be out in the daylight; it may be dark and gloomy for a little while, but soon there is light and sunshine. And in the valley it cannot be dark when the Master is there, the Good Shepherd, for He is "the light of the world."

Another word is very sweet to me, and it is that word, "walk." It means, He is in no hurry; we are going to walk through. And there is another cheering thought. You may carry a dead sheep, but it must be a living sheep that can walk through the valley. Well, here we read: "Yea, though I walk through the valley of the shadow of death."

Then the next verse tells us He is going to feed us. We are not to be hungry then. I will tell you what workers need all through this weary world — we need feeding. We need feeding to give us strength, and the Lord Jesus, the Good Shepherd, knew that. He says: "I will feed you." He brings us to the valley, and what is He going to do? He spreads a table before us in the presence of our foes, and even Satan himself shall see us satisfied. Thank God for such a Shepherd and such a Savior!

Then this verse concludes by saying he is going to anoint us. You know Moses anointed the priests just before they went into the holy presence; the last thing was to put sweet savor on them. And so it will be with all. There is to be sweet savor put on us before we go into God's presence, and the Shepherd Himself is going to anoint us. He is the Good Shepherd and giveth his life for the sheep. I need not call your attention to that last verse — the shepherd leads, and goodness and mercy bring up the rear; so that, if a poor sheep does go astray or get tired, and lag behind, goodness and mercy come along, and help the worn out one; the shepherd goes first, and goodness and mercy follow after. Now let us turn to John x. Look at the twenty-seventh verse: "My sheep hear my voice, and I know them, and they follow Me."

Is there not something very sweet there? My friend, if you want to know the mark of true sheep, they follow the shepherd; that is the mark of Christ's sheep — they know the Shepherd's voice, and go where He leads. Do we not get the Shepherd's voice in this blessed book. Sometimes we get like Peter, and follow at a distance; but you know that is a bad place to be in, at a distance. Sheep are known by following close to the Good Shepherd.

Sometime ago, when dear Mr. Sankey and myself were in Chicago, a missionary arrived from Syria, and a friend said to him: "Do the shepherds all bring their sheep to the water at once?" "Yes, they bring them down for refreshment." And that is how I think the sheep gather together for refreshment, and you know not what they are, except that they are Christ's sheep. But when the sheep have finished, they all follow their own shepherd.

Well, my friend asked if they ever refused to follow the shepherd. "Yes, sometimes a sheep gets sick, and then he will not follow." Now I want you to be charitable to everyone. I used to see Christians doing what I thought was not right, and I said: "Why, they are not Christians." But now I think every man should be taken at his word; and if he makes a profession of faith in Christ Jesus, I believe him. When you see such an one doing what is not becoming of a Christian, going apparently over to the world, do not say he is not a sheep — that may be wrong; but say he is a sick sheep, that he is not healthy; and sick sheep go their own ways, and after their own hearts, too. Healthy sheep are known by following the shepherd. "My sheep hear my voice, and I know them, and they follow Me." Now, did you ever see a sick sheep? It is a sad thing to see a sick sheep in the flock. You know that very often in England there is a very bad disease among sheep — the foot and mouth disease; and these two parts are always diseased together. The disorder breaks out in the foot, and then soon after it appears in the mouth. Well, when a Christian visits you, and by-and-by begins to talk of Brother So-and-so, and commences to tell you something bad about him, you just get as far away as you can from that one. He has the mouth disease, and it is very catching; get away from him. The Lord does not want his sheep to be sick, but to be well and healthy.

Now look at that little word "I know;" it has been one of the greatest comforts to me of any word in this blessed book: "I know them." My friends, you might pass through the busy streets of London, and they could not tell you were a Christian; you would not, perhaps, see any one you know, or get a kind word. The first time I came to London, I was walking in Oxford street, and there were thousands of people passing along that thoroughfare, but not one knew me, and I felt utterly lonely there. How sweet a thing it is for us to understand that, though the world may not know us, yet Christ says: "I know you — the Shepherd knows His sheep." In Manchester, where I come from, we have what we call our "annual festivities" in Whitsun week; every Whitsun week the schools march in procession to some place appointed, but Whit-Monday is the great day; the scholars of the Episcopal schools go out on that occasion.

Two years ago there was a poor woman standing in the street; on one side she had a little girl by the hand, and on the other she had another little girl. By-and-by the procession came along, and they could not see at all, because of the crowd between them and the scholars. The woman pushed forward, and asked some men to let the girls stand in front and they could see over them; the men good-naturedly said, "Yes, and you can stand in front as well, if you like." "Well, on came the scholars, and the first school passed, and another, and yet another. The mother did not seem to look at one of them; she had her eyes fixed right in the distance, and did not seem to see these schools. By-and-by they heard the sound of the fifes and drums of the Industrial School; as soon as ever she heard that, she turned and said, "Willie's coming." The band came up, and passed, and the elder boys passed, but the mother did not seem to mind them; but when the little fellow came, in corduroy clothes, she looked eagerly among them, and soon cried, "Willie, Willie?" In a moment the boy sprang out of the ranks, and she clasped him in her arms and kissed him. She gave him a penny and an orange, and he went on again to his place in the procession. She knew him in that vast crowd, and loved him; when he passed there was one eye saw him, and one heart loved him; she knew her boy, and she cared for her boy, though he had been wicked and had been punished. Well, the Good Shepherd cares for us, He knows us and loves us, and He says, "My sheep hear My voice, I know them, and they follow Me." I tell you friends, the more you and I know the Good Shepherd, the more closely do we follow Him; and the more do we love Him, because we understand better His mighty love to us. I will ask you to turn to 1 Sam. xvii. There we find a little illustration of what the Lord Jesus says: "My sheep shall never perish." Look at verses 33–37: Now we get two different beasts here coming against the sheep, a lion and a bear, and we find David killed them both on purpose to deliver the innocent lamb from their grasp; the shepherd went out to rescue the innocent lamb. Now, what does this teach us? There is no animal so strong as the lion, and Satan is a roaring lion; yet one thing the lion cannot do — it cannot use craft. But those who have been in America know that the craftiest thing on earth is a bear; the bear can go anywhere. The lion cannot climb a tree; the bear can. This, then, teaches the power of Satan; the lion and the bear, strength and cunning. Some people are always talking about their wonderful experience, they have got so high; but, however high you have got, the bear can follow; he can climb after you. The strength of the lion and the craft of the bear took off the lamb, but David was a match for them both, and our shepherd is a match both for the power of the devil and the craft of the devil; and neither the strength nor the wiles of Satan is going to get the lamb out of the shepherd's flock.

Now, turn to Luke xv, 3–7. I am going to read that, because I mean to ask Mr. Sankey to sing "The Ninety and Nine." I think we may get tired of this parable as soon as of that song, because it is just the parable put into verse. The shepherd went after this one sheep out of the ninety and nine. Is that not just the Good Shepherd coming after you and me, when we have gone astray? We have wandered, and He puts us on His "shoulders"— not shoulder, but shoulders; that poor sheep wants carrying; both shoulders are used for the sheep; and yet we find in Isaiah that one shoulder is enough to support the universe. Why did not he take this sheep to the ninety and nine instead of home? They would say, "Look at your wool, it is all torn and dirty;" and that sheep would have wandered away again as fast as possible; but when we understand the Shepherd's love and care, we cannot go astray. I must ask you to turn once again, not that the subject is exhausted — for there is much more in this book about the Good Shepherd — but the time is nearly spent. Turn with me to Isa. xi, 11. This is a very sweet passage. You notice here that God promised to carry the lambs "in His bosom;" when He brought back the wandering sheep it was "on His shoulder." I am thankful it was not a lamb that went astray. A great many people are afraid of young converts. Well, Scripture says the old converts go astray as well as the young. You remember when the Lord Jesus Christ was here on earth, mothers brought the little ones to Him and He took them in His arms and blessed them. The only ones He promised to take in His bosom here are the young ones — the lambs. It is for a purpose. He says He shall gently lead the mothers with the young. He carries the lamb — why? For the purpose of helping the mother sheep. Do you not think that it is very true that sometimes — I should not say sometimes, but always — the sheep are always going astray. The world is attractive, and vanity, like a beautiful bubble, is attractive; but the Lord, I doubt not, will bring the sheep back; I believe, if we do not come back, He will carry us back by main force — He will compel us to return. Sometime ago I went down to some people in the country; there were all the sheep and lambs in the fields. I thought, would it not be nice to imitate the Eastern shepherd, and have a sheep come after me. So I began to try to coax one as I would a dog. She would not mind me a bit, and my friend said, "You do not know about sheep, else you would never try to get one to run after you." However, I still kept on; I ran after the sheep and caught one of its lambs, and carried it; but the sheep did not come after me; it had a lamb still. I gave the lamb I had caught to my friend, and went after the second one, and having caught it, I put a lamb under each arm. Well, you should have seen the sheep then. Why, she fixed her eyes on me and kept as close as possible to me. When I walked she walked; when I ran she ran. But I did not want her lambs, and so I just gave them back to her. Now there is a man going to business; he takes down the Bible, and, thinking all the time of his business, reads a portion. At night he had no time, because of business; he has got some big orders, or is expecting some. But he has one little girl, who is the light and life of the whole house, and her heart is full of joy; every time her father comes home she runs to meet him. One day he does not meet her, and learns that his darling little Annie is sick; she has caught that terrible disease, diphtheria. The doctor comes. "Can you do anything for my child?" "I will do my best," he says. But by-and-by the doctor says she is dying. The father comes to gaze on that sweet face, his arms around his darling. What would he not give to make her better?—his means, his business, his all. What are "foreign orders" now? What is his bank-book now? He would give all he has in the world to make that child well. She looks at him as much as to say: "Father, won't you meet me in heaven?" And that child dies, and is carried to the cemetery and buried, and the father goes and puts flowers over her grave. But is she there? No, father; no, mother; your little child is not there. Why are you sad? She has gone home to the father. It is home up there; and He wants you to know it is all "vanity and vexation of spirit" here. The Good Shepherd wants you to follow Him; He has laid down his life for the sheep. Oh, my friends, do not follow the world, or the teachings of your own heart. Follow the Good Shepherd; keep close by his side, and then He will lead you by green pastures and still waters, and make you to love and serve Him as never before. May God, by his Holy Spirit, endear that Shepherd to us more and more, for his own name's sake! Amen.

OUR SHEPHERD.

BY A. J. GORDON.

THE relation which the Lord Jesus holds to his people as that of Shepherd to the sheep, is a perpetual relation. It extends from His first advent to his second; from His cross to His coming. If we belong to Christ's flock, so that the words of the apostle Peter apply to us, "For ye were as sheep going astray; but are now returned unto the Shepherd and bishop of your souls," it behooves us to know what our Shepherd is to us. Now, in reading the New Testament, we find three significant titles ascribed to our Shepherd, each applying to a different stage and a different office in his blessed ministry. He is called: —

"The Good Shepherd" (John x, 11).
"The Great Shepherd" (Heb. xiii, 20).
"The Chief Shepherd" (1 Pet. v, 4).

These titles are not accidental, as will appear from a glance at the passages in which they severally stand.

I. "I am the Good Shepherd; the Good Shephered giveth His life for the sheep." It is in laying down His life for the flock that He wins the eternal title of the "Good Shepherd." Here is the supreme exhibition of His love. "Who loved me and gave himself for me" (Gal. ii, 20). "Greater love hath no man than this, that a man lay down his life for his friends" (John xv, 13. See also, 1 John iv, 10; Titus iii, 4; Rev. i, 5; Rom. v, 8). It is generally said that the strongest declaration of the divine goodness is, "God is love." It seems to us that there is one which is even stronger. "God so loved the world, that he gave —" The one passage gives us goodness in essence; the other, goodness in action. Christ is the Good Shepherd, because "He giveth His life for the sheep."

II. Christ is called the Great Shephered, in connection with His resurrection: "Now the God of peace that brought again from the dead our Lord Jesus, that Great Shephered of the sheep" (Heb. xiii, 20). And what higher exhibition of Christ's greatness is there than His resurrection from the dead. His crucifiction was an exhibition of love, but, so far as men could see, only a love manifested in weakness. How significantly saith the Holy Ghost, "He was crucified through weakness" (2 Cor. xiii, 4). Of course it was the weakness of one who, for the time being, had surrendered His power and become "obedient unto death, even the death of the cross." But it was such an exhibition of helplessness as caused His enemies to triumph over Him for the time, and mock at His claim of being "The Son of God." (See Matt. xxvii, 40-42.) But in His resurrection all this was reversed. His greatness was manifested before all. On the cross they reviled Him, saying, "If thou be the Son of God, come down from the cross." And, so far as human eye can see, the taunt was only met by utter weakness. But at the sepulchre, on the third day, how all was changed. He was "Declared to be the Son of God with power, according to the spirit of holiness, by the resurrection from the dead" (Rom. i, 4). This rising again is constantly spoken of as the great exhibition of Divine power "According to the working of His mighty power which He wrought in Christ when He raised Him from the dead," etc. (Eph. i, 20; see, also, Col.

ii, 15). How different Christ dying and Christ rising. In the one instance: "Awake, O sword, against my shepherd and against the man that is my fellow, saith the Lord of hosts" (Zech. xiii, 7). In the other, the "God of peace bringing again from the dead our Lord Jesus Christ, that Great Shepherd of the sheep."

III. At Christ's second coming, He is spoken of as "the Chief Shepherd." "And when the Chief Shepherd shall appear, ye shall receive a crown of glory that fadeth not away" (1 Peter v, 4). Chieftainship is the great distinguishing attribute of Christ at His coming. Then He is not simply the King, but "King of Kings;" not simply Lord, but "Lord of Lords;" not simply a "Prince and a Savior," but the "Prince of the kings of the earth." This supreme chieftainship seems only to be fully ascribed to the Lord Jesus in connection with His second coming. See, for example, how the title "King of Kings" is used in Rev. xix, 16. It is when He has completed His final triumph, when "the kingdoms of this world have become the kingdoms of our Lord and of His Christ," that this title is found upon Him. Until He appears in glory, the rulers of this earth will continue to dispute His kingship with him. Until then, false shepherds will set themselves over God's flock only to waste and scatter. Read, in Ezek. xxxiv, the prophecy of the Lord's judgment of these unfaithful shepherds; and how, having "Delivered his flock from their mouth," He "will set up one Shepherd over them" (verses 10, 23). The Lord hasten the day "when the Chief Shepherd shall appear." And may not the bleating flock still in the desert intensely cry: "Even so, come, Lord Jesus?" We are indebted to another for pointing out the fact that the three Psalms, xxii, xxiii, xxiv, set forth very beautifully these respective offices of our Shepherd. The twenty-second is the passion psalm — the psalm of "the good Shepherd laying down his life for the sheep." Its words were used by Him to express His sorrow on the cross: "My God, my God, why hast thou forsaken me?" Its language was exactly fulfilled in the mockery and parting of His raiment, and His unutterable agony. It is emphatically the psalm of the crucified Shepherd. The twenty-third is the psalm of the Great Shepherd leading His flock in all their wilderness wanderings during His absence; spreading their table for them in the presence of their enemies, attending them through the valley of the shadow of death, and giving them the comfort which He only can give "who liveth and was dead; and, behold, is alive for evermore, and hath the keys of death and the grave." The twenty-fourth is the psalm of glory and triumph. It shows us the Chief Shepherd leading up His ransomed flock, when, as Lord of the living and of the dead, He shall bring them into heaven: "Lift up your heads, O ye gates; and be ye lift up, ye everlasting doors; and the king of glory shall come in. Who is this king of glory? The Lord, strong and mighty, the Lord, mighty in battle." "Lift up your heads, O ye gates; even lift them up, ye everlasting doors; and the king of glory shall come in." "Who is this king of glory? The Lord of hosts, He is the king of glory."

CHRIST THE SHEPHERD.

BY W. G. CARR.

John x.

I. WHAT He is: 1. The *Good* Shepherd in death, John x, 15. 2. The *Great* Shepherd in resurrection, Heb. xiii, 20. 3. The *Chief* Shepherd in glory, 1 Peter v, 4.

II. What He does: 1. Seeks and restores sheep, Luke xv, 4, 5. 2. Leads, feeds, and defends, Ps. xxiii; Romans xii, 19. 3. Heals, Ex. xv, 26. Gives rest, Matt. xi, 28. 4. Goes before, cares for, and keeps, 2 Tim. i, 12. 5. Gives eternal life, 1 John v, 13.

III. What the sheep do: Hear his voice; know his voice; follow him — listen, look, follow *Him*.

A lost sheep won't find its way back. Shepherd goes after. Shepherd don't find fault or drive, but carries sheep. The Shepherd's hand is a very safe place, Col. iii, 3. None but a satisfied sheep will lie down, Psa. xxiii. The only food for a sheep, 1 Peter ii, 2. We ought to lay down our lives for the sheep, 1 John iii, 16.

PRIESTHOOD.

SINCE the rending of the temple vail from top to bottom, a *special* class of persons on earth, exercising priestly functions according to God, no longer exist. The whole system of which earthly priesthood formed an integral part have passed away (Heb. viii, 13). Chapter vii, of the epistle to the Hebrews shows an *earthly* priesthood set aside, and a *heavenly* one established; chapter viii puts the covenant before us, contrasting them. The *old* covenant is dismissed, and the new covenant introduced. Chapter ix contrasts the sacrifice; the *one* sacrifice of Christ being of Divine and permanent value, superseding the *many* sacrifices and offerings which could never take away sins. But the Levitical system, with a temple larger and far more glorious, and sacrifices commemorative in their character, with a priesthood established in the house of Zadok, will be set up in the millennium carefully adapted to the new state of things (Ezek. xl-xlvi). But during the present interval of grace, *after* the entire abolition of Judaism, and *before* the inauguration of the new system, Christianity has come in, and the revelation of an order of priesthood, unlike what was or will be. Now all Christians are priests. *All* have an equal title to draw near, as saith the apostle: "Let *us* draw near" (Heb. x, 22). Paul's pre-eminent place as an apostle did not confer upon him any *special* place as a priest or worshipper. There is but one High Priest, even Jesus, sitting at the right hand of God; and all saints are constituted worshippers and priests. Thus the church can sing: "Unto Him that loved us, and washed us from our sins in His own blood; and hath made us *kings and priests* unto God and His Father" (Rev. i, 5, 6). What are the sacrifices which, as priests, we offer? The priest's guide-book under the law was the book of Leviticus; our guide-book and directory is the epistle to the Hebrews.

Turning to it, therefore, we learn that our sacrifices are praise to *God* and practical benevolence to *Man* (Heb. xiii, 15, 16). Further, all Christians are regarded as a *holy* priesthood in offering up spiritual sacrifices to God (1 Peter ii, 5), and a *royal* priesthood in displaying the moral virtues of Jesus to man (1 Peter ii, 9). The priesthood of Christ is exercised on high, is founded on his work and person, and is unchangeable. His object is to sustain believers in their walk, service and worship, to afford succor in temptation, and sympathy in suffering.

Priesthood is to *sustain ;* Advocacy is to *restore.* Christ is exercising His functions as a priest according to the *pattern* of Aaron, but according to the everlasting *order* of Melchisedek (Heb. vii).

OUR GREAT HIGH PRIEST

BY GEO. C. NEEDHAM.

THERE are three departments of Christ's priesthood worthy of our careful study:

1. Mediator. The explanation of this part of our Lord's priestly ministry is found in 1 Tim. ii, 3–5. "God our Savior" is "the man Christ Jesus," who is qualified to occupy the place of Mediator between God and men. When the thought of God's majesty overpowered the heart of Job, and as the imperfection of his own righteousness was brought to view by an examination of his life and character, he cried out in despair for a daysman to adjust matters between him

and his God. But there is a daysman, an umpire, an arbitrator, even Jesus, who, as Mediator, reconciles man to God by his blood, and ratifies the union in the impartation of his own nature to all who believe. Thus do they become the "sons of God." Our Great High Priest, as Mediator, opens the way of access from the scene of guilt and death to the throne of mercy and of life. And as the Priest abiding forever, whose priesthood is non-successional and untransferable, He keeps the way ever open, so that "whosoever will may come." Other aspects of the subject deal exclusively with the believer, but the Mediator is the open door of approach unto God for all who would draw nigh. This is the exclusive, blood-sprinkled pathway from sin to holiness, from guilt to remission, from judgment to salvation (John xiv, 6; Eph. ii, 18; iii, 12; Heb. iv, 16; x, 18–22).

2. Advocate. The mediator treats with God, the advocate with the Father. The mediator fulfills his office as God-man, the advocate as the righteous man. That is, sinning believers as men on the earth have on unsinning man to represent them as holy ones in heaven. Because, believers, God is their Father; and if any such man sin, "we have an advocate with the Father, Jesus Christ, the righteous" (1 John ii, 1, 2). The word translated advocate is elsewhere comforter (John xiv, 17). It also means helper, and implies that the helper is at hand, ready to strengthen, to fortify, and thus to comfort. But His advocacy is with the Father. Does my sin come before the Father's face? Then let me confess and receive forgiveness through my advocate. Is my communion with the Father interrupted? Then let me seek its recovery through my advocate. Does Satan enter the court room and lay charges against the saints? Then does our advocate take our case in hand and defeat the adversary, by showing in open court that full satisfaction has been rendered to law, to justice, and to truth. Thus sin is covered, trespasses forgiven, and Satan vanquished (Rom. viii, 33, 34).

3. Intercessor. The chief thought of intercession is one pleading for others. Thus Moses, Nehemiah, Daniel, etc., engaged in intercession. But only of one can it be truly said that He is the Intercessor. His pleadings embrace his people, and they are based on his atonement for them and their union with him. In the priestly prayer of John xvii, all the petitions are for His disciples there present, and for all who should believe through their word (v, 11, 15, 17, 21, 24). For Himself, he prayed to be with the Father again, glorified with His original glory; but all other requests are on behalf of His church. Christ's intercession is conducted for the everlasting salvation of those who come to God by Him (Heb. vii, 24, 25), and therefore none of them shall perish. All the powers, qualities, and activities of the Great High Priest are fully given to His people. 1. His hands, in

presenting sacrifices, offering incense, etc. (John xx, 24, 27; x, 27, 28; Rev. i, 17; Luke xxiv, 50). 2. His shoulders, in bearing up His church (Isa. ix, 6; Luke xv, 5). 3. His heart, the seat of love (John xiii, 2; Eph. v, 2, 25). 4. His head, seat of thought (Ex. xxviii, 36, 38; Ps. xl, 5, 17; Jer. xxix, 11). Further, as to our standing, note the teaching of Ex. xxviii, 36–39.

The mitre was the priest's head dress, or bonnet. It was made of pure linen; the plate of gold was fastened on the forefront by a ribbon of blue, and formed part of the mitre. Aaron and his successors never appeared before the Lord without this head-piece. The words: "Holiness unto the Lord," stood out in the light of the Shekinah glory, and Israel's acceptance was undisputed. Though the nation was composed of individual sinners, yet through grace they were constituted a "holy nation," and identified with their priestly representative. And here the type speaks with divine distinctness of the church's oneness with Christ, in the holiness of his unblemished character. The believer is without inherent or external righteousness. He possesses nothing which could abide under the scrutiny of God's searching light, and entitle him to a place in glory. The sinner's justification before God is by grace, through faith in Christ by his blood. It is not by works, feelings, suppositions, or arbitrary laws. If righteousness came by the law, then Christ died for nothing (Gal. iii, 21). And he who seeks heaven in self deeds, accuses the Son of God as having failed in His mission of mercy. Who will assume the place of accuser? Thou, vain man, cease thy works, and rest on His work to the saving of thy soul. Because Christ is the same, the righteousness of the believing sinner is therefore always the same, ever acceptable unto God. His righteousness is Christ; but it is only in the full recognition of this great truth that we grow in practical conformity to His image, and become gloriously changed into His likeness. Nor does this truth of our actual standing where God's grace hath placed us in His Son, lead either to a carnal walk, which disowns our responsibility, or to a legal striving after a personal holiness through the works of the flesh, which ignores His grace.

ADVOCACY.

"IF any man sin, we have an advocate with the Father, Jesus Christ the righteous" (1 John ii, 1). Advocacy is the Divine means to meet individual failure amongst Christians, and to restore communion and rest of soul when lost or interrupted. This gracious ministry by our risen Christ is founded upon his *work* of "propitiation," completed once and forever, and upon the glory of His person, as the "righteous" One ever abiding in the presence of God. Priesthood is with *God* and to preserve *from* falling; advocacy is with the *Father* and to restore *when* fallen. In the former I am regarded in my place as a *saint*, in the latter I am recognized as a *child*. In answer to the advocacy of Jesus Christ with the Father, the Holy Spirit uses the Word of God in dealing with the soiled conscience, convicting of sin, and thus leading the erring child to true and hearty confession; the fruit of this double work — Christ on *high*, and the spirit *here*—being full and happy restoration of soul, and the re-enjoyment of fellowship with the Father, and with His Son, Jesus Christ. It is well to bear in mind that the position of "child" is a fixed and eternal one, but the sense and enjoyment of it may be lost for a time, and which it is the object of "advocacy" to restore.

CHRIST GLORIFIED.

BY A. J. GORDON.

THE constant allusion in the New Testament to the ascended Savior as seated at God's right hand, is very striking. In scores of texts which describe Him in glory, this is the invariable representation; and a glance at these texts is sufficient to reveal the marked significance of this attitude. It is a position full of suggestiveness, and of itself is a powerful sermon. Among its many teachings it speaks —

I. Of the Finished Work of Christ. "Who, * * * when He had by Himself purged our sins, sat on the right hand of the Majesty on high" (Heb. i, 3). As one seats himself after completing some severe task, so Jesus, after the toil and travail of the cross, now sits down on the throne. It is the declaration, by an attitude, of what He had spoken with His mouth on the cross — "It is finished." And not only this, the complete character of Christ's sacrifice, in contrast with the incomplete and perpetually repeated Jewish sacrifices, is thus strongly brought out. The Hebrew high priest never was permitted to sit down, because his work was never done. But our High Priest, because His sacrifice is "once for all," sits down. Note this contrast, as brought out by the writer of the Epistle to the Hebrews: "Every priest standeth daily ministering and offering oftentimes the same sacrifices, which can never take away sins. But this Man, after He had offered one sacrifice for sins forever, sat down on the right hand of God" (Heb. x, 11, 12; also, viii, 1).

II. The Rest of Christ. Sitting is the attitude of repose. Here it speaks beautifully of the rest into which our Lord has entered, after His bleeding toil. "Looking unto Jesus, the author and finisher of our faith; who for the joy that was set before Him endured the cross, despising the shame, and is set down at the right hand of the throne of God (Heb. xii, 2). We who share with Christ the benefits of His redemption, enter with Him into His rest. He "hath raised us up together in heavenly places in Christ Jesus" (Eph. ii, 6). Hence the exhortation: "If ye then be risen with Christ, seek those things which are above, where Christ sitteth on the right hand of God" (1 Col. iii, 1). As though, having our citizenship in heaven, we were to be careful to make our home there —"looking down from heaven to earth, instead of looking up from earth to heaven." And this suggests—

III. The Accessibility of Christ. A sitting posture invites approach. In Christ's earthly ministry, we remember that it was when He sat on Jacob's well that the woman of Samaria held her long conversation with Him. "And when He was set, His disciples came unto Him," is the language which introduces the sermon on the mount. And so in many other instances. When a busy man sits down at his fireside at the close of day, we feel at liberty to approach him as we do not in the hurry and occupation of his counting-room. And so when Christ is seated. His very attitude seems to be an invitation, "Come unto Me." Hence, how significant, therefore, that after the description in Heb. x, of Him who, "after He had offered one sacrifice for sins forever, sat down at the right hand of God," it should be added, "Let us, therefore, draw near," etc. It is a repetition of the old story; when He was seated, "There drew near all the publicans and sinners for to hear Him." It is because "We have such a High Priest, who is set on the right hand of the throne of the Majesty in the heavens" (Heb. viii, 1), that we hear the invitation, "Let us therefore come boldly unto the throne of grace."

IV. The Exaltation of Christ. The right hand of God is the place of glory and power. Hence, hereafter "Ye shall see the Son of Man sitting on the right hand of power" (Mark xiv, 62). "So then, after the Lord had spoken unto them, He was received up into heaven and sat on the right hand of God" (Mark xvi, 19). "Therefore, being by the right hand of God exalted" (Acts ii, 33) also (v. 31), God "raised Him from the dead, and set Him at His own right hand in the heavenly places" (Eph. i, 20).

V. The Victory of Christ. "To him that overcometh will I

grant to sit with Me in My throne, even as I also overcame, and am set down with My Father in His throne" (Rev. iii, 21). This is Christ's victory over death and His crucifiers. It was to this which Peter appealed with such overwhelming force when, addressing the murderers of Jesus, he quoted David's words, "The Lord said unto my Lord, sit thou at my right hand, until I make thine enemies thy footstool;" and then showed how this same Jesus whom they had crucified, had been "made both Lord and Christ." The presence of Christ on the throne was an irresistible proof that Christ was victor, and they were condemned who had condemned Him. Spiritually, we are sharers in our Lord's victory, since His presence there is a proof that He has succeeded in His great undertaking of going through death for us. This is what gives us the triumphant assurance: "Who is He that condemneth? It is Christ that died, yea rather, that is risen again, who is even at the right hand of God."

VI. *The Expectation of Christ.* His sitting is expressive of His rest from His sacrificial toil, of His first advent, of His waiting for His final conquest at His second advent. He "sat down at the right hand of God; from henceforth expecting till His enemies be made His footstool" (Heb. x, 12, 13). The attitude of waiting for the Son of God from heaven which He enjoins on us, is the attitude which He maintains Himself. At His second coming our present humiliation will give place to glory and exaltation. When He shall leave the throne of grace where He now sits, and take the throne of judgment, we, if His saints, shall share that throne also with Him. Then will be fulfilled that which is written in Rev. xx, 4: "And I saw thrones, and they sat upon them, and judgment was given unto them: * * * and they lived and reigned with Christ a thousand years."

THE BLOOD OF CHRIST.

"The life of the flesh is IN THE BLOOD; and I have given it to you upon the altar, to make an atonement for your souls; for it is the BLOOD maketh an ATONEMENT for the soul," Lev. xvii, 11.

IN CHRIST WE HAVE THROUGH FAITH —

1. Redemption. "In whom we have *redemption through His blood, even forgiveness of sins,*" Col. i, 14.

"Feed the church of God, which he has *purchased with His own blood,*" Acts xx, 28.

"Thou wast slain, and hast redeemed us to God by thy blood out of every kindred and tongue, and people, and nation," Rev. v, 9.

"Ye were not redeemed with corruptible things, such as silver and gold, from your vain conversation received by tradition from your fathers, *but with the precious blood of Christ,* as of a lamb without blemish and without spot," 1 Peter i, 18, 19.

2. Forgiveness of sin. In whom we have redemption through His blood, *the forgiveness of sins,*" Eph. i. 7. "This is my blood of the New Testament, which is shed for many *for the remission of sins that are past,*" Rom. iii, 25.

"*Without shedding of blood is no remission,*" Heb. ix, 22.

3. Justification. "Being now *justified by His blood,* we shall be saved from wrath through Him," Rom. v, 9.

4. Cleansing from sin, both as to *the person and the conscience.* "The blood of Jesus Christ His Son *cleanseth us from all sin,*" 1 John i, 7.

THE GREAT HIGH PRIEST.

A STUDY IN THE EPISTLE TO THE HEBREWS.

1. He is a Son. i, 2, 5; iii, 6; v, 8; vii, 28.
2. He is the Son of God. i, 5; iv, 14; v, 5; vi, 6; vii, 3; x, 29.
3. He is God. i, 8–10; iii, 3, 4.
4. He is as the Son superior to angels.

    (*a*) As to name. i, 4–5; i, 7.
    (*b*) As to rank. i, 6; i, 8–9; i, 3; viii, 1; x, 12; xii, 2.
    (*c*) As to office. i, 10; i, 2; i, 13.

5. He is as the Son superior to the prophets as the mediators of Divine revelation. i, 1, 2.
6. He is as the Son superior to Moses in the House of God. iii, 5, 6.
7. He is superior to Joshua as leading into the promised rest. iv, 8–14.
8. He is the Apostle of God, above all sent from God. iii, 1; ii, 3.
9. He is man. ii, 6, 11, 14, 17; v, 1, 7.

    (*a*) And so could suffer. ii, 9–10; ii, 14–18; iv, 15; v, 8; ix, 25, 26; x, 19, 20; xiii, 12.
    (*b*) And live by faith. ii, 13, 18; v, 7; xii, 2.

10. He is the Son of Man. ii, 5–8.

    (*a*) Was a little while lower than the angels. ii, 7.

(b) Is still waiting for His dominion. ii, 8; i, 13.
(c) Is still waiting for His fellow heirs. iii, 14; iii, 1; ii, 10; iv, 9; ix, 28; x, 36, 37; x, 16; xiii, 14; xii, 25-28.
11. He is a Mediator of a *better* covenant. viii, 6-13; ix, 1-10; x, 14-18—of the *new* covenant. ix, 15-22; xii, 24.
12. He is surety of a better covenant. vii, 19-22.
13. He is the perfection of the beginnings and shadows of the old covenant. x, 1; vii, 2; v, 12-14; vi, 1-3.
14. He is a Priest from God. v, 4, 6-10; iii, 2; vii, 28; x, 5-7.
15. He is a Priest and from among men. ii, 10; iv, 15; v, 1.
16. He is a *great* Priest. x, 21. "High" is in the Greek "great."
17. He is a High Priest. ii, 17; iii, 1; iv, 14, 15; viii, 1.
18. He is a Great High Priest. iv, 14.

(a) Superior to the Aaronic order. viii, 4-6; x, 1-4; vii, 28.
(b) After the order of Melchizedek. v, 10; vii, 3.
(c) Made with an oath. vii, 20-22, 28.
(d) Abiding and with an untransferable priesthood. v, 6; vii, 16, 23-25; x, 12.
(e) Kingly. vii, 2, 14.
(f) Sinless, and separate from sinners. iv, 15; vii, 26-28.
(g) Higher than the heavens. iv, 14; x, 12; viii, 1; i, 3.
(h) Has taken away sin and brought salvation. i, 14; ii, 3, 14, 15, 17; v, 9; vi, 9; ix, 12-14, 26-28; xii, 22-24; i, 3; ii. 9.
(i) Made only one offering and once for all. vii, 27; ix, 12-14, 25-28; x, 11, 12, 18.
(j) Has entered into the Holy of Holies. iv, 14; vi, 19, 20; ix, 11, 12, 22; x, 12, 19, 20.
(k) Has purified the heavenly places and things. ix, 18-23.
(l) Is interceding now. vii, 24, 25; ix, 24; iv, 16.
(m) Is merciful. ii, 17, 18; iv, 15, 16; v, 2.
(n) Is faithful. ii, 17; iii, 2.
(o) Was perfected for His office. ii, 10, 17; vii, 7-9.
(p) Has perfected, once for all, the sanctified worshippers. x, 10-14; ix, 13, 14; x, 2. 10-22; xiii, 12.
(q) Has done what the law could not do. ix, 9; x, 1, 14; xi, 40.
(r) Is coming again out of the holy places. ix, 28; x, 37; i, 13; x, 12, 13.
19. Meanwhile He requires faith of His brethren and fellow heirs. ii, 1-4; iii, 6-19; x, 23-39; xii, 25-29.
20. Is Himself the one Son of God, who began and perfected the faith which belongs to all the sons of God. xii, 1, 2.
21. He discerns unbelief. iv, 11-13.
22. He sympathizes with and encourages the sons in the trial of their faith. ii, 18; iv, 15, 16; vi, 17-20; vii, 25; x, 23, 32, 36; xi, 1-40; xii, 1-11; xiii, 5-16; xiii, 14.
23. He requires the obedience of faith. xii,12-16; iii, 1-7; xiii, 15-19.
24. He crowns the life of faith, and closes His priestly intercessions when the sons have all entered into glory. ii, 10; iv, 9; ix, 28; xi, 16; xiii, 14.
25. He exalts all the sons to his own dignity, sovereignty, and glory. ii, 5, 11-13; iii, 6, 14; vi, 11, 12; x, 34, 35; xi, 9, 10, 17; xii, 28, 29.
THE PRAYER. xiii, 20, 21.

THE PRIESTHOOD OF CHRIST.
I. The present scene of our Lord's priestly ministry, and the characters of his ministry, Heb. i, 3; iv, 14; x, 11, 12; viii, 1, 2, 6; vii, 24, 25.
II. The necessity for such a priesthood, Job ix, 33; 1 Tim. ii, 3-5. The central idea of priesthood is mediation. The term "priest" signifies *a sacrificer*. It involves the offering of a victim to God and certain results flowing therefrom, Heb. viii,

3, "necessity." What offering? Heb. ix, 14.

III. Qualifications for the office of priesthood. These were two-fold: (1) Physical, Lev. xxi, 17, 18, 21. God guards with jealous care, even in type, the absolute perfection of His Son. So the red heifer, unblemished heifer, etc., Heb. vii, 26; 1 Peter ii, 22. Also in the choice of wife, Lev. xxi, 13; Eph. v, 25, 26; 2 Cor. xi, 2, 3. (2) Moral, called of God, Heb. v, 4, 10. Chosen from among men to represent men, Heb. v, 1; ii, 14, 16. Compassionate, Heb. v, 2; ii, 17.

IV. Duties of the high priest typical of Christ's ministry on earth and in heaven. (1) Making atonement and effecting reconciliation, Lev. xvi, 10, 21, 22; Heb. ix, 14, 26; Col. i, 21, 22. (2) Offering acceptable worship on behalf of the worshippers, Lev. xvi, 12, 13; Eph. v, 2. (3) Judging ceremonial uncleanness, Lev. xiii, 2; xiv, 2; Rev. i, 13, 14. "Eyes of flame, of fire," searching so Rev. iii, 15. Bringing to light hidden things of darkness for cleansing and absolution. (4) Deciding controversies. The high priest had the common priests in association with him in many parts of his ministry, Deut. xviii, 8–12; 1 Cor. vi, 1, 7. Believers should not drag their differences before the uncircumcised. Mutual prayer and confession before the Lord will soon right all our controversies. (5) declaring the will of God, Num. xxvii, 21; Heb. i, 1. All truth is in Jesus. (6) Presenting worshippers in full — acceptable, blameless and precious, Ex. xxviii, 12, 29; Col. i, 22; Jude 24; Eph. i, 6. (7) Blessing the people in the name of the Lord, Lev. ix, 22, 23; Num. vi, 23; Luke xxiv, 51.

V. Priestly garments typical of powers and qualities of our Great High Priest. Two sets of clothing; personal — all linen; official — of glory and beauty. (1) Girdle, Ex. xxviii, 8; Isa. xi, 5; Rev. i, 13; John xiii, 4, 5. (2) Blue robes, Ex. xxviii, 31–35, to hold up pomegranates and bells — fruit and sound. (3) Ephod, Ex. xxviii, 31–35, to sustain shoulder stones and breast plates. (4) Mitre, Ex. xxxviii, 36–39, to hold golden crown, that the people may be always accepted before God. Thus the priest's head, heart, hands and shoulders were employed to think of, love, sustain and direct those whom he represents.

VI. Three parts of priestly ministry of our Lord Jesus. (1) Mediator, 1 Tim. ii, 3–5, to keep open the way of access. (2) Advocate, 1 John, ii, 1, 2, meets the accuser in heaven's court of equity. (3) Intercessor, Heb. vii, 24. For saints only who have come unto God by Him.

GEO. C. NEEDHAM.

OUR GREAT HIGH PRIEST.

Hebrews, iv.

Great, better than angels; Heb. i, 4; better than Moses, Heb. iii, 3; better than Aaron, Heb. v, 4; better than Melchizedek, Heb. vii, 22. Prophet, Priest, King; past, present, future.

In heaven, There by virtue of His own blood, so we, Heb. ix, 12, there once for all, work of atonement never repeated, Heb. ix, 26; work of our advocate never interrupted, Heb. vii; He represents us there; we represent Him here, Heb. ix, 24; He presents our gifts and sacrifices, Heb. xiii, 15. Only a perfect man could be a perfect priest, Heb. v, 9.

Able and willing. Our friend in court, the Judge's Son, verse 14. Our advocate with the Father if we do sin, 1 John ii, 1. Our helper that we may not sin, John xvi, 13. He died to make us clean, Heb ix, 14. He lives to keep us clean, Heb. x, 21, 22.

Hold fast what you have, verse 14; Heb. x, 23. Come boldly for what you need, verse 16.

W. G. CARR.

CHRIST AS THE HIGH PRIEST.

I. "He is able to save," Heb. vii, 24–27; completely, perfectly, unto the end, altogether, forever, Rom. v, 10; x, 9, 10; Eph. ii, 8, 9; 1 Tim. i, 15; Tit. iii, 5–7.

II. He is able to succor, Heb. ii, 18. Same word is used in 2 Cor. vi, 2; elswhere translated "help," 2 Cor. xii, 9, 10; 2 Tim. iv, 17, 18; 2 Cor. i, 10; 2 Pet. ii, 9.

III. He is "A merciful and faithful High Priest," Heb. ii, 17; Jude 21; Rev. i, 5; iii, 14; xix, 11; Heb. xiii, 5, 6; Rom. viii, 31–39. He is so merciful He never inflicts a needless stroke; so faithful He never fails to inflict the needed stroke, nor to make good to us the promise of His sustaining grace.

IV. He is a sympathizing High Priest, Heb. iv, 14–16. His sinlessness "without sin," 2 Cor. v, 21; "who knew no sin," 1 Pet. ii, 22; "in Him is no sin," 1 John iii, 5. "We have not an High Priest which can not be touched with the feeling of our infirmities." Ou, and mee, the former expressing objective negation, the latter subjective, according to Wener, show that He is most completely the reverse of not being able to sympathize, Heb. v, 7–9; Rom. xv, 3; 2 Cor. i, 5; Eph. v, 25–27; Phil. 5–7; Col. i, 24.

V. He is constituted a priest after the power of an endless life, Heb. vii, 16; v, 9; ix, 12, 14, 15; xiii, 20; 1 Pet. v, 10; 2 Pet. i, 11; 1 John v, 11–13.

VI. He "Now appears in the presence of God for us," Heb. ix, 24; 1 John iv, 17; Rom. viii, 24; 26; the word rendered "helpeth," meaning "to take hold with anyone," 1 John ii, 1. "Advocate" is the same word translated "comforter" in John xiv, 16, 26; xv, 26; xvi, 7; v, 11. He is an High Priest forever after the order of Melchizedek, Heb. vi, 20; vii, 1–3; Gen. xiv, 18–20; Heb. i, 5–8; Phil. ii, 9–11; Col. iii, 4; Rev. xix, 16. The dignity to which He has exalted all who believe on Him as their Savior, Heb. ii, 11; 1 Pet. ii, 5, 9; Rev. i, 6; v, 9, 10; xx, 5, 6.

It is not scriptural to tell unbelieving sinners that Christ is pleading for them before the Father's throne. God is already merciful, and is beseeching them to be reconciled, 1 John iv, 9, 10; Heb. x, 10, 14, 17. Then for all who trust in the blood for cleansing, there remains the privilege described in Heb. x, 19–22; No wonder the Apostles could write, "we have such an High Priest," Heb. viii, 1.

OUTLINE OF CHRIST'S PRIESTHOOD IN HEBREWS.

ITS CHARACTERISTICS.

I. Sin purging, Heb. i, 3.
II. Suffering, Heb. ii, 17, 18, 20, 7–9.
III. Sympathizing, Heb. iv, 15.
IV. Kingly, Heb. vi, 20; vii, 1, 2.
V. Interceding, Heb. vii, 25.
VI. Sinless, Heb. vii, 26.
VII. Coming, Heb. ix, 24–28; x, 11–13.

HIS RELATION TO US IN GIVING.

I. Succor, Heb. ii, 18.
II. Grace, Heb. iv, 16.
III. Cleansing from dead works, Heb. ix, 14.
IV. Entrance into the holiest, Heb. x, 19.
V. Separation, Heb. xiii, 13.
VI. Praise, Heb. xiii, 15.
VII. Acceptable service, Heb. xiii, 16.

HIS RELATIONS AS PRIEST TO GOD.

I. Things of God, Heb. ii, 17.
II. The word of God, Heb. iv, 12–14.
III. Called of God. Heb. v, 10.
IV. The council of God, Heb. vi, 17–20.
V. The throne of God, Heb. viii, 1.
VI. A sacrifice to God, Heb. ix, 14.
VII. Accomplishing God's will, Heb. x, 5–10.

THE RESURRECTION.

1. Ancient Belief in the Resurrection—Heb. ii, 19; Luke xxii, 37; Job xix, 19, 25-27; Isa. xxvi, 19; Dan. xii, 2, 3, 13; Hos. xiii, 14.

2. Witnesses to Christ's Resurrection.—Matt. xxviii, 5,6; Acts ii, 24; Acts iv, 33; Acts xiii, 37; Mark xvi, 9; Luke xxiv, 15; John xx, 19.

3. Fruits of Christ's Resurrection. —1 Cor. xv, 20, 23; John vi, 39, 40; 1 Thess. iv, 13, 14.

4. Faith in the Resurrection. — Acts xxiii, 6, 8; 1 Cor. xv, 26; 1 Thess. iv, 16; John ii, 23, 24.

5. The Resurrection Body.—1 Cor. xv, 37, 38; 1 Cor. xv: 32-44; 1 Cor. xv, 53; 2 Cor. v, 1; Matt. xxii, 30.

6. The Hope of the Resurrection. —Acts xxiv, 15; Acts xxvi, 6-8; 2 Cor. v, 4; Rom. viii, 23; Phil. iii, 2; 1 Thess. iv, 13-18; Rev. xx, 5, 6.

CHRIST IN HEBREWS.

It has been suggested that each chapter in the Epistle to the Hebrews presents to us a different picture of Jesus; thus:

CHAP. 1. Sin-purger.
" 2. Captain of Salvation.
" 3. Head of His house.
" 4. Rest of His people.
" 5. Great High Priest.
" 6. Forerunner.
" 7. Surety of the better Covenant.
" 8. Minister of the Sanctuary.
" 9. Perfect Offering.
" 10. Obedient One.
" 11. Object of Faith.
" 12. The Prince and Pattern of Faith.
" 13. Shepherd of the Sheep.

THE RESURRECTION.

I. The fact of a resurrection is asserted in the Old Testament. The primary proofs used by the Hebrew doctors: 1. God's covenant to give the land to Abraham and to his seed forever. (*a*) Deed of gift; (*b*) to Abraham; (*c*) his seed; (*d*) in perpetuity, Gen. xiii, 14-18; Gen. xvii, 1-8. 2. God to Moses at "the bush," Ex. iii, 1-8. This *after* Abraham, Isaac, and Jacob were dead. Their seed now go into the land. 3. But Abraham has no inheritance in it. Yet God promised to give it to him, Acts vii, 1-5, and to Isaac and Jacob personally, and forever, Ex. vi, 4, 8 (note it). 4. They were pilgrims and strangers in the land of promise, Heb. ii, 8-10. They never yet possessed it in their persons as their own. And yet it was promised "to him," Abraham, and "to them;" viz.: Abraham, Isaac and Jacob.

Has the covenant failed? No. Its fulfillment is due at the resurrection. Now see Matt. xxii, 23, 24. The answer of Christ does not mean immortality, but resurrection. Unless Abraham, Isaac and Jacob, are raised up to inherit the land, God's covenant is a failure. But the strength of Israel will not lie. Ergo, the land will be given to Abraham, Isaac and Jacob, at the resurrection, and that is at the second coming.

Now in view of this, and on the basis of this covenant, all the other promises to Israel rest, and all are to be fulfilled through the Messiah. Other proofs are found, (1) In the song of Moses, Deut. xxxii, 36, 39-43; Rev. xv, 1-5. Moses predicts Israel's future. (2) David's hope of the resurrection, Ps. xlix, 6-15. Here the resurrection is represented as the peculiar reward of the righteous, Ps. i, 1-6, in the far future. No hint of the resurrection of the wicked here. Only of the righteous. (3) We come to the prophets, In Hosea, the prophet of the ten tribes, xiii, 14, we find a prediction of Israel's resurrection. (4) Isa. xxvi, 19, 13, 14; xxv, 7-9; xxvi, 1-4. (5) Ezekiel, compare xxxvii, 12-14, 26-28. (6) All accomplished at the second coming of Christ, 1 Cor. xv, 51-54. (7) Now read Dan. xi, 45; xii, 1-4, at the time of antichrist's destruction.

We come now to consider the doctrine of the simultaneous resurrection of all the dead. There is no such doctrine taught in all the Scriptures.

The texts on which it is rested, are Dan. xii, 2; John v, 28, 29; Acts xxiv, 15. These do not prove a simultaneous resurrection of all the dead. Dan. xii, 2, is limited to Israel's hope. One resurrection, *i. e.*, the righteous. "Many *out from* among," the Hebrew participle *min*, is the source of the Greek *ek*, out of. The resurrection of the wicked is implied, but not at this time. Hence there are only two texts where both resurrections are simultaneously mentioned, John v, 29; Acts xxiv, 15. But this is not simultaneous occurrence. (*a*) Thus Luke iv, 19, 20, comyared with Isa. lxi, 2. Why did he stop where he did, when quoting Isaiah? Because the "day of vengeance" was future. Even if that day of vengeance was A. D. 70, there are 43 years between! (*b*) Thus in Matt. xxiv, 28, 29, there is a whole dispensation between the verses, 1800 years of which has passed already. Even supposing both resurrections are mentioned in Daniel, it does not follow that both occur at the same time. (*e*) So Dan. ix, 26, "unto the end." The end of Jerusalem's desolation, yet future, the whole period between A. D. 70 and the second advent. (*d*) So Dan. xi, 45, and xii, 1, between these a period from B. C. 160 to The Second Coming, 2640 years already! Prophecy grasps in one conception the whole future, and even calls a dispensation a day, an hour; speaks of both ends of an age in one breath. But Paul settles it, 1 Cor. xv, 23, 24. Three ends: (1) Of the Jewish age, A. D. 70; (2) of this age, at the coming of Christ; (3) of the kingdom surrendered at the end of 1000 years. This brings us to John's apocalypse. John settles it and calls The Resurrection at Christ's coming, "The *first* Resurrection, Rev. xx, 1–6: (1) A period of time 1000 years, was well known to the Jews. It is that period predicted by the prophets, inaugurated by the Resurrection at Messiah's coming in the clouds of heaven. (2) The first Resurrection opens this period because the raised "Live and reign" 1000 years, etc. (3) It follows the destruction of antichrist, the beast, chap. 19. (4) They who rise are those who have been martyrs under the Beast, now destroyed. We share in it, but the martyrs are prominent in it. (5) But Antichrist is destroyed by the Epiphany of Christ's Appearing, 2 Thess. ii, 8; Isa. xi, 4. (6) And this antichrist is Daniel's "Little horn," and Paul's "man of sin," and John's "beast," and eighth head. (7) And this resurrection is that predicted to occur by Hosea, Isaiah, Ezekiel and Daniel, when Messiah comes in clouds, at the time of Israel's deliverance.

It is not a spiritual one, for it is of believers already spiritually raised. Not a figurative one, for it is precisely that spoken of by Daniel; it is to "everlasting life," and figures enjoy no such immortality. Not a general one, for it is here only of the martyrs and companions of Jesus.

But is: (1) A partial one, separated from the "rest of the dead" by 1000 years. (2) A literal one, for it is of the bodies of the slain for Jesus, named in vi, 9; xii, 11; xiv, 13. It is not the "*souls*" that are raised, but "*they*," "*them*" that were beheaded."

The events immediately connected with the coming of Christ are: (1) The resurrection of the righteous; (2) The conversion and glorification of Israel. Second great pentecost. (3) The destruction of antichrist; "the little horn;" the beast. Armageddon. Jerusalem. (4) The end of Gentile supremacy over Israel. The metallic image goes down. (5) The field of christendom cleared of the tares. (6) The judgment of the professing church and the nations. (7) The restoration of the kingdom to Israel, the 1000 years. (8) The binding of Satan in the abyss. All inaugurating a new age, all constituting the bisecting epoch between "this world" and the "world to come."

The coming of Christ is the hope of the church. This is proved by Christ's word "watch." It is also proved by apostolic teaching. I only name: Peter's pentecost sermon, Acts ii, 19. Peter's two Epistles; Paul's letter to the Thessalonians; Paul's letter to the Romans, chap. viii; Paul's letter to the Hebrews; John's apocalypse. Were Christ and the Apostles mistaken? No. The advent is certain. The time is uncertain. The advent is possible in any generation. Times and seasons are with the Father, not with Christ. It is a bad argument that because 1800 years have gone by, therefore the advent never could have occurred before. It might have occurred in any generation. God's government is not fate, but a wise one. All depends on His sovereign will to make the time long or short as He chooses. It is ours to expect as possible in our own day the Lord's return. Then the Resurrection!

N. WEST.

THE SECOND COMING OF CHRIST.

I. It is a personal coming, John xiv, 2, 3; xxi, 22, 23; Mark viii, 38; xiii, 34–37; xiv, 62; Matt. xxv, 31; Acts i, 11; Luke xxiv, 51–53; 1 Thess. iv, 16; Rev. i, 7.

II. It is the hope set before us in the gospel, Titus ii, 13–15; Heb. ix, 28; 2 Tim. iv, 6–8; 2 Peter iii, 12; 1 Cor. i, 7; 1 Thess. i, 10; Phil. iii, 20, 21; Rom. v, 2; viii, 23–25; xv, 13.

III. It is held forth as a powerful motive and incentive, Matt. xxiv, 42–44; xxv, 14–19; Luke xxi, 33–36; Acts iii, 19–21; 1 Thess. ii, 19; iii, 12, 13; v, 1–6, 23; 2 Thess. i, 7; 1 John ii, 28.

IV. It is presented as our consolation amid sorrow and trial, 1 Thess. iv, 13–18; Heb. x, 34, 37; Jas. v, 7, 8; 1 Peter i, 7; Col. iii, 4, 5; 1 Cor. iv, 3–5; xv, 23; Rev. ii, 25; iii, 3, 11.

V. The state of the world at the time of our Lord's return, and during the entire interval of His absence from the earth, shows the folly of the common expectation of a spiritual millennium, or the conversion of the nations by the church, Luke xvii, 26–30; xviii, 8; Matt. xiii; John xvi, 33; Acts xiv, 22; Phil. i, 29; 1 Tim. iv, 1, 2; 2 Tim. ii, 1–5, 12, 13; 2 Peter iii, 3; 2 Thess. ii, 1–8; Rev. xiii.

VI. This personal coming of the Lord may occur at any moment, Luke xii, 35–40; Matt. xxv, 13. Titus ii, 13; Rev. xxii, 7, 12, 16, 20; But it will not be seen by the world, Gen. v, 24; 2 Kings ii, 16, 17; vi, 17; Dan. x, 7; John xii, 29; Acts ix, 7; Rev. iii, 19.

VII. The judgments. (1) Our first parents, Gen. iii, 16–24; (2) The old world, Gen. vii, 17–24; (3) Israel, Matt. xii, 41–50; (4) The judgment of sin on the cross, Rom. viii, 3; Col. ii, 14; 1 Peter ii, 24. Putting the believer beyond judgment as touching the question of his salvation, John v, 24; 1 Cor. vi, 2, 3; 1 John iv, 17; (5) The judgment of the believer works, 2 Cor. v. 10; Rev. xxii, 12; (6) The judgment of the living nations, Matt. xxv, 31–46; Joel iii, 11–15; (7) The judgment of the great white throne, ushering in the eternal state, Rev. xx, 11–15.

J. H. BROOKES, D.D.

THAT BLESSED HOPE.

AN ACROSTIC.

*T*his same Jesus which is taken up from you into heaven, shall so come in like manner as ye have seen Him go into heaven, Acts i, 11. He that shall come, and will not tarry, Heb. x, 37.

*A*nd when the Chief Shepherd shall appear, ye shall receive a crown of glory that fadeth not away, 1 Peter v, 4.

*T*herefore, be ye also ready, for in such an hour as ye think not the Son of man cometh, Matt. xxiv, 44.

*B*e ye also patient, stablish your

hearts, for the coming of the Lord draweth nigh, Jas. v, 8.

Little children abide in Him, that when He shall appear, we may have confidence, and not be ashamed before Him at His coming, 1 John ii, 28.

Every man that hath this hope in Him purifieth himself, even as He is pure, 1 John iii, 3.

So Christ was once offered to bear the sins of many; and unto them that look for Him shall He appear the second time without sin unto salvation, Heb. ix, 28.

So that ye come behind in no gift, waiting for the coming of our Lord Jesus Christ, 1 Cor. i, 7.

Every eye shall see Him, and they also which pierced Him, Rev. i, 7.

Death is swallowed up in victory, 1 Cor. xv, 54.

Holding forth the word of life, that I may rejoice in the day of Christ, that I have not run in vain, neither labored in vain, Phil. ii, 16.

Our conversation is in heaven, from whence also we look for the Savior, the Lord Jesus Christ, Phil. iii, 20.

Patient waiting for Christ, 2 Thess. iii, 5.

Even so, come, Lord Jesus, Rev. xxii, 20.—*The Truth.*

COMPLETENESS IN CHRIST.

BY GEO. C. NEEDHAM.

MAN out of Christ is "dead in trespasses and sins." Through faith in Christ he becomes the possessor of a new life, and is "justified from all things" (Acts xiii, 38, 39). "There is, therefore, now no condemnation to them which are in Christ Jesus" (Rom. viii, 1). The believer is beautified with Christ's beauty, made righteous in His righteousness. The apostle, in writing to the Colossian saints, as by a master-stroke of his inspired pen, sets forth the position of every Christian in these words: "Ye are complete in Him" (Col. ii, 10). Observe the language. Not, Ye may be complete, nor seek to obtain completeness; but "ye are complete." This is no cold, theological expression, nor empty doctrinal statement. It is a sublime fact made known to us by the living Word. It is God's estimate of His people — those having life in His Son. Habitual fellowship with God in the power of this truth, insures constant victory over sin, and daily deliverance from its despotic power.

In order to apprehend the believer's present completeness in Christ Jesus, we need to understand the two-fold nature of the saved sinner — that which is born of the flesh, and that which is born of the spirit.

The unbeliever is identified with the flesh; hence he is continually under condemnation (Rom. viii, 8; John iii, 18). The believer is identified with the new nature, which is "born of God;" hence the expression, "Ye are complete in him." The believers' completeness is not the purification of the flesh, nor its utter extinction. He is not complete in Himself, but in Christ. The "flesh" is in him, but he is not in the flesh (Rom. viii, 9). The flesh does not control him when walking in the spirit. He lives a conqueror, by the power of God through faith.

What do we mean by "the flesh?" It is not the human body of flesh and blood, but "the carnal mind" which is "enmity against God" (Rom. viii, 7). Not alone at enmity, but the very essence of enmity—enmity against God. "The flesh" is the evil inherent in man, as seen in the alienated affections, the self-will and self-emulation in the man "without God in the world." "It is not subject to the law of God, neither, indeed, can be." It opposes that law, which is "holy, just, and good;" it frets and chafes under it. Like the tamed lion, quiescent at times, yet when infuriated, breaking his cage and killing his keeper, "the flesh" breaks through law, being utterly lawless and insubject. The mind of the flesh is death, opposing the mind of the spirit, which is life and peace. The apostle says, "I know that in me (that is, in my flesh) dwelleth no good thing;" "the imaginations and thoughts of man's heart are only evil continually."

The history of man "in the flesh" is a black record. Outside Eden's garden he raised the bludgeon, and smote to the earth the first saint, and afterward built a city in order to have a paradise of his own, independent of God. It was the vile workings of the flesh which brought a flood upon the earth, and afterward would fain build a tower whose top might reach heaven. At the foot of Sinai man in the flesh obeying the lusts thereof, became an idolater, whilst Jehovah commanded, "Thou shalt have no other gods before me." Previous to law, under law, during the life-time of Jesus, and throughout this present dispensation, the flesh is ever the same, unchangeable, ungovernable, unimprovable, vile beyond comparison. "That which is born of the flesh, is flesh" (John iii, 6).

Like the croaking raven sent forth from the ark, supplying its needs from the floating dead, the flesh feeds on corruption. Pompous and vain, presumptuous and self-willed, it alike opposes the law of Moses and the grace of Christ. Man "in the flesh" is filled with self-glory, madly trampling under foot the glory of God.

The works of the flesh which are manifest are these: "Adultery, fornication, uncleanness, lasciviousness, idolatry, witchcraft, hatred, variance, emulation, wrath, strife, seditions, heresies, envyings, murders, drunkenness, revelings, and such like" (Gal. v, 22). "Out of the heart proceedeth all evil thoughts." "The heart is deceitful above all things and desperately wicked." There are many names by which this evil root is designated. It is called "the carnal mind," "the law of sin and death," "the old man," "the flesh." Thus its history, character, works and names identify it as the concentration of all evil, and it is evil continually.

The completeness of the believer in Christ, then, is not the improvement of "the flesh" in him, for vain are his attempts in this direction. As the common instinct of nature is to bury our dead out of sight, so the "old man" is consigned to the tomb. "Knowing this, that our old man is (has been) crucified * * * reckon ye also yourselves to be dead indeed unto sin? * * * Let not sin therefore reign * * * that ye should obey it."

2. "That which is born of the spirit is spirit." Of believers it is said : "Ye are not in the flesh but in the spirit." The moment we believe on the Lord Jesus Christ, we receive a new life, which is in nature His own. It is a Divine life, called the "Divine nature" (2 Peter i, 4), the "new man" (Eph. iv, 24), the "new creature," literally, creation (2 Cor. v, 17), the "inner man" (Eph. iii, 17).

Here, then, are two opposites in the one individual man, like Esau and Jacob, struggling for the mastery; nevertheless, "the last shall be first." "Jacob have I loved, but Esau have I hated."

God looks at the believer — the one "born of the spirit," through Christ — and sees him in Christ; and as Christ is, so is the Christian (1 John iv, 17); loved by the Father, even as He is loved (John xvii, 23); "accepted in the beloved" (Eph. i, 6); "sanctified by God the Father" (Jude 1); "complete" in Christ (Col. ii, 10); "sealed in Him" (Eph. i, 13); "comely" (Cant. i, 5); "all fail" (Cant. iv, 7). This, then, is our true condition now, as "sons of God," "heirs of God," and "joint heirs of Christ" (Rom. viii, 16, 17). But, beloved, "it doth not yet appear what we shall be; but we know that when He shall appear, we shall be like Him" (1 John iii, 2). Soon the whole church, at the coming of our Lord, will be manifested in the fullness of glory, without spot or wrinkle, or any such thing, unblemished and unchargeable before God, even our Father. The Christian, living in the spirit, must exemplify the Christ-life in practical consecration to God. His growth will be growth "in grace." His evil nature will be kept in daily subjection. Through communion with God, prayer, and feeding on the truth, the germ of spiritual life will develop into full maturity, changing the personal man into the image of Christ.

To recapitulate : —

1. The believer has "the flesh" still in him, and his completeness does not consist in its purification.

2. The believer is already "complete" in Christ, being made "a partaker of the Divine nature."

3. The believer is responsible to nourish the dispositions of this nature, and exhibit growth in grace, manifesting Christian character.

4. The believer must keep "the flesh" in subjection, mortifying his members which are upon the earth, and gain victory over sin by faith in Christ Jesus, and the constant application of the blood of sprinkling, through realizing the perpetual efficacy of the atonement.

Apprehending our completeness in Christ Jesus gives great peace to the soul, and power to overcome the workings "of the flesh." It also produces joy and gratitude to God, and checks the thought of "sinless perfection," which is legal and hurtful.

The full knowledge of our completeness in Christ is not Antinomian in its tendencies. Shall we continue in sin that grace may abound? God forbid! On the contrary, it leads away from self, and occupies the soul with Christ, who is our "wisdom and, righteousness, and sanctification, and redemption." "Ye are complete in Him."

May reader and writer seek to honor God by a life of practical separation unto Him, not seeking to improve self or give it full play in daily experience, but rather to cross its will by refusing to submit to its demands. "No man can serve two masters." Let us wholly aim, then, to do those things which shall please our Lord, in whom we stand perfect and accepted.

THE LOVE OF CHRIST.

I. Eternal, Prov. viii, 22–31.
II. Infinite, John xv, 9.
III. Unmerited, Rom. v, 8.
IV. Unchanging, John xiii, 1.
V. Inseparable, Rom. viii, 35.
VI. Perfect, 1 John iv, 17.
VII. Constraining, 2 Cor. v, 14.

FRIENDSHIP WITH CHRIST.

BY CHAS. M. WHITTELSEY.

FRIEND is a human word, which, in the Scripture, is especially defined and guarded, lest its ordinary use should limit or betray its full significance.

It is also suggestive, before we look up the specific scriptural definition, to note it as compared with other human words, used to picture Divine relations. To the king in a royal family, as head over all the kingdom as well, every soul in the realm has some relation. The nearest is that of the queen and this in Scripture is taken to represent the relation to the Lord which will be borne by the church in glory (Eph. v, 27, and Rev. xix, 7-9). In succession follow the full grown sons, who, being of age, share in all the plans and powers of the king; the friends and counsellors, who are not indeed in the affectionate nearness which comes by birth, and yet by intimacy and fellowship know the king's plans, and participate in his government; the younger children, who are as dear as the full grown sons, but who, for their good are put under law, because they have not yet come to be of one mind with the king; the loyal and intelligent subjects who delight to do his will; the refractory subjects who are limited in their privileges; and those who are utterly and forever banished from the face and realm of the king, because there is no hope of their ever being brought into harmony with his will. Following some of these analogies in Scripture, we find the royal seed, the sons come of age in the kingdom of Christ, are the saints of this dispensation. The children under age were believers of former dispensations, some of whom by faith, like Enoch and Abraham, were friends of God. Believers of future dispensations will be loyal and intelligent subjects of the kingdom; while there will be some who shall be forever destroyed from the presence of the Lord and the glory of His power. As every higher relation includes all the privileges and blessing of those below it, Jesus distinctly opened to us, who in this age have believed, all the privileges of friendship, and this the friendship of full grown sons who with Himself are "heirs of the kingdom." It is, therefore, cause of grief to Him, and to all who know His will, when any Christian falls from this grace into the legal bondage of a child under age, remaining in ignorance of both His love and His purposes, both of grace and glory.

Without further introduction turn to Proverbs for the Divine analysis and definition of friendship. A friend is (1) one who (Prov. xvii, 17) loveth at all times; (2) who by conversation quickens our intelligence (Prov. xxvii, 17), as iron sharpeneth iron; (3) who by hearty counsel is to us, in our difficulties and worries (Prov. xxvii, 9) what ointment and perfume are to those dwelling in the east; (4) who in faithful love speaks the truth to us (Prov. xxvii, 6), even when it wounds us; and (5) who, having friends (Prov. xviii, 24), shows himself friendly by participation in our plans, gaining us favors within his power as a "friend at court," and rendering us practical service. Nor are we left in doubt for what this definition and analysis is given us. All points forward unmistakably to Christ, that we might know "What a friend we have in Jesus;" for it is written (Prov. xviii, 24), "And there is a friend that sticketh closer than a brother." But weak faith and human wisdom are slow to believe that Jesus is willing, or able, to be to us such a friend. It is objected that all this must of necessity be mystical and unreal, that conversation with Jesus, when He is in heaven and we on earth is impossible, and to think of such intimacy with the Eternal Son of God, our Creator, Redeemer and King and High Priest, is the height of presumption.

But such friendship with the invisible Jehovah has been, and, therefore can be (Gen. xviii, 19; Ex. xxxiii, 11). Moreover, Jesus made special arrangements that the intercourse of this friendship might be really enjoyed (John xiv, 20, 27, compare 2 Cor. iii, 18; iv, 6; note 1 John iii, 2).

Nor is this friendship too good to be true, though we be altogether unworthy of it. When on earth He was "The friend of sinners" (Matt. xi, 19), eating with them (Luke xv) in saving love. And beyond this He laid down His life for us (John xv, 13), and refused to let us who have believed, remain any longer in the distance, and with only the privileges of servants (John xv, 15, Rev. iii, 20).

In connection with Prov. xvii, 17, read Rom. v, 6-8; John xv, 9, 11. With Prov. xxvii, 17, read Luke xxiv; John xiv, 20-27; John xv, 15; 1 Cor. ii, 9, 10. With Prov. xxvii, 9, read Isa. ix, 6; John xvi, 13; Ps. xxxii, 8. With Prov. xxvii, 6, read 2 Tim. iii, 16; Heb. xii, 6; Rev. iii, 19 (Judas).

(Prov. xviii, 24.) Jesus has shown Himself our friend on the cross (John xv, 13) and in the gift of the Holy Spirit (John xiv, 15, 16; xv, 15; xvi, 12-15). He is showing Himself our friend in His priesthood and advocacy (John xiii, 3, 10, compare Rev. i, 12, 13, 20; Heb. vii, 25; ix, 24; 1 John i, 9; ii, 1). He will show Himself friendly in the glory (John xvii, 20, 26; Rom. viii, 17; Rev. iii, 20, 21).

But this same analysis of friendship must hold good, according to our measure, in our relations to our living Lord (Prov. xviii, 24, first clause; John xv, 13-20).

John xv, 13, compare Rev. ii, 10. John xv, 14, compare Jas. ii, 23, and context, Gen. xxii. John xv, 15, compare John iii, 29; Gen. xviii, 1, 8, 17, and the contrast in xix, 2. John xv, 16, compare 2 Cor. iii, 18. John xv, 17, compare verse 12; xiii, 34, 35; Col. i, 4, 6. John xv. 18-20, compare Jas. iv, 4; John xvii, 15, 16; Col. ii, 8. Phil. v, 17; 1 John ii, 15-18; 3 John 5, 6; 1 John ii, 15, 16; Titus ii, 11-14; 2 Cor. vi, 14-17.

The Lord give us to walk in such fellowship with Him, as friends, that He may have no word like Zech. xiii, 6, to say to us; but rather may say to us, in that day of our family gathering together unto Him, "Ye are my friends, because ye have done whatsoever I commanded you." Amen.

CHRIST AND ANTICHRIST.

BY REV. H. M. PARSONS.

The personality of the antichrist who has been predicted and foreshadowed by many persons as types, is seen to be real and finally visible in human form. From noting the contrasts of personal and moral qualities in Christ, the true prophet and victor king, we see

CHRIST.	ANTICHRIST.
John iii, 31: "Comes from above."	Rev. xi, 7: "Comes from below."
John v, 43: "Comes in His Father's name."	John v, 43: "Comes in His own name."
Phil. ii, 8: "Humbled Himself and became obedient."	2 Thess. ii, 4: "Exalts Himself above all."
Isa. liii, 3: "Was despised and rejected, and we esteemed Him not."	Rev. xiii, 3, 4: "All the world wonder after the beast, saying, Who is like unto him."
John vi, 38: "Comes to do His Father's will."	Dan. xi, 31: "Does according to His own will."
John xvii, 4: "Glorifies God on earth."	Rev. xiii, 6: "Blasphemes the name of God."
John x, 14, 15: "The Good Shepherd that giveth His life for the sheep."	Zech. xi, 16, 17: "The evil shepherd or idle shepherd who shall tear the flesh."
Phil. ii, 9, 10: "God highly exalts Him, and gives Him a name above every name, that at the name of Jesus every knee should bow."	Isa. xiv, 14, 15: "Exalteth Himself above the heights of the clouds, yet is brought down to hell."
Matt. xxiv, 30: "Shall be seen coming in the clouds with power and great glory."	Isa. xiv, 16: "They that see thee shall narrowly look upon thee, saying, Is this the man that made the earth to tremble, that did shake the kingdoms?"
Rev. xi, 15: "Shall reign forever and ever."	Dan. vii, 26: "They shall take away His dominion, to consume and destroy it to the end."
Heb. i, 2: "The heir of all things."	2 Thess. ii, 4: "The son of perdition."

From these Scriptures it is plain that antichrist in His development must be more than a principle, or a system, or a typical form. He must finally be *a person*. The very term intimates, in place of, or opposed to the Christ. As the long preparation for the revelation of Christ as the victorious person is manifest in the former dispensation, so the present development of the age is to reveal the personal antichrist whom He (Christ) conquers.

"THAT BLESSED HOPE."

THE HOPE.

For the grace of God hath appeared, bringing salvation to all men, instructing us, to the intent that denying ungodliness and worldly lusts, we should live soberly, righteously, and godly in this present world, looking for the Blessed Hope and appearing of the glory of our great God and Savior. Tit. ii, 11–14.

Christ, having been once offered to bear the sins of many, shall appear a second time, apart from sin, to them that wait for Him, unto salvation. Heb. ix, 28.

For our citizenship is in heaven; from whence also we wait for a Saviour, the Lord Jesus Christ. Phil. iii, 20.

When Christ who is our life shall be manifested then shall ye also, with him, be manifested in glory. Col. iii, 4.

Watch therefore, for ye know not on what day your Lord cometh. Matt. xxiv, 42.

THE GROUND OF OUR HOPE OF HIS COMING.

Readings by the pastor. 1. His own words, John xiv, 1–3. 2. Two men at His ascension, Acts i, 10, 11. 3. He established His supper in memory of His death "till He come," 1 Cor. xi, 26. 4. Paul taught it, 1 Thess. iv, 13–18. 2 Thess. ii, 1 12; Phil. iv, 5. 5. So also James and Peter, Jas. v, 7, 8; 1 Pet. v, 4. Read responsively, 2 Pet. iii, 1–12.

THERE IS NO HOPE BUT THIS SET BEFORE THE CHURCH.

Think ye that I am come to send peace on the earth; I tell you nay, but rather division. Luke xii, 51.

If ye were of the world the world would love its own; but because ye are not of the world, but I chose you out of the world, therefore the world hateth you. John xv, 19.

These things have I spoken unto you, that in me ye may have peace. In the world ye shall have tribulation. John xvi, 33.

If they persecute me they will also persecute you. John xv, 20.

To you it hath been granted in the behalf of Christ, not only to believe on Him, but also to suffer in His behalf. Phil. i, 29.

Yea, and all that would live godly in Christ Jesus shall suffer persecution. But evil men and impostors shall wax worse and worse. 2 Tim. iii, 12, 13. Read responsively also, 1 Pet. iv, 12, 18

FOR WHAT PURPOSE IS HE TO COME?

1. To raise the dead saints. 2. To change the living to immortal. 3. To inaugurate His kingdom and destroy His enemies. 4. To perfect His millennial reign. Read responsively, Rev. xix, 11–16; xx, 1–6; Isa. ii, 1–4; Mic. iv, 1–4; Zech. xiv, 16–22.

REV. JOHN C. HILL.

THE JUDGMENT SEAT OF CHRIST.

2 Cor. v, 10.

I. FOR WHOM?

Believers (see context), "we know" — "we labor." No unbeliever at judgment seat of Christ. No believer at Great White Throne.

II. FOR WHAT?

1. Not for Sins. That question is settled, John v, 24. For God to raise the question of the believer's sins would be to call in question the perfection of Christ's work and the completeness of the believer's justification. To appear in judgment with sin secures only condemnation. "No flesh living shall be justified in His presence."

2. Judged for Service. Matt. xxv, 14–30 (Read). Notice the quality of service as well as quantity. Luke xix, 12–26; xii, 41, 48. Rom. xiv, 10–12. 1 Cor. iii, 11, 15. Notice repetition of the word "work." Person saved — work burned. Paul labored as a saved man, but as one who felt that all his work would be tried by God's searching judgment. Eph. vi, 8, 9. Col. iii, 23, 25. 1 Cor. iv, 1-5.

3. Judged with a view to reward. God speaks much about reward in New Testament. See (Matt. vi, 4) Alms giving. (Verse 6.) Unostentation (Verses 44, 46.) Loving enemies. Matt. x, 32, for confessing Christ. (Verse 37.) Making sacrifice for Christ. (Verse 38.) Cross bearing. (Verse 39.) Martyrdom. (Verse 40.) Receiving Christ's messengers. (Verse 41.) A prophet's reward; a righteous man's reward. (Verse 42.) For service done to Christ through His own. The martyr's reward. The crown of life, Rev. ii, 10. Jas. i, 12. The evangelist's reward. The crown of rejoicing, 1 Thess. ii, 19, 20. The pastor's crown, 1 Pet. v, 1-4. The victor's crown, 1 Cor. ix, 24, 29. The crown of righteousness for "loving His appearing." 2 Tim. iv, 8. Ten cities, five cities, two, Luke xix, 12, 26.

Do not confound eternal life which is a gift, with reward in the kingdom which is acquired.

III. WHEN WILL THE JUDGMENT SEAT BE SET?

2 Tim. iv, 8. "In that day." 1 Thess. iv. First resurrection. 1 Cor. iv, 5. At coming of the Lord. 2 Tim. iv, 1. Appearing and kingdom, Luke xiv, 14.

"Behold I come quickly and my reward is with me." Rev. xxii, 7, 12, 30.   W. H. W.

QUESTIONS ABOUT CHRIST'S SECOND COMING ANSWERED.

I. WHY IS IT SO IMPORTANT A DOCTRINE?

1. Because of its prominence in the Scriptures. It is mentioned 318 times in the 260 chapters of the New Testament, or it occupies about one in every twenty-five verses.

2. Because we have a sure word of prophecy whereunto we do well to take heed, 2 Peter i, 19; "*Take heed.*" Mark xiii, 33; Heb. ii, 1.

II. WILL CHRIST'S COMING BE SPIRITUAL OR PERSONAL?

1. It does not mean death, John xxi, 23. Death not certain, 1 Cor. xv, 51. Nothing is promised the believer at death but "Rest in Jesus," 2 Thess. i, 7; Rev. xiv, 13; but there is at His coming. Not commanded to watch for death, but His coming, Mark xiii, 35.

2. It does not mean the Holy Spirit, John xiv, 18-23. Christ, through John, long after this was fulfilled, still spoke of His coming. We, therefore, conclude that it does not mean death, the Holy Spirit the destruction of Jerusalem, or any other event of a spiritual character; but,

3. It is to be literal and personal, John xiv, 3; Acts i. 11; Acts iii, 20, 21; 1 Cor. xv, 23; Phil. iii, 20; Col. iii, 4, etc.; Rev. i, 7.

III. WHAT IS TO BE THE CONDITION OF THE WORLD WHEN HE COMES?

There is no hint of the universal sway of righteousness preceding Christ's coming in the Scriptures, rather the opposite is set forth, 2 Tim. iii, 1-5. 12, 13; 2 Tim. iv, 1-4; Heb. x, 30, 37; 2 Peter iii, 3, 4, also Matt. xiii, 24-30; Luke xviii, 8; Rom. viii, 17-24.

IV. WHAT IS TO TAKE PLACE WHEN HE COMES?

1. Believers are to be caught up to be "Forever with the Lord," John xvii, 24; 1 Cor. xv. 23, 51-53; Phil. iii, 20, 21; 1 Thess. i, 10; 1 Thess. iv, 15-18: 1 Thess. v, 10.

2. The unbelieving dead will not rise until a thousand years later, left behind, Matt. xxiv, 37-42; Rev. xx.

3. There is a difference between His coming for and with His people. Not two appearings, but two stages in the one—the first, 2 Thess. ii, 1;

the second, 2 Thess. i, 7. A start for earth ; a delay ; a manifestation.

4. Coming with all His saints, Zech. xiv, 5; Col. iii, 4; 1 Thess. iii, 13; iv, 14; Rev. xix, 14; or between the coming of the Lord and the appearing of the Lord there will be a period in which the saints caught up to be with Him will be judged— their works, not their persons, will be judged. It is a question of rewards — not of salvation — that has already been settled.

5. The judgment of believers, John iii, 18; John v. 24; Rom. viii, 1. Believers who are now asleep in Jesus are certainly not troubled about the results of the judgment, and those who are still living have just as little reason for fear of trusting in His word, Luke xii, 32; John x, 27-29; 1 Cor. xv, 50-57; 2 Cor. v, 6-8; Phil. i, 23. Solemn thought all the works of Christians must appear in judgment, and nothing will stand the test except that which is built on the foundation — done solely for Christ. Matt. xxiv, 14-31; Mark ix. 41; Rom. xiv, 10-12; 1 Cor. iii, 11-15; Col. iii, 23, 24 2 Tim. iv, 8; Jas. i, 12; Rev. xxii, 12.

6. While this is taking place in the air, events of an entirely different character will be fulfilled on earth, as follows : 1. A literal restoration of the Jews to their own land — part of them to return in unbelief, Isa. vi, 9, 13; xvii, 10-14; Dan. ix, 24, 27; comp. Zech. xi, 14, 17; xii, 8-14; Isa. xviii, 3-7; Eze. xxii, 1-9; Zech. xiii, 1-9; Isa. xxiv, 2; Jer. xvi. 2. The temple to be rebuilt, 2 Thess. ii, 4; Rev. ii, 1-8. 3. The Jews enter into covenant with antichrist, Dan. ix, 27; John v, 43; who reveals His true character, Dan. vii, 19-25; viii, 23-25; ix, 27; Dan. xi, 36; 2 Thess. ii, 3, 9; Rev. xiii. 4. He stops the sacrifice in the temple and sets up His own image for worship, Dan. ix, 27; Dan. xi, 31; Matt. xxiv, 15; Rev. xiii, 14-17; Dan. xii, 11. 5. The two witnesses shall be killed, Rev. xi, 7. 6. The Devil cast out of the air into the earth, Rev. xii, 7, 12. 7. The holy city (Jerusalem) trodden down, Dan. ix, 26; Rev. xi, 2; Luke xxi, 24. 8. Great tribulations come upon the world, Jer. xxx, 7; Dan. xii, 1, Matt. xxiv, 21; Rev. vii, 14; Rev. iii, 10; Luke xxi, 34-36; Zech. xiv, 12. 9. Israel is saved from this by personal appearance of Christ, Zech. xiv, 1-3; Rev. xix, 1; 2 Thess. ii, 4-7.

V. WHAT IS THERE PRACTICAL ABOUT THE DOCTRINE?

The following practical duties taught :

1. It leads to watchfulness, Matt. xxiv, 42-51; Mark xiii, 33-37; Luke xxi, 28, 34, 36; Rev. iii, 3; Luke xii, 45, 46.

2. Faithfulness, Matt. xxv, 14-20; Matt. xxiv, 48-51; Luke xix, 13-15.

3. Wakefulness, Matt. xxv, 1-13; 1 Thess. i, 8.

4. Joy, Acts i, 11; cf. Luke xxiv, 52; Col. iii, 4; Phil. iv, 4. 5; 1 Peter i, 7, 8; Rom. v, 2; Rom. viii, 24.

5. Patience, Heb. x, 36, 37; 1 Cor. iv, 5; Jas. v, 7, 8. In anticipation of trouble, John xiv, 1-3. In actual trouble, 1 Thess. iv, 13-18.

6. Will make us like Christ — to watch for Him, 1 Thess. i, 10; Col. iii, 23, 24; Phil. i. 10; Mark viii, 38; 1 Peter v, 1-4; 2 Tim. iv, 1-5.

7. It helps in living a consecrated life, 1 John iii, 2, 3; Luke xxi, 34, 36; 2 Peter iii, 10, 11, 12; Titus ii, 11-15. The Westminister Confession of Faith says that Christ would have men always watchful, because they know not at what hour the Lord will come, and may ever be prepared to say: "Come, Lord Jesus, come quickly."

8. It gives assurance of sonship to believers; peace in believing, security, etc., Phil. iii, 20, 21; Col. i, 12-14; 1 John iii, 2, 3; 2 Tim. i, 12; 2 Tim. iv, 8.

9. Gives comfort in affliction, 1 Thess. iv, 13-18; 1 Peter iv, 12, 13.

JOHN H. ELLIOTT.

PROPHETIC OUTLINES.

Prophecy is important: One-fourth of the Bible is prophetic.

Full one-half of the book is concerning Israel.

Three classes in Scripture: Jew, Church and Gentile.

Prophecy always refers to time; Church not of time.

Prophecy always refers to earth; Church is heavenly.

Church chosen in him *before* foundation of world.

Israel chosen *from* the foundation of world.

Prophecy always associated with the first or second coming of Lord.

Prophecy always comes in when man breaks down.

Man failed in Eden, in the antediluvian world, and the end of Noahic dispensation was idolatry, Josh. xxiv, 2.

Abraham called out. Promise unconditional, Gen. xii.

Stars of heaven represent spiritual seed, Gen. xv, 5.

Dust of earth represent literal seed, Gen. xiii, 16.

Abraham died without a foot of land. Promise is good.

Israel's history foretold in furnace and lamp, Gen. xv, 17. Furnace. Bondage in Egypt, Canaan, Babylon and dispersion.

Lamp. Deliverance from Egypt, Canaan, Babylon by Christ appearing.

Jacob foretells the future of the twelve tribes, Gen. xlix. .

Israel dwells alone, not numbered with nations, Numbers xxiii, 9.

Song of Moses. Past, present and future of Israel, Deut. xxxii.

When obedient, God gave them authority over the nations.

When disobedient, uses the nations to chastise them.

He reigns as their king till they reject him, Sam. viii, 19.

Jewish history divided into four periods of 490 years each: (1) From call of Abraham to the exodus of Egypt. (2) From exodus to completion of Solomon's temple. Infidels say this was 621 years, but God does not count the seven different times of captivity in Canaan of 131 years. (3) From Solomon to the Babylonish captivity. (4) From captivity to cutting off of Messiah, 483 years; the last seven years of this period are *postponed.*

For idolatry (Israel) ten tribes carried to Asyria, 2 Kings xvii, 6.

For idolatry (Judah) two tribes carried to Babylon, 2 Chron. xxxvi.

All this was foretold in 1 Kings xi. 31.

A remnant of Judah and Benjamin returned from Babylon, but the ten tribes have never yet. They will.

The second temple was built, but no Shekinah appeared.

In the three prophecies written after the return from Babylon, God never addressed them as "my people."

Here the times of the Gentiles begin, and will continue until Christ's *second* coming, Luke xxi, 24.

ISRAEL'S PRESENT CONDITION.

Kingdom taken away, Matt. xxi. 43. *Blindness,* Rom. xi, 25. *Vail over eyes,* 2 Cor. iii, 15. *House desolate,* Matt. xxiii, 28; Shekinah gone, Ezek. xi, 23. Without king, Hosea iii, 4, 5. Not owned. Hosea v, 14. Power to Gentiles, Dan. ii, 37.

ISRAEL'S FUTURE.

Returned to own land, Isa. xiv, 1, 2; also, xi, 11, 16.

As in days of old, Isa. xxvii, 12; Jer. xvi, 14.

Resurrected, regathered, re-united, Ezek, iii, 1; Jer. xxx, 31.

Sheltered like Noah, Lot or Egypt, Isa. xxvi, 20, and xxvii, 1, 6.

Restoration, baptism of fire and coming Lord one, Isa. lxvi, 15.

Joel ii. Pours out spirit on *all* flesh, not *some* as at pentecost. Deliverance of the elect (Jew), v. 32.

Judgment and great tribulation; destruction of their enemies, iii, 1, 2.

Three things in all prophecy: Restoration of Israel, judgment on her enemies, millennial blessedness.

Tabernacle of David restored *forever*, Amos ix, 11, 14.

Temple rebuilt, Micah iv, 1; same as Isa. ii.

Judgments on nations precedes the kingdom, Zephaniah iii, 8.

Spirit of repentance on Israel, Zechariah, xii, 9, 10.

Two-thirds die; one-third refined in the fire, Zechariah xiii, 29.

Tribulation; escape; Lord comes, Zechariah xiv.

Captivity and time of Gentiles begin together.

Daniel's seventy weeks the key to prophecy.

Thy people, *thy* holy city; *Jews* and *Jerusalem*, Chap. ix, 24.

Just closing seventy years' captivity. Gabriel announces seventy weeks of years: (1) A period of forty-nine years; wall and city rebuilt; Ezra records it. (2) A period of 434 years; Messiah cut off; no throne or kingdom yet.

(Here is an interval during which the church is called out.)

(3) Last week of seven years, during which the Jews return to their own land; a covenant with antichrist is made; worship restored; abomination of desolation set up; great tribulation, ending with the appearing of the Lord.

SECOND COMING OF CHRIST.

WHEN.

After gathering Israel, abomination and desolation, Matt. xxiv, 29.

Not till "times of the Gentiles" are fulfilled, Luke xxi, 24.

Not till the falling away and antichrist appears, 2 Thess. ii, 3.

Not till Israel shall say: "Blessed be He," Matt. xxiii, 39.

Not till Holy Ghost as a dispensational agent is taken away. 2 Thess. ii, 7.

Not till the body is complete, and the bride taken home. Acts xv. 14.

Not till the restitution of all things. Acts iii, 21.

Not till after the first resurrection. 1 Thess. iv, 15.

HOW.

Actually: I will come. Not send. John xiv.

Literally: All tribes earth *see* and mourn. Matt. xxiv, 30. All who look shall see. Phil. iii, 20; Heb. ix, 28.

Visibly: Lord *himself* descends. 1 Thess. iv, 16.

Acts i, 11. In glory, not humiliation as before. Titus ii, 13; 2 Thess. 2, 9, 10.

WHERE.

In the air: For his saints. 1 Thess. iv.

Mt. Olives: With his saints. Zechariah xiv, 4; Jude 14.

Jerusalem: God's earthly center. Dan. ix, 24.

SEVENTIETH WEEK, OR LAST SEVEN YEARS.

Church in heaven; marriage and supper. Rev., from iv to xix chapter.

Saints come *with Him* to judgment. Rev. xix; Jude 14.

Israel returns to Jerusalem. Temple rebuilt.

Covenant with antichrist, beast — false prophet.

Abomination of desolation set up.

Vials of God's wrath poured out.

Great tribulation cut short by Lord's coming.

MILLENNIAL REIGN — RIGHTEOUSNESS AND PEACE FILL THE EARTH.

THE GENTILES OR NATIONS.

Always separate from the church and Israel. Not dealt with yet. Deut. vii, 1, 3, 6.

When Israel obedient, power over nations.

When Israel disobedient, made captive by nations. Deut. xxviii.

Egypt and Assyria, her worst enemies, will yet share her blessings. Isa. xix.

Israel, God's center, Jerusalem, seat of God's government till Nebuchadnezzar.

Now Israel cut off. Rom. xi. (Church called out.) *Then* Israel restored. Hosea v, 15.

Not till then will the Gentiles be dealt with. Acts xv, 14.

PROOF.

He shall judge the nations. Isa. ii, 4. They shall *come to Israel.* Isa. lv, 5.

Nations who wont serve shall perish. Isa. lx, 12.

The remnant shall be preachers of the Word. Isa. lxvi, 19.

Nations shall *know* the Lord. Ezekiel xxxvii, 28, and xxxviii, 23.

The image of Daniel ii, represents the only *four* kingdoms of *this* world. Babylon, Medo-Persia, Greece and Rome.

The four beasts. These span the whole period of Gentile supremacy, from the time of Nebuchadnezzar to the second coming of our Lord. Dan. vii.

After these, God of heaven sets up His *everlasting* kingdom. Dan. ii, 44.

After these, Son of man receives a kingdom, *never to be destroyed.* Dan. vii, 14.

Rome (the last) was, is not, and yet is (future). Rev, xvii.

Israel gathered, and nations judged at the *same time.* Joel iii, 2-12.

Nations worship at the *Lord's* house. Micah iv, 2; also v, 9, 15.

Baptism of fire on the nations. Zech. iii, 8; Isa. lxvi, 16.

Nations shall come to Jerusalem. Zech. viii, 22, and xiv, 16.

Those who reject Christ shall be destroyed. Zech. xiv, 2, 3.

Word yet to be taught to all nations. Matt. x, 23, and xxviii, 19.

When this is done the *end will come.* Matt. xxiv, 14.

Judgment of the *nations,* as they have treated *these my brethren.* Matt. xxv.

WM. G. CARR.

THE COMING OF THE LORD.

1 Thess. iv, 13–18; 2 Thess. i–iv.

HE WILL COME.

How? For his saints, 1 Thess. iv, 17. With his saints, 2 Thess. i, 10. Literally, as he went, Acts i, 11. Personally (I will come), John xiv, 3. As the bridegroom, Matt. xxv, 6. As the judge, Matt. xxv, 31; Acts xvii, 31.

Where? In the air, 1 Cor. xv, 51; 1 Thess. iv, 17. On the earth (Mt. of Olives), Zech. xiv, 4. "Coming of the Lord." Saints only will see him, Luke xiii, 35. Day of the Lord. Appearing of the Lord. Day of tribulation and judgment. All shall see Him. Rev. i, 7.

For His Saints. When? With His Saints. At any time, when "the body" is complete, Eph. v, 27–30. Before the hour of trial of them that dwell on earth, Rev. iii, 10. Before the seals are broken or vials poured out. Proof: the church is in heaven, from Rev. iv–xix. After the "falling away," 2 Thess. ii, 3. After the great tribulation, Matt. xxiv, 29. After the marriage supper, Rev. xix, 14.

ORDER OF EVENTS IN CHRIST'S COMING.

Dead in Christ and the living caught up. 1 Thess. iv.

Jews return to their own land. Jer. xxx, 3.

Temple will be rebuilt. Rev. xi.

Jews enter into covenant with antichrist. John v, 43; Dan. ix, 27.

After three and a half years he reveals his true character. Rev xiii; Dan. vii, 9.

Stops sacrifice, sets up his own image. Rev. xiii. 15; 2 Thess. ii, 4.
Kills two witnesses. Rev. xi, 7.
Satan cast out of the air into the earth. Rev. xii, 7-9.
Holy city trodden down. Lu. xxi, 24; Rev. xi, 2.
The great tribulation. Dan. xii, 1; Matt. xxiv, 21; Rev. vii, 14.
Christ appears. Zech. xiv, 1-3; Rev. xix; 2 Thess. i, 10.
"Be patient, brethren, unto the coming of the Lord." Jas. v, 7.
Let your moderation be known unto all men; the Lord is at hand. Phil. iv, 5.

W. G. CARR.

CHRIST'S METHOD OF TEACHING.

"Never man spake like this man," John vii, 46. All believers should preach, teach, or talk the Gospel, and Christ is our model in matter and manner. Let us study some characteristics of His method.

1. He spoke with the authority of Divine majesty (and so may we, in His name), and the assurance of absolute and positive truth. He was a personal witness concerning Divine and unseen things. He was not a debater or reasoner, Isa. lv, 4; Matt. v, 21, 22; vii, 29; John iii, 11.

2. He taught much in parables, similitudes and illustrations, Matt. xiii, 1; vii, 24-27; v, 14, 15; Luke, vii, 31-35. The Old Testament Scriptures, all nature, and all the occupations of man. constituted his cyclopedia of illustrations.

3. He was frank and free from sophistry, and exposed the shams, hypocrisies and wiles of his enemies, Matt. xxii, 15-46 and xxxiii. 14.

4. He did not seek to excite sensation, or gratify idle curiosity, Matt. xii, 39; xiii, 28, 24; Luke vii, 24-26. Let this apply to "curious questions" about Old Testament history.

5. He used wisdom and tact in dividing the word of God to different classes, ever revealing truth to one class, and concealing it from another in the same assembly by use of parables, John iv, 14; xvi, 12; Matt. xiii, 10-16. In Luke iv, 16-19, He closes the book at a comma, thus dividing the acceptable year and the day of vengeance.

6. He sought no applause from His hearers, John v, 41; Rom. xv, 8. The motto of the play-actor is "we study to please," but of the preacher, "we study to save."

7. He preached with great boldness, regardless of the fear or favor of man, Matt. xi, 20-24; xxiii. 33. Men who want us to "preach as Christ did," are unwittingly asking for almost unparalleled severity.

8. He taught with patience, repetition, self control, meekness and kindness, Matt. vii, 7, 8; ix, 36; xi, 29; xxiii, 37; Mark ix, 43; Luke xix, 41.

9. He taught with unequaled simplicity, so that the old and young, persons of all grades of understanding and attainment, listened with rapture on his words. He brought to them in the simplest language, the grandest truths that the universe contains or eternity can reveal, Matt. xi, 25, 26; John xv, 22; 2 Cor. iv. 6.

10. He used great plainness and simplicity of speech, and not the fine rhetoric and elocution of the schools. Study any of His discourses and you see that He used the unadorned language of common life. In like manner Paul never wreathed the "sword of the Spirit" with garlands. Study 1 Cor. ii, 1-11. He quoted and used the Old Testament Scriptures constantly, Matt. xii, 5; Mark xii, 26; Luke xxiv, 27, 44; John v, 39-46.

11. He taught that the great and constant theme of the Old Testament was His own Divine person and redeeming work.

12. He preached with profound seriousness and intense earnestness. He did not trifle, and people did not expect Him to "entertain" them

with the Gospel message, Mark xvi, 16; Luke ii, 49; xii, 50; John iv, 34; ix, 4.

The results of His teachings were:
1. Universal astonishment, Matt. vii, 28, 29; Mark vi, 2; xi, 18; Luke iv, 32.
2. The violent opposition of many, Luke iv, 28; vi, 11; John v, 16-18.
3. The conversion of some, Luke iv. 15; John i, 40-45; x, 27.

Thank God for this and take courage. The duty of all who hear the Gospel is found in Acts iii, 22, and their danger in Acts iii, 23.

E. P. M.

DID JESUS CHRIST TEACH HIS DEITY?

The answer to the above question is to be found in the four Gospels, in the words spoken by our Lord Himself. We have this statement in John x, 30: "I and My Father are one;" and that by this he meant more than one in sympathy, desire, etc., the following texts will show:

They are one in work, John v, 7, 19, 21; x, 28, 29; xv, 26; xvi, 7; xx, 22; Luke xxiv, 49.

One in possessions, John xvi, 15: xvii, 9, 10; v, 26.

One in glory, Mark viii, 38; Matt. xvi, 27; Luke ix, 26; Matt. xxv, 31; John xvii. 5.

One in person, John x, 38; xiv, 10, 11, 23; viii, 19; xiv, 7, 9; xii, 45; xv, 23, 24; v, 23; Matt. xxviii, 19.

He teaches His omnipotence, Matt. xi, 27; Luke x, 22; John xvi, 15; Matt. xxviii, 18; John vi, 39; ii, 19; x, 18.

His omniscience. John v, 20; Luke v, 4; John xxi, 6; i, 48; iv. 18; vi, 70; xxi. 18.

His omnipresence, John iii, 13; Matt. xviii, 20; xxviii, 20.

His eternal existence, John viii, 58; xvii, 5, 24.

His holiness, John vii, 18; viii, 46.

He teaches His deity in what He says: —

1. As to His words, Matt. xxiv, 35; Mark xiii, 31; Luke vi, 63; John vi, 63; xv, 3.
2. As to what He is in Himself, John viii, 12; ix, 5; xii, 35; xi, 25; xiv, 6, 19; xvii, 3.
3. As to what He does, Matt. ix, 2, 6; Mark ii, 5, 10; Luke v, 20, 24; vii, 48; xxiv, 47; Matt. xi, 28; Luke xxiv, 36; John xiv, 27; iv, 14; vi, 35; Matt. xvi, 19.

"My Lord and my God."—Thomas.

R. A. ORR.

CHRIST REJECTED AND FORSAKEN.

I. By the world, John i, 10.
II. By His nation, John i, 11.
III. By His country, Mark vi, 1-4.
IV. By His city, Luke iv, 16, 29;
V. By His kindred, John xii, 5.
VI. By His friends, Matt. xxvi, 56.
VII. By His God, Matt. xxvii, 46.

THE TRANSFIGURATION.

Matt. xvii, 1-13; Mark ix, 2-13; Luke ix, 28-36; 2 Pet. i, 16-21.

Six persons on the mount; two groups of three.

First group, James, John and Peter. Their call, Matt. iv, 18, 21.

In the garden, Matt. xxvi, 37; Mark xiv, 33.

Second group, lawgiver, prophet, savior.

Moses, fasted forty days, Ex. xxxiv, 28. Transfigured, Ex. xxxiv, 29. Burial, Deut. xxxiv, 5, 6.

Elijah, fasted forty days, 1 Kings xix, 8. Translated, 2 Kings, ii, 11.

Christ, fasted forty days, Matt. iv, 2. Transfigured, Matt. xvii, 2. Ascended, Acts i. 9.

Each heard the "voice," Ex. iii, 4; 1 Kings xix, 12; Matt. xvii, 5. Peter desired a Tabernacle, Matt. xvii, 4; which must perish, 2 Pet. i, 14.

J. E. BROWN.

THE STONE.

Acts iv, 11.

1. It was laid in death and resurrection, Gen. xlix, 23, 24.
2. It thus became a sure foundation, Isa. xxviii, 16; 1 Pet. ii, 6.
3. It was set at naught, Matt. xxi, 42.
4. It is the head of the corner, Ps. cxviii, 22.
5. It is the living stone, 1 Pet. ii, 4.
6. It will grind to powder those that rise up against it, Matt. xxi, 44.
7. It will fill the earth, Dan. ii, 34, 35; Rev. xxi.

JAS. H. BROOKES, D. D.

WHAT WE HAVE IN CHRIST.

Psalm ciii.

In celebrating Christ's glory three things are specially mentioned: His accomplished and certain salvation given to believers, ver. 1–12; His present and loving care, ver. 13–18; His universal and everlasting Kingdom, ver. 19–22. There can be no singing and making melody in our heart to the Lord (chap. v, 19), unless faith accepts it as true that He hath forgiven all trespasses, that He watches over us with unceasing tenderness, and that He will receive us into His kingdom at His coming. "He hath not dealt with us according to our sins, nor rewarded us according to our iniquities. For as heaven is high above the earth, so great is His mercy toward them that fear Him. As far as the east is from the west, so far hath He removed our transgressions from us." This is the base of the anthem of praise that ascends to our Risen Lord, and this leads us to behold Him with joy in His various offices here described.

First. He is the Forgiver, "Who forgiveth all thine iniquities." It is not simply that He forgives some of them, but He forgives them all, casting them behind His back, Isa. xxxviii, 17; blotting them out, Isa. xliv, 22; "Sought for and not found," Jer. i, 20; "Cast into the depths of the sea," Mic. vii, 19; "Remembered against us no more," Heb. x, 17; Pet. ii, 24; 1 John i, 7.

Second. He is the Healer, "who healeth all thy diseases," Acts x, 38; Matt. viii, 16; Isa. xxxiii, 24.

Third. He is the Redeemer, "who redeemeth thy life from destruction," 1 Pet. i, 18, 19; Isa. xliv, 22; Rev. iv, 9.

Fourth. He is the Crowner, "who crowneth thee with loving kindness and tender mercies." Among the crowns bestowed with His loving kindness and tender mercies may be mentioned the Holy Spirit, of whom the oil is the type." Lev. xxi, 12; Christ Himself at His coming, Isa. xxviii, 5: "An incorruptible crown," 1 Cor. ix, 25; a "Crown of rejoicing," 1 Thess. ii, 19: a "Crown of life," Jas. i, 12; a "Crown of righteousness," 2 Tim. iv, 8; a "Crown of glory," 1 Pet. v, 4.

Fifth. He is the Satisfier, "who satisfieth thy mouth with good things," Isa. lv, 2; Ps. xvii, 15; Ps. xxii, 26; Ps. xxxvi, 8; Ps. xxxvii, 19; Ps. lxiii, 5; Ps. cvii, 9; Isa. lviii, 11.

Sixth. He is a Pitier, "Like as a father pitieth his children, so the Lord pitieth them that fear him," Matt. ix, 36; Matt. xiv, 14; Matt. xx, 34; Mark i, 41; Luke vii, 13; Luke x, 33; Luke xv, 20.

Seventh. He is the Preparer of His throne, "The Lord hath prepared His Throne in the heavens, and His kingdom ruleth over all," Luke xix, 12; Ps. lxxii, 7, 8.

Thus do we find Him sufficient for all our need from first to last. He forgives, He heals, He redeems, He crowns, He satisfies, He pities, He prepares His throne, and He is preparing the faithful in the midst of declension to share His throne, Rev. iii, 21.

J. H. BROOKES.

THE POWER OF CHRIST UPON THE BELIEVER.

There are two meanings of the word *power*. Authority or right, Matt. xxviii, 18; and ability or power to execute, 2 Cor. xii, 9. The latter word in the original is found one hundred and twenty-one times in the New Testament. It is translated seventy-seven times *power;* in other places *strength, might,* etc. Consider the power of Christ:

I. The power which characterized Christ, and became manifest also in the life of Paul: (1) In the form of sympathy; in our Lord, Heb. ii, 17; Mark i, 41; vi, 34; Luke xix, 41. In Paul, Acts xx, 31; Phil. iii, 18; Phil. i, 8 (literally, the tender heart of Christ). (2) Power of motive, our Lord's motive, John v, 30; vi. 38; John xvii, 3, 4, finished. Motive impelling Paul, 2 Thess. ii, 4. Acts xx, 24; *finished,* 2 Tim. iv, 7; (3) Power of a definite purpose controlling the whole life. Jesus, John ix, 4. Where did such work lead Him? To death? Power of death, John xii, 24. Paul, Phil. i, 21, was likewise led to the cross, 1 Cor. iv, 11-13; 2 Cor. xi, 26-31; Galatians vi, 14; Acts xx, 22-24; 1 Cor. xv, 31. If these characteristics of Christ, which in measure rested upon Paul, rest upon us in conflict and service, we shall have the power of Christ upon us.

II. The power of His presence with His people. Promised, Matt. xxviii, 18. With Old Testament saints, Ex. iii, 11, 12; iv. 10, 11; xxxiii, 14; Judges iv, 16, 17. His presence with Paul, Acts xxiii, 11; 2 Tim. iv, 16, 17. With all His saints, Heb. xiii, 5, 6.

III. Power of His Spirit within us and upon us. Believers possess a new life through the Spirit. He is also the sustainer of that life. Christ Himself is our life, 1 John v, 10; John x, 10, *abundant.* Hence Phil. iv, 13, "upon us." The word "*rest*" in 2 Cor. xii, 9, is *Tabernacle.* Think of the Shekinah cloud resting down on the Tabernacle, the outward symbol of God's power and glory.

IV. Christ's power is the power of His Word. Knowledge is power. Through His words we come to know Himself. Human speech alone is impotent for spiritual results, 1 Cor. ii. 1. 4; 1 Cor. iv, 19. Jesus is fully identified with Scripture : "Me and and My words." Read, also, Matt. xxii, 29; Jer. xxi, 9. Every word of God is pure.

V. Power of His name. Acts iii, 6, 16; iv, 10, 22-30. David faced Goliath in the name of the Lord.

VI. Power of His resurrection. Phil. iii, 10; Col. ii, 12; iii, 1.

VII. How are we made partakers of Christ's power? (1) Through humbling, Gen. xxxii, 24-32. He wrestled with Jacob until he deprived him of all strength, and taught him to prevail by weakness. So Paul in 2 Cor. xii. (2) Through self denial, 1 Cor. ix, 25-27. (3) Through faith, Luke vii, 7, 8. The centurion recognized Christ as one under authority, having all the power of heaven behind Him, even as he himself was under authority with the resources of the Cæsars to draw upon. So said Jesus : "I have not found so great faith, no, not in Israel." Let us beware of counterfeiting Divine power, as Jannes and Jambres copying Moses. See, also, Acts viii, 10. Do not trade with unfelt truth, or traffic in stolen experience.

GEO. C. NEEDHAM.

THE JOY OF CHRIST.

I. When He made the world, Prov. viii, 22-31; John i, 1-3; Heb. i, 2.

II. When He found the church, Matt. xiii, 44; Phil. ii, 6-8; Heb. xii, 2.

III. When He found His lost sheep, Luke xv, 5; xix, 10; Matt. xviii, 11-13.

IV. When His people abide in Him, John xv, 10, 11; xiv, 21, 23; 1 John ii, 28.

V. When He comes for believers, 1 Thess. iv, 16; John xiv, 3; Matt. xxv, 21.
VI. When He receives His bride, Rev. xix, 7; Eph. v. 25–27; Ps. xlv, 11–15.
VII. When He presents us to God, Jude 24; 1 Cor. xv, 24; Rev. xxi, 3, 4.

IN CHRIST.

We have redemption, Rom. iii, 24.
We are new creatures. 2 Cor. v, 17.
We are sanctified, 1 Cor. i, 2.
We are wise. 1 Cor. iv, 10.
We are created unto good works, Eph. ii, 10.
We have peace, 1 Peter v, 14.
We have hope, 1 Cor. xv, 19.
We have consolation, Phil. ii, 1; 2 Cor. i, 15.
We have liberty, Gal. ii, 4.
We rejoice, Phil. iii, 3.
We triumph, 2 Cor. ii, 14.
We are saints, Col. i, 2.
We are perfect, Col, i, 28.
We shall sleep, 1 Cor. xv, 18.
We shall rise, 1 Thess. iv, 16.

P. AUGUSTUS WIETING.

LOOKING TO CHRIST.

I. For salvation, Isa. xlv, 22.
II. In prayer, Ps. v, 3.
III. For light, Ps. xxxiv, 5.
IV. In service, Ps. cxxiii, 2.
V. For consolation, 2 Cor. iv, 18.
VI. For consecration, Heb. xii, 2.
VII. As the hope, Phil. iii, 20; Tit. ii, 13.

CHRIST'S GIFTS TO HIS PEOPLE.
John xvii.

This prayer opens to us a view within the veil, whither the forerunner for us is entered, and shows us the nature of our High Priest's perpetual ministry of intercession. The frequent recurrence of the word "give" suggests the following line of study. He gives us —

1. The Life He has, v, 2; 1 John v, 11, 12; Col. iii, 3.
2. The Truth He has, v, 8; Ps. xxiv, 14; John xvi, 14, 15.
3. The Joy He has, v, 13; John xv, 11; 1 John i, 4.
4. The Glory He has, v, 22; Romans viii, 17; 1 Thess. ii, 14.
5. The Place He has, v, 24. Heaven anywhere with Him, 2 Cor. v, 8; Rev. vii. 7; Rev. xxii, 3, 4.
6. The Love He has, v, 26. Through Him that love flows to us. Compare v, 23, last clause.
7. Himself, v, 26. "Is in them," is the crown and consummation of all. Gen. xv, 1; Ps. xvii, 25; Ps. xviii, 4.

REV. W. H. MARQUESS.

THE MIND OF CHRIST.
Phil. ii, 1-13.

Our Model a Little Child. He thinks as the Father thinks. He wills as the Father wills. He acts as the Father acts.

Verse 2. Only as we are Christlike do we approach oneness.

Ver. 7. Christ acted out His own doctrine; took the lowest place; Christ a servant, with one hand on the throne of God, with the other washing the disciples' feet, John xiii, 14.

Ver. 9. The way to go up is first to go down, Luke xiv, 11.

Ver. 10. Lord in three worlds, two yet to be reconciled, Col. i, 50.

Ver. 11. Even His enemies shall confess, Rev. vi, 16.

Ver. 12. Don't lean on Paul; lean on God; work out has already been worked in. Save yourself now; try to save others.

A Mind like Jesus. To work first recorded words of Jesus, Luke ii, 49. Kind, true hearted, Eph. iv, 32; Forbearing, forgiving, Col. iii. 13; Pitiful, courteous, 1 Peter, iii, 8 — lowly, loving, loyal.

W. G. CARR.

WHAT CHRIST IS TO US.

Christ's blood the sinner's redemption, 1 Peter i, 18, 19.
Christ's blood the believer's justification, Rom. v. 6-9.
Christ's blood the believer's cleansing, 1 John i, 7.
Christ's resurrection the believer's confidence, 1 Cor. xv, 12-20.
Christ's intercession the believer's surety, Heb. vii, 25.
Christ's life the believer's example, 1 Peter ii, 21-24.
Christ's coming again the believer's hope, 1 John iii, 2, 3.

L. W. MUNHALL.

WHAT IS CHRIST TO US?

He is our example, 1st. In meekness and lowliness of heart, Matt. xi, 30; John xiii, 5; 2d. In beneficence, 2 Cor. viii, 9; 3d. In suffering, Heb. xii, 2, 3; 1 Peter ii, 21; iv, 1; 1 John iii, 16.

He is our justification, Acts xiii, 39; Rom. iii, 24-26; iv, 25; v, 9; Gal. ii, 16.

He is our propitiation, Rom. iii, 25; v, 8; 2 Cor. v, 18, 19; Col. i, 14.

He is our sanctification, Heb. x, 10-14; xiii, 12.

He is our life, John xiv, 19, 1 Thess. v, 10; 2 Tim. ii, 11; 1 John iv, 9.

He is our Mediator, John xiv, 6; xvi, 26; Rom. viii, 34; 1 John ii, 1.

He is our Priest, Heb. iv, 14; v, 10; viii, 1; ix, 11, 12.

He is our Savior, Matt. xviii, 2; Luke ii. 11; John iii, 17; Acts iv, 12.

Is not this inducement enough for every one to accept the Beloved? How can men refuse to accept Christ when there is so much offered in and through and by Him?

W. E. BASKETTE.

CHRIST OUR LIFE.

I. "Bread of Life." John vi, 35.
II. "Fountain of Life," Ps. xxxvi, 9.
III. "Tree of Life," Rev. ii, 7.
IV. "Light of Life." John viii, 12.
V. "Path of Life." Ps. xvi. 11.
VI. "Word of Life," 1 John i. 1.
VII. "Prince of Life," Acts iii, 15.

CHRIST OUR HIDING PLACE.

I. From wrath, John iii, 36; Rom. v, 9; 1 Thess. i. 9, 10; v, 9.
II. From sin. Matt. i, 21; Luke vii. 50; Acts xiii, 38, 39; Eph. i, 7.
III. From fear, Rom. viii, 15; 2 Tim. i, 7; Luke xii, 32; 1 John iv, 17, 18.
IV. From temptation, 1 Cor. x, 13; 2 Peter ii, 9; Heb. ii, 18; iv, 15, 16.
V. From trouble. Ps. xxvii, 5; xci, 15; John xiv, 1, 27; 2 Thess. 1, 7.
VI. From death, 1 Cor. xv, 54-57; 2 Cor. v, 1, 8; Phil. i, 23; 1 Thess. iv. 14-18.
VII. From judgment, John iii, 18; v, 27; 1 Cor. vi, 2, 3; Rev. iii, 21.

"If ye then be risen with Christ. seek those things which are above, where Christ sitteth on the right hand of God, not on things of the earth. For ye are dead [ye died]. and your life is hid with Christ in God. When Christ, who is our life. shall appear, then shall ye also appear with Him in glory," Col. iii, 1-4.

REV. J. H. BROOKES.

THE CHRISTIAN'S PLACES OF REFUGE.

1. At Christ's Cross — the place of Peace, Col. i, 20; Gal. vi, 14. Here we find refuge from the curse of the law and the conscience.

2. Before His Face — the place of Light, 2 Cor. iv, 6; Ps. lxvii, 1, 2. The face is an expression or revelation of the man. Here we find refuge from the darkness of our natural states.

3. On His Shoulders — the place of Strength. Exod. xxvii, 9-12; Luke xv, 2. Here we find refuge from the weakness of our own characters.

4. On His Bosom — the place of Love, John xiii, 23; John xxi, 20;

Exod. xxvii, 29, 30. Here we find refuge from the unsatisfied cravings of our nature, relief from care, and disappointment, and reproach.

5. At His Feet — the place of Instruction, Deut. xxxiii, 3; Luke x, 39; Col. i, 9. Here we find refuge from our own ignorance, follies and mistakes.

6. By His Side — the place of Service, Luke viii, 1-3. "With Him," and "ministered unto Him," Col. iii, 23, 24. Here we find refuge from the emptiness of our own life and the ignobleness of its pursuits.

7. In His Steps — the place of Holiness, 1 Peter i, 21; 1 John ii, 6. Here we find refuge from the passions and habits of our own evil nature.

REV. W. H. MARQUISS.

THE WAY, THE TRUTH, AND THE LIFE.

John xiv, 6.

We have here one of the well-known seven "I Am's" of this Gospel. Jesus says:

1. "I AM the Bread of Life," John vi, 35.
2. "I AM the Good Shepherd," x, 11.
3. "I AM the Door." x, 7.
4. "I AM the Resurrection," xi, 25.
5. "I AM the Light of the World," ix, 5.
6. "I AM the true Vine," xv, 1.
7. "I AM the Way, the Truth, and the Life," xiv, 6.

It is interesting to trace out all that is said in the Bible about "the way" to heaven, remembering that way is Christ.

He is the way of peace, Luke i, 79; Eph. ii, 14.

The way of life, Prov. xv, 24; Col. iii, 4.

The way of pleasantness, Prov. iii, 17; Cant. i, 16.

The way of holiness, Isa. xxxv, 8; 1 Cor. i, 30.

The way everlasting, Ps. cxxxix, 24; Isa. ix, 6.

The way into the holiest, Heb. ix, 8; Heb. x, 19, 20.

The one way, Jer. xxxii, 39; John x, 7; Acts iv, 12.

Like the ladder of, Gen. xxviii, 12, He is the connecting medium between heaven and earth (see John i, 51). The only way of approach to God ; the only channel of blessing to man.

"I am the truth." For every one who has found the world false, and scepticism a vain refuge, this is a word to be tested. God says: "Prove Me now." Jesus says: "If any man will (i.e. be willing to) do His will, he shall know of the doctrine, whether it is of God, or whether I speak of myself," John vii, 17. The inquirer honestly pleading this verse, and taking the ground it gives him to stand on, shall find the fetters that have bound him fall off.

"Ye shall know the truth, and the truth shall make you free," John viii, 32. Light shall dawn on the darkness, and you will know Christ, the truth, as a reality. "I am the life." No warmth, no love, no feeling, no power, until Christ is yours. In Him, only, we get life. Having life, we have all these things, and much more, for, "If any man be in Christ, he is a new creature. Old things are passed away; behold all things are become new," 2 Cor. v, 17.

G. M. TAYLOR.

CHRIST, OUR EXAMPLE.

"For I have given you an example."

"Let this mind be in you, which was also in Christ Jesus."

"He that saith He abideth in Him, ought Himself also so to walk, even as He walked."

Our example :

1. In prayer, Mark i, 35; Luke v, 15, 16; John xii, 27, 28; xvii, 1-20; Matt. xvi, 39-42; Luke xxiii, 34-40.

2. In fidelity, Luke ii, 49; Matt. iv, 1-11; John xvii, 4-8; xviii, 37; xix, 30.

3. In tenderness, Luke vii, 11-15; Mark i. 40, 41; vi, 34; Matt. ix, 20-22; Luke xix, 41; John xi, 35.

4. In courage, John ii, 14-16; Mark xi, 15-18; Matt. xxiii, 13-33.

5. In patience, Isa. liii, 7; Matt. xxvii, 11-14; 1 Peter ii, 19-24; Heb. xii, 1-3.

FRED. S. GOODMAN.

CHRIST IS EVERYTHING.

I. Look unto me. Isa. xlv, 22.
II. Come unto me, Matt. xi, 28.
III. Learn of me, Matt. xi, 28.
IV. Abide in me, John xv, 4.
V. Lovest thou me, John xxi, 15.
VI. Follow thou me, John xxi, 22.
VII. Watch with me, Matt. xxvi, 48.

THE HOLY SPIRIT.

All we can know of the Spirit is contained in the Bible. As we are now more intimately related to the Spirit than any other person of the Trinity, a correct knowledge of His person and work is of the utmost importance to the believer. The doctrine of Scripture is that the Spirit is the executive of God. What God does is done by the Spirit.

I. Hence, at the very first, we find Him presiding at the creation, Gen. i, 2; Job xxiv, 13; xxxiii, 4; xxxii, 8; Ps. civ, 30

II. This creative power is made the symbol of the new creation; hence we find that the soul is like chaos, until the spirit acts; no order, no life, the soul is desolateness and emptiness. Compare John iii, 5; 1 Cor. xii, 3; 1 Thess. i, 5; Titus iii, 5, illustrated by Gen. xli, 38; Num. xi, 17, 25-29; 1 Sam. x, 6-16; xiii, 14; Isa. lxi, 1.

III. The field of the Spirit's work at first seems to have been confined to a few, Joel ii, 28; Isa. xliv, 3. His dispensation had not yet arrived. He was to take Christ's place, John xiv, 16; xxi, 7. "The promise of the Father" was fulfilled, Acts i, 11. The history in the book of Acts is the record of the Acts of the Holy Ghost, indicating the part he was to take thereafter in the economy of the church, Acts iv, 8-13; v, 32; vi. 3-5; li, 55; viii. 15; ix, 17-31; x, 44-47; xi, 15, 16; xiii, 2, etc.; xix, 26.

IV. In the epistles the doctrine is based on the history — the actual experience, Rom. xv, 13; 1 Cor. ii, 13; vi, 19; 2 Cor. xiii, 14; Heb. vi, 4; 2 Tim. i, 14; Jude 20.

V. "Therefore," grieve not the Holy Spirit of God, Eph. iv, 30.

REV. JOHN C. HILL.

PERSON OF THE HOLY SPIRIT.

A BIBLE READING.

The Holy Spirit, as a Person, is associated with the Father and the Son, Matt. xxviii, 19; 2 Cor. xiii, 14; Matt. iii, 16, 17; Eph. ii, 22.

The Holy Spirit is represented as a distinct agent, John xiv, 16; John xv, 26; John xvi, 7-15: 1 Cor. xii, 8-11; Acts vii, 51; Acts xiii, 2, 4; Acts xxviii, 25.

Divine attributes are ascribed to the Holy Spirit, Acts xxviii, 25; Heb. x, 15; Jer. xxxi, 33; 1 Cor. ii, 10, 11; John iii, 5; John i, 13.

Will and feeling are ascribed to Him, 1 Cor. xii, 11; Eph. iv, 30; Isa. lxiii, 10.

He is a sent Messenger and Teacher, John xiv, 16, 26; John xv, 26; John xvi, 7, 13, 15.

The Holy Spirit and Spirit of God are identical in some passages, Acts ii, 17; Joel iii, 1-5; Acts x, 38; Luke iv, 18; Isa. lxi, 2; Mark xii, 36.

The Holy Ghost is called God, Acts v. 3, 4; 1 Cor. iii, 16, 17; 2 Cor. vi, 16; Eph. ii, 22; 1 Cor. vi, 19.

The Holy Spirit quickens the mind, Rom. xii, 6, 8; 1 Cor. xii, 27, 28; Ex. xxxi, 3, 6; Ex. xxxv, 31, 35; Jud. iii, 10; Jud. vi, 34; 1 Sam. xi, 6; 1 Sam. xvi. 14.

The Holy Spirit inspires to teach God's will, John xiv, 26; John xv, 26; John xvi, 13; Luke i, 67; Acts xxi, 11; 2 Peter i, 21; 2 Sam. xxxiii, 2; 2 Chron. xx, 14; Micah iii, 8; Judges vi, 34; 1 Chron. xii, 18; 2 Chron. xxiv, 20; Luke xxiv, 49.

The Holy Spirit effects whatever is done in the soul by special Divine agency to accomplish justification and sanctification.

STEPHEN H. TYNG, JR.

THE HOLY SPIRIT.

I. WHO THE HOLY SPIRIT IS.

1. He is a person, not a mere influence or power, but a real person, who lives and loves and acts. He makes intercession, Rom. viii, 26; testifies, John xv, 26; teaches, John xiv, 26; hears and speaks, John xvi, 13; Acts x, 19, 20; xiii, 2; gives spiritual gifts, 1 Cor. xii, 8. 11.

2. He is a Divine Person. He is called God, Matt. xii, 28, compared with Luke xi, 20; 1 Cor. vi, 19, compared with 1 Cor. iii, 16; Acts v, 3, 4.

The acts of God are wrought by Him, and He possesses the attributes of God, Ps. cxxxix, 7, 13; Rom. xv, 19; 1 Cor. ii, 10; Heb. ix, 14; 1 Peter iv, 14.

II. WHAT THE HOLY SPIRIT DOES.

He convinces the world of sin, etc., John xvi, 8; strives with sinners, Gen. vi, 3.

He glorifies Christ, John xvi, 14; testifies of Him, John xv, 26; is sent by Him, John xv, 26; xvi, 7.

He dwells with Christians, John xiv, 17; teaches and guides them, John xiv, 26; xvi, 13; comforts, helps, and sanctifies them, Acts ix, 31; Rom. viii, 26; xv, 16; 1 Cor. vi, 11.

He is the unction, the seal, and the earnest, 2 Cor. i, 21, 22. What is the unction? 1 John ii, 20. There was the anointing in the Levitical dispensation, Ex. xxx, 23-33; typical of the anointing of the Holy Spirit in the Gospel, Luke iv, 18; Acts x, 38; and this unction of the Spirit is our enlightenment. 1 Cor. ii, 12; 1 John ii, 27. What is the seal? The ordinary use of a seal will explain this. It implies certainty, security. It authenticates, it confirms, Dan. vi, 17; Matt. xvii, 66; see 2 Tim. ii, 19. Thus the Holy Spirit assures and confirms the truth to His believing people, Eph. i, 13. What is the earnest? The word means foretaste, or pledge; and this the Spirit is to us of Heaven, 2 Cor. v, 5. He produces in the believer love, joy, peace, and every blessed fruit, Gal. v, 22; these, like the grapes of Eshcol, are an earnest of the inheritance promised to the people of God.

The Spirit pleads and strives. Oh, beware lest you resist Him, Acts vii, 51; Gen. vi, 3; Isa. lxiii, 10. He is not an enemy. He is resisted when in spite of pleading and striving He is refused admittance. Seek Him. He is given in answer to prayer, Luke xi, 13. Then when He dwelleth in you, 1 Cor. iii, 16; John xiv, 17; Isa. lvii, 15; grieve Him not by inconsistency and unholiness, Eph. iv, 30, lest He be altogether quenched, 1 Thess. v, 19.

DIVINITY OF THE HOLY SPIRIT.

Definition : The Holy Spirit, one with the Father and the Son, is the personal, eternal agent of the power and might of God, by whom the fullness of the Divine life, revealed in the Son, is communicated to the creature.

I. HE IS A PERSON.

1. Personal acts are ascribed to Him.

(*a*) He teaches, John xiv, 26; xvi, 13; 1 John ii, 27.

(*b*) Bears witness, John xv, 26; Rom. viii, 16; 1 John v, 6.

(*c*) Calls and separates men to the ministry, Acts xiii, 2; Ex. xxxi, 3; Gal. ii, 8.

(*d*) Distributes gifts, 1 Cor. xii, 11.

2. He is distinct from the Father and the Son.

Is said to be sent by and to proceed from them, John xiv, 16, 17; John xv, 26; Acts ii, 33; Rom. viii, 15; Eph. iv, 4.

3. The sin against Him can never be forgiven, Matt. xii, 31, 32; Mark iii, 29; 2 John v, 16.

II. HE IS GOD.

1. Old Testament proofs: The name Jehovah, the incommunicable name applied to Him, Ex. xvii, 7, with Heb. iii, 7–9; Jer. xxxi, 31–34, with Heb. x, 15–17; Isa. vi, 8–10, with Acts xxviii, 25.

2. New Testament proofs: Acts v, 3, 4; 1 Cor. iii. 16, with 1 Cor. vi, 19. Like God, He is said to be:

(a) Eternal, Heb. ix, 14.
(b) Omniscient, 1 Cor. ii, 10.
(c) Sovereign, Dan. iv. 35, with 1 Cor. xii, 6.
(d) Omnipotent, Luke i, 35; Rom. xv, 19. Like God, He is said:
(a) To create, Ps. xxxiii, 6; Job xxxiii, 4.
(b) To re-create, John iii, 3, 8; Titus iii, 5; 1 Cor. vi, 11.
(c) Is a source of miraculous power, Matt. xii, 28, with Luke xi, 20; Acts xix, 11, with Rom. xv, 19.

Like God, He inspires, 1 Tim. iii, 16, with 2 Peter i, 21.

Like God, He is divinely honored, 1 Cor. iii, 16, 17; Acts v, 4.

III. HE IS CALLED THE SPIRIT OF GOD, BECAUSE :

(a) This expresses His Divinity, 1 Cor. ii, 11.
(b) His intimate relation to God, the Father, John xv, 26; 1 John v, 6.
(c) As the immediate agent of God, Ps. civ, 30; 1 Peter iv, 14.

Also called *Spirit of Christ*, Gal. iv, 5; Rom. viii, 9; Phil. i, 19; 1 Peter i, 11.

IV. EMBLEMS OF THE HOLY SPIRIT.

1. Water, John vii, 38, 39.

(a) Cleansing, Ez. xvi, 9; xxxvi, 25; Eph. v, 26.
(b) Refreshing, Ps. xlvi, 4; Isa. xli, 17, 18.
(c) Freely bestowed, Isa. lv, 1; Rev. xxii, 17.

2. Oil, Ps. xlv, 7; Matt. xxv, 4.

(a) For healing, Isa. i, 6; Rev. iii, 18.
(b) For illuminating, Zech. iv, 12, 14; Matt. xxv, 3, 4; 1 John ii, 20, 27.
(c) For consecrating, Ex. xxix, 7; Heb. i, 9; Ps. lxxxix, 20.

3. Wind, John iii, 8.

(a) Powerful, 1 Kings xix, 11, with Acts ii, 2.
(b) Reviving, Ezek. xxxvii, 9, with 14.

4. Fire, Matt. iii, 11.

(a) Purifying, Isa. iv, 4; Matt. iii, 2, 3.
(b) Illuminating, Ex. xiii, 21; Ps. lxxviii, 14.
(c) Searching, Zeph. i, 12, with 1 Cor. ii, 10.

V. HIS WORK.

1. In regard to the world.

(a). He regenerates the sinner, John iii, 5.
(b) He quickens, John vi, 63; Rom. viii. 11; Eph. ii, 1.
(c) He is sovereign in this, John iii, 8; John i, 13.
(d) He reproves and convicts, John xvi, 8; of sin, John xvi, 9; Rom. iii, 9; Gal. iii, 22; of righteousness, Isa. xlii, 6; John xvi, 10; of judgment, Col. ii, 15; John xvi, 11; Heb. iv, 13.
(e) He strives with men, Gen. vi, 3; Heb. iii, 7.
(f) He aids the word preached, 1 Thess. i, 5; 1 Peter i, 12.
(g) He washes, justifies, 1 Cor. vi, 11; Heb. x, 22.
(h) He gives liberty, 2 Cor. iii, 17; Luke iv, 18.

2. In regard to Christians.

The Spirit has renewed them. Jas. i, 18; Tit. iii, 5. Strengthens them, Eph. iii, 16; Rom. viii, 26. Intercedes for them. Rom. viii, 27. Dwells in them. John vi, 14; John xiv, 17; Rom. viii, 9. Comforts them. John xv, 26; 1 John ii, 11. Gives joy, Rom. xiv, 17; Gal. iii, 22; 1 Thess. i, 6. Imparts the love of God, Rom. v, 3–5. Inspires hope, Rom. xv, 13; Gal. v. 5. He teaches us as the Spirit of wisdom, Isa. xi, 2. Reveals the things of God, 1 Cor. ii, 10, 13. Those of Christ, John xvi, 14; 1 Peter i, 11. Directs in the way of holiness, Isa. xxx. 21; Ezek. xxxvi, 21; Rom. viii, 1. Teaches us to wield the sword of the Spirit, Eph. vi, 17; Heb. iv, 12. Guides into all truth, John xvi, 13; 1 John ii, 20.

3. *Our relations to Him.*

(a) We live in Him, Gal. v, 25; Col. iii, 1, 2.

(b) Are led by Him, Gal. v, 18; Rom. viii, 14.

(c) As such He is a witness to us, 1 John v, 6; John xv, 26.

(d) A seal, Eph. i, 13; Eph. iv, 30; Lev. xiv, 25.

(e) An earnest, Rom. viii, 17; 2 Cor. i, 22; 2 Cor. v, 5.

VI. WARNINGS IN REGARD TO THE SPIRIT.

1. *To the unconverted:* Resist not the Holy Spirit, Acts vii, 51; Heb. iii, 15, 19. How to avoid resisting Him, Acts, xvi. 31; Isa. xlv, 22.

2. *To Christians:* Grieve not the Spirit, Eph. iv, 30. How to avoid grieving Him, Eph. iv, 27, 29; Col. iii, 8.

3. *Quenching the Spirit is the final result of grieving Him:* 1 Thess. v, 19. How to avoid this, Rom. xii, 2; 1 John ii, 5; 1 Tim. iv, 13, 14.

VII. TWO IMPORTANT EFFECTS OF THE SPIRIT.

1. *Renewing of the Holy Ghost:* Titus iii, 5; Acts iv, 31; Acts ii, 4.

2. *Joy in the Holy Ghost:* Acts xiii, 52; Rom. xiv, 17; Gal. v, 22.

ANON.

THE WORK OF THE HOLY SPIRIT.

John xvi.

Let us try and realize the position of the disciples as the Lord spake to them the words of this chapter. The truths we are familiar with were then understood, but very imperfectly. The doctrine of three persons in one God was only beginning to find entrance into their minds. They knew, doubtless, that in old times * * * "Holy men of God spake as they were moved by the Holy Ghost," 2 Pet. i, 21; that God gave His people His "good Spirit to instruct them," and also testified against their evil deeds by His "Spirit in His prophets," Neh. ix, 20, 30; but of the abiding indwelling of the Holy Ghost as a person, they could know nothing. Here, in John xiv, in prospect of His speedy removal from them, the Lord gives the disciples two comforts for their troubled hearts. One was the promise, "I will come again" (verse 3, 18; 1 Thess. iv, 18; v, 11). The other was the promise of "the Comforter, which is the Holy Ghost," verse 26. The coming of this Comforter was dependent on the ascension of Christ. As the mantle of the ascending Elijah, by which he crossed the waters of Jordan (judgment), fell upon Elisha, and with it a "double portion of his spirit," 2 Kings ii, so "power from on high," such as enabled the church to do the works that Jesus did, and "greater works" (verse 12), was "shed forth." He was exalted to the right hand of God, Acts ii, 33. Till then the Spirit could not be given, John vii, 39; but then He came to be the abiding comforter of the church until the Lord returns (verse 16). He is as much with us now as Jesus Himself was with the disciples while His bodily presence was on earth; as truly with us as Rebekah's guide, who led her all the journey long, from her father's house to the house of Isaac, Gen. xxiv. He never leaves us though He may be grieved, Eph. iv, 30. We have not to call Him from on high, as though He had returned to heaven. He "abides with us forever," according to the promise of Christ, John xiv, 16. This is the perseverance of the

Christians. It is *the perseverance of the Holy Spirit.* John Bunyan's picture of the fire of grace is a true one. In spite of every effort of the evil one to extinguish it, it burns, for it is continually replenished by the oil of the Spirit. Let us look at His work as revealed to us in John's Gospel — a twofold work, in the church and in the world, to the saint and to the sinner.

In the world, —

1. The Holy Ghost convinces of sin, John xvi, 8, 9, margin.
2. Convinces of righteousness, John xvi, 8, 10.
3. Convinces of judgment, John xvi, 8, 11.
4. Regenerates the sinner, John iii, 5–8.

In the church, —

1. The Holy Ghost indwells, John xiv, 17.
2. Comforts, John xiv, 16.
3. Teaches, John xiv, 26.
4. Guides, John xvi, 13.
5. Testifies of Christ, John xv, 26.
6. Glorifies Christ, John xvi, 14.
7. Shows things to come, John xvi, 13.

Let us seek to realize the mighty power we have with us, able and willing to do all these things for us and in us; and so continually shall we find ourselves "strengthened with might by his Spirit in the inner man," Eph. iii, 16.

THE HOLY SPIRIT.

1. God is three in one and one in three. The name (not names) of the three in one God, is Father, and Son, and Holy Spirit. Matt. xxviii.
2. All that is out of God is from the Father. All that can be seen of God is in the Son. All that can be felt of God is by the Holy Spirit.
3. In the covenant of grace it has pleased the Son to become the servant of God the Father. Phil. ii. Now, also, the Holy Spirit is acting as the servant of the Son. John xvi. The Spirit draws us to Christ, and through Christ we come to the Father. We are strengthened with might by the Spirit, in order that Christ may dwell in our hearts, and that thus we may be filled unto all the fullness of God. Eph. iii.
4. The Son comes forth from the Father. The Holy Spirit proceeds from the Father and from the Son. Rom. viii.
5. Now that Christ has been rejected here and departed to the Father, the cardinal feature of God's ways with the world throughout this dispensation, is the personal presence of the Holy Spirit. John xiv, 16, 17. He did not come down personally unto the world, until the Son of man had been received up into glory. As in Genesis i we read of light ere we hear of the sun, so it was of the Spirit of God that a people was led to fear God, even in those times after the fall, but previous to the Word becoming flesh. But as the light now shines forth from the sun, so the Holy Spirit is poured out from the ascended Christ. Acts ii, 17 with 33.
6. Now, inasmuch as the presence of the Holy Spirit in person here is only consequent on Christ's rejection by man, and on the reversal of man's sentence by God in His Son's resurrection and ascension, it follows that this very presence here convicts the world of sin, of righteousness and of judgment. But this reproof of the world is not His object in coming; this only comes to pass incidentally. He is never called a Reprover. He has come down to display in Christ's acceptance the infinite grace and long suffering of God. He has come down whence Christ has gone up. Therefore, here we have proof of Christ's exaltation to the right hand of God. The bells are sounding whilst the High Priest is in the holiest of all. Exodus xxviii, 35.

W. LINCOLN.

THE HOLY SPIRIT AND THE GODHEAD.

Personality. Matt. xxviii, 19; John i, 18; xv, 26; 1 John iv, 14; John xiv, 26; 1 Cor. xiv, 33; Ps. xi, 6; John xvi, 13. 14; Rom. xv, 30; xv, 19; viii. 6, 14; Eph. iv, 30; Acts vii, 51; 1 John v, 7; Job xxvi, 13; Phil. ii, 1; John vi. 63; 2 Cor. v, 17; 1 John iii, 9; John iii, 6; Col. i, 27; Isa. viii, 20; 2 Tim. iii. 16; 1 Pet. iii, 25; Rom. viii, 16; ix, 1; 1 John v, 9-11; Heb. x, 15; Rom. viii. 14; 1 Peter iv, 6.

I. Name implies personality, on account of personal relation; certain acts of each not performed by other persons of the Godhead.

Pronouns:

I am. Thou art. He is.
Father. Son. Holy Spirit.

II. *Personal attributes of the Spirit.* Intelligence, affection, will. Our relation to the Holy Spirit, as implied in "grieve," "led," etc., imply personality—distressing the Holy Spirit. Life imparted—"Seed of a rose bush dropped into a corpse." born of the Spirit — "Holy thing," "Seed," "Christ in us." The Spirit forms Christ in us, then dwells with Christ in us; not making the old man over, but putting a new man in. *Absolute sanctification is the new creature's state or nature. Progressive sactification is the growth of the new creature.* As a babe Christ grew. Flesh never looks over the border of the new creation. There is nothing of flesh in the new creation.

God has done the best He could in His Word to meet all the requirements of the new nature He has made; nothing to be added.

"Testifies to, not with our spirits." And by the Word; Spirit brings the Word into my heart and writes it there. REV. GEO. BISHOP, D. D.

HOLY SPIRIT AND CHURCH.

"*Personality of the Spirit.*" The Scriptures show that He possesses all personal attributes, and that He is the equal of the Lord Jesus in nature. Whatever the Savior was to His disciples, that the Spirit now is to believers. Jesus was their companion, Luke xxiv, 32; so the Spirit abides with us, John xiv, 16, 17. The first instance where the Spirit is said to abide is John i, 32. In virtue of our union with our risen Lord, He abides with us, Acts ii, 3; 1 Peter iv, 12. Jesus was a Father to them, anticipating their wants, etc. And so is the Spirit. Mark vi, 30, 31; John xxi, 9: Phil. i, 19. Jesus was at hand to help them; so the Paraclete, Matt. xiv, 30, 31; Rom. viii, 26. Jesus was a witness, and the Spirit is also, John xv, 26; Acts ii, 4.

GEO. C. NEEDHAM.

THE RELATION OF CHRIST TO THE HOLY SPIRIT.

Passive relation. Conceived by the Spirit, Matt. i, 20. The Spirit descending on Him, Luke iii, 22; cf., iv, 18. Anointed with the Spirit, Luke ix, 1. The Spirit not given by measure to Christ, John iii, 34. Christ full of the Spirit, Luke iv, 1.

Active relation. Returned in the power of the Spirit, Luke ix, 14. Gave commandments through the Spirit, Acts i. 2. Cast out devils by the Spirit, Matt. xii, 28. Offered Himself a sacrifice through the eternal Spirit, Heb. ix, 14.

H. STANLEY.

THE HOLY SPIRIT — HIS NAMES, TITLES AND ATTRIBUTES.

The word for "Spirit" occurs 383 times in the Old Testament, 385 times in the New. But it is not by any means always so rendered, nor does it always refer to the Holy Spirit. Still it will be seen that He is revealed everywhere in the Scriptures: and it may be helpful to Bible students to have a condensed statement of the testimony concerning Him, as gathered from the Word of God. The same title is sometimes frequently given Him, but of course it will appear but once in the following table:

I. HIS NAMES.

Spirit of God, Gen. i, 2.
" of the Lord, Jude iii, 10.
" of our God, 1 Cor. vi, 11.
" of the Lord God, Isa. lxi, 1.
" of the living God, 2 Cor. iii, 3.
" of your Father, Matt. x, 20.
" of His Son, Gal. iv, 6.
" of Christ. Rom. viii, 9.
" of Jesus Christ, Phil. i, 19.
" of glory and of God, 1 Peter iv, 14.
Spirit of grace and of supplication, Zech. xii, 10.
Holy Spirit, Luke xi, 13.
Holy Spirit of promise, Eph. i, 3.
Holy Spirit of God, Eph. iv, 30.
Eternal Spirit, Heb. ix, 14.
Spirit of truth, John xiv, 17.
" of holiness, Rom. i, 4.
" of adoption, Rom. viii, 15.
" of power, 2 Tim. i, 7.
" of love, 2 Tim. i, 7.
" of a sound mind, 2 Tim. i, 7.
" of revelation, Eph. i, 17.
" of grace, Heb. x, 29.
" of prophecy, Rev. xix, 10.
" of judgment, Isa. iv, 4.
" of burning, Isa. iv, 4.
" of wisdom, Isa. xi, 2.
" of understanding, Isa. xi, 2.
" of council, Isa. xi, 2.
" of might, Isa. xi, 2.
" of knowledge, Isa. xi, 2.
" of the fear of the Lord, Isa. xi, 2.
Spirit which is of God, 1 Cor. ii, 12.
Comforter, John xiv, 16.
One Spirit, Eph. iv, 4.
Good Spirit, Neh. ix, 20.
Free [liberal, princely] Spirit, Ps. li, 12.
Seven Spirits of God, Rev. iii, 1.
Holy Ghost occurs ninety times in the New Testament.

II. HIS WORK.

He is represented in the Old Testament as—
Engaged in creation work, Gen. i, 2.
Striving with man, Gen. vi, 3.
Recognized in Joseph. Gen. xli, 38.
Devising the high priest's robes, Ex. xxviii, 3.
Planning the Tabernacle, Ex. xxxi, 2–5.
Filling Bezaleel, Ex. xxxv, 31.
Put upon the seventy elders, Num. xi, 17.
Coming upon Balaam, Num. xxiv, 2.
Qualifying Joshua to lead Israel, Num. xxvii, 18.
Coming upon Othniel, Jud. iii, 10.
Clothing Gideon (margin), Jud. vi, 34.
Coming upon Jeptha, Jud. xi, 29.
Moving Samson at times, Jud. xiii, 25.
Enabling Samson to kill a lion, Jud. xiv, 6.
Enabling Samson to slay thirty men, Jud. xiv, 19.
Enabling Samson to slay one thousand men, Jud. xv, 14.
Coming upon Saul, 1 Sam. x, 10.
Coming upon David, 1 Sam. xvi, 13.
Coming upon Saul's servants, 1 Sam. xix, 20.
Speaking by David, 2 Sam. xxiii, 2.
Coming upon Amasai, 1 Chron. xii, 18.
Planning the temple, 1 Chron. xxviii, 12.
Coming upon Azariah, 2 Chron. xv, 1.
Coming into the congregation, 2 Chron. xx, 14.
Clothing Zechariah, 2 Chron. xxiv, 20.
Instructing God's people, Neh. ix, 20.
Testifying against them, Neh. ix, 30.
Garnishing the heavens, Job xxvi, 13.
Giving life to men, Job xxxiii, 4.

Needful for spiritual life, Ps. li, 11.
Needful to uphold, Ps. li, 12.
Creating animals, Ps. civ, 80.
Everywhere present, Ps. cxxxix, 7.
Benevolent and merciful, Ps. cxliii, 10.
Making known God's Word, Prov. i, 23.
Unsearchable in His ways, Ecc. xi, 5.
Promised to rest upon Christ, Isa. xi, 2.
Making the wilderness fruitful, Isa. xxxii, 15.
Gathering God's executioners, Isa. xxxiv, 16.
Withering man's glory, Isa. xi, 7.
Above human counsel, Isa. xi, 13.
Qualifying Christ for service, Isa. xliii, 1.
To be poured out on Israel's seed, Isa. xliv, 3.
Sending Christ upon His work, Isa. xlviii, 16.
Lifting up a standard for truth, Isa. lix, 19.
Never to depart from believers, Isa. lix, 21.
Anointing Christ for His ministry, Isa. lxi, 1.
Vexed with rebellion, Isa. lxiii, 10.
Causing His people to rest, Isa. lxiii, 14.
Directing God's agencies, Ezek. i, 12.
Taking and lifting up Ezekiel, Ezek. iii, 12.
Falling upon the prophet, Ezek. xi, 5.
Leading to obedience, Ezek. xi, 19.
Causing to walk in God's statutes, Ezek. xxxvi, 27.
Imparting life to the dead, Ezek. xxxvii, 9.
Restoring Israel, Ezek. xxxix, 29.
Making the man he uses seem mad, Hos. ix, 7.
To be poured out on all flesh, Joel ii, 28.
Not straightened in His resources, Mic. ii, 7.
Able to give power, Mic. iii, 8.

Remaining with God's people, Hag. ii, 5.
Indispensable for service, Zech. iv, 6.
Communicating God's word, Zech. vii, 12.
God has the residue of the Spirit, Mal. ii, 15.
Hence we find advanced thoughts upon this important subject in the New Testament, where He is represented as —
Forming the body of Jesus, Matt. i, 18.
Descending upon Him at His baptism, Matt. iii, 16.
Inspiring the apostle's words, Matt. x, 20
Casting out devils. Matt. xii, 28.
Terrible to the blasphemer, Matt. xii, 31.
Named in baptism, Matt. xxviii, 19.
Baptizing believers, Mark i. 8.
Speaking by David, Mark xii, 36.
Coming upon the virgin, Luke i, 35.
Filling John the Baptist, Luke i, 15.
Filling Elizabeth, Luke i, 41.
Filling Zecharias, Luke i, 67.
Coming upon Simeon, Luke ii, 25.
Revealing Christ to Him, Luke ii, 26.
Leading him into the temple, Luke i, 15.
Filling the Lord Jesus Christ, Luke iv, 41.
Leading the Lord Jesus Christ, Luke iv, 31.
Attending Christ with power, Luke iv, 14.
Anointing Christ for service, Luke iv, 18.
Giving to them that ask for Him, Luke ix, 13.
Abiding upon Christ, John i, 32.
The author of the new birth, John iii, 5.
Imparting His own nature, John iii, 6.
Giving without measure, John iii, 34.

Quickening the dead soul, John vi, 63.
Flowing out of the believer, John vii, 39.
Abiding with the believer, John xiv, 16.
Dwelling in the believer, John xiv, 17.
Sent by the Father in Christ's name, John xiv, 26.
Teaching all things, John xiv, 26.
Bringing Christ's word to memory, John xiv, 26.
Sent by Christ from the Father, John xv, 26.
Testifying of Christ, John xv, 26.
Coming after Christ's going, John xvi, 7.
Reproving the world, John xvi, 8.
Guiding into all truth, John xvi, 13.
Showing things to come, John xvi, 13.
Glorifying Christ, John xvi, 14.
Breathed upon the disciples, John xx, 28.
Communicating Christ's commands, Acts i, 1.
Promised as the baptism, Acts i, 5.
The power for witnessing, Acts i, 8.
Speaking by David's mouth, Acts i, 16.
Coming like a mighty wind, Acts ii, 2.
Appearing as cloven tongues, Acts ii, 3.
Filling the disciples, Acts ii, 4.
Inspiring their very words, Acts ii, 4.
Beginning His final display, Acts ii, 17.
Sent as the Father promised, Acts ii, 33.
Bestowed in the name of Jesus, Acts ii, 38.
Filling the apostle Peter, Acts iv, 8.
Filling all of the disciples, Acts iv, 31.
Spoken of as God, Acts v, 3, 4.
Refusing to be tempted, Acts v, 9.
Given to them that obey Him, Acts v, 32.
Filling Stephen, Acts vi, 5.
Making His words resistless, Acts vi, 10.
Resisted by unbelievers, Acts vii, 51.
Preparing Stephen for death, Acts vii, 55.
Given to Samaritan believers, Acts viii, 15.
Not to be purchased with money, Acts viii, 20.
Telling Philip where to go, Acts viii, 29.
Catching him away at the end of work, Acts viii, 39.
Filling the converted Saul, Acts ix, 17.
Comforting the church, Acts ix, 31.
Speaking to Peter, Acts ix, 19.
Given to Gentile believers, Acts x, 44.
Filling Barnabas, Acts xi, 24.
Predicting a dearth, Acts xi, 28.
Preparing unto service, Acts xiii, 2.
Sending forth His servants, Acts xiii, 4.
Rebuking resistance, Acts xiii, 9.
Filling the disciples with joy, Acts xiii, 52.
Visiting Jew and Gentile alike, Acts xv, 8.
Releasing Gentiles from bondage, Acts xv, 28.
Forbidding Paul to preach in Asia, Acts xvi, 6.
Suffering him not to go to Bythinia, Acts xvi, 7.
Coming upon John's disciples, Acts xix, 6.
Witnessing to Paul's sufferings, Acts xx, 23.
Giving overseers to the church, Acts xx, 28.
Forbidding Paul to visit Jerusalem, Acts xxi, 4.
Foretelling his imprisonment, Acts xxi, 11.
Announcing Israel's rejection, Acts xxviii, 25.
Declaring Christ's sonship, Rom. i, 4.
Pouring out the love of God, Rom. v, 5.

Freeing from the law of sin, Rom. viii, 2.
Fulfilling the law in believers, Rom. viii, 4.
Having a mind of life and peace, Rom. viii, 6.
The dwelling place of believers, Rom. viii, 9.
Dwelling in believers, Rom. viii, 9.
Raising up believers, Rom. viii, 11.
Mortifying their fleshly deeds, Rom. viii, 13.
Leading the sons of God, Rom. viii, 14.
Not a spirit of bondage, Rom. viii, 15.
Exciting the cry, Abba, Father, Rom. viii, 15.
Bearing witness with our spirit, Rom. viii, 16.
The first fruits of glory, Rom. viii, 23.
Helping our infirmities, Rom. viii, 26.
Making intercession for us, Rom. viii, 26.
Known in his mind to Christ, Rom. viii, 27.
Witnessing with the conscience, Rom. ix, 1.
The present Kingdom of God, Rom xiv, 17.
Making us abound in the hope, Rom. xv, 13.
Sanctifying the offering up of Gentiles, Rom. xv, 16.
Giving power to Paul's preaching, Rom. xv, 19.
Loving like Christ Himself, Rom. xv, 30.
Imparting power to the word, 1 Cor. ii, 4.
Revealing what awaits us, 1 Cor. ii, 10.
Searching all things, 1 Cor. ii, 10.
Knowing the things of God, 1 Cor. ii, 11.
Given that we might know them, 1 Cor. ii, 12.
Dictating the words of Scripture, 1 Cor. ii, 13.
Enabling us to discern them, 1 Cor. ii, 14.
Making the church His temple, 1 Cor. iii, 16.
Washing, sanctifying, justifying, 1 Cor. vi, 11.
Dwelling in the body as His temple, 1 Cor. vi, 19.
Speaking through Paul, 1 Cor. vii, 40.
Leading to the confession of Christ, 1 Cor. xii, 3.
Bestowing all gifts for service, 1 Cor. xii, 4–11.
Baptizing into one body, 1 Cor. xii, 13.
The earnest of our inheritance, 2 Cor. i, 22.
Writing Christ on our hearts, 2 Cor. iii, 3.
Unlike the law, giving life, 2 Cor. iii, 6.
More glorious than the law, 2 Cor. iii, 8.
Carrying with Him liberty, 2 Cor. iii, 17.
Changing into Christ's image, 2 Cor. iii, 18.
Approving true ministers, 2 Cor. vi, 6.
Invoked with the Father and Son, 2 Cor. xiii, 14.
Received by Faith, Gal. iii, 2.
The beginning of Christian life, Gal. iii, 3.
Ministered by the hearing of faith, Gal. iii, 5.
Imparting the blessing of Abraham, Gal. iii, 14.
Raising us to full grown sons, Gal. iv, 6.
Opposed by the natural man, Gal. iv, 29.
Causing us to wait for the hope, Gal. v, 5.
Inviting us to walk in Him, Gal. v, 16.
At ceaseless war with the flesh, Gal. v, 17.
Leading us from under law, Gal. v, 18.
Desiring us to live in Him, Gal. v, 25.
Giving us to reap everlasting life, Gal. vi, 8.

Sealing the believer, Eph. i, 13.
Revealing the knowledge of God, Eph. i, 17.
Giving access to God, Eph. ii, 18.
Building us for His habitation, Eph. ii, 22.
Revealing the church, Eph. iii, 5.
Strengthening believers, Eph. iii, 16.
Making the unity of the body, Eph. iv, 3.
Not to be grieved, Eph. iv, 30.
Sealing unto the day of redemption, Eph. iv, 30.
Offering to fill us, Eph. v, 18.
Using the Word as His sword, Eph. vi, 17.
Inditing true prayer, Eph. vi, 18.
Supplying all our need, Phil. i, 19.
Having fellowship with us, Phil. ii, 1.
The power of true worship, Phil. iii, 3.
Causing love for the brethren, Col. i, 8.
Making effectual the Gospel, 1 Thess. i, 5.
Imparting with it joy, 1 Thess. i, 6.
Given to seal the Word, 1 Thess. iv, 8.
Not to be quenched, 1 Thess. v, 19.
Source of sanctification, 2 Thess. ii, 13.
Justifying Christ, 1 Tim. iii, 16.
Foretelling apostacy, 1 Tim. iv, 1.
Keeping that committed to us, 2 Tim. i, 14.
Renewing the soul, Tit. iii, 5.
Confirming the word, Heb. ii, 4.
Saying to men, To-day, Heb. iii, 7.
Asking men to partake of Him, Heb. vi, 4.
Signifying what the Tabernacle means, Heb. ix, 8.
Leading Christ to offer Himself, Heb. ix, 14.
Witnessing that our sins are forgotten, Heb. x, 15.
Making it fatal to insult Him, Heb. x, 29.
Jealously desiring us, Jas. iv, 5.
Sanctifying the elect, 1 Peter i, 2.
Testifying beforehand of Christ, 1 Peter i, 11.
Sent down from heaven, 1 Peter i, 12.
Leading to obedience, 1 Peter i, 22.
Quickening Christ, 1 Peter iii, 18.
Inspiring holy men of old, 2 Peter i, 21.
Causing us to know Christ in us, 1 John iii, 24.
Recognizing Christ, 1 John iv, 2.
Witnessing to the blood, 1 John v, 6.
Witnessing with the Word, 1 John v, 8.
Separating from the sensual, Jude 19.
Instructing us how to pray, Jude 20.
Taking His place before the throne, Rev. i, 4.
Looking on to the Lord's day, Rev. i, 10.
Raising up the slain witnesses, Rev. xi, 11.
Pronouncing the dead blessed, Rev. xiv, 13.
Showing the mother of harlots, Rev. xvii, 3.
Showing the beauty of the church, Rev. xxi, 10.
Calling upon Christ to come, Rev. xxii, 17.— *The Truth.*

THE HOLY SPIRIT.

HISTORY.

Formed the World, Gen. i, 2: "The Spirit of God moved upon the face of the waters."

Spoke through Prophets, 2 Peter i, 21: "The prophecy came not in old time by the will of man; but holy men of God spake *as they were* moved by the Holy Ghost."

Was promised to all classes, Joel ii, 28: "It shall come to pass afterward, *that* I will pour out my Spirit upon all flesh."

Was given as promised. Acts ii, 4: "They were all filled with the Holy Ghost."

OFFICE.

Convinces of Sin, John xvi, 8: "When He is come, He will reprove the world of sin."

Gives Spiritual life, John iii, 6: "That which is born of the flesh is flesh; and that which is born of the Spirit is Spirit."

Leads into all truth, John xvi, 13: "He will guide you into all truth."

Produces all Christian graces, Gal. v, 22, 23: "The fruit of the Spirit is love, joy, peace, long suffering, gentleness, goodness, faith, meekness, temperance."

Anoints for service, Isa. lxi, 1: "The Spirit of the LORD GOD is upon me; because the LORD hath anointed me to preach good tidings unto the meek."

Freely offered, patiently waiting, Luke xi, 13; Rev. iii, 20: "If ye then, being evil, know how to give good gifts unto your children, how much more shall *your* heavenly Father give the Holy Spirit to them that ask him?" "Behold, I stand at the door, and knock."

H. E. BROWN.

THE PROMISE OF THE HOLY SPIRIT.

1. To convince of sin, etc., John xvi, 8.
2. To teach, John xiv, 26.
3. To testify of Christ, John xv, 26.
4. To glorify Christ, John xvi, 14.
5. For vital union and indwelling, John xx, 22; xiv, 17.
6. For anointing for service, Acts i, 8.
7. Overflowing to the world, John vii, 38, 39.

THE NEED OF THE HOLY SPIRIT.

1. Human nature in us, Rom. viii, 5-8.
2. Presence of the world, 1 Cor. ii, 12-14.
3. Presence and power of Satan, Eph. vi, 12.
4. Absence of the Lord, John xvi, 7.
5. Power to witness for Christ, Acts i, 8.
6. Keeping and perfecting the saints, Eph. iv, 13, 14.
7. A building for God, Eph. ii, 22.

HINDRANCE TO THE WORKING OF THE HOLY SPIRIT.

1. Legalism, Gal. iii; 2, 3.
2. Denying the Deity of Christ, 1 Cor. xii, 3.
3. Denying the Spirit's words, 1 Cor. ii, 13.
4. Denying His gifts, 1 Cor. xii, 7-11.
5. Resisting Him, Acts vii, 51.
6. Grieving Him, Eph. iv, 30.
7. Quenching Him, 1 Thess. v, 19.

THE SPIRIT AND SONSHIP.

PREFACE. — Gifts and acts of the Spirit same in many respects in new and old. The special promise to new dispensation.

Five points of difference:
1. Joel ii, 28, 29. All flesh proved.
2. Isa. xxxii, 15. From on high. Acts ii, 2; John xiv, 26.
3. Isa. xliv, 3. On all thirsty. John vii, 37-39.
4. Ezek. xxxiv, 27; xxxvii, 14. Within.
5. Isa. lix, 21. Forever. John xiv, 16, 17.

1. All conditions and classes of society. Poured not scattered drops.
2. From on high. From the glorified Christ.
3. Within. "Upon," mostly the word used in the Old Testament.
4. Forever.

Jesus repeated specifically all of these promises. John foretold the same baptism.

Promise fulfilled to believers as sons, for, —
1. Filial experiences.
2. Service. The main question is not so much what the disciples received on the day of pentecost, but rather who were they that received it — even sons. In Acts, sons not

used because sons were acting as servants. In John's Gospel, and in the Epistles, the sonship is prominent.

Adoption. Eph. i, 5; Rom. viii, 15, 23. Not correct translation of the word Paul used. It is most briefly "sonship." Only one way to enter into the family of God—by birth. Proper rendering—setting in place of a son. Gal. iv, 7. In the place of a full grown son. Eph. i, 5. Children same word as sons. Redemption must first be accomplished, before promise could be fulfilled. John vii, 39; Gal. iv, 1-5; Isa. xxxii, 15.

Old Testament saints were minors. Gal. iv, 1-6. Never called God "Father," as Jesus called Him, or as we now call Him, being one with Christ.

Confession by Son of God of believers as sons of God.

John xiii to xvii. Belong to the confessed disciples of Christ.

See John ii, 23; xii, 37. All the way between these verses He was testing professed disciples.

John xiii. He reveals truth to those who had borne the testing; "His own" peculiar ones.

See John xiii, 10; Luke xxii, 24-27; Before God they were sinless sons. Type of standing of churches in all times. John xv, 26; Rom. v, 5.

W. F. ERDMAN.

THE HOLY SPIRIT AND THE CHURCH.

I. The Holy Spirit must be present to make the church "the Body." The grouping of the disciples about Jesus, in John xiv-xvii, is a living picture on earth of this truth; but, in place of the departing Jesus, the Holy Spirit from the glorified Jesus is about to come. The result is that, linked by the Spirit to the Christ in glory, they henceforth know neither themselves nor Jesus any more after the flesh, John xvii, 26; 1 Cor. xii, 12, 13; 2 Cor. v, 16, 17; John xx, 16, 17; xi, 51, 52; Eph. iv, 4.

II. The Holy Spirit must be present to make a ministering church; in teaching and in manifold work. What Jesus began both to do and to teach, the Holy Spirit finished, Acts i, 1.

The acts of Jesus were finished in the acts of the Holy Spirit through the Apostles, so far as the founding of the church was concerned; but this self-same adding of living stone to stone on the foundation since the Apostles passed away, is still done by the same Spirit through "Faithful men," 2 Tim, ii, 2; 1 Cor. iii, 9-15; John xiv, 12.

The book of the Acts of the Apostles is a permanent mirror of the world and the church, and all the varied forms of service until the Lord returns. Likewise, the teaching Jesus began, the Holy Spirit finished as to substance and form in His writings through the inspired Apostles and Prophets, John xiv, 25, 26; xvi, 13; Rev. xx, 19.

The Spirit is present to teach of Christ that the church may teach of Christ; and to testify that the church may testify; and always and only of Christ, John xv, 26, 27; xvi, 13, 14; Acts i, 8.

The Spirit having convinced some of sin and of righteousness and of judgment, is present in them to convince others also, John xvi, 7-11; Acts ii, 4, 33, 37; vii, 51; 1 Cor. ii, 4.

The church is ministered to that the church may minister in word and work, Acts xx, 28. In Eph. iv, 12, omit the comma after the word "saints," and the meaning of the passage is brought out.

The Spirit gives Himself in every gift, 1 Cor. xii, 14. Compare the two promises in Matt. vii, 11; Luke ii, 13; Acts xiii, 2-4.

And all this service is priestly service before God on the one unended day of pentecost. See Acts xiii, 2; Heb. x, 11; Rom. xv, 27; xv, 16; 1 Peter ii, 5-9; Lev. xxiii, 15-18. And to the maintaining of such holy priestly life and work and teaching, the church is exhorted and urged, and what is noteworthy, by the frequent use of a word and words kindred to the name Paraclete, the literal word for comforter. This gives a touching and energetic meaning to every ministry of comfort, exhortation, beseeching, and consolation between the saints one to another. It would always hint that all attempts at edification, except "in the Spirit," are of no avail. It must ultimately be the Spirit Himself who is paracleting the saints.

From and through the Acts on throughout the Epistles, such a word in different forms and variously translated, is found over one hundred times.

Evangelists, pastors, teachers, all who have a gift for service, are wholly dependent upon the Holy Spirit, the Paraclete.

III. The Holy Spirit must be present to sustain and comfort the suffering church. The suffering for Christ's sake is the normal, ideal state of the church until He comes, Rom. viii, 18, 26, 27; 1 Peter iv, 13, 14; v. 1; 2 Cor. xii, 9.

IV. The Holy Spirit will be in the glorified church, Eph. ii, 19-20; 1 Peter ii, 5; Rev. i, 4-6.

W. J. ERDMAN.

THE ABIDING PRESENCE OF THE SPIRIT.

All are agreed that there cannot be any *spiritual life* until the Holy Spirit comes into the heart. The spiritual man must be "born of the Spirit," or experience the renewing of the Holy Ghost." The very *source* of all spiriutal life is, therefore, the Spirit of God. Hence, just as a fire goes out, when nothing is left for it to feed upon, so will any spiritual life become extinct, if ever that to which it owes its existence is removed. Therefore the importance of the question: When the Spirit comes, does He come as an *abiding* guest?

The question must be settled alone on the Divine testimony. Leave it to human experience and judgment, and the decision would be against the Spirit's abiding, because the child of God does so many things in which he is conscious, he does not act from the impulse of the Spirit. The Divine testimony, John xiv, 16, 17, "abide," "forever," "dwelleth;" Gal. iv, 6, 7, "are" abidingly "sons."

There is never a time when the child of God may not cry: "Abba Father," verse 7; "If son, then heir," but if Spirit depart, one is no longer son or heir, Rom. viii, 9; 1 Cor. iii, 16; Jude 20, 21; Eph. vi, 18.

This ever present Spirit may be treated in various ways, 1 Thess. v, 19, "quench;" Acts viii, 51, "resist;" Heb. x, 29, "does despite;" Eph. iv, 30, "grieve, not," "grieve away." If the Spirit were grieved away, one could have no possible hope, Heb, vi, 4-6.

JOHN P. KENDALL.

POWER BY THE SPIRIT.

1. He is the power of life, John iii, 5; vi, 63; Rom. viii, 2; 2 Cor. iii, 8, 6; Rev. xi, 11. In imparting this new and eternal life, He uses the Word, 1 Cor. ii, 15; Jas. i, 18; 1 Pet. i, 23.

2. He is the power of testimony, Acts i, 8; ii, 1-4; iv, 8-12; vi, 5, 10; 1 Cor. ii, 4; John xv, 26; Matt. x, 20; Acts iv. 8-12, 31; vii, 51-55.

3. He is the power of prayer, Rom. viii, 15, 26; Eph. vi, 18; Phil. iii, 3; Gal. iv, 6; Jude 20; Acts xi, 5, 12; Rev. i, 4.

4. He is the power of knowledge, Ex. xxxi, 3-5; Neh. ix, 20; John xiv, 26; xvi, 13; 1 Cor. ii, 9-14; Eph. i, 17; 1 John ii, 20, 27; Rev. ii, 11.

5. He is the power of guidance, Luke iv, 1, 14; Acts xvi, 6, 7; Rom. viii, 14; Gal. v, 16, 18; 1 John iv, 1-3; Jude 19; 1 Thess. v, 19.

6. He is the power of service, Acts viii, 29; x, 19, 38, 44–47; xiii, 1–4; Eph. vi, 17; John vii, 39; Rom. viii, 5; xv, 13; 1 Cor. xii, 7.

7. For all these purposes He is the abiding Spirit, John xiv, 16, 17; Rom. viii, 9; 1 Cor. vi, 19; Eph. i, 13; iv, 30; 2 Cor. v, 5, 6; i, 21, 22.

JAS. H. BROOKES, D.D

THE HOLY SPIRIT AS OUR TEACHER.

1. Who is the teacher? The Spirit of God in all ages, Job xxxv, 10, 11; Rom. i, 19; Ps. cxlv, 10; cxix, 18.

(a) He is especially the teacher as the Spirit of truth, the Spirit of Christ, the Spirit of God, Heb. i, 1; John iii, 34, 35; xiv, 26; Acts i, 1; 1 John ii, 20, 27; Rom. viii, 29.

2. Whom does He teach?
(a) Believers as forgiven sinners, Acts ii, 38; Isa. xliii, 45; xliv, 1–3.
(b) Believers as the body of Christ, 1 Cor. xii, 12–14.

3. What does the Spirit teach? He teaches the truth of the personal Word of God, John i, 1, 18; xiv, 6, 17; xv, 26.

(a) He especially teaches the facts of the four Gospels of the Son of God.

(b) He teaches in detail the words of the truth of Christ, 1 Cor. ii, 10–13; i, 30.

4. How does the Spirit teach?
(a) By using the word of God, 1 Cor. ii, 13; John xvi, 13; 1 John i, 1–3, the word *show* meaning *rehearse.*

(b) By opening eyes, Ps. cxix, 18; 1 John ii, 20.

(c) By Jesus' method, John xvi, 13; Acts viii, 31; Mark viii, 31; Matt. xvi, 21; Luke xxiv, 27, 44, 45; Matt. iv, 7.

(d) By the apostle's method, Acts xvii, 2, 3.

(e) By the method of the early church, Eph. v, 18.

5. When does the Spirit teach? John xiv, 23, 24; 1 Cor. iii, 1, 2; Heb. v, 11–14; when a soul is empty and humbled.

6. Through whom does the Spirit teach? 1 Cor. xii; Acts xi, 19; xviii, 26; Jas. iii, 1, 2.

7. Why does the Spirit teach?
(a) To renew and edify saints.
(b) To enable saints to teach others.
(c) To glorify Christ, Luke xxiv, 44; John xvi, 14, 15.

W. J. ERDMAN.

THE HOLY SPIRIT AND THE CHURCH AS THE BODY.

1. The Spirit must be present to make the church, or a church. First proof — the grouping of the disciples around Jesus in the Gospels, a picture of the church, see John xiii to xvii. In John neither Jesus nor the disciples should be regarded as after the flesh, John xx, 16, 17; John xi, 51, 52; Eph. iv. 4; 1 Cor. xii, 12, 13. Another Comforter, but not a different one — another person, but not another being.

2. He must be present to make a ministering church, Acts, i, 1; John xiv, 12–15; 1–8; 1 Cor. iii, 9–15; 2 Tim. ii, 2; John xv, 25, 26; xvi, 13; Acts xx, 28; xiii, 2–4; 1 Cor. xii–xiv.

3. The Spirit makes a witnessing and preaching and teaching church, John xv, 26, 27; xvi, 13, 14; Acts i, 8. Seven witnesses in John to Christ as the Son of God : 1. Old Testament ; 2. John the Baptist ; 3. The Father ; 4. Jesus; 5. His works: 6. The Spirit; 7. The disciples. Spirit in believers to witness, John xvi, 7–11; 1 Cor. ii, 4; Acts ii and iii; vii, 7. Pentecost is one day, yet unended. The passover lamb has been slain. We are now keeping the seven days' feast. Ministering as priests, Lev. xxiii, 15–18; Acts xiii, 2; Heb. x, 11; Rom. xv, 16, 27; 1 Peter ii, 5–9; Rom. xii, 1.

4. The Holy Spirit must be present to sustain a suffering church, Rom. viii, 18–27; 1 Peter iv, 13, 14; 2 Cor. xii, 9.

5 Must be present to raise the

church in resurrection. Commandments, 1 John iii, 28; Eph. i, 15; Col. i, 4.
W. J. ERDMAN.

THE HOLY SPIRIT AND MINISTRY.

John xv, 16; Christ, the trunk — not fruit through Him — until branches are found.

I. The Holy Spirit is called the Spirit of Christ.

Jesus the Son of God is in Heaven, John xiv, 12; not one act of believing. but continual believing.

John xiv, 16: "Ye know Him"— not see Him. We are not conscious of the Holy Ghost apart from Christ. He represents Jesus.

Comes in Christ's name; identified with Christ.

John xv, 26: Personal knowledge of Jesus foundation of all ministry.

John xvi, 13 and 14: Things to come. Faith in prayer answered.

Acts ii, 33: Get near Jesus; He sheds forth the Spirit.

II. The Promise of Old Testament was Jesus in the flesh. Of New, the Holy Spirit.

Matt. xxviii, 18, 20: Am with you always; no break.

Luke xxiv, 49; Acts i, 7, 8: Going out from Jerusalem — widening — must not cease work; power will cease.

Acts xiv, 28: Question on rest — as losing power.

Hosea ii: Rest with Jesus present. One God revealed in the Son by the Holy Ghost — all one — no difference in going in prayer,

1 Cor. ii: Presenting spiritual things to the spiritual.

Acts iv, 31: Must keep filled.

Acts vi, 3; Acts vi, 5; Acts xiii, 2–4: Ministered to the Lord in prayer and fasting.

III. The best way to find God in prayer is to accept the fact of His indwelling presence, and in quiet turn to Him. Not cry aloud as though He was far off.

Acts xvi, 6: Can we not, giving up our will. wait on God, and be guided by the Holy Spirit.

2 Tim. i, 6, 7: In you; stir it up; the spirit of power, of love, of sound mind.

Love is a gift; go to Christ; He can put in us a heart of love.

Heb. xii, last verse.

Col. i, 29, last verse.

Not to throw away our individuality or endowments, but to give them to Christ.

Power will come as we need; not all at once; could not bear it.

REV. MR. SIMPSON.

SYMBOLS OF THE HOLY SPIRIT.

1st. Air, John iii, 8; John xx, 22. Around us; but must breathe it for life — in close room — poor air — come out — constant breathing — so constant dependence, 1 Cor. xii, 14; freemen of air, Eze. xxxvii, 10–12.

2d. Light, Luke xi, 34–36; we make obstacles to reception of light, Eph. i, 18; Ps. lxxxix, 37; moon reflects light of sun; sometimes earth intervenes — so with us in our relations to Christ.

3d. Fire, Matt. iii, 2; Acts ii, 3.

4th. Oil, Lev. xii, 15, 16, 17. Ear; man fell by wrong use of ear. Ps. civ, 15; xxiii, 5; oil in lamp; wick will have no power of endurance if oil is lacking, Zech. iv, 3; sons of oil; consecrated ones full of spirit strengthening others.

5th. Water, Lev. xiv, 16: blood applied by spirit, Num. ix, 17; red heifer, John iv. 14: vii, 38. 39; underdrain carrying off water, Eze. xlvii, 1–12; 2 Kings iii, 16, 17; get the channels ready; water comes in various ways, Deut. xxxii, 2; dew storm; gentle rain; early and latter rain; trees (saints)draw rain.

SARAH F. SMILEY.

THE GOSPEL IN THE INQUIRY ROOM.

BY R. C. MORSE.

The object of all our work with unconverted young men, is to bring them to the point of inquiring the way of life. We all know what it is in our meetings to rejoice to see one after another brought to this point, and rising for prayer. We also remember how utterly weak and ignorant we have felt, as we have sat down to talk to these inquirers. Until three years ago, I confess I was among the number who felt painfully ignorant, and at a loss in approaching an inquirer. I rejoiced to see him manifest the interest he did. It was easy and pleasant to express my joy to him. If he seemed troubled, and wanted light, I fell back on my own experience ; and was surprised oftentimes that this did not seem to be of much comfort to him. Mr. Moody, in his talk to Christians, in Brooklyn, about how to deal with inquirers out of the Bible, gave me more practical suggestions on this subject than I have ever received up to that day in December, 1875. Since that time, in dealing with scores, perhaps hundreds, of individual inquirers, I have learned something of what is to me now the most delightful sort of Christian work. In this paper I try to give some hints borrowed from this three years' experience.

1. How to obtain inquirers at our meetings. It may be well to say a word in opening about the appeal made in many of our meetings to the unconverted, asking them to become inquirers.

2. It should never be made as a matter of form. If the leader does not feel, at the moment, a genuine and earnest conviction that it is a fitting time for such an appeal, it is worse than useless for him to make it.

3. If it is to be made, you want the sympathy and prayers of every Christian present. Ask for this. Appeal for it, if desirable. One reason why there are not more inquirers is that we are not enough in earnest about awakening them. It is a good plan, before making your appeal for inquirers, to ask Christians to bow their heads in silent prayer for God's blessing on the truth we have been considering in the meeting, and its application to those without a

knowledge of Christ. While they are in the act of praying, a solemn appeal can be fitly made to the unconverted.

4. But the meeting is now over. The inquirer has remained. The room is quiet. It is important to insist on this. If there are in the room several knots of brethren talking and laughing, the whole atmosphere is uncongenial. Yet I have often seen brethren try to deal with inquirers in just such an uncongenial atmosphere. It is your duty to be honest with the inquirer in this matter, and if you ask him to remain for serious conversation, it is your duty to see that the room is cleared of gossiping intruders, and that a fair opportunity is given for such calm, quiet conversation as befits the serious subject of the hour.

5. As you now turn to engage in talk with the inquirer, lift up your heart in prayer to God. Remind yourself that without the presence, help and power of the Holy Spirit, even the truth of His Word will not be discerned. Blessed is the sense and knowledge of your weakness, when they lead you to depend wholly on Christ.

6. At the outset of your talk with the inquirer, let him be the chief speaker. He is the patient in this case, and you want at first to find out his symptoms. This you can only do by letting him talk. Ask him what the trouble or difficulty is. Often the reply will be: "I am out of employment;" or, "I have no money;" or, "I am away from home, and want to get back to my friends." Then follows a story of destitution, and God's hard dealing with him. You had thought he was burdened with his sins, and was seeking Christ. But you find all he wants is relief in his temporal distress. Do not refuse him your sympathy, but let him know that this is not just the time when you can attend to his case; and if other inquirers are waiting, pass on to them.

7. Let us suppose the next case to be of quite an opposite description. The inquirer is in earnest to become a Christian. The truth uttered in the meeting has made genuine impression on him. Your whole dependence should now be upon the Word of God. Remembering Paul's words to the jailer (Acts xvi, 31), and Philip's to the eunuch (Acts viii, 37), ask the inquirer: "Do you believe and trust in Christ as your Savior, according to the Scriptures?" Upon the reply made to this question, the whole character of the conversation must turn. Let us consider, one by one, some of the usual replies made to this question.

8. The answer which has most frequently been given me by inquirers has been: "Yes, I do believe in Christ," and to show the man he don't believe, and how it is that he is deceiving himself, is, in such cases, the best way to give him a clear idea of what it is to believe in Christ. Turn, therefore, to 1 Peter ii, 24: "Who His own

self bare our sins, in His own body on the tree;" and to Isa. liii, 4, 5: "He bore our sins; was wounded for our iniquities." Let the inquirer read for himself aloud this and every other passage you refer to; it impresses the words on his attention. After he has read the above verses, ask him: "Do you believe Christ bore your sins?" After some hesitation, the reply is generally "Yes." "If He is bearing them, then you are wholly relieved of the burden. He must be your greatest benefactor. Have you ever thanked Him for having pardoned and borne away your sins?" The usual reply is: "No." His want of faith is revealed to him in his want of lively gratitude to Christ. The importance of appealing to this sense of gratitude to Christ was deeply impressed on my mind years ago by the following incident, told me by one experienced in Christian work : An English gentleman, who was an earnest Christian, had a servant whom for a long time he had sought to lead to Christ; but the man's constant and amiable reply was: "I am trying to believe and lead a Christian life. I read my Bible and pray regularly every day; but I feel sure I am not yet a Christian." These replies for a long time baffled and puzzled the master, until one day it occurred to him to say: "John, you tell me you pray every day." "Yes." "What do you pray for?" "Why, sir, that God would forgive my sins and bless me." "Have you ever thanked him, John, for having forgiven your sins?" "No," said John. "Why should I?" The master turned to 1 John i, 9, saying: "These words were written to believe in, and you tell me you believe and pray." John read: "If we confess our sins, he is faithful and just to forgive us our sins." John found he could never pray after that without hearing the question: "Have you ever thanked God for having forgiven your sins?" In the light of his ingratitude he saw his own unbelief, and was led to a real, saving, grateful and rejoicing faith. Since hearing this true story, I have seen many inquirers convicted of their unbelief in the same way. But sometimes the inquirer will confess to having felt grateful to God in view of his promise to forgive sins; yes, he has thanked Christ for bearing his sins. Then ask him: "Have you ever told your wife or any of you nearest friends of this fact?" By your own acknowledgment, Christ is your best friend and benefactor. He wants you to confess him (Luke xii, 8, and Rom. x, 9). Have you told to others what a Savior you have found? Have you acted in this matter as if you really believed in it, as you say you do? I do not recall any unbelieving inquirer who said "yes" to this question. Once convicted of his unbelief, the inquirer is ready to ask and see what it is genuinely to believe. He has now become an inquirer in deed and in truth. To believe in Christ is not to assent to a creed; it is not feeling bad and then feeling good, but it is trust in a person. Take the inquirer to John i, 12: To believe in Christ is to receive him. "As many as receive Him, to them gave He power to become the sons of God." Mr. Moody says he has known many to be led to Christ in the light of these words, with whom the word *believe* had become so mixed up with the notion of a creed, or of some peculiar mystical operation, that it was a relief — a joy — to find that believing was just receiving Christ as a personal Savior and friend. But Mr. Moody's favorite passage is, I think, the words of our Lord, John v, 24: "Verily, verily, I say unto you: He that heareth my word, and believeth on Him that sent me, hath everlasting life * * * is passed from death unto life." Mr. Sankey's favorite passage is John vi, 47: "Verily, verily, I say unto you: He that believeth on me hath everlasting life." Another friend who has led many to Christ, tells me he finds John iii, 36, has become quite a favorite with him: "He that believeth on the Son hath everlasting life." It seems to me they all agree upon the same words of our Lord, but find them in different verses, because he repeated them so often. In the case of some inquirers, the word "trust" seems to be the one they most easily grasp and rest upon. It is the Old Testament word; you can take them to Isa. xxvi, 3: "Thou wilt keep him in perfect peace whose mind is stayed on Thee, because he trusteth in Thee." In response to the truth presented, the inquirer says: "I believe in Christ; I accept Him as my personal Savior; I confess, and will confess Him." We all know something of the joy and gratitude that comes into our hearts when the Lord Jesus grants such answer to our prayers and appeals. With what thankfulness we then kneel with the inquirer, and ask the Lord to seal this surrender with the revelation of Himself. After offering a brief prayer, ask the inquirer to pray audibly for himself. If he is unable to do so, ask him to follow you, sentence by sentence, in prayer. Do not encourage yourself or him to look for any immediate outburst of feeling. A calm, deliberate act of the will is the accepted and acceptable token. If he has not a copy of the Bible or Testament, give him one, and mark in it the verses which have most interested him in your talk. In any event write these on a slip of paper for him, urging him to look them up and commit them to memory. Never tell him he is converted. You don't know. Let God, who does know, tell him in his own way and time. Be warned by Jer. vi, 14: "Peace, Peace," etc. As the inquirer goes away, urge him to be faithful to Christ as his newly found almighty friend. To confess Him (Rom. x, 9); to consult Him (Matt. xxviii, 20); to depend on Him (John xv, 5): "Without me ye can do nothing." Treat Him fairly. Be true to Him, and He will never fail you. The cause of all backsliding is our leaving Him. I have spoken of one class of inquirers, viz., those who profess a sort of faith, and have shown how they may be dealt with and led to see what it is genuinely to believe in Christ. Every sort of inquirer must be led up to this final inquiry: What is it for me to believe? But the beginning of each talk varies endlessly with the states of the minds of different inquirers. Only a few classes can be mentioned, and very briefly:

I. The Backslider. Mr. Moody has well said: "All the prophecy of Jeremiah was written to backsliding Israel." Point the backsliders to Jer. ii, 13. The two sins of every backslider (Jer. iii, 12). The remedy for every backslider (Hos. xiv, 4). The encouragement offered; and the backslider needs encouragement. He feels he is the chief of sinners. Remember to tell him that Peter, on the day of pentecost, rejoicing in three thousand converts, was a healed backslider.

II. Another says: "I am too great a sinner." "To save yourself? Yes; but not too great to be saved by the infinite power, and infinite love pledged to do it (Isa. xliii, 24). "I am He that blotteth out thine iniquities" (1 John i, 7).

III. Another says: "I am not enough of a sinner to need Christ. I lead a good moral life." "Before men?" Perhaps. But, before God? (See 1 John i, 10; Matt. v.) Anger — murder — in God's esteem. Matt. v: Lust — adultery — in God's esteem. Penetrating nature of sermon on mount.

IV. Another says: "I cannot understand what it is to be born again" (1 John v, 1). "Whosoever believeth * * * is born of God."

V. "I am sceptical — a confirmed doubter," says another. These are depressing persons to meet. What a doubter wants is to know of the doctrine of the Bible, whether it be of God. John vii, 17: "If any man will do His (God's) will, he shall know of the doctrine." What is the will of God? John vi, 40: "This is the will of God, that every one that believeth should have eternal life."

VII. Says another: "The inconsistencies of professing Christians stumble me." Many answer:

(a) Moody's: "You are choosing to be in their eternal company."
(b) John xx, 21. What is that to thee?
(c) Rom. xiv, 10.

VIII. "I have committed the unpardonable sin." If you had you would be indifferent to the fact. Your anxiety shows the Spirit is still striving with you, and has not abandoned you, as the devil is trying to persuade you He has done.

IX. In a time of religious interest, two men who were at feud with one another, became impressed, and were inquirers. They would not be reconciled, nor speak to each other, and they could find no peace. They complained greatly of this, and resisted for many days the efforts and urging of Christian friends. At last, one evening as they sat in the inquiring room, one of the brethren was led to ask one of the two this question: "Do you think a murderer should be admitted to Heaven?" "Certainly not," was the prompt reply. "But the word of God says you are a murderer." "Where?" The accuser pointed to Matt. v: "Whosoever is angry with his brother is a murderer." The accused man thought for a few moments. What all appeals and arguments of man had failed to do, the Word of God accomplished. He crossed the room to speak to his enemy. That night they were reconciled, and found peace in believing.

X. An inquirer said to me once: "It seems to me God could have brought me into the world without sin." Your child might find fault with you because he was born into the world naked. You would reply: "But, my child, I provide you with clothes, don't I?" So your Heavenly Father says to you "that I have provided for you a Savior. Believe in Him and you shall be saved from guilt and corruption of sin. Refuse and reject Him, and for that neglect you are condemned." I pointed him to John iii, 18: "Condemned already." Why? Because he is born a sinner? No. Because he has broken God's law? No; but "because he hath not believed in the name of the only begotten Son of God." You are condemned now, not because you were born a sinner, but because you are rejecting the Savior God has provided for born sinners. He accepted Christ that night. "I am afraid I will fall," says another. Yes; you certainly will if you depend on yourself. Every one before you, who has so depended on himself, has fallen. But read Jude 24: "Christ is able to keep you from falling." If your confidence and trust are in Him, you are secure.

XI. Another said to me: "I don't believe a man can be a sinner one day, and then become perfectly holy the next day." "Is it possible?" I replied. "You have lived forty years in a Christian community, and this is your idea of what it is to become a Christian?" We turned to John i, 12, and iii, 16.

GRACE.

BY D. L. MOODY.

GRACE.

1. Its source, John i, 14–17; Rom. v, 15; 1 Cor. i, 3, 4.
2. All grace comes from God, 1 Peter v, 10.
3. To whom does He offer grace? Matt. xxi, 31; Hosea xiii, 9; John viii, 4–12.
4. Not of works, Eph. ii, 8, 9; 2 Tim. i, 9; Rom. xi, 6.
5. It bringeth salvation, Titus ii, 11–14.
6. We are justified freely by His Grace, Titus iii, 7; Rom. iii, 24.
7. Sin reigned unto death, but grace unto life eternal, Rom. v, 20, 21; vi. 1, 2.
8. We are not under law, but under grace, Rom. vi, 14, 15.
9. The difference between law and grace, Deut. xxi, 18; Luke xv, 12–24.
10. How are we to get it? Heb. iv, 16.
11. His grace sufficient at all times, 2 Cor. ix, 8; xii, 9.
12. Who have it more freely? Eph. vi, 24, James iv, 6.
13. We are going to sing with grace in our hearts, Col. v, 16.
14. What is falling from grace? Gal. v, 1–5.
15. Difference between government and grace. (No text; but retributive dealings with Lot, Jacob, David, brought out, as contrasted with the prodigal son, and the surpassing love revealed in the Gospel.)
16. Last words of Peter and John, 2 Peter iii, 18; Rev. xxii, 21.

THE GOSPEL.

I. AUTHORITY.

The Holy Scriptures, 2 Tim. iii, 14–17.
Search the Scriptures, John v, 39; Acts xvii, 11.
Law and testimony, Isaiah viii, 20.
Sure word, 2 Peter i, 19.
Eternal, Matt. xxiv, 35.
Born of the word, 1 Peter i, 23.
Freedom by the word, John viii, 32.

II. ALL SINNERS.

None righteous, Rom. iii, 10–12.
All guilty, Rom. iii, 19, 23.
All included, Gal. iii, 22.
One sin, Jas. ii, 10.
God made a liar, 1 John v, 10.

III. CONDEMNATION.

Wrath of God, Rom. i, 18.
Condemned already, John iii, 18.
Darkness chosen, John iii, 19.
Reproved of sin, John xvi, 8, 9.

IV. CONSEQUENCES.

Wages, Rom. vi, 23.
Sin finished, Jas. i, 15.
Everlasting punishment, Matt. xxv, 46.
Without, Rev. xxii, 15; Rev. xxi, 27.

V. SACRIFICE.

Curse for us, Gal, iii, 13.
Bare our sins, 1 Peter ii, 24.
Sin for us, 2 Cor. v, 21.
Once offered, Heb. ix, 28; Heb. x, 10.
Wounded for our transgressions,

Isaiah liii, 5, 6; Rom. iv, 25; Rom. viii, 3; 1 Cor. xv, 3.

VI. SACRIFICE APPROVED.
The Father well pleased, Matt. iii, 17.
Approved of God, Acts ii, 22.
Declared His Son with power, Rom. i. 4.
Highly exalted, Phil. ii, 9–11.

VII. SALVATION APPREHENDED.
Believe, John iii, 15, 36; Mark xvi, 15, 16.
With all the heart, Acts viii, 37.
The jailer, Acts xvi, 30, 31.
Power of God, Rom. i, 16.
Faith in His blood, Rom. iii, 25.

VIII. SALVATION SECURE.
Passed from death to life, John v, 24.
Have redemption, Eph. i, 7.
Heirs, Titus iii, 7; Rom. viii, 17.
Who shall separate us, Rom. viii, 35.
Never perish, John x, 27–29.

IX. CONFESSING JESUS.
Confess me, Matt. x, 32; Luke xii, 8.
Deny and be denied, 2 Tim. ii, 12.
Mouth and heart, Rom. x, 9, 10.
Ashamed of Jesus, Mark viii, 38.
Their testimony, Rev. xii, 11.

X. HOLY LIFE.
The motive—"If ye love me," John xiv, 15; John xv, 14. "Constraining love," 2 Cor. v, 14, 15.
Walk as He walked, 1 John ii, 6.
Purifying hope, 1 John iii, 3.
Dead to sin, 1 Peter ii, 24.
How we know, 1 John ii, 3; Jas. i, 22–27; Gal. v, 22.

XI. THE GLORIOUS END.
Return of ransomed, Isa. xxxv, 10.
With Jesus, John xvii, 24; Phil. i, 21, 23.
Ever with the Lord, 1 Thess. iv, 17.
Name confessed, Rev. iii, 5.
Seat on Christ's throne, Rev. iii, 21.
White robes, Rev. vii, 13–17.
Forever and ever, Rev. xxii, 3–5.

D. W. WHITTLE.

A MESSAGE FROM GOD.

THOU ART A SINNER.
1. There is no man that sinneth not, 1 Kings viii, 46.
2. The Lord looked down from heaven upon the children of men to see if there were any that did understand and seek God. They are all gone aside, they are all together become filthy (margin, stinking): there is none that doeth good, no, not one, Ps. xiv, 2, 3.
3. There is not a just man upon earth that doeth good and sinneth not, Eccl. vii, 20.
4. All have sinned and come short of the glory of God, Rom. iii, 23.
5. In many things we offend all, Isa. iii, 2.
6. If we say that we have not sinned, we make Him a liar, and His word is not in us, 1 John i, 10.
7. If we say that we have no sin, we deceive ourselves, and the truth is not in us, 1 John i, 8.

THY VERY NATURE IS CORRUPT.
1. God saw that the wickedness of man was great in the earth, and that every imagination of the thoughts of his heart was only evil continually, Gen. vi, 5.
2. Behold, I was shapen in iniquity, and in sin did my mother conceive me, Ps. li, 5.
3. The heart is deceitful above all things, and desperately wicked, Jer. xvii, 9.
4. I know that in me (that is, in my flesh) dwelleth no good thing, Rom. vii, 18.
5. Because the carnal mind is enmity against God, for it is not subject to the law of God, neither indeed can be, Rom. viii, 7.
6. The flesh lusteth against the spirit, and the spirit against the

flesh; these are contrary, the one to the other, Gal. v, 17.

7. You hath he quickened, who were dead in trespass and sins, * * * and were by nature the children of wrath, even as others, Eph. ii, 1-3.

THE GOSPEL INVITATION.

Subject: Matt. xi, 28: "*Come unto me all ye that labor and are heavy laden, and I will give you rest.*"

1. *The one who invites is the Mediator*, Matt. xi, 3. The question asked in this verse is answered in the 28th verse of the same chapter.

(*a*) Commissioned of God the Father, Matt. xi, 27; xxviii, 18.

(*b*) Fitted to be Mediator, because knowing the Father's will, and revealing His love, Matt. xi, 27; John i, 18.

(*c*) Reveals the way to God, John xiv, 6.

(*d*) Mediates before God, in Divine and human nature, pleading his own merits. Heb. vii, 25; xii, 24.

(*e*) Appeals to men by showing His wounded hands and side, John xx, 20, 27.

2. Who are invited, Matt. xi, 28, "all"— and yet especially here:

(*a*) The convicted, Acts ii, 37, Peter's hearers; Acts ix, 4; Saul: Acts xvi, 29, 30, the jailer.

(*b*) The thirsting, John vii, 37; Isa. lv, 1; Matt. v, 6.

(*c*) The penitent, Jer. xxxi, 18; Luke xviii, 13, the publican; Luke xv, 17, the prodigal.

3. The promise to those that come, Matt. xi, 28, "*Rest.*"

(*a*) Saved and brought into communion with God's people, and into the light, Acts ii, 41; ix, 18.

(*b*) Forgiven, Isa. xliv, 22; Micah vii, 19; Ps. li, 17.

(*c*) Quickened, John iv, 14.

(*d*) Justified, Rom. v, 1; Luke xviii, 14.

(*e*) Prevailing in prayer, John xvi, 23.

(*f*) Grounded in love and understanding God's love, Eph. iii, 12.

(*g*) At rest from one's own works, Heb. iv, 9.

(*h*) Restored to sonship, Luke xv, 20.

(*i*) Heirs to an eternal inheritance, Heb. ix, 15.

Rev. J. N. Crocker.

THE GOSPEL OF THE GRACE OF GOD.

1. Sinful by nature, Gen. iii, 16-19; Rom. v, 12; Ps. li, 5; Mark vii, 21-23.

2. Sinners by practice, 1 John i, 8, 10; 2 Chron. vi, 36; Eccles. vii, 20; Rom. iii, 23.

3. Consequences— spiritual death, Gen. iii, 17; physical death, Gen. iii, 19; the second death, Rev. xxi, 8; Rom. vi, 23; Ezek. xviii, 4.

4. Remedy, Lev. xvii, 11; Heb. ix, 22; 1 John i, 7; John iii, 16; Heb. ii, 9; 1 John ii, 2; John v, 24.

5. Exhortation, Jas. iv, 17; Luke xii, 47; Heb. xii, 25; Prov. xxix, 1; Gen. vi, 3; 2 Cor. vi, 2.

L. W. Munhall.

THE GOSPEL FOR THE UNSAVED.

CHRIST AS SAVIOR.

1. Sin in nature found its end in Him, John i, 29; 2 Cor. v, 14; Rom. vi, 3, 6, 7.

2. Condemnation came upon Him, Rom. viii, 1.

3. Penalty met by Him, 2 Cor. v, 18-21.

4. Obedience rendered by Him, Phil. iii, 9.

5. New standing in Him, Rom. vi, 8.

6. New nature through Him, 2 Cor. v, 17; Rom. viii, 15, 16.

D. W. Whittle.

IF THERE BE NO RESURRECTION.

1 Cor. xv, 13-19.

Then, 1. *Christ is not raised*, verse 13.

Then, 2. *Our preaching is vain,* verse 14.
Then, 3. *Your faith is also vain,* verse 15.
Then, 4. *We are false witnesses,* verse 16.
Then, 5. *Ye are yet in your sins,* verse 17.
Then, 6. *They which are fallen asleep are perished,* verse 18.
Then, 7. *We are of all men most miserable,* verse 19.

EXCUSES ANSWERED.

"I intend to be a Christian."
1. "*But I am too great a sinner.*" Come, though sins scarlet (blood red), Isa. i, 18.
2. "*But I do not know how.*" Forsake sin, Isa. lv, 7; Ps. lxvi, 18, 19. Believe, John iii, 16; Acts xvi, 31. Receive, John i, 12. Acquaint, Job. xxii. 21. Taste and trust, Ps. xxxiv, 8.
3. "*But I must prepare myself.* I must pray and read my Bible before I can be saved." Salvation a gift, Eph. ii, 8, 9. The dying thief, Luke xxiii, 42, 43.
4. "*But I want to have a good time.*" Rich fool, Luke xii, 16-21. We reap what we sow, Gal. vi, 7, 8.
5. "*But I have not enough feeling.*" Faith, not feeling, demanded, John iii, 36. Look and live, John iii, 14, 15.
6. "*But I lead a moral life.*" None righteous, Rom. iii, 10. Guilt in thought of sin, Matt. v, 28. Not by works, Titus iii, 5.
7. "*But not to-night.*" Seek now, Isa. lv, 6. Now, 2 Cor. vi, 2.
8. "*But there are so many hypocrites.*" What is that to thee, John xxi, 21, 22. Look unto me, Isa. xiv, 22. — *Y. M. C. A. Watchman.*

GOOD TIDINGS OF GREAT JOY.

I. *Freedom for the slave,* John viii, 34, 36; Rom. vi, 16-22; 2 Cor. iv, 3-6.
II. *Health for the sick,* Matt. viii, 16, 17; ix, 12, 35; Acts x, 38, 1 John i, 7.
III. *Water for the thirsty,* John iv, 13, 14; vi, 35, vii, 37; Rev. xxi, 6; xxii, 17.
IV. *Pardon for the guilty,* Matt. xxvi, 28; Acts xiii, 38, 39; Eph. i, 7.
V. *The way for the lost,* John xiv, 6; Luke xix, 10: xv, 4, 6, 8, 9, 10-24.
VI. *The truth for the ignorant,* John xiv, 6; xvi, 13; xvii, 17; Eph. iv, 21.
VII. *Life for the dead,* John xiv, 6; v, 24, 25; xi, 25, 26; Col. iii, 3, 4.

THE GOSPEL IN NAMES.

Genesis, chapter v.
Adam. — Man in God's image, ver. 5.
Seth. — Substituted, ver. 7.
Enos. — Man in misery, ver. 7.
Canaan. — Lamenting, ver. 9.
Mahalaleel. — The blessed God, ver. 12.
Jared. — Will come down, ver. 15.
Enoch. — Teaching, ver. 19.
Methuselah. — His death will bring, ver. 21.
Lamech. — To the weary, ver, 28.
Noah. — Rest; comfort, ver. 30.

RECEIVING THE TESTIMONY.

Receiving the testimony of Jesus, John iii, 33.
1. *His testimony,* John i, 12; iii, 15, 16; v, 24; vi, 29, 37, 39, 47; x, 9, 27, 28, 29; xi, 25, 26 (see 1 Thess. iv, 16, 17): xiv, 6; xvii. 3; xx, 31.
2. *His power,* John iii, 35; x, 17, 18; v, 23; xvii, 2: Matt. xxviii, 18 (see 1 Cor. xv, 24, 26, 28).
3. *Result of rejecting His testimony,* John viii, 24; Mark xvi, 16: 1 John v, 10 (12, last clause); iii, 36. He that believeth not. Must believe with the heart (see Rom. x, 9, 10).
THOMAS DARK, JR.

GOSPEL RAILROAD.

1 *Road bed.* The Bible, Ps. cxix, 105; Heb. iv, 12; 2 Tim. iii, 16; 1 Peter i, 25.
2. *Engine.* Love, 1 John iv, 16;

John iii, 16; Deut. vi, 5; 1 John ii, 5; iv, 19; Rom. xiii, 10.
 3. *Engineer.* God, Ps. xlvi, 1; xlviii, 3; Matt. xix. 17; John xvii, 3.
 4. *Conductor.* Jesus Christ, Rom. v, 8; Heb. xiii, 8; Rom. viii, 1; Col. iii, 1–4.
 5. *Train.* (Made up of) Believers, Acts xvi, 31; 1 Tim. iv, 10; iv, 12; Mark ix, 23, 24.
 6. *Destination.* Heaven, 2 Cor. v. 1; 1 Peter i, 3, 4; John xiv, 1–3; Rev. viii, 9–17. — *Y. M. C. A. Watchman.*

RANSOM MONEY.

I. *Every man needed a ransom.*
 a. Birth in the flesh profited nothing, John iii, 3, 5, 6.
 b. All in same condition, Rom. iii, 19, 22; Ps. xlix, 7.

II. *Ransom or plague.*
 a. Man shut up to an *alternative*, John iii, 18–36.
 b. Ransom or bondage, Job xxxiii, 24.
 c. Ransom rejected no deliverance, Job xxxvi, 18.

III. *God fixed the price of the ransom.*
 a. Within the reach of all (30c.), half a shekel.
 b. Perfect in quality — "pure silver."
 c. Perfect in quantity, "half a shekel." Coming up to Divine requirement — "*shekel of the Sanctuary.*"
 d. Nothing left to human discretion.
 e. Atonement is for God. Comp. Rom. v, 11, *margin.* We receive reconciliation — God receives atonement.

IV. *The effect of ransom.*
 a. Deliverance from plague, Job xxxiii, 24, etc.; Rom. iv, 25; v, 1.
 b. Numbered among God's family, verses 12, 13; Eph. ii, 19; Luke xv, 22.
 c. Fit for warfare, Num i, ii.

NOTE 1. *The only standing before God must be of atonement — Law teaches this.*

 2. The redemption money used for sockets of the Tabernacle, Ex. xxxviii, 25–31.

 3. And for purchasing lambs for atonement, comp. 1 Peter i, 18, 19.
W. H. W.

"PUT THAT ON MY ACCOUNT."

The word so rendered is translated *impute* in Rom. v, 13. When, therefore, all that Christ did for our salvation is imputed to us, it is put on our account; and on the other hand. He is saying to the Father for every believing sinner, as the Apostle wrote to Philemon concerning Onesimus: "If he hath wronged thee, or oweth thee ought, put that on mine account."

(1) *Our sins are put on His account,* 1 Cor. xv, 1–3; Gal. i, 4; Heb. i, 3; 1 Peter ii, 24; iii, 18; 1 John iv, 10; Rev. i, 5; Isa. liii, 5, 6; Heb. x, 17.

(2) *Our sin, for there is a difference between sin and sins,* Rom. viii, 3; 2 Cor. v, 21, Heb. ix, 26; 1 John i, 7; iv, 17; Rom. vi, 6; Gal. ii, 20; Col. iii, 3.

(3) *Our failures,* John iii, 6; Matt. vii, 16–18; Rom. vii, 20; 1 John i, 8; Luke xxii, 32; John xiii, 7, 10; Heb. vii, 25.

(4) *Our weaknesses,* Matt. xxvi, 41; Rom. xiv, 1, 2; 1 Thess. v, 14; 2 Cor. xii, 9, 10; Heb. xi, 34; xii, 1, 2; 1 John ii, 1.

(5) *Our cares,* Matt. vi, 25, 34; Luke x, 41, 42; xii, 29; 1 Cor. vii, 32; Ps. lv, 22; Isa. xlix, 15; Phil. iv, 6; 1 Peter v, 7.

(6) *Our sorrows,* Ex. iii, 7; Isa. liii, 3, 4; Lam. i, 12; Matt. viii, 17; 2 Cor. vi, 10; Phil. iv, 4; 1 Thess. iv, 13.

(7) *Death,* Heb. ii, 14, 15; 2 Tim. i, 10; Rev. ii, 8; John xi, 25, 26; 1 Cor. xv, 54–57; 1 Thess. iv, 16, 17; 1 Sam. xx, 3.

JAS. H. BROOKES, D.D.

BRIEF EXPOSITION — "WITHOUT FAITH."
Hebrews xi, 6.

1. What faith is, Heb. xi, 6. The confident expectation of things hoped for. Double aspect of faith — present trust and future hope. Example: God called Abram without any promise. In present trust he obeyed. Afterward, God showed him the stars and the land, and hope fastened on a definite promise. Consider the manslayer fleeing, and the manslayer as a Levite, safe in the city, Josh. x, 1–6.

2. The object of faith, Heb. xii, 2. This looking away from all else to Jesus. There are two kinds of faith — saving and worthless. Cain had faith, centered in his fruits and his own way. Abel trusted God's way, in God's Lamb, and it saved his soul. The Bible is the only standard for saving faith. Conscience must be thus regulated. A watch never compared with the sun will deviate and mislead.

3. Christian faith and other faith, Rom. x, 10. It is the belief of the heart; the consent of the affections. The one relates to things heavenly; the other to things earthly. The one concerns the life to come; the other pertains to this life. Geography is believed with the intellect; the Bible must be believed with the heart. We must believe in a Savior, not about a Savior.

4. The simplicity of faith, Matt. xviii, 4. It is not reason. It looks and lives. Brazen serpent, Num. xxi, 9. It believes and rejoices. Israelites before Jericho, Josh. vi, 20. It trusts and rests, John vi, 20. Mary sat still. Illustration.—"How can you be so gay, my little girl, when a little while ago you were so naughty?" "Why, I went and confessed my sin to Jesus, and I am sure he does not want me to worry about it now."

5. Jesus, and not faith, saves. Faith is not salvation, but the channel through which salvation flows to the soul. The eye is not the light, but we discern light by means of the eye. A coupling beside the railroad track is a bit of useless iron; linked to the train, it joins the power of the steam to the inert passengers in the cars. Faith only saves as it grasps a Savior.

6. Sin of unbelief. The crowning sin of the Bible, Mark xvi; 16; Rom. xiv, 23, 25. Without faith, no other merit will please God, Heb. xi, 6. Treatment of Jesus in this life will be the basis of judgment in the world to come. Simply to negatively believe not will condemn the soul forever, John iii, 36; viii, 24. Unbelief is counted disobedience, Rom. xi, 30, 32. Same Greek word in Eph. ii, 2; v, 6. Let us heed the exhortation of Heb. iv, 2.

MRS. GEO. C. NEEDHAM.

FAITH, IMPORTANCE OF.

A full and perfect trust in God is one of the most important elements in the life of a believer. In the Word we find the widest grounds for such a trust. To all who have been born into the kingdom, who are truly His dear children, comes the command: "Ye that fear the Lord, trust in the Lord," Ps. cxv, 11. And this trust is fully defined.

We are told how much we are to trust. "Commit all thy way unto the Lord," Ps. xxxvii, 5. The promises that follow this are manifold: "I will guide thee with mine eye," Ps. xxxii, 8. That eye is all seeing; far beyond the "pillar of cloud" that is before us, right through the darkest night we may be in, even unto the perfect day it can see. "He shall direct thy paths," Prov. iii, 6. "He will be our guide even unto death," Ps. xlviii, 14. There are in our journey so many perplexing positions, so many times when we know not which way to go; is it not an easy thing to submit to the guidance of one who posesses at one the tender, loving kindness of a father and omniscience? "And verily thou shalt be fed," Ps. xxxvii, 3. "My God shall supply all your need according to His richness in glory, by Christ Jesus," Phil. iv, 19. In things temporal, and in things spiritual we may be sure of having each day our "daily bread."

We are told when we are to trust: "Trust in Him at all times," Ps. lxii, 8. "Trust ye in the Lord forever," Isa. xxvi, 4. So there is no phase of life in which we may not trust. In every time of joy or sorrow, of sunshine or shadow, it is the same.

Is there danger of any kind? Do waters overflow the soul? "What time I am afraid I will trust in thee," Ps. lvi, 3; and the blessed assurances are ours. "Fear thou not, for I am with thee; be not dismayed, for I am thy God; I will strengthen thee; yea, I will uphold thee with the right hand of my righteousness," Isa. lxi, 10. He shall cover thee with His feathers, and under His wings shalt thou trust; His truth shall be thy shield and buckler," Ps. xci, 4. There is a peace which "passeth all understanding" that comes only from trusting fully, and "at all times." "Rest in the Lord," Ps. xxxvii, 7.

"And thou wilt keep him in perfect peace, whose mine is stayed on thee, because he trusteth in thee," Isa. xxvi, 3.

FAITH—WHAT IT IS AND WHAT IT DOES.

Faith defined, Heb. xi. Now faith is the assurance of things hoped for, the conviction of things not seen.

I. Faith necessary.

1. To access to God, Heb. xi, 6. It is impossible to please Him without faith.
2. To salvation, Mark xvi, 16.
3. To success in the Christian warfare, 1 Tim. vi, 12.
4. Christ the author and finisher of faith, Heb. xii. 2.

II. Faith is to be exercised.

1. In God, Mark xi, 22.
2. In Christ, John xiv, 1; Acts xx, 21.
3. In the Gospel, Mark i, 15.
4. In the promises, Rom. iv, 21.

III. What faith does for us.

1. It saves, Mark xvi, 16.
2. Makes us Sons of God, John i, 12.
3. Justifies, Acts xiii, 39.
4. We live by faith, Gal. ii, 20.
5. By faith ye stand, Rom. xi, 20; 2 Cor. i, 24.
6. By it we may obtain a good report, Heb. xi, 2.
7. Overcomes the world, 1 John v, 4, 5.
8. Overcomes the Devil, 1 Peter v, 8, 9; Eph. vi, 16.
9. Supports in trying circumstances, Ps. xxvii, 13.
10. Through it the Word worketh effectually, 1 Thess. ii, 13.
11. Secures eternal life, John iii, 15.

IV. What faith does in us — produces:

1. Peace and hope, Rom. v, 1, 2.
2. Joy unspeakable, 1 Peter i, 8.
3. Confidence also makes Christ precious, 1 Peter ii, 6, 7.
4. Christ dwells in the heart by faith, Eph. iii, 17.

V. The power of faith.

1. All things possible, Mark ix, 23.
2. Removes mountains of difficulties, Mark xi, 23, 24.
3. Secures answers to prayer. Secures the pardon of sin, Matt. ix, 2.

VI. Examples and illustrations of the power of faith.

1. Heroic examples, Heb. xi. 7; Noah, Heb. xi, 17; Abraham, Heb. xi, 24; Moses, Heb. xi, 29, the Israelites passing through the Red Sea.
2. Examples on the part of common people: Matt. viii, 5, 10, 13; the centurion; Matthew ix, 20, 22, the woman with the issue of blood;

Matt. xv, 22–28, the Canaanitish woman.

VII. Christians should —
1. Abound in faith, 2 Cor. viii, 7.
2. Be strong in faith, Rom. iv, 20.
3. Pray for the increase of faith, Luke xvii, 5.
4. Extraordinary faith secured by prayer and fasting. Mark ix, 29.

VIII. The word of faith to the unconverted.
1. The command, Mark i, 15, repent and believe.
2. The promise, John iii, 15, whosoever believeth shall have eternal life.

REV. H. G. DAY.

FAITH — WHAT IT DOES.

1. Rests in the Divine promises, Heb. xi, 1 (Heb. xi, 13; 1 Peter i, 8): "Faith is the substance of things hoped for, the evidence of things not seen."

2. Finds forgiveness in Christ, John iii, 18 (Acts xiii, 38, 39; Acts iv, 12): "He that believeth on Him is not condemned; but he that believeth not is condemned already, because he hath not believed in the name of the only begotten Son of God."

3. Is essential to life, John iii, 36 (John vi 35; John 40): "He that believeth on the Son hath everlasting life; and he that believeth not the Son shall not see life."

4. Works by love, Gal. v, 6 (James ii, 26; Titus iii, 8): "In Jesus Christ neither circumcision availeth anything, nor uncircumcision; but faith which worketh by love."

H. E. BROWN.

FAITH, OBJECT OF.

"WHOSOEVER BELIEVETH ON ME" — (JESUS).

1. Believeth on Him that sent me, John xii, 44.
2. Hath eternal life, John iii, 15.
3. Overcometh the world, 1 John v, 5.
4. Shall never thirst, John vi, 35.
5. Shall not abide in the darkness, John xii, 46.
6. Shall walk in the light, John xii, 35, 36.
7. Shall not be ashamed, Rom. x, 11.
8. Shall not be confounded, 1 Peter ii, 6.
9. Shall do the works that I do, John xiv, 12.
10. Shall never die, John xi, 26.
11. Shall be raised up at the last day, John vi, 40.

FRANK G. PERKINS.

THE SWEET WORD "COME."

BY HENRY MOORHOUSE.

The first "Come" in the Bible is a "Come of Salvation," when God invited Noah and his family into the ark (Gen. vii, 1). The last "Come" in the Bible is a "Come of Salvation," too. "The Spirit and the bride say come" (Rev. xxii, 17). After John had seen all the glories of heaven, the Lord Jesus Christ sent him the message: "Come"—the last message Jesus sent from heaven to this earth. Luke xix, 5: "Make haste and come down, for to-day I must abide at thy house." People say Zaccheus was very much in earnest; but if he was he would have been like the woman who pressed through the crowd to touch Jesus, instead of hiding himself up in a tree. We do not read that Zaccheus saw Jesus, but Jesus saw Zaccheus. We are naturally proud, and, like Zaccheus, we wish to exalt ourselves; but before Jesus can do us any good, we must come down. Matthew xi, 28: "Come unto me all ye that labor and are heavy laden, and I will give you rest." This is a very important "Come;" there must be a coming unto the person of the Lord Jesus Christ.

Many people think salvation depends on receiving the doctrines of the Bible; but we may receive every doctrine in the Book and not be a Christian. I was crossing the Atlantic, and on board the ship there was an American who argued on every question that came up, no matter what it was. Christianity was spoken of, and he wanted to prove to me that he was as good a Christian as anybody in the ship, because he believed all that was in the Bible. He was too smart for me, and I could not argue with him; but I said: "I have been to America three times. I have gone right from New York to California and back again. If you were to ask me my opinion of America, suppose I should say it was just as good as yours, and that I was as much an American as you?" Views about Christ do not make us Christians; we must come to Him as a person; "Come unto me."

In 2 Cor. vi, 17, we have another "Come" from the lips of God: "Come out from among them, and be ye separate." Some people think that should be the first "Come"—that coming out and being separate makes them Christians. But this is Jesus' message to His people. I do not come out — come out to make myself a Christian, but because I am a Christian.

John xxi, 12: "Come and dine." As soon as we cease to let the world satisfy us, God satisfies us. These are three sweet words of the Savior to Peter in this chapter: "Come and dine;" "Feed my sheep" "Follow thou Me." God never sends a hungry Christian to feed his sheep; they must themselves first be fed. If we dine with the Master, we are able to go and satisfy some one else. Therein we shall follow Him. John xi, 43: "Lazarus, come forth!" Jesus had but to speak the word, and the dead will live. Ah, but that was Jesus, you say. "Greater things than these shall ye do." We have not got this power, simply because we have not the other "Comes" that go before.

Another sweet "Come" (Mark vi, 31): "Come ye yourselves apart into a desert place and rest awhile." The disciples had received power to cast out devils; they had come back and told Jesus of the sermons they had preached, and the mighty deeds they had done, expecting Him to pat them on the back, and say: "Ye did well." There is something we need just as much, and that is to be with Christ. Notice one point; Christ did not say: "Go into a desert place." He never sends us into the desert; He takes us there. The desert is a sweet place when the Master is with us. God sends us these seemingly mysterious visitations of His providence that we may "come apart." John xiv, 3: "I will come again and receive you unto myself." Christ said He would go away, and He did. He has promised to come back, and this word is as sure as the other. Then His word will be: "Come home." Salvation begins with "Come down," and ends with "Come home." Put these six sweet "Comes" together: "Come down;" "Come to Me;" "Come out;" "Come and dine;" "Come forth;" "Come apart;" "Come home." And may God open our ears to hear the Master's voice.

"THE LAST DAY" IN JOHN'S GOSPEL.

THE first day in the year may well remind every thoughtful believer, and even every thoughtless unbeliever, of the last day that is coming soon. The fact that it may be forgotten, or, if remembered, that it may be pushed away as an unpleasant reflection, does not change the fact that each successive sunset finds us twenty-four hours nearer that last day. If saved, we are rapidly approaching a day that has no night; if unsaved, the call is swelling into louder and more piercing accents to flee from the wrath to come. In either case, the connection in which "the last day" occurs in John's Gospel is worthy of prayerful attention.

First. *Invitation.* "In the last day, that great day of the feast, Jesus stood and cried, saying, 'If any man thirst, let him come unto me and drink'" (vii, 37). It was the feast of Tabernacles; but amid the outward demonstrations of gladness that specially distinguished the last great day, His searching eye saw the multitudes longing with a soul-thirst that was still unsatisfied. It was like the hollow laugh that rings around many a convivial circle, like the mockery of joy the world is so eagerly pursuing in business and pleasure, like the heartless sham of what is called "society." Man, in his stupid depravity, is disposed to try every source of earthly happiness, in the vain expectation of finding something that can gratify his desire, while Jesus is pointing to the beauties and glories of heaven, and saying in tender love: "I will give unto him that is athirst of the fountain of the water of life freely" (Rev. xxi, 1–6. See, also, Isa. lv, 1; John iv, 10–14; Matt. xi, 28–30; Luke xiv, 17; Rev.xxii, 17).

Second. *God's sovereign grace.* "No man can come to me, except the Father which has sent me draw him; and I will raise him up at the last day" (vi, 44). It is strange that any Christian retaining the slightest recollection of his own conversion, or observing with the least degree of interest the conduct of those who hear the Gospel, or knowing the alphabet of revealed truth, can doubt for a moment our absolute dependence upon God's unmerited kindness for every right emotion, for every proper word, for every real step from darkness into light. If it is argued that such total inability lessens the sense of responsibility, the answer is that it manifestly increases both the responsibility and the guilt of the sinner, because it indicates the utter alienation of the will. Joseph's brethren "could not speak peaceably unto him" (Gen. xxxvii, 4); but the "could not" only proves the intensity of their hatred. So Jesus says: "Why do ye not understand my speech? even because ye cannot hear my word" (John viii, 43); and the "cannot" He explains when He says: "Ye will not come to me, that ye might have life" (John v, 40). So then the unregenerate are "dead in trespasses and sins" (Eph. ii, 1), and the will of a dead man is a very poor thing, making him wholly unable to come to Christ, except the Father draw him.

Third. *Believing.* "This is the will of Him that sent me, that every one which seeth the Son, and believeth on Him, may have everlasting life, and I will raise him up at the last day" (vi, 40). The believer, therefore, need not fear the last day, for "he that believeth on him is not condemned [or rather, judged]; but he that believeth not [the not implies refusal] is judged already, because he hath not [refusal again] believed in the name of the only begotten Son of

God" (John iii, 18). There is no judgment, then, for the believer in the last day, but certain acceptance and everlasting glory. Men are continually asking, in view of that last day, what they must do that they may work the works of God, and Jesus still answers and says to them : "This is the work of God, that ye believe on Him whom He hath sent" (John vi, 29).

Fourth. *Safety.* "This is the Father's will which hath sent me, that of all which He hath given me I should lose nothing, but should raise it up again at the last day" (vi, 39). In another place He says: "I give unto them eternal life ; and they shall never perish; neither shall any pluck them out of my hand" (John x, 28); and in yet another place: "Because I live, ye shall live also" (John xiv, 19). As long, therefore, as He lives, they shall live ; and if the weakest believer should perish, there would be a mutilated Christ in heaven, "for we are members of His body, of His flesh, and of His bones" (Eph. v, 30).

Fifth. *Nourishment.* "Whoso eateth my flesh, and drinketh my blood, hath eternal life ; and I will raise him up at the last day" (vi, 54). The context shows that as the body is sustained by daily food, which it assimilates and makes its own, so we must receive Christ Jesus the Lord every day, resting on Him, trusting in Him, having nothing apart from Him, living by Him, through Him, in Him, for Him, with Him, at every step of our pilgrim journey. Thus our path shall be as the shining light "that shineth more and more unto the perfect day" (Prov. iv, 18).

Sixth. *Resurrection.* "Martha saith unto him, I know that he shall rise again in the resurrection at the last day. Jesus said unto her, I am the resurrection and the life ; he that believeth in me [till I come again], though he were dead, yet shall he live ; and whosoever liveth and believeth in me [when I come again] shall never die" (xi, 24–26). If the body of the believer is in the grave, it cannot appear in the last day until it comes forth arrayed in the likeness of Christ's glorious body ; and if still on the earth at His coming, it will be changed in a moment, and caught away to meet Him in the air (1 Thess. iv, 17).

Seventh. *Judgment.* "He that rejecteth me, and receiveth not my words, hath one that judgeth him ; the word that I have spoken, the same shall judge him in the last day" (xii, 48).

Solemn, indeed, is this announcement of the faithful witness to the unbeliever. The Gospel, now heard with indifference or contemptuous rejection, is to face Him again, and to face Him in the last day, when its spurned or neglected invitations and entreaties will be a more terrific sound than the crash of ten thousand thunders, chasing the self-condemned sinners to the darkness of hell. — *The Truth.*

THE SINNER'S REPENTANCE UNTO THE FORGIVENESS OF SINS.

BY CHAS. M. WHITTELSEY.

Jesus, after His resurrection, sent His disciples forth as witnesses, to preach repentance and the remission of sins in His name (Luke xxiv, 44-47).

The Greek word for repentance occurs in the New Testament fifty-seven times, and is literally translated an "after mind." John preached to God's ancient people of Israel that after mind, or change of mind, necessary to the reception of their promised Messiah (Matt. iii, 1-3).

Jesus preached to them that change of mind which should accept Him as their Messiah and King, though He had come in humiliation when they were expecting Him to come in power and glory (Mark i, 14, 15).

Peter, on the day of pentecost, preached to them that change of mind which should accept Jesus, whom they had crucified and God had raised from the dead, as both Lord and Christ (Acts ii, 36-38).

Another Greek word, which means an "after sorrow," and occurs only five times in the New Testament, is also translated in our version, repentance. Sometimes this "after sorrow" is merely "regret," as when Paul writes (2 Cor. vii, 8).

Sometimes this "after sorrow" is so deep as to be remorse, as in the case of Judas, who afterward hanged himself and went to his own place (Matt. xxvii, 3, 4).

Every sinner must, therefore, remember that remorse for sin is not saving repentance. 2 Corinthians vii, 9, 10, was written to Christians who had sorrowed unto repentance in that, grieved by Paul's letter, they had changed their mind toward the man in the church who had committed a grievous sin. In this repentance they were saved from being a continual reproach to the name of Christ (2 Cor. vii, 9, 10).

So, while "the sorrow of the world worketh death," as in the case of Judas, it is equally necessary to notice that it is impossible for the unsaved sinner to exercise "godly sorrow." He is himself ungodly; nothing "godly" can come out of ungodliness.

Repentance unto life is, accordingly, no reformation of life, no protracted agony of soul, which the sinner works out for himself before accepting salvation as the gift of God. He truly repents when he changes his mind, and instead of longer rejecting Christ, accepts Him. And it is the Gospel that leads him to repent, or in the language of Scripture: "Give him repentance to the acknowledging of the truth" (2 Tim. ii, 24, 25).

The important question, therefore, is: "What truth must I acknowledge in order to be saved?" And it is answered for us in the Gospel, that asks every sinner to change his mind about himself and about God. Saving repentance is the sinner's forsaking his own ways and giving up his own thoughts, to turn to God and believe in Christ (Acts xvii, 29, 30).

God had paid no attention to the idolatry of the nations, and had sent them no messages, such as He had sent to Israel, to correct their ignorance of God. But now the revelation of Himself, in the person of His Son, is sent to all men everwhere, that they may know Him as the giving God, whose righteous demands, in order to pardon, are all met in the cross of Christ, so that He gives salvation to those entirely unworthy, without money and without price. Therefore, the only thing to be done for salvation is that the sinner should at once change his mind about God on account of this revelation, and believe in Christ (Isa. lv, 7-9; 2 Kings v, 11-14; Acts xx, 17, 18, 21).

A sinner, therefore, exercises "repentance unto life," when he turns from resting upon anything in himself, and begins to rest upon Christ (Luke v, 31, 32; 1 Cor. iii, 11).

The repentance which God commands is that the sinner should suffer himself to be brought home to God through the Shepherd's work (Luke xv, 1-7).

True repentance is the sinner's yielding to the Gospel that has sought him out in his sins (Luke xv, 8-10).

It is genuine repentance when one is persuaded to come to God in all his need and sin, because in his Father's house there is bread enough and to spare (Luke xv, 17-24).

Thus it is "the goodness of God," in having given His Son, that whosoever believeth in Him might not perish, which leads to genuine saving repentance (Rom. ii, 4).

Indeed, neither sorrow for sin nor reformation of life is true repentance, and it is further true that both together can not save a soul; yet there is nothing like grace to give a true sense of unworthiness (2 Sam. ix, 3, 5-8).

And the repentance which accepts the goodness of God in Jesus Christ will always manifest itself in a life of service and devotion to God. Paul, in his defense, declares that Jesus appeared to him and sent him to the Gentiles (Acts xxvi, 18-20). Of the fact just stated, the Thessalonian Christians were a notable example. Paul wrote to them (1 Thess. i, 2, 3, 5, 7, 9, 10).

The Word of God accordingly demands of the sinner immediate repentance, bidding him turn from all his excuses to accept the gift of God, and from himself and his sins unto Christ and His service (Rom. vi, 23; 1 John v, 11, 12; John iii, 36).

REGENERATION.

"VERILY, verily I say unto thee, except a man be born again he cannot see the kingdom of God" (John iii, 3).

These are the words of Him to whom the kingdom belongs. He also speaks of the time when He shall sit on the throne of His glory, as the regeneration (Matt. xix, 28). Hence we are sure that none can be with Him in His kingdom who are not regenerate. We could not enter into this world until we are born; it is just as certain that we shall not "obtain that world" unless we are born again.

The reason is plain. "That which is born of the flesh is flesh" (John iii, 6). It is, moreover, sinful flesh; and "they that are in the flesh cannot please God" (Rom. viii, 8); "who can bring a clean thing out of an unclean? Not one" (Job xiv, 4). "There shall in no wise enter into it (heaven) anything that defileth" (Rev. xxi, 27). It is no marvel, therefore, that the Lord should say to inquiring sinners, "Ye must be born again" (John iii, 7).

Regeneration is not, as some say, merely an alteration in outward conduct, or change in the sinner's nature; but a new creation. "That which is born of the Spirit is Spirit" (John iii, 6; 2 Cor. v, 17; Gal. vi, 15). "The new man" (Col. iii, 10); "The life of Jesus" (2 Cor. iv, 11); "The Spirit of life in Christ Jesus" (Rom. viii, 2); "Christ" (Gal. ii, 20; Col. i, 27; Gal. iv, 19).

The author of generation can, therefore, be no less than the creator of all things — God (John i, 13); as the Father of lights (James i, 17); the Savior (Titus iii, 4); the Spirit (John iii, 5, 6, 8). By the light of these Scriptures we learn that regeneration is not of blood (natural descent or relationship), nor of the will of the flesh (natural desire), nor of the will of man (so that an appointed person, at any hour he will, may make or declare any to be regenerate); but solely of God. The reviving cause in this mighty work of regeneration is "His own will" (James i, 17); "His mercy" (Titus iii, 5). By the light of these Scriptures we learn that regeneration cannot be produced by any forms whatsoever.

The channel of this mercy is Jesus Christ (Titus iii, 6). By the light of this Scripture we learn it is not in the hands of any particular set of men.

The instrument whereby regeneration is effected is "incorruptible seed, the Word of God, which liveth and abideth forever" (1 Pet. i, 23). "The Word is truth" (James i, 18). By the light of these Scriptures we learn the instrument of regeneration is not, as some affirm, water, nor is regeneration a work that can pass away, or be undone.

The power communicated by regeneration, is power to do righteousness (1 John ii, 29); power to overcome the world (verse 4). It is, therefore, fitly called "the washing of regeneration." By the light of these Scriptures, false professions may be discovered, and the question is at once answered whether baptism is regeneration.

The mode by which any can ascertain their regeneration, is by simple faith in Jesus. "As many as receive Him — even they that believe on His name — were born of God" (John i, 12, 13).

"Whosoever believeth that Jesus is the Christ, is born of God" (1 John v, 1). Whatever may be affirmed of the believer may be affirmed of the regenerate, and every regenerate person is a believer. "Whatsoever is born of God overcometh the world; and this is the victory that overcometh the world, even our faith" (1 John v, 4). The power of regeneration and the power of faith is, therefore, the same.

All the truths of God are as links in one chain, and ought neither to be confounded together, nor put asunder. Regeneration and faith are parts of one "great salvation," so are justification, sanctification, etc., etc. Yet, neither regeneration nor faith is the Savior, but the mighty operation of God bringing the believer into union with Christ. Regeneration fits the poor sinner to be the temple of the Holy Ghost now, and prepares him for an entrance into the everlasting kingdom of the Lord Jesus Christ.

In conclusion, let it be remembered that, as in the natural family, so in the spiritual family; the newborn babes or the little children have not the strength of the young men, nor the maturity of the fathers; yet all are equally members of the family.

The prevention of growth is stated in Cor. iii, 1–3; Heb. v, 11–14. The counsel to the new born is found in 1 Pet. ii, 1, 2: "Wherefore, laying aside all malice, and all guild, and hypocrisies, and envies, and all evil speakings, as new born babes desire the sincere milk of the Word, that ye may grow thereby."

THE NEW BIRTH.

The new birth is not the improvement of man, or the sanctification of his old nature, but it is the entire ignoring of the old life, with all its motions, works and tenderness, and the impartation of a totally new life or nature. This new and divinely imparted life is as true and real in the soul of the believer as it is now in Christ's ("which thing [eternal life] is true in *Him* and in *you*"), 1 John ii, 8. We are born again or anew of water and of the Spirit, that is of the Word of God and the Spirit of God. The "water" of John iii, 5, must not be confounded with baptism, which latter is important in its place, but is not in a single instance connected with eternal life. The following Scriptures show clearly enough that "water" symbolizes the Word of God in its life-begetting. 1 Peter i, 23: "Being born again, not of corruptible seed, but of incorruptible, by the Word of God, which liveth and abideth forever." Cleansing, Eph. v, 25-27, and sanctifying power, John xv, 3. By the reception in faith of God's testimony in the power of the Spirit, I get communicated an actual, real, and eternal life. The measure and character of this life is Christ; thus "Christ our life." It is a *subjective* condition, as "regeneration," with which it is often erroneously confounded, is an *objective* one. The new birth is as distinct and positive as the life received from Adam. We believers have both, but it is our responsibility and privilege to deny the life of the first man, and to walk in the power of the second man, who is our life, as to its source, measure, character and blessedness, and who has also quickened us, the agent being the Holy Spirit planting the incorruptible seed of the Word in our souls.

Arranged by W. H. W.

REGENERATION.

This word occurs but twice in the New Testament. In Matt. xix, 28, it is applied to the new state of things commonly called the millennium. In Titus iii, 5, it is used to describe the believer's new place on earth as patterned in baptism. It is almost regarded as equivalant to the new birth, but it is not so in Scripture. Regeneration is an *objective* state or condition, while the new birth is an inward and *subjective* state. The washing of regeneration can be discovered by the eye of man, as it is an outward change. The renewing of the Holy Ghost can alone be seen by God, as it is an internal condition.

REGENERATION.

1. Corruption of human nature, John iii, 18; Rom, viii, 7, 8; John iii, 3.

2. Trinity engaged in new birth.
  (*a*) *Word of God*, James i, 18; 1 Peter i, 23; 1 Cor. iv, 15.

(b) *A new creation*, 2 Cor. v, 17; Gal. vi, 15; Eph. ii, 10.

(c) *A spiritual resurrection*, Rom. vi, 4–6; Eph. ii, 1, 15; Col. ii, 12.

(d) *A new Spirit*, Ezek. xxxvi, ii, 6; Rom. vii, 6. John i, 13; 1 Peter i, 3; John iii, 6; Titus iii, 5.

(e) *A new man*, Eph. iv, 24; 2 Cor. iv, 16.

(f) *Likeness to God in Christ*, Eph. iv, 24; Col, iii, 10; Rom. viii, 28.

HENRY MOREHOUSE.

THE NEW BIRTH.

1. Its necessity, Gen. 5; Job xiv, 4; Ps. li, 5; Prov. xxviii, 26; Eccl. ix, 3; Jer. xvii, 9; Mark vii, 21–23; Rom. viii, 7, 8; 1 Cor. ii, 14; Eph. ii, 1.

2. Its source, John i, 13; Titus iii, 5; James i, 18; 1 John ii, 29.

3. How described, new creation, 2 Cor. v, 17; Gal. vi, 15; Eph. ii, 10. Spiritual resurrection, Rom. vi, 4–6; Eph. ii, 1–5; Col. ii, 12; iii, 1. New heart, 1 Sam. x, 9; Ezek. xxxvi, 26. Circumcision of the heart, Deut. xxx, 6; Rom. ii, 29; Col. ii, 11. New man, 1 Sam. x, 6; Eph. ii, 15; iv, 24. Inward man, Rom. vii, 22; 2 Cor. iv, 16. Washing of regeneration, Titus iii, 5. Born again, James i, 18; 1 Peter i, 23.

4. Its effect. Begets likeness to God, Eph. iv, 24; Col. iii, 10. To Christ, Rom. viii, 29.

5. Evidences of faith in Christ, 1 John iii, 9; v, 1; i, 18. Love of God's law, Rom. vii, 22. Brotherly love, John xiii, 35; 1 John iii, 14–24; iv, 7; v, 1, 2. Victory over the world, 1 John v, 4.

6. Instrumentality of the Word of God, James i, 18; 1 Peter i, 23. Ministry of the Gospel, 1 Cor. iv, 15.— *Y. M. C. A. Watchman.*

NEW BIRTH NECESSARY.

Text: John iii, 7: "Ye must be born again."

1. All have sinned, Rom. iii, 23 (Gal. iii, 22): "For all have sinned, and come short of the glory of God."

2. Under condemnation, Rom. iii, 19 (1 John iii, 20): "Now we know that what things soever the law saith, it saith to them who are under the law; that every mouth may be stopped, and all the world may become guilty before God."

3. Taken captive, Rom. vii, 23 (Gal. v, 17): "I see another law in my members, warring against the law of my mind, and bringing me into captivity to the law of sin which is in my members."

4. Doomed to death, Rom. vii, 24 (Jas. i, 15): "O wretched man that I am! who shall deliver me from the body of this death?"

5. A better life possible, 2 Tim. i, 9, 10 (1 Cor. xv, 53, 54): "Who hath abolished death, and hath brought life and incorruptibility to light through the Gospel."

6. Condemnation removed, Rom. viii, 1 (Col. ii, 13–15): "*There is* therefore now no condemnation to them which are in Christ Jesus, who walk not after the flesh, but after the Spirit."

7. Liberty through Christ, Isa. lxi, 1 (2 Cor. i, 9, 10): "He hath sent me to bind up the brokenhearted, to proclaim liberty to the captives, and the opening of the prison to *them that are bound.*"

8. Eternal life through faith, John v, 24 (Rom. vi, 11): "He that heareth my Word, and believeth on Him that sent Me, hath everlasting life, and shall not come into condemnation; but is passed from death unto life."

H. E. BROWN.

FAITH, TRIUMPHS OF.

Hebrews xii.

Verse 1. Faith is believing and doing what God commands.

Ver. 2. Best way to die in faith is to live in it.

Ver. 4. Abel's faith saw the blood brought nothing of his own. Abel

brought *sin* offering. Cain, *thank* offering.
Ver. 5. Enoch walked with and pleased God. God took him. A type of the heavenly family who shall meet the Lord in the air.
Ver. 6. To please God believe *that* He is, and *what* He is.
Ver. 7. Noah, just and perfect. God's one man, Gen. vi, 9. A type of those saved through the tribulation.
Ver. 8. Abraham, God's friend, obeyed and asked no questions.
Ver. 10. Looked for a city, though he never saw even a house.
Faith never refers to self; always to God. Object of faith always outside. Enjoy results of it inside.
To have faith grow, feed it well on the Word. To have great faith, exercise what you have.
Faith never overdraws its account.
Profitable mixture. Word of God and faith not feeling, Heb. iv, 2.
W. G. CARR.

FAITH AND WORKS.
James ii, 14–26.

Verse 14. Pious words without pious works, so much air. Millions say on Sunday: "I have faith," "I believe," and give practical denial all the rest of the week.
Ver. 16. Inward principles and outward practice go together.
Genuine faith has no respect of persons, James ii, 1; makes no friends of world, James iv, 4; pays as well as prays, James v, 4.
Ver. 19. Right believing is followed by right living.
Ver. 23. Faith made Abraham the friend of God. Faith makes us sons of God.
Living faith — laying hold of God — is salvation.
W. G. CARR.

FAITH AND FORGIVENESS.
Mark xi, 24, 25.

Successful prayer is here made to depend on two conditions — faith and forgiveness. The same double truth is elsewhere stated thus: "Let him ask in faith, nothing wavering; for he that wavereth is like a wave of the sea driven with the wind and tossed. For let not that man think that he shall receive anything of the Lord," James i, 6, 7. "If I regard iniquity in my heart, the Lord will not hear me," Psa. lxvi, 18.

I. Look at the faith: —

It must be definite faith, Matt. xx, 31–33.
It must be joyful faith, Josh. vi, 16.
It must be steadfast faith, 1 Kings xviii, 43.
It must be prompted of the Spirit, Gen. xviii, 17, 19.
It must wait in patience, Psa. xl, 1; Luke ii, 25, 29, 30.
It must rejoice in hope, 1 Sam. i, 17, 18.
It must persevere in importunity, Luke xviii, 5, 7.
It must defy impossibilities, Matt. xv, 22–28.

II. Look at the forgiveness: —

It must make Jesus its example, Luke xxiii, 34.
It must spring from knowledge of personal forgiveness. Col. iii, 13.
It must be unlimited, Matt. xviii, 21, 22.
It must be unconditional, Matt. x, 8.
It must be done in forbearance, Gen. xiv, 4, 5.
It gives opportunity for counsel and prayer, Gen, xiv, 24; Matt. v, 44.
It provokes love, Rom. xii, 20.
It is imperative to the soul's well-being, James ii, 13.
Read the promise for prayer and forgiveness, James v, 16.
Consider a few who exemplified this: —

Joseph, Gen. l, 20, 21.
David, 1 Sam. xxiv, 6, 7; 2 Sam. xix, 19, 23.
Stephen, Acts vii, 60.

Paul, 2 Tim. iv, 16; Philem. 17-19. Remember what forgiveness has done for us: —

Borne our sins away, Isa. vi, 7.
Blotted them out, Isa. xliii, 25.
Forgotten them forever, Ps. ciii, 12.
"Blessed are they whose iniquities are forgiven," Rom. iv, 7.
Be exhorted. "Forgive as ye have been forgiven."

MRS. GEO. C. NEEDHAM.

REPENTANCE.

In our revered "King James' Bible," the work *repent*, together with its six derivatives — *repenteth, repentest, repented, repenting, repentings,* and *repentance,* occurs one hundred and seven times.

In the original Hebrew and Greek Scriptures, *four* root words are used to express the idea of *repentance* — two in the Old Testament and two in the New. All theories of repentance must be tried by these four words.

(A) ETYMOLOGY.

1. Two Old Testament roots, signify repentance.

(*a*) *Nokham,* to change purpose, Jer. xviii. 7-10. This properly means the *inward* mental change. Pure repentance, Job xlii, 1-6.

(*b*) *Shoov,* to turn, return, repent. This word gives the *outward,* moral change. Strictly, *conversion* from the error of one's way, Jas. v, 19, 20.

Note. Ex. xiii, 17, contains both terms. See "repent," and "return."

2. Two New Testament roots indicate repentance.

(*a*) *Metamelomai,* Matt. xxi, 28, 29.

1. To feel repentance, to rue, repent.
2. To change one's purpose.
3. To change one's line of conduct.

(*b*) *Metanoeo,* Matt. iv, 17. Pure repentance. See *Nokham.*

1. To *perceive afterward,* and thus sometimes too late, Heb. xii, 15, 17, Esau; Matt. xxvii, 3-5, Judas.
2. To change one's mind or purpose.
3. To repent, Godly sorrow, 2 Cor. vii, 9-11.

3. Summary of Ideas in repentance :

(a) To perceive [sin] afterward.
(b) To *feel* repentance, Acts v, 31.
(c) To change one's mind, and *think* differently about sin.
(d) To change one's purpose.
(e) To turn from one's ways, and *do* differently.

4. Corresponding Ground of Moral Obligation.

(a) "The Spirit of the Mind" *perceives,* Eph. iv, 23; Job xxxiii, 14-17.
(b) Conscience *feels conviction* for sin, John viii, 9.
(c) Reason *thinks* about righteousness, temperance, and judgment to come, Isa. i, 8-20; Acts xxiv, 25.
(d) The will *changes its purpose,* and submits to God, 1 Peter iv, 3; iv, 19; Luke xxii, 42.
(e) The whole man seeks *to learn and to do* the will of God, 1 Peter iv, 1, 2; Eph. vi, 6, 7.

Golden Texts on Repentance, Isa. lv, 6, 7; i 16-20.

(B) CALLS TO REPENTANCE.

(*a*) *Sinners to Repent,* Mark ix, 13.
(*b*) Churches to repent :

1. *Fallen,* Rev. ii, 5.
2. *Balaam,* Rev. ii, 16.
3. *Jezebel,* Rev. ii, 20.
4. *Dead,* Rev. iii, 1-3.
5. *Lukewarm,* Rev. iii, 19.

(*c*) "All men everywhere to repent," Acts xvii, 30; Mark vi, 12.

REV. GEO. J. BROWN.

REPENTANCE.

1. Calls to Repentance, Acts xvii, 30; Mark i, 14, 15; Luke xxiv, 47; Rev. ii, 5; Ezek. xviii, 30-32.

2. Motives to Repentance, Rom. ii, 4; Rom. vi, 1, 2; Job xxxiii, 27-30;

Hos. xi, 4; 1 Kings viii, 47; Rev. iii, 19; Psa. cxix, 75; lxxi, 67.

3. Time for Repentance, 2 Cor. vi, 2; Psa. xcv, 7, 8; viii; Heb. iv; 7; Luke xiv, 17.

4. True Repentance, 2 Chron. vii, 14; James iv, 9, 10; Job xlii, 6; Lev. xxvi, 40; 1 Kings viii, 33; Acts viii, 22.

5. Fruits of Repentance, Acts iii, 19; 2 Chron. vi, 26; Ezek. xiv, 6; Acts viii, 22; 2 Cor. vii, 11.

6. Examples of Repentance, Jud. x, 15, 16; 2 Sam. xii, 13; 2 Chron. xxxiii, 12, 13; Jonah iii, 5-8; Matt. xxvi, 75; Luke xix, 8; Luke xxiii, 40, 41.

7. False Repentance, 1 Sam. xv, 24-30; 1 Kings xxi, 27-29; Matt. xxvii, 3-5.

REPENTANCE.

Acts iii, 19; Mark i, 15; Acts ii, 38; xxvi, 20; Luke xxiv, 47; Acts xx, 21; 2 Cor. vii, 10.

These Scriptures show the important place — repentance — occupied in the preaching of the Apostles. Alas! that it should be to such an extent overlooked in modern preaching and evangelistic work generally. Where repentance is not pressed upon the hearers, solid results cannot be expected.

If repentance is not conversion, nor baptism, nor faith, nor godly sorrow, as these and other Scriptures clearly show, what is it? In spite of its etymological signification (*change of mind*), it carries with it a deeper thought in the Scriptures of truth. It refers to the moral judgment of self — my state and ways — and that, too, in the presence of the goodness of God. It is the thorough wakening up of conscience, to realize what sin is. It is a deep, soul-searching process, most needful to insist upon in these days when the conscience is but feebly dealt with by preachers. Repentance in the Old Testament, when spoken of God, signifies a change of action or dealing; but in the New Testament there are but two instances in which repentance is directly spoken of in regard to God, and in both cases the *unchangeableness* of His action is declared. See Rom. xi, 29; Heb. vii, 21. What a stay to the heart! Repentance is a Divine gift, Acts xi 18. Is preceded by Godly sorrow, 2 Cor. vii, 10. In view of the goodness of God, Rom. ii, 4, is unto life and without recall.

W. H. WALKER.

THE FORGIVENESS OF SINS.

Who can forgive sins but God only? Mark ii, 7. If we were to ask: "Who need the forgiveness of sins?" the ready answer would be: "Sinners." But who are sinners? All men are sinners. See what God says, Rom. iii, 10, 12, 23, and 1 John i, 8, 10. Mark the distinction. We deceive ourselves if we say we have no sin in our nature; we make God a liar if we say we have not sinned in our life. The dreadful reality of sin in us, and of sin on us, making us sinners in the deepest sense, gives the teaching of the Word touching forgiveness a large and living interest to us all. In the following Scriptures we have:

I. The fact that God forgives sins. 1. Stated, Exod. xxxiv, 6, 7; 2 Chron. vii, 14; Ps. lxxxvi, 5; cxxx, 4. 2. Illustrated in David, Ps. xxxii, 5. Sick of the palsy, Matt. ix, 2. Woman in Simon's house, Luke vii, 48.

II. The meritorious ground on which God forgives is Christ Jesus, Col. i, 14; 1 John ii, 12; Acts x, 43; Rom. iii; 24, 25. The question may be asked: "What has Christ done that God forgives for His sake?" See Heb. ix, 22-26; 1 Peter iii, 18; Isaiah liii, 5, 6.

III. The conditions in us necessary to forgiveness: Faith, Acts xiii, 38. Repentance, Acts iii, 19. Confession, 1 John i, 9. Forsaking sin, Prov. xxviii, 13.

IV. The perfection of this forgiveness of God. 1. Sins are blotted out, Isa. xliii, 35. 2. Totally removed from sight, Isa. i, 18. 3. Forgotten forever, Jer. xxxi, 34; Heb. x, 17.

V. The consequences of forgiveness. We have: 1. Life, Col. ii, 13. 2. Blessedness in the soul, Ps. xxxii, 1, 2; 1 John v, 10. 3. Praise in the heart, Ps. xii, 1–4. The fear of God, Ps. cxxx, 4; Jer. xxxiii, 8, 9. 5. Reconciliation with God, Luke xxv, 12, 32. 6. Peace with God, and joy in the hope of the glory of God, Rom. v, 1, 2.

J. A. R. DICKSON.

SIN AND FORGIVENESS

SIN.

"Sin is any want of conformity unto, or transgression of the law of God."

1. Sin pervades our nature, Ps. xiv, 2, 3; Rom. iii, 10; vii, 14; viii, 7, 8; manifesting itself in:

1. Sins of omission, Rom. vii, 18, 21; Gal. v, 17.
2. Sins of commission, Isa. lix, 12; Rom. vii, 15, 19, 21; John iii, 4; involving:
3. Guilt (liability to punishment), Rom. iii, 19; v, 12–21.
4. Corruption, Jer. xvii, 9; Matt. xv, 18–20; Gal. v, 17; Eph. ii, 1–3.

It is in the *former sense only* that Christ is our sin bearer, Isa. liii, 4–6; 2 Cor. v, 21; Gal. iii, 13; Heb. vii, 26; iv, 15; 1 Peter ii, 22.

2. Sin is antagonistic to God and opposite to the Divine character, Hab. i, 13; Rom. viii, 7; Heb. xii, 14.

3. Sin and salvation are therefore mutually exclusive, Eze. xviii, 4; Rom. vi, 23; Gal. iii, 10; James ii, 10.

4. Sin unforgiven makes terrible:

1. The thought of God, Gen. iii, 9, 10; Luke xii, 45; Heb. xii, 29.
2. The thought of death, Heb. ii, 15; 1 Cor. xv, 56.
3. The thought of judgment, Isa. xxxiii, 14; Heb. x, 27.
4. The restlessness of the heart, Isa. lvii, 20, 21; and,
5. Itself, loathing, Job xlii, 6; Isa. vi, 5.

5. The fearfulness of sin is measured by:

1. Its punishment in the lost sinner, Matt. xxv, 41; Mark ix, 44, 45.
2. Its punishment in the sin bearer, Matt. xxiv, 36–39; xxvii, 46.

FORGIVENESS (ONE ELEMENT IN JUSTIFICATION).

1. God only forgives. man does not merit, Mic. vi, 6, 7; Heb. x, 1, 2; Gal. iii, 10–13; Ps. cxliii, 2; cxxx, 3; Rom. iii, 19, 24.

2. Forgiveness grounded on the atonement of Christ, Isa. liii; Heb. ix, 22, 23; Eph. i, 7; 1 Peter i, 18, 19; 1 John i, 7; ii, 2.

3. The atonement originates in the love of God, Ex. xxxiv, 6, 7; Isa. xliii; 25; xlviii, 9; John iii, 16; 1 John iv, 10.

4. Freely applied, Isa. lv, **1, 8, 9;** Rev. xxii, 17; upon conditions of

1. True repentance, Acts ii, 38; 2 Cor. vii, 9–11.
2. Faith, Rom. v, 1; Acts xvi, 31; Eph. ii, 8.

5. Fruits:
Peace, Rom. v, 1; Matt. ix, 2.
Fear of God, Ps. cxxx, 4.
Rest, Matt. xi, 28; Isa. lvii, 18–21.
Love to God, 1 John iv, 10, 19.
Return to God, Isa. xliv, 22.
Assurance, Rom. viii, 33, 34; Heb. x, 21, 22.

6. Evidences, Matt. xviii, 35; Tit. ii, 11, 12; 1 Peter i, 22; 1 John iii, 13.

REV. T. G. DARLING.

HOW GOD FORGIVES SIN.

It seems as though God had exhausted the resources of language, and the stores of natural imagery in the effort to set forth the fullness and completeness of His forgiveness of the penitent. We call attention to some of the most striking illustrations which the Spirit has used to set forth the fullness of Divine pardon. What, then, does God do with the sins of the Christian?

I. "*Thou wilt cast all their sins into the depths of the sea.*" Micah vii, 19. The stone cast into the deep ocean is quite safe from the danger of discovery. "Tell the people," said a thoughtful child, when he had listened to a sermon on these words from his father, "tell them to remember that sin is heavy, and it will sink itself. They might think it was light and might float." Indeed, it will sink of its own weight. And God puts it not into the shallow brook, where it may be laid bare, or into the treacherous river, which may uncover its bed in the time of drought; but He casts it into the depths of the sea, where no search can find it.

II. "*For thou hast cast all my sins behind my back.*" Isa. xxxviii, 17. David, in his penitence, cried out, "Thou has set may iniquities before Thee; my secret sins in the light of Thy countenance." We see, at once, what a change forgiveness effects. Our sins are behind God now, instead of before Him. He is between us and Him. He thus hides us from our transgressions, instead of our transgressions hiding us from Him.

III. "*As far as the east is from the west, so far hast thou removed our transgressions from us.*" Ps. ciii, 12. Wonderful promise, this! For who can tell how far the east is from the west? The sailor that navigates the globe says that he never finds the west, and that it is always before him, but never found. He sails to one point which lies west, and when he is there he hears them telling of the west still as farther on. So God's forgiveness puts our sins into a far off land, which we never can find, as well as into a deep which we can never fathom.

IV. "*I have blotted out as a cloud thy transgressions, and as a thick cloud thy sins.*" Isa. xliv, 22. When God accuses His people, He says: "But your iniquities have separated between you and your God, and your sins have hid His face from you." Here the cloud is between the Lord and His children, hiding His face and bringing darkness upon them, clouding their hearts and glooming their minds. But in forgiveness the sky is swept of clouds, the sun shines once more undimmed; God's hand, sweeping through the heavens, has cleared it, and in so doing, has cleared the soul of its gloom.

V. "*Their sins and their iniquities will I remember no more.*" Heb. viii, 12. Forgetfulness is the greatest boon to a sinner. The ancients dreamed of Lethe, the river of forgetfulness, into which the soul should plunge at death. There is but one such stream — the fountain that cleanses us, blots our sins from memory. God can forget — blesssed assurance to the sin-ridden, conscience-stung soul! "The true penitent," says Neuman, "never forgives himself." God forgives, we say, and God forgets; and He invites us to lose the very memory of our sins in the sweet oblivion of His grace.

A. J. GORDON.

FORGIVENESS.

The Scriptures do not speak of past, present, and future forgiveness. "Having forgiven you *all* trespasses" (Col. ii,13), refers to all they *had* done. All our sins (believers) were necessarily future when laid by God on Jesus and full atonement made, but atonement and forgiveness are distinct truths, although closely connected. Forgiveness means the complete remission of all sin and trespass, up to the moment of believing on Jesus and resting on His finished work. After sins and failure are, upon confession, forgiven, 1 John i, 9. Forgiveness of sins is Divine, Rom. iii, 25; eternal, Col. i. 14; full, and founded solely on the shed blood of Jesus, Heb. ix, 22. There is another kind of forgiveness which is neither for God nor eternity, but administrative in its character, and for earth, as in John xx, 21–23; and certainly *not* priestly absolution.

Arranged by W. H. W.

ADOPTION.

Adoption is God receiving us into His family, and is:
1. An act of His sovereign grace, Eph. i, 4–12.
2. Imparted by God's uniting His people by faith to Christ, John i, 12, 13; Rom. viii, 14–16; Gal. iii, 26; Gal. iv, 4, 5.
3. God is their Father, because Christ's Father, John xx, 17.
4. Sealed by the Holy Ghost, Eph. i, 13.
5. Producing the filial cry of prayer, Gal. iv, 6.
6. Fruit of the Spirit — conformity to Christ, Rom. viii, 29.
7. Renewal in image of our Father, Col. iii, 10.
8. Privileges. God's special love and favor, 1 John iii, 2.
9. Union with God to be perfect hereafter, John xvii, 23–26.
10. Access to God with filial boldness, Matt. vi, 8, 9.
11. Not slavish fear, Gal. iv, 1–7; John iv. 17, 18.
12. Fatherly correction, Heb. xii, 5–8.
13. Provision and protection, Matt. vi, 31–33.
14. Heavenly inheritance, 1 Pet. i, 3, 4; Rev. xxi, 7.

REV. W. M. GRIMES, M. A.

JUSTIFICATION.

The use of the word in the New Testament, a judicial sentence, declaration of right.
1. Man's need, Ps. li, 3–5; Job xxv, 4–6, Gal. iii, 10.
2. Wants to justify himself, Job xi, 2; xxxii, 2; Luke xvi, 15; x, 29.
3. Cannot do it, Job ix, 2, 3, 20, 21, 30–33; Ps. cxliii, 2; Rom. ii, 13; iii, 19, 20; Gal. ii, 16.
4. If God justifies man, He must be just in doing it, Isa. xlv. 21; Rom. iii, 26; 1 John i, 9; Acts vii, 52; xxii, 14.
5. The source of justification is God's grace, Titus iii, 7; Rom. iii, 24.
6. The ground of justification is the death of Christ in our stead, Rom. v, 9; Heb. x, 18,19; Heb. ix, 7–11.
7. Justification is received by faith in Christ, Rom. iv, 5; iv, 24, 25; v, 1, 2; Gal. iii, 13, 14.
8. Position of a justified man before God, Luke xviii, 14; Acts xiii, 39; 1 Cor. vi, 11; Rom. viii, 30
9. Blessings of the just, in Proverbs: "He blesseth the habitation of the just," iii, 33; "Path as the shining light," iv, 18; "Teach a just man and he shall increase," ix, 9; "Blessing upon the head of the just," x, 6; "Memory of the just is blessed," x, 7; "Tongue as choice silver," x, 20; "Mouth bringeth forth wisdom," x, 31; "Delivered through knowledge," xi, 9; "Shall come out of trouble," xii, 13; "No evil shall happen to him," xii, 21; "Wealth of the sinner laid up for him," xiii, 22; "Walketh in his integrity," xx, 7; "Joy to the just to do judgment," xxi, 15; "Falleth seven times but riseth up again," xxiv, 16.

D. W. WHITTLE.

JUSTIFICATION.

Many persons use the word "justification" in the same sense as sanctification. Webster gives the true Bible meaning of the word when he defines it to be not "made holy," but "the treating of sinful man as though he were just."

Justification is the opposite of condemnation. Now, as condemnation does not make a man wicked, but only pronounces sentence upon him according to his wickedness, so justification does not infuse righteousness into a person and make him holy, but pronouncs the person free from the penalties of the law.

The question came up in the oldest theological discussion of which we have any record. "How should man be just with God?" Job ix, 2. Bildad answered the question by saying there could be no justification before God, Job. xxv, 4–6.

The Bible presents two methods of justification:

1. *By keeping the whole law*, Rom. ii, 13; x, 5; Gal. iii, 12; v, 3, 4. Perfect obedience, spotted innocence was and is required of him who would be saved by works. The Bible nowhere says that partial obedience will be accepted. To do as well as a man knows how, which no man ever did, will never satisfy the demands of law.

(*a*) Now, was any mere man ever saved in this way, or can one be? The Bible is very explicit in the negative, Rom. iii, 20–25; Gal. ii, 16; James ii, 10; Eph. ii, 8; Gal. iii, 21, 22.

(*b*) Was our Savior justified by works? The typical lamb was always one without spot. Jesus claimed perfect holiness for Himself; His enemies admitted it; and His apostles preached His spotless perfection, 1 Tim. iii, 16; Heb. iv, 15; vii, 26; 1 Cor. v, 21; 1 Pet. ii, 22; 1 John iii, 5; John viii, 46; xix, 5; Matt. xvii, 5.

2. *The second plan of justification proposed in the Scripture is through the Lord Jesus Christ.*

(*a*) It is of the pure grace of God, Rom. iii, 24; vi, 23; iv, 16; v, 17; Eph. ii, 8; Titus iii, 5–7; Heb. iv, 16.

(*b*) Justification through Christ consists of two things:

1. The forgiveness of sin, Eph. i, 7; Rom. viii, 33, 34; Acts xiii, 38, 39; Rom. viii, 1.

2. The imputation of righteousness, Isa. liii, 11; Rom. v, 19; x, 3, 4; 1 Cor. i, 30; 2 Cor. v, 21; John iii, 16, 17.

When a sinner is forgiven, he is freed from the penalties of the law. Jesus secures this by bearing the penalty of sin — death. With Christ's righteousness, or holiness, imputed, He stands before God, not simply a pardoned outlaw, but a saint. This Christ also secures by His holy, sinless life. If we could believe that Jesus sinned in one point, then we have no Savior. Once we are said to be justified by the name of Christ — the name is put for the person. In Rom. v. 9. Paul says we are justified by "His blood." His death is the ground of justification. Again Paul says, in Rom. iv, 25, that Christ "rose for our justification." With the resurrection He would have been a dead Savior.

We are frequently said to be justified by faith. God in Christ is the ground cause of justification: faith is the instrument or means of securing it. James says we are justified by works. A faith that produces no change of life, no fruit of righteousness is a "dead faith," or no faith at all. Christ is still the cause and source; faith, the means; works, the proof of it.

REV. H. B. GAGE.

JUSTIFICATION.

I. We are justified by grace, the source of it, Rom. iii, 24; 2 Cor. viii, 7; Eph. ii, 8; Titus iii, 7.

II. We are justified by the obedience of Christ. the ground of it, Rom. v, 19; Phil. ii, 8; 1 Peter ii. 24.

III. We are justified by the blood of Christ, the price of it, Rom. v, 9; Eph. i, 7; 1 Peter i, 18, 19.

IV. We are justified by faith, the hand that receives it, Rom. v, 1; Gal. ii, 16; Acts xiii, 39.

V. We are justified by the resurrection of Christ, the proof of it, Rom. iv, 25; vi, 6–9; Eph. ii, 6.

VI. We are justified by works, the fruit of it, James ii, 20–26; Matt. v, 16; Titus iii, 8.

VII. We are justified by Him who

rules the universe, Rom. viii, 33; Isa. l, 8; Zech. iii, 1–5.

"THE JUST."

Shall live by faith, Heb. x, 38.
Shall have their hearts sprinkled from an evil conscience, Heb. x, 22.
Shall receive the promise of the Spirit, Gal. iii, 14.
Shall receive remission of sins, Acts x, 43.
Shall have peace with God, Rom. v, 1.
Shall not perish, John iii, 16.
Shall not come into condemnation, John v, 24.
Shall be saved, Mark xvi, 16.
Shall be raised up. John vi, 40.
Shall have joy and peace, Rom. xv, 13.
Shall have a crown of life, Rev. ii, 10.
Shall have power over the nations, Rev. ii, 26.
Shall have a seat on the throne, Rev. iii, 21.

OUR SONSHIP.

Father bestows, 1 John iii, 1. By faith in *Christ Jesus*, Gal. iii, 26. Led by the *Spirit*, Rom. viii, 14.

Received by adoption. Gal, iv, 5. Accept the adoption crying "abba," Gal. iv, 6. No more servant, Gal. iv, 7.

Partakers of Divine nature, 2 Pet. i, 4. Partakers of suffering, Heb. ii, 10; 1 Pet. v, 10; Rom. viii, 17; 2 Tim. ii, 12; Phil. i, 29. Partakers of work, Luke xix, 10; 2 Cor. vi, 1.

He gives us, Jas. i, 17, His peace, John xiv, 27; His consolation, 2 Thess. ii, 16, 17.

If children, then heirs, Rom. viii, 17; Gal. iv, 7.

Heirs to,
1. A royal throne, Rev. iii, 21.
2. A royal kingdom, Rev. ii, 26.
3. A royal crown and jewels, Rev. ii, 10, 17, 28: iii, 11.
4. A royal name, Rev. iii, 12.
5. Royal apparel, Rev. iii, 5.
6. Royal food, Rev. ii, 7, 17.
7. All this eternally, Rev. ii, 11; iii, 5.
8. Royal residence, John xiv, 2.
" I'm a child of the king."

J. E. BROWN.

SONSHIP.

Christians are termed "sons" and "children," the former expressing their dignity, the latter their filial relationship. Angels, because of their place and greatness in the scale of creation, are termed "sons of God." Jesus is called *the* Son of God because of the pre-eminent and personal place and glory, but not once is he termed "child of God." In Acts iv, 27, "child" should be "servant" Jesus. The Apostle John in his Epistles and Gospel does not once style us "sons," but always "children," as the family, and not the dignity, of its members is his main theme. In John i, 12, and 1 Eph. iii, 2, "sons of God" reads *children* of God. Paul often treats both of relationship and dignity; hence the abundant use of the terms "children" and "sons" in his writings.

Arranged by W. H. W.

ASSURANCE.

1 John v, 13. (R. V.)

Those who lack, do so often because they only know of justification by faith; in theory, not in practice.

Stopped short of Christ, Isa. lxv, 2. Trying to get rest without coming to Christ; laboring for rest, Matt. xi, 28.

Without Christ the disciples toiled all night and took nothing, Luke v, 5. All religion without Christ is toil. Nothing short of rest on Him can satisfy — or give peace — assurance.

"THESE THINGS."

I. Sin, 1 John i.
Verse 8. Sinners by nature.

Ver. 9. Sinners by practice.
II. Christ manifested, 1 John iii.
Verse 5. To take away our sins.
Ver. 8. To destroy works of devil.
III. How appropriated, 1 John v.
Verse 1. Believing Jesus is *the* Christ.
Ver. 9-12. Believing God's record concerning Jesus, *the* Christ.
IV. The result.
Verse 13. Assurance.
Ver. 20. Knowledge, growth.

JOHN H. ELLIOTT.

ASSURANCE.

WE MAY KNOW.

John vii, 17, and viii, 31, 32.

If any man will do His will, he shall know of the doctrine, whether it be of God.

1. Christ is our personal friend, Jno. x, 14 (Rev. iii, 20): "I am the Good Shepherd, and know My *sheep*, and am known of Mine."

2. Our eternal life is begun, 1 John v, 13 (1 John iii, 14): "These things have I written unto you that believe on the name of the Son of God; that ye may know that ye have eternal life."

3. We have a home in heaven, 2 Cor. v, 1 (John xiv, 2): "We know that, if our earthly house of *this* tabernacle were dissolved, we have a building of God, a house not made with hands, eternal in the heavens."

CAUTIONS.

4. Profession is not proof, Titus i, 16 (1 John ii, 4): "They profess that they know God; but in works they deny *Him*."

5. All present knowledge is incomplete, 1 Cor. xiii, 12 (1 Cor. viii, 2): "Now I know in part; but then shall I know even as also I am known."

CONCLUSION.

6. Press forward, Phil. iii, 13, 14: "Forgetting those things which are behind * * * I press toward the mark for the prize of the high calling of God in Christ Jesus."

SOME THINGS WE OUGHT TO KNOW.

1. Our state by nature, Rom. viii, 18; Isa. lix, 12; Gen. vi, 5; Psa. li, 5; Jer. xvii, 9; Mark vii, 21, 22; Rom. viii, 7; Eph. ii, 1, 2; John iii, 6.

2. The purpose for which Christ was manifested, 1 John iii, 5; Isa. liii, 6; Heb. ix, 26; 1 Peter ii, 24.

3. The way of justification, Gal. ii, 16.

(a) Rom. iii, 20; Titus iii, 5; Gal. iii, 11.

(b) Rom. iii, 24; Eph. i, 7; Rom. v, 1. We work not for but from justification, Gal. ii, 16-21; Rom. viii, 1-4.

4. That we have eternal life, 1 John v, 13; John v, 24; ix, 25; vi, 47; xx, 31.

5. That all things work together for good, etc., Rom. viii, 28; Phil. iv, 19.

6. That when Christ shall appear, we shall be like Him, 1 John iii, 2; Psa. xvii, 15.

7. That if death comes first, we have "a home in heaven," 2 Cor. v, 1-7

J. H. ELLIOTT.

REDEMPTION.

This word implies deliverance from captivity or punishment by the payment of a ransom. All believers were once in captivity to the law, to their own folly, to iniquity, to the devil, to death; and the ransom price paid for their deliverance was the precious blood of Christ. It is most important to see that, the price having been paid, the deliverance has already been effected; and the slightest doubt of the present, certain, and eternal salvation of the believer, shows a low estimate of the value of the ransom, and casts the dishonor of a foul suspicion upon the Divine Redeemer.

I. He redeemed us from the law, as it is written: "Christ hath redeemed us from the curse of the law, being made a curse for us" (Gal. iii, 13). According to Young's Analytical Concordance, the word here used means to acquire out of the forum. He appeared in heaven's high court of justice, and exhibited the ransom which perfectly met all the demands of the law; he led us forth forever free. It will be observed also that He hath redeemed us, or rather He redeemed us once for all and completely, so that "there is therefore now no [or not one] condemnation to them which are in Christ Jesus. * * * For what the law could not *do*, in that it was weak through the flesh, God, sending His own Son in the likeness of sinful flesh, and for sin, condemned sin in the flesh" (Rom. viii, 1-3). His redemption reached effectually to the hidden root of sin in our depraved and ruined nature.

II. He redeemed us from our foolish behavior: "Forasmuch as ye know that ye were not redeemed with corruptible things, as silver and gold, from your vain conversation [foolish behavior, Dr. Young renders it], received by tradition from your fathers; but with the precious blood of Christ, as of a lamb without blemish and without spot" (1 Peter i, 18, 19). Here the word means to loose by a price, and He loosed us from the control of sinful and foolish self by a most costly price to Himself. This He does by "the expulsive power of a new affection," as Dr. Chalmers admirably called it, substituting His love as the governing principle, instead of the abominable selfishness that has degraded and disgraced the race ever since the fall. For specimens of fools in the Bible, see Ps. xiv, 1; Prov. xiv, 9; Luke xii, 22; xxiv, 25; Rom. i, 26; 1 Cor. xv, 36; Eph. v, 15.

III. His redemption does not stop until it has secured deliverance from all iniquity: "Who gave Himself for us, that He might redeem us from all iniquity, and purify unto Himself a peculiar people, zealous of good works" (Tit. ii, 14). Here, too, the word means to let loose by a price, and if not loosed from all iniquity, redemption would not be worth having. It is sin that gives to hell its awful significance more than the burning of unquenchable fire ; and if not loosed from its thralldom, heaven would be no heaven. Hence at the birth of the Savior it was announced that "He shall save his people from their sins" (Matt. i, 21); and at His resurrection it was proclaimed: "God, having raised up His Son Jesus, sent Him to bless you, in turning away every one of you from His iniquities" (Acts iii, 26).

IV. He redeems from all evil. The dying Jacob could say : "The angel which redeemed me from all evil bless the lads" (Gen. xlviii, 16). Here the word means to free by avenging, and it is the same word employed, where God says of His people : "I will redeem them from death" (Hos. xiii, 14). It is sweet to know that our kinsman Redeemer is also our God, our avenger Redeemer, and that He will take vengeance on the monster that has desolated so many homes, and made so many hearts bleed : "Forasmuch, then, as the children are partakers of flesh and blood, He also Himself likewise took part of the same ; that through death He might destroy Him that had the power of death — that is, the devil — and deliver [rid judicially, Luke xii, 58] them who through fear of death were all their life-time subject to bondage" (Heb. ii, 14, 15).

V. Hence He redeems from death. The Psalmist looks forward to the coming of Christ, when death shall feed upon those who reject Him, and the upright shall have dominion over them in a morning that is without a cloud and without an evening, and he exclaims in joy : "God will redeem my soul from the power of the grave; for He shall receive me" (Ps. xlix, 15). In this instance the word means to free, and there will be entire and eternal freedom from death, and all that is associated with death : "There shall be no more death, neither sorrow, nor crying, neither shall there be any more pain" (Rev. xxi, 4).

VI. This glorious redemption is through His blood: "In whom we have redemption through His blood, according to the riches of His grace" (Eph. i, 7). In all parts of the Bible, from the time God made coats of skins for fallen Adam and Eve, down to the millennial day, the blood is seen as the purchase price of man's salvation : "Thou wast slain, and hath redeemed us to God by thy blood," sing the happy saints (Rev. v, 9). Here the word means "to acquire at the forum," as if Jesus stands there, and claims their acquittal on the ground of the law satisfied. Nor would the true-hearted Christian have it otherwise. To him heaven would not be more desirable than hell, if obtained at the cost of the slightest detraction from God's holiness, or the smallest infraction of God's law.

VII. His redemption, in all of its fullness and power and everlasting efficacy, is applied to us the moment we believe in Christ: "Being justified freely by his grace, through the redemption that is in Christ Jesus; whom God hath set forth to be a propitiation through faith in his blood" (Rom. iii, 24, 25). It is not faith and something beside; it is faith alone; faith without resolutions, faith without ordinances, without looking to results. Indeed the sinner must quit struggling and trying, before he will ever know the blessedness of Christ's wonderful redemption: "To him that worketh not, but believeth on Him that justifieth the ungodly, his faith is counted for righteousness" (Rom. iv, 5). — *The Truth.*

REDEMPTION.

Colossians i, 14.

The necessity of redemption is set forth —

1. In man's condition under the law. See Gen. vi, 5; Ps. xiv, 1-3; Isa. i, 5, 6; Rom. iii, 9-19; Eph. iv, 17-19.

2. In man's inability to redeem himself. See Jer. xiii, 23; xvii, 9; Micah vi, 5, 6; Phil. iii, 8-11; Rom. vii, 24.

With the first sin came a promise of redemption. See Gen. iii, 15; which promise was reiterated all along through the history of God's people until "the fullness of time." See Deut. xviii, 15; Ps. cxxxii, 11; Isa. ix, 6; Jer. xxxiii, 14, 15; Ezek. xxxiv, 23; Dan. ii, 44; Hosea xiii, 14, Mal. iii, 1.

By the offerings, sacrifices and worship of the Tabernacle and temple service, God was teaching His people the great fact and need of redemption. Not only by these, but this wonderful truth was incorporated into the organic law, by which they were governed. See the law of redemption of servants, Lev. xxv, 49, 54; of lands, Lev. xxv, 27; of name, Deut. xxv, 5-9; of beasts, Ex. xiii, 13. It thus appears that God, in His great mercy, desired to remind them continually of His purposes in grace.

THE REDEEMER.

Redemption must needs come by one worthy and able. Search was made throughout the universe, and it was found that the Lamb of God alone could meet the inexorable demands of the law against the transgressor. So He, "in whom dwelleth all the fullness of the godhead bodily," became man's Redeemer. See Matt. xx, 28; Rom. iii, 24; 1 Cor. i, 30; 2 Cor. v, 18, 19; Gal. iii, 13; Eph. i, 7; Phil. ii, 7; 1 Tim. ii, 6; Titus iii, 5-7; Heb. ix, 24-26; 1 Peter i, 18, 19.

THE METHOD.

The carping, caviling children of darkness say to the children of the light, yours is a bloody religion, inhuman and unjust, and should therefore be rejected. Many in the orthodox church, ministers as well as others, accept the teachings of men rather than God's Word. Any method of redemption devised by any man, would be acceptable to very few other men, except as it should recognize man's morality as meritorious, and permitted him to roll sin as a sweet morsel under his tongue. God did not consult the wishes of rebellious men, who are constantly seeking a truce with their own consciences upon the grounds of their own choosing, or vain in their own conceits. In the counsels of eternity He determined upon His own plan; and, though He knew what men would think and say of it, He went right forward and perfected it just as He might reasonably be expected to.

The declaration that death is the result of sin is made over and over again in the Scriptures. See Gen. ii,

17; Ezek. xviii, 4, 20; Rom. v, 12; vi, 23.

The law is imperative in its demands. Life must be given. The life is in the blood. Hence God has said: "For the life of the flesh is in the blood; and I have given it to you upon the altar, to make an atonement for your souls; for it is the blood that maketh an atonement for the soul," Lev. xvii, 11; "And without shedding of blood is no remission," Heb. ix, 22. If these words do not mean what they imply, then there is no significance in the passover, and the bloody rites of the olden dispensation have no interpretation whatever. The plain statements of Scripture, on this subject, are, that redemption is alone through the blood of the cross. See Matt. xxvi, 28; Acts xx, 26; Rom. iii, 25; v, 9; 1 Cor. x, 16; Eph. i, 7; ii, 13; Col. i, 19, 20; Heb. ix, 12, 14; x, 19; xiii. 12; 1 Peter i, 2, 18, 19; 1 John i, 7; Rev. i, 5; v, 9; xii, 11.

REDEMPTION AND PURCHASE.

The church has been purchased by the blood of God's Son, Acts xx, 28. Even false teachers spreading their damnable heresies have been bought by the Lord, 2 Peter ii, 1. And so their judgment will be all the more swift and sure. Christ has tasted death for everything (see Greek of Heb. ii, 9). Christ has bought the world. God loved it, John iii, 16; and Christ bought it, Matt. xiii, 44. Thus the world has been loved and bought. Redemption is a very different thing from "purchase;" the former refers to a change of state or condition, while the latter merely intimates a change of masters. You may purchase a slave, but that is not deliverance from the state of slavery: "Until the redemption (future) of the 'purchased' (past) possession," Eph. i, 14. The creation is purchased, but its redemption is yet future; *that* will be effected when it passes from its present condition of bondage unto the liberty of the children of God, from its present groans to praises, and from its pain to rest. See Rom. viii, 19–22.

By purchase you change masters. We belonged to Satan, Eph. ii, 2, 3. Now by purchase we belong to God; are his willing slaves, and gladly doing his will, Rom. vi, 22. Redemption gives freedom — an entire change of state. The believer is no longer in the flesh, Rom. vii, 5. Although the flesh may be in him, Rom. vii, 23, A totally different thing. The change of *position* and *state* from Adam to Christ, from the flesh to the Spirit, is true in God's sight, and is so presented as a doctrine and truth for the saint to make practically his own, and in this sense he is already redeemed. The soul is redeemed, but not the body; for that we wait, Rom. viii, 23. Redemption in its fullest extent for *Israel* — *Creation* and the *church* is yet future. The right to redeem is founded on the blood of the lamb, and the power to effect it on the glorious person of the Redeemer.

Selected by W. H. W.

SALVATION.

I. Fundamental Truth, Jer. iii, 23; 1 Thess. v, 5. Salvation of God is of His appointment.

II. Comes to us through Christ, John iii, 17; Heb. v, 9; Matt. xviii, 11; John iii, 14, 15; Rom. iv, 25; Acts v, 31. Christ, "the author of eternal salvation;" "delivered for our offences;" "raised again for our justification;" "exalted to give repentance to Israel and forgiveness of sins."

III. Design of Salvation, Matt. i, 21; Rom. v, 9; Gal. i, 4; John iii, 16, 17. Brings not only pardon, but purification. Saves not only from wrath of God, but from the power of a present evil world to hurt or lead astray. Delivers from eternal death and makes partakers of everlasting life.

IV. *Evidences of a State of Salvation*, Rom. xiv, 17; 1 Peter i, 8; 1 John iii, 14; Ps. i, 2; cxix, 81; xcvii, 102; Heb. vi, 9, 10. Peace and joy through the Holy Ghost. Brotherly love. Delight in God's word. Works of faith and labors of love.
Illustration of Fruits, Gal. v, 22, 23. These the glorious results of a soul saved by Christ and under the influence of the Holy Ghost.
V. *Salvation Emphasized and Illustrated*, Jude 3; Heb. vii, 25; Heb. v, 9; Heb. ii, 3; 2 Tim. iii, 10. "Common,"—for each, for all, to be preached throughout the world, to every creature. "To the uttermost"—none too far away; none too low in sin. "Eternal"—not a mere temporary deliverance. "Great"—in the price paid for it. "Glorious" saints before the throne, washed, purified, without spot or wrinkle, will be glorious. Heaven is glorious. Christ is glorious.
VI. *A present Salvation*, 2 Cor. vi, 2; Heb. iv, 7. Delay dangerous.
VII. *How Obtained*, John iii, 36; Matt. xi, 28; vii, 7; Isa. xlv, 22; Rev. xxii, 17. "Believe;" "Come;" "Seek;" "Look;" "Take freely." We have but to open our hearts to receive the grace of God through our Lord Jesus Christ.

REV. H. G. DAY.

MAN AND HIS SALVATION.

I. *Original condition of all alike*, Rom. iii, 22; Gal. iii, 22; Eph. ii, 3.
1. A condition of darkness, Col. i, 13; 1 Peter ii, 9; John i, 4, 5.
2. This made permanent in death, Eph. ii, 1, 5; Col. ii, 13.
3. This voluntary, John iii, 19, 20; viii, 12.

II. *Present condition of salvation.*
1. By grace, free, unmerited favor, Rom. xi, 6; Eph. ii, 5, last clause.
2. Through faith, Eph. ii, 8; Rom. iv, 16.

III *The Father is the author of this salvation.*
1. The characteristic of His relation to us is love, John iii, 16; Rom, v, 8; 1 John iv, 10.
2. This love finds its expression in our adoption, Hos. i, 10; 1 John iii, 1.

IV. *This salvation is made possible by the work of the Son*, John i, 12; 2 Cor. v, 18, 19; Gal. iii, 26.
1. The characteristic of His relation to us is love, Gal. ii, 20, last clause; John xiv, 9, 13.
2. The same work finds its expression in our justification, Rom. iii, 24, 26.

V. *This salvation is communicated to us by the Holy Spirit*, under whose dispensation we are living, John xvi, 17.
1. In our call, convincing us of sin, John xvi, 8.
2. In our enlightening, John xvi, 13–15.
3. In our regeneration, John iii, 3, 5.
4. In our sanctification, 2 Thess. ii, 13.
(*a*) The means generally employed by the Spirit is the truth, 2 Thess. ii, 13; John xvii, 17.
(*b*) This truth is but the expression of Christ, John i, 14; xiv, 6.
The work of Father and Son is an external work, of the Spirit internal. This work is a complete work; our salvation is spoken of as present, not future or indefinite; *are* saved, not *shall* be.

VI. *In this saved life there is conflict and weakness*, because of
1. The world—the aggregate of temptation, natural and external, James iv, 4; 1 John ii, 15, 16.
2. The flesh—the aggregate of temptation, natural and internal, Rom. vii, 14–19; Gal. v, 17; Eph. ii, 8.
3. The devil—the aggregate of temptation, supernatural, internal, and external, Eph. vi, 11, 12. These are all hostile to God and His people.

VII. *In this saved life there is strength and triumph*, because
1. As to God.
(*a*) The Father is for us, Rom. viii, 31

(b) The Son is for us. He has overcome the world for us, John xvi, 33; and the flesh, Rom. vii, 24, 25; lives in us, Gal. ii, 20; and gives all needed grace, 2 Cor. xii, 9, etc.
(c) The Spirit is for us, strengthening us within, Eph. iii, 16.
2. As to the renewed nature, there are powers, e. g.
(a) Faith, 1 John v, 4.
(b) Hope, Heb. vi, 19, 20.
(c) Love, John xiv, 23.

VIII. *This saved life is evidenced*
1. By works of service, Jas. ii, 17.
2. By love underlying service, 1 John iii, 10; iv, 8, 20.

IX. *Among its benefits.*
1. In this life, are
(a) Peace with God and hope of glory, Rom. v, 1, 2.
(b) Absolute assurance of God's protecting care, Deut. xxxiii, 27; Ps. xxiii, 1; Rom. viii, 28.
(c) Deliverance from death, John xi, 25, 26; John v, 24.
(d) In general all that comes from sonship, Rom. viii, 16, 17.
2. In the life to come.
(a) Negatively — freedom from all imperfections of the earthly state, 1 Cor. xv, 53; Rev. xxi, 4.
(b) Positively — the realization of sonship in full, Rev. xxi, 7; perfect knowledge, 1 Cor. xiii, 12; closer life with Christ, Phil. i, 23; closer likeness to Him, 1 John iii, 2.

REV. T. G. DARLING.

OUR THREEFOLD SALVATION.
(FOR CHRISTIANS.)

"*Being* justified," Rom. v, 1.
Past, Stand in grace, Rom, v, 2.
Present, "Rejoice in hope," Rom. v, 2.
Future, All "by faith;" hence shows up more *our* past.
Past, "Hath," Heb. ix, 26.
Present, "Now," Heb. ix, 24.
Future, "Shall," Heb. ix, 28.
All Christ's own work *standing alone*. Hence Christ's past. "A threefold cord is not quickly broken,

Eccl. iv, 12. The same thought is brought out in the three "delivers" of 2 Cor. i, 10.

F. G. PERKINS.

SEALING.

Sealing is the marking of one for God. It implies that those thus marked or sealed are *appropriated* and *preserved* for God, Rev. vii, 1–8. The believers are sealed with the Holy Spirit, He being the seal. The consequence of this posessing the Holy Ghost is to impart the consciousness of relationship, for it is by the Spirit we cry, Abba, Father. The Holy Ghost dwelling in us is also our power for walk, Rom. viii, 14, 15; and for worship, John iv, 23; and for enjoyment, John vii, 38, 39. By this also we *know* that we are in Him, and also, that He is in us. Sealed with the Spirit, and born of the Spirit are distinct actions, Eph. i, 13. The interval between believing may be brief or prolonged, but the one follows the other. The indwelling Spirit is the *seat* of salvation and the *earnest* of glory to come, Eph. i, 13, 14.

Selected by W. H. W.

SANCTIFICATION.

The root idea in this word, wherever it occurs in the Scriptures, means *setting apart* toward an object, and its measure is Christ on high, John xvii, 19. We have *absolute* sanctification taught in 1 Cor. i, 30; vi, 11; Heb. x, 14. We have *positional* sanctification unfolded in Heb. xiii, 12, and progressive sanctification in John xvii, 17; 1 Thess. v, 23. Sanctifying and cleansing are both ascribed to the Word of God, Eph. v, 26; the former setting an object before the soul, the latter completely removing all blemish and defilement. We *are* sanctified and are *being* sanctified. It is as we realize the former, and live in its power, that the latter is produced.

Both truths should be held with an even hand, both weighed and held in the sevenfold light of the sanctuary.

Selected by W. H. W.

SANCTIFICATION.

I. We are sanctified by God the Father, Jude 1; Eph. i, 3, 4; 1 Peter i, 15, 16; 1 Thess. iv, 3.

II. We are sanctified in Christ Jesus, 1 Cor. i, 2, 30; Heb. ii, 11; x, 10, 14; Phil. i, 1.

III. We are sanctified by the Holy Ghost, Rom. xv, 16; 1 Cor. vi, 11; 2 Thess. ii, 13.

IV. We are sanctified by faith, Acts xxvi, 18; xv, 9; Gal. v, 6; 1 John v, 4.

V. We are sanctified by the blood of Christ, Heb. xiii, 12; ix, 13, 14; 1 John i, 7.

VI. We are sanctified by the truth, John xvii, 17, 19; 1 Tim. iv, 5; 1 Pet. i, 22.

VII. We ought to be sanctified wholly, 1 Thess. v. 23; 1 Pet. iii, 15; Heb. xii, 14.

HOLINESS NECESSARY.

Text: Heb. xii, 14.

1. God is holy, Lev. xix, 2 (Psa. cxlv, 7; Isa. vi, 3; Rev. iv, 8): "Ye shall be holy; for I the Lord your God am holy."

2. He cannot endure iniquity, Hab. i, 13 (Ex. xix, 10, 11; Psa. v, 4, 5; Isa. i, 13–15): "Thou art of purer eyes than to behold evil, and canst not look on iniquity."

3. Christ was sinless, 1 Peter ii, 22, 23 (Heb. iv, 15; Heb. vii, 26; Isa. liii, 9): "Who did no sin, neither was guile found in His mouth."

4. He came to destroy sin, 1 John iii, 5 (Heb. ix, 26; 2 Cor. v, 21; Col. i, 21, 22): "Ye know that He was manifested to take away our sins."

5. Heaven is pure, Ezek. xliii, 12 (Zech. xiv, 20, 21; Rev. xxi, 2, 11, 21; Rev. xxii, 1): "The whole limit thereof round about shall be most holy."

6. The pure alone can enter heaven, Rev. xxi, 27 (Eph. v, 5; Isa. lii, 1; Rev. xxii, 14, 15): "There shall in no wise enter into it anything that defileth."

H. E. BROWN.

THE HOLINESS WHICH GOD REQUIRES.

Text: Ezek. xliv, 23.

1. Puts away all sin, 2 Cor. vi, 16, 17 (1 John iii, 3–10, and i, 7; Ezek. xxxvi, 25): "Let us cleanse ourselves from all filthiness of the flesh and Spirit, perfecting holiness in the fear of God."

2. Boasts not, Rom. iii, 27 (1 Cor. x, 12; Rom. iv, 2, and xi, 20): "Where is boasting then? It is excluded. By what law? Of works? Nay; but by the law of faith.

3. Endures temptation, 1 Peter i, 6, 7 (James i, 2, 3, 12; 1 Cor. x, 13; Eph. vi, 12): "Wherein ye greatly rejoice, though now for a season, if need be, ye are in heaviness through manifold temptations."

4. Suffers patiently, 1 Peter ii, 20 (Col. i, 24; Phil. iii, 10; Heb. ii, 10): "If, when ye do well, and suffer for it, ye take it patiently, this is acceptable with God."

5. Begins in a Divine baptism, 1 John iii, 9 (1 John v, 18; Isa. vi, 7; Hos. x, 12): "Whosoever is born of God doth not commit sin; for his seed remaineth in him; and he cannot sin, because he is born of God."

6. Progresses by Divine help, Eph. iv, 13 (Eph. iii, 16–19, and v, 27; 1 Thess. iii, 12, 13): "Till we all come in the unity of the faith, and of the knowledge of the Son of God, unto a perfect man, unto the measure of the stature of the fullness of Christ."

H. E. BROWN.

PERFECTION.

This word is used in the Scriptures in a way very different from that usually ascribed to it. Were the believer either perfect in himself, or in his ways, there would be no room for the exhortation, "Be ye therefore perfect." Paul would not venture to affirm that he was perfect, Phil. iii, 12, save in Christ risen and glorified, Col. ii, 10. We are, however, to be perfect as our Father in heaven is, in the principle of our walk amongst men. Grace should characterize our ways and actions toward *all;* in this sense only are the words used: "Be ye therefore perfect, even as your Father, which is in heaven, is perfect," Matt. v, 48.

This is perfection as to the principle of walk and action in the world.

"Perfection" is employed in Heb. vi, 1, to express Christian progress and growth, in contrast to the state under Judaism; and in Phil. iii, 12–15, it refers to the object set before the Christian — Christ on high and glorified.

There is a passage, and a blessed one it is, which declares that we *are* perfected, and that *forever*, Heb. x, 14; but that is perfection for God — what we are in *His sight* — the answer to the present place of Jesus on high, as having finished the work which the Father gave Him to do. But our full and absolute perfection *in fact* will be accomplished only and when "we see Him as He is," 1 John iii, 2. If bodily and moral likeness to Christ (Phil. iii, 21, and John iii, 2) await His coming, there cannot be perfection short of *beholding* Christ in glory.

Selected by W. H. W.

PEACE OF GOD.

I. Peace defined: The opposite of fear, Jud. vi, 23. The opposite of disquietude and trouble, Mark iv, 39; John xiv, 27.

II. Its source: Peace with God and man comes from being in a right relation toward them. "Great peace have they which love thy law," Ps. cxix, 165. "The end of the perfect and upright man is peace," Ps. xxxvii, 37. "And the work" — or working — "of righteousness shall be peace," Isa. xxxii, 17. Melchisedek is said to be "first king of righteousness, and after that, king of peace," Heb. vii, 2; so Christ is the Prince of *Peace, because* he is the Lord, our *righteousness.*

III. The author of peace is God.
1. The Father, Hag. ii, 9; Rom. xv, 33.
2. The Son, Isa. ix, 6, 7; 2 Thess. iii, 16.
3. The Spirit, Gal. v, 22; Rom. viii, 6.

IV. Peace an object to be desired. Daily invokes as a blessing upon Israel, Num. vi, 26. Made an object of prayer, Ps. cxxii, 6, 7, 8. The office of proclaiming and making peace a blessed one, Isa. lii, 7; Matt. v, 9. Peace proclaimed by the angels at *Christ's birth,* as the object of His coming, Luke ii, 14. Peace proclaimed by Christ Himself to His disciples just *before His crucifixion,* John xiv, 27. Peace, the first word to His assembled disciples *after His resurrection,* John xx, 19, 21. The Gospel described as one of peace, Eph. vi, 15. God's peace upon the churches invoked by the apostles, Rom. i, 7; 1 Pet. i, 2; Jude i, 2; Rev. i, 4.

V. Characteristics of this peace. Imparts to nature fresh life and beauty, Isa. lv, 12. Compare to the even, quiet, majestic flow of the river, Isa. xlviii, 12. It is *Christ's* peace, in distinction from the world's. The one is real and enduring, the other superficial and transient, John xiv, 27: Ps. iv, 8; compare Jer. viii, 11.

VI. How peace is secured:
1. God's part.
Isa. liii, 5, "The chastisement of our peace," *i. e.,* the chastisement which secured our peace " was upon Him." Col. i, 19, 20, Peace through *the blood of the cross.* John xvi, 33,

Peace from *the words of Jesus.* Heb. xii, 11, Peace through *chastening or affliction.*
2. Man's part,
Rom. v, 1, Peace obtained by *faith.* Phil. iv, 6, 7, By *prayer.* 2 Pet. i, 2, "Through the *knowledge of God* and Jesus our Lord."
VII. *The promise of peace.* Isa. xxvi, 3, "Thou wilt keep him in perfect peace whose mind is stayed on Thee, because he trusteth in Thee."
Concluding exhortation.
Col. iii, 15, *Let* the peace of God *rule* in your hearts.
O. C. MORSE.

PEACE.

I. *Who have peace?* Not the wicked, Isa. lvii, 20, 21; Isa. lix, 8 (read the preceding context); Rom. iii, 17, 2. God's believing children, Ps. cxxv, 5; xxix, 9; cxix, 165; Gal. vi, 16; Rom. viii, 6. These passages clearly indicate that it is only God's believing people that have peace.
II. *The character of the peace.*
1. Great peace, Ps. cxix, 165.
2. Perfect peace, Isa. xxvi, 3.
3. God's peace, Phil. iv, 7, first clause; John xiv, 27; xvi, 33.
4. Passeth understanding, Phil. iv, 7; 1 Cor. ii, 9; Eph. iii, 20.
5. Defensive (keeps), Phil. iv, 7, 8; 1 Peter i, 5.
III. *How obtained.*
1. From God, Eph. i, 2.
2. Through Christ, Col. i, 12–14, 20; Eph. ii, 13, 14.
3. By faith, Rom. v, 1; Rom. xv, 13; Isa. xxvi, 3.
4. Fruit of the Spirit, Gal. v, 22.
REV. WALTER REID.

THE PEACE LEFT AND THE PEACE GIVEN.

I. God is the God of peace, Rom. xv, 33; xvi, 20; 1 Cor. xiv, 33; 2 Cor. xiii, 11, 1 Thess. v, 23; Heb. xiii, 20; Jud. vi, 24.
II. The king and kingdom of peace, Jud. vi, 24; Isa. ix, 6; Heb. vii, 1, 2; Isa. xxxii, 17; Isa. lii, 7; Ps. xxix, 11. xxxvii, 11; lxxii; Mic. v, 5; Hag. ii, 9; Matt. v, 4, 9; Luke ii, 14; xix, 38.
III. Peace! I leave, Luke vii, 5; Rom. v, 1; Eph. ii, 13–17; Col. i, 20; Job xxii, 21; Isa. liii, 5.
IV. "My peace I give unto you." John xvii, 26; 1 John iv, 17 ; Phil. iv, 6, 7; Rom. v, 1.
W. J. ERDMAN.

THE CHRISTIAN'S JOY.

His strength, Neh. viii, 10.
Prayers for, Ps. liii, 12, 13 ; Rom. xv, 13.
Reasons for joy, Luke x, 17.
Commanded to rejoice in time of persecution, Luke vi, 23.
In God's presence is fullness, Ps. xvi, 11.
GEO. A. WARBURTON.

JOY IN PHILIPPIANS.

I. In connection with prayer, i, 3, 4; iv, 6, 7, 19.
II. In the preaching of the Gospel, i, 18, 25, 26.
III. In brotherly love and sympathy, ii, 2, 28; iv, 10.
IV. In the day of Christ, ii ; 16; i, 6; iii, 20, 21.
V. In the sacrifice and service of faith, ii, 17, 18: iv, 17, 18.
VI. In the Lord Jesus Christ, our Savior, iii, 1, 3; iv, 4.
VII. In the crown of a faithful ministry, iv, 1; 1 Thess. ii, 19.

THE CHRISTIAN'S CALLING.

Called by God, Rom. viii, 30 ; 2 Thess. iii, 14.
Called of Jesus Christ, Rom. i, 6 ; 1 Pet. v, 10.
Called according to His purpose, Rom. viii, 28–30; 2 Tim. i, 9.
Called the sons of God, 1 John iii, 1, 2; Gal. iv, 6, 7.
Called in one body, Col. iii, 15.
Called to be saints, Rom. i, 7; 1 Cor. i, 2; 1 Thess. iv, 7.
Called into fellowship, 1 Cor. i, 9.

Called into the grace of Christ, Gal. i, 6.
Called out of darkness into the light, 1 Pet. ii, 9.
Called in hope, Eph. i, 18; iv, 4; Rom. v, 2.
Called to virtue, 2 Peter i, 3.
Called by the Gospel, 2 Thess. ii, 14.
Called to eternal life, 1 Tim. vi, 12.
Called to an eternal inheritance, Heb. ix. 15; 1 Pet. i, 4.
Called to blessing, 1 Pet. iii, 9.
Called to liberty; Gal. v, 13.
Called to peace, 1 Cor. vii, 15; Col. iii, 15.
Called to suffer, 1 Peter, ii, 21.
Called to glory, 1 Thess. ii, 12; 2 Thess. ii, 14; 1 Pet. v, 10; 2 Pet. i, 3.
A heavenly calling, Heb. iii, 1.
A holy calling, 1 Thess. iv, 7; 2 Tim. i, 9.
That worthy name by which ye are called, Acts. xi, 26; James ii, 7.
Ye see your calling, brethren, 1 Cor. i, 26.
The prize of the high calling, Phil. iii, 14.
Faithful is He that calleth you, 1 Cor. i, 9; 1 Thess. v, 24.
Walk worthy of, Eph. iv, 1; Col. i, 10; 1 Peter i, 15, 16; 2 Peter i, 10.

GEO. A. HALL.

THE CHRISTIAN'S WALK.

"Rise up and walk," Acts iii, 6.

This is what Peter said to the lame man at the beautiful gate of the temple; and this is what Jesus says to every one He saves. First — "Rise up;" then — "Walk." What a beautiful comment we get on these words in the Epistle to the Ephesians! The first three chapters are: "Rise up." Then you see every believer on Christ quickened into life with Christ, Eph. ii, 5. Raised up together with Christ, ii, 6. Seated in Christ, ii, 6. Blessed with all spiritual blessings in Christ, i, 3. All this is of grace; and it is true of the believer before he puts a foot to the ground to walk. It is his position. The last three chapters say "walk."
Walk worthy of the calling, ch. iv, 1.
Walk in love, v. 2.
Walk as children of light, v. 8.
Walk circumspectly, v. 15.
Walk not as other Gentiles, iv, 17.
This is the believer's practice. Some try to walk without having to "rise up." This is impossible. Others talk a lot about being "high up," but forget to walk. Both are wrong. God's way is right. "Rise up and walk." Reader, have you been raised up? If so, do you walk? Contrast now the downward walk in sin with the upward walk in grace. David gives us a negative description of the first: "The man that walketh not in the counsel of the ungodly, nor standeth in the way of sinners, nor sitteth in the seat of the scornful." The second, the walk of grace, is described thus: "And he, leaping up, stood and walked, and entered with them into the temple, walking and leaping, and praising God," Acts iii, 8.

WALKING.

1. *With God*, Gen. v, 22.
2. *Before God*, Gen. xvii, 1.
3. *After God*, Deut. xiii, 4.

WALKING WITH GOD.

Gen. v. 22–24; Heb. xi, 5; 1 Cor. x, 31; 1 Kings iii, 6; 2 Kings xx, 3; Luke i, 6; 2 Cor. v, 7; Col. ii. 6; Acts iii, 6; Luke v, 22–24; Rom. vi, 4; Rom. viii, 1; Rom. xiii, 13; 2 Cor. iv, 2; Gal. v, 16; Col. i. 10; Eph. v, 2; Peter xiv, 28, 29; Dan. iii, 25; Isa. iv, 2; Ps. xxiii, 4.

Results: 1 John i, 7; John viii, 12; Rev. iii, 4.

GEO. A. HALL.

THE CHRISTIAN WALK.

1. *God's commands*, Ezek. xx, 19; Jer. vii, 23; Jer. vi, 16.
2. *How to walk*, Eph. v, 8; Rom.

vi, 4; Rom. xiii, 13; Eph. v, 15; Col. iv, 5; Thess. ii, 12; Col. i, 10; Eph. iv, 1; Eph. v, 2; Col. ii, 6; Gal. v, 25; 2 Cor. v, 7.

3. Results of the walk: 1 John i, 7; Gal. v, 6; Rom. viii, 14; Rev. iii, 4, 5; Rev. xxi, 23, 24.

C. E. DYER.

"FRUIT BEARING."
Gal. v, 22; vi, 1-9.

1. Life — Live in the Spirit, ver. 25.
2. Communion — Walk in the Spirit, ver. 16.
3. Fruit — Be led by the Spirit, ver. 18.
Result — Fruit of Spirit.

NATURAL FRUIT.

Works of flesh, Psa. xiv, 3; Rom. ii, 10; Rom. iii, 4.
Grafted Fruit — Spirit's work, Eph. v, 9.
Nine characteristics of this fruit, verses 22, 23.
No "off years" in this fruit bearing, 1 Cor. xv, 58.
Every perfect fruit tree, seven branches, 2 Peter i, 5, 7.
No fruit until grafted in the vine, John xv, 4.
Knife needed for more fruit, John xv, 2.
When a man has deceived himself, all other deceit easy, Gal. vi, 7.
Men sow as they live, upward or downward, Gal. vi, 8.
Be sure you get your "seed" out of God's granary.
"In due season," when the books are opened, Gal. vi, 9.
God makes no mistakes in His book-keeping.
"What shall the harvest be?"

W. G. CARR.

CONVERSATION — BIBLE READING.
James iii.

Titus iii, 2, speak evil of no man.
James iv, 11, of brethren.
Eph. iv, 31, four things.
1 Pet. ii, 1, malice.
Matt. xv, 19.
Isa. vi, 5.
Isa. vi, 7, cure.
Ps. xix, 14, pray for.
Phil. iv, 8, think of good things.
Rom. xii, 9.
1 Pet. i, 22.
Matt. viii, 15.
Phil. i, 27.
Phil. iii, 20.
Col. iv, 6.
Psa. cxli, 3, set a watch.

GEO. A. HALL.

MEEKNESS.
Zeph. ii, 3,

"Seek righteousness." Seven New Testament precepts:
I. "Put on meekness," Col. iii, 12.
II. Follow after meekness, 1 Tim. vi, 2.
III. "Be * * * gentle, showing all meekness unto all men," Titus iii, 2.
IV. "Walk * * * with all lowliness and meekness," Eph. iv, 2.
V. "Receive with meekness the engrafted Word," Jas. i, 21.
VI. Be adorned with "the ornament of a weak and quiet Spirit," 1 Peter iii, 4.
VII. "If a man be overtaken in a fault, restore * * * in the spirit of meekness," Gal. vi, 1.
"Learn of Me, for I am meek and lowly in heart; and ye shall find rest unto your souls," Matt. xi, 29.

Zeph. ii, 3.

Seek meekness. Seven Old Testament promises:
I. "The meek shall increase their joy in the Lord," Isa. xxix, 19.
II. "The meek shall inherit the earth," Ps. xxxvii. 11.
III. "The Lord lifteth up the meek," Ps. clxvii, 6.
IV. The meek shall He teach His way, Ps. xxv, 9.
V. "The meek shall be satisfied," Ps. xxii, 26.
VI. "He shall beautify the meek with salvation," Ps. clxix, 4.

VII. "The meek shall He guide in judgment," Ps. xxv, 9.
"All the promises of God in Him are Yea, and in Him Amen, unto the glory of God by us," 2 Cor. i, 20.

ENDURANCE.

We count them happy which endure, James v, 11.

ENDURE WHAT?

Temptation, James i, 12.
Chastening, Heb. xii, 7.
Hardness, 2 Tim. ii, 3.
Afflictions, 2 Tim. iv, 5; Heb. x, 32.

ENDURE HOW?

As seeing Him who is invisible, Heb. ii, 27.

PROMISE TO THOSE WHO ENDURE.

Shall be saved, Matt. x, 22; xxiv, 13; Mark xiii, 13.

EXAMPLES — ABRAHAM.

Obtained the promise, Heb. vi, 15.

PAUL.

Persecutions, 2 Tim. iii, 11.
All things, 2 Tim. ii, 10.

CHRIST.

Contradiction of sinners, Heb. xii, 3; cross, Heb. xii, 2.

J. E. BROWN.

CHRISTIAN COURAGE.

Based on Deut. xx, 1-8.
The soldier the type, 2 Tim. ii, 4; 1 Tim. i, 18; vi 12.

I. Three things necessary for a soldier.

1. Courage, 2 Chron. xix, 11; Josh. i, 6, 7, 8, 9; x, 24, 25; Ps. xxvii, 14; xxxi, 24.
2. Obedience, Jer. vii, 23; Acts v, 29.
3. Endurance, 2 Tim. ii, 3.
(*a*) Promises Matt. xxiv, 13; Mark xiii, 13.
(*b*) Examples — Moses, Heb. xi, 27; Abraham, vi, 15; Christ, xii, 2, 3; 1 Cor. xiii, 7.

II. Our enemies.
1. Outward, Eph. vi, 12.
2. Inward, Rom. vii, 22, 23.

III. The end — Victory!
1. By faith, 1 John v, 4; 2 Cor. x, 4.
2. Organization, Heb. ii, 10; 1 Cor. ix, 7.
3. Drill, etc., 1 Tim. iv, 7, 8; Eph. vi, 13-17.

REV. JOHN. C. HILL.

CONSECRATION.

A call. 1 Chron. xxxix, 5.
A duty. Ex. xxxii, 29; Num. vi, 12; Rev. i, 6; Ezek. xliii, 26; 2 Cor. vi, 17; Acts xxiv, 16; Rom. xiii, 14; xii, 1; Eph. vi, 11; 2 Cor. v, 15; 1 Cor. vi, 19, 20.
A first duty. See 1 Chron. xxxix, 5; read Matt. vi, 33; 1 Tim. iv, 8; 1 Kings iii, 5-13; Mark x, 29, 30.
Must be willing. See 1 Chron. xxxix, 5; Gen. xxxv, Ps. cx, 3; Jud. v, 2; 1 Chron. xxix, 9; 1 Pet. v, 2.
Must be entire. Matt. vi, 24; Rom. xiii, 14: 1 Cor. x, 31; Col. iii, 16; 2 Tim. ii, 19-22.
Illustrations. Luke v, 11; Ex. xxix, 20.

J. H. ELLIOTT.

PATIENCE.

Rom. v, 3 — Produced by tribulation.
Heb. vi, 12 — Difference between idleness and patience.
Heb. xii, 2 — Let us run with patience.
Heb. x, 30 — Receive the promise.
Luke viii, 15 — Bringing forth fruit with patience.
2 Peter i, 6 — Between temperance and Godliness.
1 Thess. v, 14, 15 — Patient toward all and in all.
1 Peter ii, 20 — When persecuted for well-doing.
Jas. i, 3, 4 — Makes perfect.
Isa. liii, 7 — Christ our example.

W. E. W.

THE HOPE OF THE GOSPEL IS:

I. A good hope, 2 Thess. xi, 16.
II. A blessed hope, Titus ii, 13.
III. A joyful hope, Heb. iii, 6; Rom. v, 3.
IV. A sure, firm hope, Heb. vi, 18.
V. A living or lively hope, 1 Peter i, 3.
VI. A saving hope, Rom. viii, 24.
VII. A glorious hope, Col. i, 27.
VIII. A purifying hope, 1 John iii, 3.

THANKSGIVING.

I. For God's goodness. O give thanks unto the Lord; for he is good; for His mercy endureth forever, 1 Chron. xvi, 34; Ps. cvii, 1; cxviii, 1.

II. For His holiness. Sing unto the Lord, O ye saints of His, and give thanks at the remembrance of His holiness, Ps. xxx, 4; xcvii, 12; cxl, 13.

III. For revealing Himself. Unto thee, O God, do we give thanks, unto to thee do we give thanks; for that thy name is near, thy wondrous works declare, Ps. lxxv, 1; cxxxviii, 2; 1 Thess. ii, 13.

IV. For the gift of His Son. Thanks be unto God for His unspeakable gift, 2 Cor. ix, 15. For God so loved the world that He gave His only begotten Son, that whosoever believeth in Him should not perish, but have everlasting life, John iii, 16; Rom. vi, 23.

V. For a present salvation. Giving thanks unto the Father, which hath made us meet to be partakers of the inheritance of the saints in light; who hath delivered us from the power of darkness, and hath translated us into the kingdom of His dear Son, Col. i, 12, 13; John vi, 47.

VI. For victory. The sting of death is sin; and the strength of sin is the law. But thanks be to God, which giveth us the victory through our Lord Jesus Christ, 1 Cor. xv, 56, 57; Rom. vii, 25.

VII. For everything. In everything give thanks; for this is the will of God in Christ Jesus concerning you, 1 Thess. v, 18. Be careful for nothing; but in everything by prayer and supplication, with thanksgiving, let your requests be made known to God, Phil. iv, 6; Eph. v, 20.

THANKSGIVING AND PRAISE.

1. Things to be thankful for, 1 Thess. v, 8; Isa. xlviii, 20; Ps. xxviii, 7; Luke xv, 24; 1 Peter iv, 12, 13; Dan. vi, 22; 1 Tim. i, 12; Col. i, 12.

2. Ground of thanksgiving. 1 Cor. xv, 57; Gal. vi, 14.

Profit of thanksgiving, Ps. xcii, 1; 1 Tim. iv, 5; Ps. cxix, 54; Luke xvii, 18, 19; Acts xvi, 25, 26.

The fellowship of Praise, Luke xix, 37, 38; Rev. vii, 11, 12.

H. MOREHOUSE.

LET US SING UNTO THE LORD.

O come, let us sing unto the Lord; let us make a joyful noise to the rock of our salvation, Ps. xcv, 1.

Who? Rejoice in the Lord, O ye righteous, for praise is comely for the upright, Ps. xxxiii, 1.

Let everything that hath breath praise the Lord. Praise ye the Lord, Ps. cl, 6.

Of what? They shall abundantly utter the memory of thy great goodness, and shall sing of thy righteousness, Ps. cxlv, 4-7.

Give thanks unto the Lord, call upon His name, make known His deeds among the people.

Sing unto Him, sing psalms unto Him, talk ye of His wondrous works, 1 Chron. xvi, 8, 9.

How? I will pray with the Spirit, and I will pray with the understanding also; I will sing with the Spirit, and I will sing with the understanding also, 1 Cor. xiv, 15.

By Him, therefore, let us offer the sacrifice of praise to God continually, that is, the fruit of our lips, giving thanks to His name, Heb. xiii, 15.

When? Seven times a day do I praise thee, because of thy righteous judgment, Ps. cxix, 164.

I will sing unto the Lord as long as I live; I will sing praise to my God while I have my being, Ps. civ, 33.

May wanderers sing? How shall we sing the Lord's praise in a strange land? Ps. cxxxvii, 4.

The mirth of taberts ceaseth, the noise of them that rejoice endeth, the joy of the harp ceaseth. They shall not drink wine with a song, Isa. xxiv, 8, 9.

H. E. BROWN.

PRAISE.

Who shall praise Him? Isa. xxxviii, 12; xliii, 21; Ps. li, 15; 1 Pet, ii, 9.

Why should we praise God? Ps. xcix, 9; cvi, 1; 1 Pet. 1, 3; Eph. i, 8.

What shall we praise Him for? Ps. xxx, 4; xxxv, 27, 28; lxiii, 3; ci, 1; ciii, 1–4; cxvii, 1, 2; cxxxviii, 1, 2.

How should we praise Him? Ps. xxviii, 7; lxix, 30; lxxxvi, 12; xlvii, 67; xxxiii, 1, 2; Eph. v, 20; Heb. xiii, 15.

Where shall we praise Him? Ps. xxii, 25; lvii, 9; c, 4; Heb. ii, 12; 2 Cor. iii, 17.

When shall we praise Him? 1 Chron. xxiii, 30; Ps. cxix, 62–64; cxiii, 2; xcii, 12; xlii, 4; lxxi, 15; xxxiv, 1.

How long shall we praise Him? Ps. civ, 33; lxi, 8.

"And after these things I heard a great voice of much people in heaven saying, Alleluia, Salvation and glory, and honor and power unto the Lord our God."

PLINY FRY.

PRAISE TO GOD.

When to praise, 1 Chron. xxiii, 30; Ps. cxix, 62, 164; cxiv, 2; xcvi, 1, 2; xlii, 4.

What to praise for, Ps. xxx, 4; xxxv, 28; lvi, 10; lxiii, 3; lxxi, 15; xcii, 1, 2; ci, 1; cxvii; cxxxviii, 2;

Where to praise, Ps. xxii, 25; xlii, 4; lvii, 9; xxxiv, 1.

How to praise, Ps. xxxiii, 2, 3; xlvii, 6, 7; lxix, 30; lxxxvi, 12; cxix, 7; cxxxviii, 1.

Why to praise, Ps. xcix, 3; cvi, 1.

Who shall praise, Ps. lxvii, 3; Isa. xxxviii, 19.

How long to praise, Ps. civ, 33; lxi, 8. — *Y. M. C. A. Watchman.*

THE FLESH AND THE SPIRIT.

I BELIEVE the Scriptures teach that the old man and the new are together in the believer, and contrary, the one to the other, to the end of the life on earth. I believe this teaching, when rightly understood, avails toward a walk of sweet, strong and uninterrupted service and communion.

I wish, therefore, to read upon "The Flesh" and "The Spirit," with direct reference to the privilege of a daily and unbroken fellowship with God, and an unremitting and effective service in the name of Christ.

I. Definition: The word "flesh" has various shades of meaning. Without attempting an exhaustive analysis, it will be sufficient for my purpose to notice:

1. "The flesh," as a phrase, often means the race, man, men (Ps. lxv, 2; Isa. xl, 5, 6; Matt. xxiv, 22; Rom. iii, 20).

2. It accordingly is used for human nature as sinless (John i, 4; Rom. i, 3; compare Luke i, 35).

3. Though it came specially and most frequently to mean human nature as sinful (Rom. vii, 18).

4. In "the flesh," or human nature as affected by sin, the Scripture is careful to include the whole man, not merely the bodily lusts and appetites, but also (*a*) the mind, with its desires, understanding, and judgment; (*b*) the will, and (*c*) the soul, with its natural and religious instincts. Accordingly, refined, cultured, poetic, philosophic and moral human nature is as truly of "the flesh" as degraded and ignorant human nature, sunken in vice (Matt. xvi, 17; John i, 13; viii, 15, 43, 47; Rom. iv, 1; 1 Cor. ii, 14; i, 26; iii, 1–4; 2 Cor. i, 17; vii, 1; x, 2; Gal. iii, 3; Phil. iii, 3–7; Eph. ii, 1–3; Rom. vi, 6; Eph. iv, 22; Col. iii, 5–7).

5. Other Scripture names of "the flesh" are "the old man" (Rom. vi, 6); "nature" (Eph. ii, 3; compare 2 Peter i, 4); "the evil man" or "heart" (Matt. xv, 18, 19; xii, 33–35); "the natural (soulish) man" (1 Cor. ii, 11–14; compare 1 Cor. xv, 44–46; James iii, 15; Jude 19).

II. The flesh incapable of improvement. In regeneration "the flesh" is not changed over into the Spirit, or in any way improved. To the very end it is still "the flesh" in all its varied and irremediable hostility to God (John iii, 3–8; Rom. viii, 7; 1 Cor. ix, 24–27). See, also, the Biblical history of the race.

III. Regeneration a new creation — the conflict. By the new or second birth, a new "man" is created; a new and spiritual "nature" is possessed; and the believer, as a partaker of the Divine nature, has as distinct and positive and holy tendencies toward all sin. The man, or the "I" of the believer, can walk or act in either nature. When he acts in his flesh, he sins; when in the Spirit, he pleases God. The man, distinct, of course, from both natures (see Rom. vii), can now, therefore, identify himself with which ever he choose, and can act either in and according to "the flesh," or in and according to "the Spirit."

There is, therefore, of necessity, an irrepressible conflict, which must continue so long as we are in this body of humiliation (John iii, 3–8; i, 13; 1 Peter i, 27; ii, 3; 2 Peter i, 4; 1 John iii, 9; 2 Cor. v, 14–17).

The whole epistle to the Galatians is on this theme; but notice particularly: Gal. iv, 28–31; v, 16–25; Gal. vi, 7, 8; "His flesh." Every man has his own variety of flesh; but there is no difference as to its essential character or result (Gal. vi, 12–15; Eph. ii, 10; iv, 22–24; Phil. iii, 20, 21).

IV. The conflict to be experimentally a victory. In this conflict between the flesh and the Spirit, the Word of God calls the believer to be constantly setting aside the flesh and acting in the Spirit. The normal, and, indeed, only Christian experience, as set forth in the Scriptures (however rare among those who are really Christians), is one of habitually enjoying the peace that passeth all understanding, constantly winning the victory over the world, the flesh, and the devil, and always ministering with the demonstration and power of the Spirit. There is need to insist, and so I repeat, that this experience of abiding in Christ and walking in the Spirit, is not merely opened to us as a privilege, but is both expected of us and urged upon us that we may glorify God (Gen. v, 21–24; Num. xiii, 25; xiv, 10; Josh. i, 1–10; John xiv, 22–27; xv, 3–8; xvi, 33; Rom. vi–viii; 1 Cor. ix, 24–27; 2 Cor. vi, 14; vii, 1; x, 1–6; Eph. v, 18; vi, 16–18; Phil. iii, 8–14; iv, 6, 7, 13, 19; Col. ii, 6–10; iii, 1–5, 15–17; 1 Thess. v, 4–11; 2 Tim. i, 7; ii, 19–21; iii, 16, 17; Heb. xiii, 20, 21; 1 John ii, 14, 27, 28; iv, 4; v, 4; Jude 20–25; Rev. ii, 7, 11, 17, 26–29; iii, 5, 10–13, 19–22).

From these Scriptures it is plain that every discovery in the believer of the character of the flesh, whether we come upon it in the Bible or in our own experience, has quite another mission than discouragement. Instead, every such fresh occasion to confess what God says, and we know that we are, is a new opportunity to learn:

1. The grace that has nevertheless put the power of victory into our hands. 2. The value that God puts upon the death and everlasting priesthood of Christ, since we are, notwithstanding the existence of the flesh, without condemnation (Rom. viii, 1-3). 3. The pressing necessity we are under, if we would glorify God or satisfy Christ (Rom. viii, 4; John xv, 8-11, 16; xvii, 9-21; 2 Thess. i, 11, 12), to yield ourselves to the Holy Spirit in unreserved subjection (Rom. viii, 12, 14; 2 Tim. 11-21; iii, 16, 17; Eph. iv, 30; v, 8, 9, 14-21, especially verse 18). 4. The character and power (2 Tim. i, 7) of the nature in which we have been partakers (2 Peter i, 4), or what it means experimentally to say I am born of God (John i, 12, 13; 2 Cor. vi, 14; vii, 1).

Permit, in closing, four suggestions to those who may be asking how they may practically keep themselves in the love of God, the victory over the flesh and the power of the Spirit.

1. Since both duty and privilege call every believer to a daily experience of the walk in Spirit, and with God, set the heart upon possessing it. To say because the flesh is in us, "I cannot" keep my body under; "I cannot" overcome the world, and the flesh, and the devil, but must be content with an experience that makes life something beside Christ (Phil. i, 21), is not only faithless, it is an unutterable libel upon grace. Nothing in all the world should have such a charm, and can have such irresistable attraction to all who are in Christ, as this walk with God in knowing Christ Jesus, our Lord (Phil. iii, 8-14).

2. Any relation must be uninterrupted in order to allow its experience to be permanent. Unless I see and know that Christ and the Holy Spirit are assuredly and ceaselessly maintaining my relations with God, intact and uninterrupted, I may be driven any moment (1) from my Father's side by the question, whether I am a child; (2) from appealing to Christ by the thought that possibly my union with Him is broken, and a divorce decreed, and from drawing upon the Holy Spirit in present need by the suggestion that He has left me, being grieved away; (3) we need, therefore, continually to give affectionate heed in our spirits to the unimpeachable witness of the Holy Spirit by the Scriptures; (1) to the value of the death of Christ as an eternal redemption perfecting us forever; (2) to the ceaseless exercise of the priesthood of Christ as our advocate; (3) to the abiding presence in us of the Holy Spirit whom, even when we greatly grieve, we cannot grieve away; and (4) to our never lapsing sonship and access as born of God. Every one may say, giving such heed to the witness of the Spirit, I shall be able unceasingly to identify myself, first, with Christ upon the cross, as having died in Him (Gal. ii, 19, 20); second, with the living

Christ in glory as risen in Him (Eph. i, 3, ; ii, 4–6, 10; Col. ii, 6, 7; iii, 1–5); third, with the Holy Spirit in me, taking His side in every controversy He has with my flesh, or the world, or the devil (Rom. viii, 14; Gal. v, 18); and fourth, with my new nature, walking "after," or "in" my Spirit instead of my flesh (2 Tim. i, 7; Rom. viii, 4–6; Gal. v, 16, 22–25).

3. Mark the fact that this identification is not theoretic, but practical. Receiving the testimony that God so identifies me, I am now to practically live out the union. Therefore, I really and fully identify myself with Christ on the cross, only as self is not allowed to speak when deciding what I shall do, any more than dead men are allowed to vote when the nation makes a decision. I really and fully identify myself with the Holy Spirit only as I yield Him instant and unreserved obedience. I really and fully identify myself with my new nature only as what I am by nature is entirely hidden and inactive, and what I am by grace, both shines without the darkening of any shadow, and acts without any restraint.

4. With such a standard of Christian life, and an open door to such an experience, there is no one who can escape for a moment the sense of short coming. Hence, uninterrupted communion involves, also, uninterrupted searching and believing, confession both of the sin in me, and the forgiveness in Christ. The soul that is walking through a desert "in the light" of the most Holy Place, standing before the unclouded shining of the glory of God upon the mercy seat, sees both His own flesh and the sprinkled blood as God sees them. The walk with God, therefore, says of no moment, "in it I have not sinned," but every moment, and immediately upon the slightest sense of something wrong, not only "Father, I have sinned," but also with humbled joy and exultant praise, "the blood of Jesus Christ cleanseth from all sin." There is no secret of communion which I think the church so much needs to hear as that God cannot be fully pleased with any confession of sin that is not at the same instant accompanied by a confession of Christ and His faithfulness, and righteousness. Study 1 John ii, 2. Finally, Eph. iii, 14, 21. Amen.

THE NEW NATURES.

The first Adam was Lord over creation, Gen. i, 26; ii, 20. The second Adam was driven off into the wilderness among the wild beasts, Mark i, 12, 13. Brought sin into the world, Gen. ii, 17; iii, 6. Was made sin for us, 2 Cor. v, 21. Brought death, Rom. v, 12. Brought life, John xi, 25. Gen. iii chap. tells how we lost life. John iii chap. tells how we find life. First Adam fell in a garden. Second Adam rose in a garden. Was disobedient unto death, Gen. ii, 17. Was obedient unto death, Phil. ii, 8. Was a living soul, 1 Cor. xv, 45. Was a quickened Spirit, 1 Cor. xv, 45. Was of the earth, earthy, 1 Cor. xv, 47. Was the Lord from heaven, 1 Cor. xv, 47. Was tempted by his bride, Gen. iii, 12. Came for a bride, Rev. xix, 7-9. Charged his guilt upon God, Gen. iii, 12. Bare our sins in his own body, 1 Peter ii, 24. Was driven from the Tree of Life, Gen. iii, 22-24. Has transplanted the Tree of Life into the midst of his paradise, Rev. xxii, 2. If the first Adam, on account of one sin, was driven out of a garden on earth, how can a man with many sins hope to enter the paradise above? All men must get out of the first Adam into the second Adam in order to enter heaven. This is done only through the cross of Christ.

THE OLD MAN AND THE NEW.

The flesh and the spirit both in the Christian are contrary, the one to the other.

Read Cruden (unabridged) upon the words "flesh" and "spirit." In Scripture, the word flesh often means man, Ps. lxv, 2; Isa. xl, 5, 6; Matt. xxiv, 22; Rom. iii, 20; 1 Cor. i, 29. Hence it came to be used for what is characteristic of man — for human nature as affected by sin, including the mind, soul, will, understanding, judgment, religious instincts, affection and appetites — the whole sinful man, Matt. xvi, 17: John i, 13; viii, 15, 43, 47: vi. 63; 1 Cor. ii, 14; i, 26; iii, 1-4: Rom. iv, 1; 2 Cor. i, 17; vii, 1; x, 2: Gal. iii, 3; Phil. iii, 3-7; Eph. ii, 1-3; Rom. vi, 6; Eph. iv, 22; Col. iii, 5-9.

In regeneration the old man is not changed over into the new, or in any way improved. To the end of the life on earth, flesh is still flesh in all its varied hostility to God. By the new birth, a new man, a spiritual or Divine nature is superadded.

Of necessity there is an irrepressible conflict. But it is the believer's privilege habitually to set aside and overcome the flesh, and walking in the Spirit to continually glorify God. Consequently, every discovery in the Bible, or his experience of the character of the flesh, instead of producing discouragement should only lead to new confession before God, new understanding of the value of the death and ever living priesthood of Christ, and deeper appreciation of the power of the Holy Spirit, who is dwelling in him. And we shall know the joy and victory of the walk with God in the measure we practically identify ourselves with Christ, and yield ourselves to be led by the Spirit, John iii, 3–8; 1 Pet. 1, 22; ii, 3; Rom. vi–viii; Eph. ii, 5, 10; iv, 14; Gal. v, 3–26; vi, 7, 8, 15; 2 Cor. v, 17; Col. iii, 10–17; 2 Pet. i, 4–11; 1 Cor. ix, 24–27; Gal. ii, 19, 20; Eph. iv, 30; v, 18; vi, 10–18; John xv, 3–8; Phil. iii, 3, 8–14; iv, 6, 7, 13; 1 John v, 4; ii, 27, 28.

CHARLES M. WHITTELSEY.

SEVEN THINGS THE BELIEVER SHOULD REMEMBER ABOUT THE FLESH.

1. That he is under no obligation to it. We are debtors not to the flesh, Rom. viii, 12; viii, 8; Gal. vi, 8; Rom. viii, 6; margin, Rom. vii, 25; viii, 7, margin.

2. That he must not make it his companion. Who walk not after the flesh, Rom. viii, 4; Eph. iv, 19; Phil. iii, 19; Gen. xiii, 9.

3. That he must not make any allowance for it. Make no provision for the flesh, Rom. xiii, 14.

4. He must not give it an opportunity to show itself. Use not liberty for an occasion to the flesh, Gal. v, 13.

5. That he must not trust it under any circumstances. For we have no confidence in the flesh, Phil. iii, 3.

6. That he must not expect any good thing from it. In my flesh dwelleth no good thing, Rom. vii, 18; it is sinful, Rom. viii, 3; unclean, Gal. v, 19; filthy, 2 Cor. vii, 1; corrupt, Gen. vi, 12; Job xiv, 4.

7. He must look upon it as a dead thing. And they that are Christ's have crucified the flesh, Gal. v, 24; Rom. vii, 24. May the Lord Jesus grant that we may all through the Spirit mortify the deeds of the body, Rom. viii, 13; and not fulfill the lust of the flesh, Gal. v, 16.

R. A. ORR.

THE THREEFOLD CONFLICT OF THE CHRISTIAN.

1. The old against the new nature, Rom. vii, 18–25.

2. The flesh against the Holy Spirit, Gal. v, 16, 17, etc.

3. The soul against evil spirits, Eph. vi, 10–17.

REV. JOHN C. HILL.

DAILY.

WHAT WE SHOULD DO DAILY.

I. Praise. Daily shall he praised, Ps. lxxii, 15. Blessed be the Lord who daily loadeth us with benefits, even the God of our salvation, Ps. lxviii, 19.

II. Pray. Be merciful unto me, O Lord, for I cry unto Thee daily, Ps. lxxxvi, 3. Give us this day our daily bread, Matt. vi, 11.

III. Read God's Word. These were more noble than those in Thessalonica, in that they received the Word with all readiness, and searched the Scriptures daily, whether these things were so, Acts xvii, 11 ; 2 Tim. iii, 14–17 ; 2 Pet. i, 12.

IV. Watch. Blessed is the man that heareth Me, watching daily at My gates, waiting at the posts of My doors, Prov. viii, 34. Watch and pray, that ye enter not into temptation, Matt. xxvi, 41; Mark xiii, 33–37.

V. Fight. Be merciful unto me, O God; for man would swallow me up: He, fighting daily, oppresseth me. Mine enemies [margin, observers] would daily swallow me up, Ps. lvi, 1, 2. Fight the good fight of faith, 1 Tim. vi, 12.

VI. Exhort. Exhort one another daily, while it is called To-day, Heb. iii, 13. And they, continuing daily with one accord in the temple, and breaking bread from house to house, did eat their meat with gladness and singleness of heart, praising God and having favor with all the people. And the Lord added to the church daily such as should be saved, Acts ii, 46, 47.

VII. Take the cross. If any man will come after me, let him deny himself, and take up his cross daily and follow me, Luke ix, 23 ; 1 Cor. i, 18. — *The Truth.*

CONTRASTS BETWEEN CHRISTIANS AND THE WORLD.

Servants of sin — Rom. vi, 16, 23.
Entangled — Gal. v, 1.
Sinners — Rom. iii, 23.
Children of the devil — John viii, 44.
Prodigal away from home — Luke xv, 13, 14.
Sold under sin — Rom. vii, 14.
Led captive by the devil — 2 Tim. ii, 26.
Wicked flee — Prov. xxviii, 1.
Shall perish — Luke xiii, 3.
Jesus "knows not" — Matt. xxv, 12.
Depart — left hand — Matt. xxv, 41, 46.

Servants of God — 1 Peter ii, 15, 16.
Free — Rom. vi, 22.
Saints — 1 Cor. i, 2.
Children of God, Gal. iv, 3-7.
Child at home — Luke xv, 20-24.
Bought with a price — 1 Cor. vi, 20.
Led by the Spirit — Rom. viii, 14.
Righteous bold — Prov. xxviii, 1.
Shall never perish — John x, 25.
Jesus knows His sheep — John x, 27.
Come — right hand — Matt. xxv, 31, 34.

GEO. A. HALL.

I. THE DISCIPLES' WATCH.

Though the garden and the agony are forever past for the Lord of Glory, yet by the Holy Ghost Christ still travails in the redemption of souls. In such travail it is our duty to be sharers, having fellowship with the sufferings of Christ. There are times in the history of the church and in the lives of Christians, when the destiny of souls is hanging in awful suspense. "Watch with me," Christ seemed to say again. Prayer and tears and agonizing intercessions are demanded on the part of Christians. Woe to the disciple who is sleeping at such a moment! "What, could ye not watch with me one hour?" is the Master's astonished question to such an one; and yet here is one of the most serious perils of Christians — that they may be careless and drowsy in these critical hours, and that souls may fail of life eternal through their indifference. The travail of Christ's soul is still going on as the Spirit strives with souls. Like Paul, we must be able to say: "My little children, of whom I travail in birth again until Christ be formed in you." The suffering of Christ for sinners must still go on in us, His disciples, since we are enjoined to "fill up that which is behind of the afflictions of Christ." Happy is the Christian who has so watched and wept with souls, that like Paul, he can repeat the Master's command, because he repeated the Master's intercessions, saying: "Watch, and remember that by the space of three years, I ceased not to warn every one, night and day, with tears," Acts xx, 31.

II. THE STEWARD'S WATCH.

Now that Christ has gone away for awhile, He has left us in charge of His house and of His goods. As the keepers of God's house, the church of Jesus Christ, the utmost vigilance is demanded against those enemies that are ever ready to steal in secretly. Hence, as the Master of the house went away, "He commanded the porter to watch." Mark xiii, 34. As guardians of "the faith once delivered to the saints," and which the devil is always seeking to destroy, the command is to us: "Watch ye, stand fast in the faith," 1 Cor. xvi, 13. Prayer is our all powerful defence against the foe, but it must be accompanied with vigilance. Hence the injunction: "Watch unto prayer," 1 Peter iv, 7; and "Praying always with all prayer and supplication in the Spirit, and watching thereunto with all perseverance," etc.. Eph. vi, 18; also see Col. iv, 2, and Matt. xxvi, 41. As Christ's stewards, we are not only the keepers of His house, and the keepers of the faith, but we are keepers of souls. Hence the saying: "Obey them that have the rule over you, and submit yourselves; for they watch for your souls as they that must give account," Heb. xii, 17.

III. THE SENTINEL'S WATCH.

Rev. xvi, 15—An eminent Jewish writer tells us how, on the watch tower of the temple, a sentinel was stationed to catch the first rays of the sunrise, and to give the signal to those below, that the morning service might begin. So Christians are commanded to watch for the day-dawn of Christ's second advent. This injunction is one of the most solemn and constant in Scripture: "Watch, therefore; for ye know not what hour your Lord doth come," Matt. xxiv, 42; xxv, 13; Luke xxi, 36. Because we know not the day nor hour of our Lord's return, we are to be always waiting for Him, and looking for the signs of His coming. Woe to that servant who shall be beguiled into sleep, because some have made mistakes in regard to times and seasons! The pious John Cox, of England, says: "Because some have made mistakes in fixing dates, let us beware of saying: 'My Lord delayeth His coming.'" Very solemn are the words of God in Ezekiel xii, 22, 28. And the saintly Fletcher of Madely, said, a hundred years ago: "I know many have been grossly mistaken as to the years, but because they were rash, shall we be stupid? Because they said 'to-day,' shall we say 'never?'" The true posture of the Christian is to have his hand always on the plow, occupying till Christ come; and his eye upon the heavens watching for His appearing. Blessed is the man who can say, with David: "My soul waiteth for the Lord more than they that watch for the morning. I say more than they that watch for the morning." If any count it fanatical or eccentric to talk thus about watching; if any say it may have been a practical duty for the early Christians, but cannot be such for us, answer by repeating the Master's own words: "What I say unto you I say unto all, Watch," Mark xiii, 37. The uncertainty of the hour of the Lord's return is especially designed to beget this spirit of watchfulness in the church of all ages. The time of Christ's absence is always spoken of as the night time, and His coming as that of a "thief in the night;" but the hour is absolutely uncertain. "Watch ye, therefore; for ye know not when the Master of the house cometh, at even, at midnight, at cock crowing, or in the morning; lest coming suddenly He find you sleeping," Mark viii, 35. Edersheim, in his work on the Jewish temple, says that if the temple watchmen were caught sleeping at their posts at night, the penalty was that their garments should be stripped from them and burned, in token of their degradation. Perhaps this explains Christ's solemn words in Rev. xvi, 15: "Behold, I come as a thief. Blessed is he that watcheth, and keepeth his garments."

WATCHFULNESS.

1. Define soberness, vigilance, 1 Pet. v, 8. Faithfulness to one's own interest, Rev. ii, 10.

2. Who are to be watchful? The Christian. Those building upon the foundation, Jesus Christ, 1 Cor. iii, 10. Young men exhorted, see 1 Tim. iv, 12. Word, conversation, charity, etc., 1 Tim. iv 16. Take heed to thyself, not your neighbor.

3. Why are Christians to be watchful? 1 Pet. v, 8, Devil roaring lion. 2 Cor. xi, 14, Satan angel of light. 1 Tim. iv, 16, To save thyself and others.

4. What demands watchfulness? Prov. iv, 23. Thy heart. My lips and tongue, Psa. xxxiv, 13; John xv, 10. Keeping Christ's commandments. Watchfulness against *entering* into temptation, Matt. xxvi, 41. Watching for Christ's coming, Matt. xxiv, 42–44; Matt. xxv, 1–13; Mark xiii, 32–37.

5. Where is the Christian to be watchful? Did you ever watch a deceitful person? Did the place or a position you may have placed them in cause you to wholly relax your vigilance when your interests were at stake? Jer. xvii, 9, The heart is deceitful.

6. When is the Christian to be watchful? Luke viii, 13, Time of temptation. Luke xxi, 36 (New Version), Every season.

7. How shall the Christian watch? Mark xiv, 38, With prayer. Eph. vi, 18, With perseverance. Ezek. iii, 17, 21, Lifting up warning voice. Matt. xxvi, 40, Watch with me (Christ). "For without me ye can do nothing," John xv, 5.

WATCHWORDS OF SCRIPTURE.

One of the most frequent and most solemn injunctions of Scripture is contained in the single word "watch;" and a careful study of the matter will indicate that it is a word which does not call our attention in one direction merely, or fix our eye upon any single point. It is a word which indicates that we must not only be expectant, looking earnestly forward to the things that are to come, but circumspect, looking diligently about us on every side, to guard against the manifold perils that beset us. Recall some of these solemn injunctions;

"Watch with me," Matt. xxvi, 38.
"Watch and pray," Matt. xxvi, 41.
"Watch thou in all things," 2 Tim. iv, 5.
"Watch ye stand fast in faith," 1 Cor. xvi, 13.
"Watch and be sober," 1 Thess. v, 6.
"Watch unto prayer," 1 Peter iv, 7.
"Watch, therefore, for ye know not what hour your Lord doth come," Matt. xxiv, 42.

PRAYER.
Luke xi, 11.

I. What it is to pray, Matt. xxvi, 39; Eph. iii, 14; Ps. xcv, 6, 7; 1 Kings viii, 22; Ps. xxviii, 2; v, 3; iv, 1; Lam. iii, 41; 1 Sam. i, 12–18; Ps. xxvii, 7; 2 Chron. xxxii, 20; Ps. xl, 1; Job viii, 5; Ps. lxii, 1, 8; cxvi, 4, 5; Ex. xxxiv, 5–7; Rom. x, 13; Matt. vii, 7, 8; vi, 6; Luke ix, 28, 29; Heb. x, 22.

II. Why should I pray? Matt. vii, 8; Ps. lxv, 1–4; cxvi, 1, 2; 1 John v, 14, 15; Ps. lxxii, 12; James i, 5; 1 Kings viii, 38; Jer. xvii, 9; 1 Pet. iv, 7; John xv, 5; Phil. iv, 12, 13, compare 6, 7; Heb. iv, 14–16.

III. To whom I should pray, Matt. vi, 9; Acts vii, 59.

IV. In and through whom, Eph. ii, 18; Heb. x, 19–22; John xiv, 13, 14; Matt. xviii, 19, 20.

V. In and by whom, Zech. xii, 10; Rom. viii, 15, 26; Eph. ii, 18; vi, 18; Jude 20.

VI. With what arguments, Gen. xxxii, 9–12; Ex. xxxii, 11–13; 1 Kings viii, 26; Ps. cxix, 49; Dan. ix, 4, 8, 9, 16–21; Ps. li, 1; cxliii, 1; 1 John i, 9; Acts iv, 30; Ps. lxxix, 9; John xii, 28; 2 Thess. i, 11, 22; iii, 1.

VII. After what manner, 1 Cor. xiv, 14, 15; Matt. vi, 6; xiv, 23; Acts xvi, 3; iii, 1; 1 Thess. v, 17 (*i. e.*, "without omission," observing one's hours of prayer regularly); 1 Peter iii, 7; 1 Tim. ii, 8; 2 Chron. vii, 14; James iv, 3, 4; John xv, 16; Prov.

xv, 18; John ix, 30, 31; James v, 16; Heb. vii, 25; Matt. vi, 9; vii, 9–11; Dan. ii, 17–23; Ps. ciii, 10–14; Luke xxii, 42; John xvii, 23, 25, 26; Matt. xxi, 22; Heb. xi, 6; Jas. i, 6; v, 15; John xv, 7; Ps. lvi, 9; Rom. viii, 32; Gen. xxxii, 26; Luke xviii, 1-7; Jas, v, 16, 17; Jer. xxix, 12, 13; Ps. xxxvii, 3–7; Neh. i, 4–17; Matt. xvii, 21; Ps. xvii, 1; cxlv, 19; Heb. x, 22; Matt. vi, 5–8; Ecc. v, 2; Ps. xl, 1; Eph. vi, 18; Ps. lxii, 5; Col. iv, 2; Phil. iv, 6; 1 Thess. v, 18; Ex. xxx, 7, 8, 34–38; Ps. cxli, 2; Luke, i, 10; Rev. v, 8; viii, 3, 4.

VIII. At what times, Ps. v, 3; cxix, 147; lv, 16, 17; Dan. vi, 10; 1 Thess. iii, 10; 1 Tim. v, 5; Acts xii, 5; Rom. xii, 12; 1 Thess. v, 17 (see above); Col. i, 3; iv, 2; John vi, 11; 1 Tim. iv, 5; 1 Cor. x, 13; compare Matt. vi, 13; Ps. i, 15; xci, 14–16; Jas. i, 5; Phil. iv, 6.

IX. For what, Matt. vi, 9–13; John xv, 11; Eph. i, 16–19; iii, 14–21; Col. i, 9–14; 1 Tim. ii, 1–3; Gen. xvii, 18, 20; Matt. xv, 21–28; Isa. xxxviii, 1-5; Isa. xxxix; Jas. v, 15; Matt. xix, 13–15; Job xlii, 8; Rom. x, 1; Matt. v, 44; Luke iv, 5–13; Matt. ix, 2; xvii, 16, 17; Ps. xxvii, 11; Ex. xxxi, 3–6; 2 Chron. i, 7–12, 1 Thess. iii, 11–13; 2 Thess. i, 11, 12; ii, 16, 17; iii, 1, 5; Eph. vi, 18–20, 23, 24; 2 Peter i, 2; Rev. xxii, 20, 21.

X. Suggestions for home study. Review, looking up all the references. "Beginning at Genesis, trace out the account of every prayer, and the answer; consider the circumstances under which these prayers were made; the great variety of blessings desired, and the readiness with which God responded. It is an exercise in which I have found peculiar delight."—Extract from letter of C. H. Payson, in "All for Christ," published by American Tract Society.

Collect all the teaching about prayer, under appropriate headings. Make a "prayer-book" for yourself, letting it grow by every day's reading, that you may appeal to it from time to time for refreshment, direction and quickening, when consciously weak, and if ever discouraged or in any darkness.

Add at the back of the book a record of personal answers to prayer, Ps. cxi, 2, 4.

Keep on a loose slip of paper, in the front of your book, easily placed before your eyes when you kneel, the names of persons you would remember, the besetting sins you discover in your life, any Christ-likeness not yet developed in you, etc., etc., that you may pray for definite things, and may recognize the answers, watching thereunto with all perseverance and supplication for all saints and for me.

CHAS. M. WHITTELSEY.

ACCEPTABLE PRAYER.

The impenitent unsaved person cannot offer acceptable prayer; see Prov. xv, 8; xxviii, 9. There is the promise of salvation to the penitent person only; all the promises otherwise are to the saved — the children. As rebels we must first lay down our arms and surrender unconditionally; then our prayers will be regarded favorably. The following are elements of acceptable prayer:

1. Confessing, Ps. lxvi, 18; 1 John i, 6; If as children, we sin, our first duty is to make acknowledgement of the same and ask God's forgiveness, else communion is interrupted.

2. Thanksgiving, 1 Tim. ii, 1; Phil. iv, 6; We should cultivate more than we do the Spirit of thankfulness.

3. Adoration, Matt. vi, 9; Ps. xcv, 6, 7; man never rises above the object of his worship, hence he should worship the living and true God as the only being above him and therefore worthy of worship.

4. Supplication, Ps. vi, 9; Luke xi, 5–13; the ground of our asking is our need, there is no inopportune time with God. He is a liberal giver, He is a willing giver. In the gift of the Holy Spirit we have the indispensable gift.

5. *Submission*, Rom. viii, 26, 27; 1 John v, 13, 14. God cannot grant us that which is not in accordance with His will. He is not a capricious being. His ways are past finding out. Therefore should we be submissive to the Holy Spirit, that He may guide and help us to know what is the will of God.

6. *Intercession*, John xvi, 23, 24; xiv, 6. The method of approach is to the Father by the Son, through the Holy Spirit. God has in all ages found it necessary to bend Himself to the comprehension of finite man, else he could not know the infinite. Hence Christ became a man.

L. W. MUNHALL.

PRAYER.

What is prayer? Phil. iv, 6.
Its natural divisions:
(a) Invocation, 1 Tim. i, 2.
(b) Adoration, Psa. cxiii.
(c) Confession, Psa. li, 4.
(d) Thanksgiving, Psa. ciii.
(e) Petition, Psa. iv, 1.

Postures in prayer: Standing, 1 Kings viii, 22; Mark xi, 25. Kneeling, Psa. xcv, 6; 2 Chron. vi, 13; Luke xxii, 41; Acts xx, 36. Prostrate, Matt. xxvi, 39; 1 Tim. ii, 8; Num. xvi, 22. Lifting up hands, Ps. xxviii, 2; Lamentations ii, 19; 1 Tim. ii, 8; Isa. i, 15. Sitting, 2 Sam. vii, 18.

Places for prayer, 1 Tim. ii, 8.
Time, Psa. lv, 17; 1 Tim. v, 5; Psa. lxxxviii, 1.
Kinds of prayer.
1. Audible, 1 Kings viii, 22-30; Psa. lv, 17.
2. Secret, Matt. vi, 6, 7; Luke v, 16.
3. Mental, 1 Sam. i, 12-17.
4. Social, Matt. xviii, 19.

Its necessity, Heb. iv, 16; Ezekiel xxxvi, 37. A command, Isa. lv, 6; Matt. vii, 7; Phil. iv, 6.

To whom should be addressed.
1. Father, Matt. vi, 6-9; Psa. v, 2.
2. Son, Luke xxiii, 42; Acts vii, 59.
3. Holy Spirit, Eph. ii, 18.

The nature of acceptable prayer.
1. It must be in faith, Heb. xi, 6; Jas. i, 6, 7.
2. It must be with confession and repentance, Dan. ix, 3-24.
3. It must be in obedience, John ix, 31; 1 John iii, 22.
4. It must be in submission, Luke xxii, 42.
5. It must be in humility, 2 Chron. vii, 14; xxxiii, 12.
6. It must be in a forgiving spirit, Matt. vi, 12; Mark xi, 25.
7. It must be importunate, Luke xi, 8.
8. It must be with perseverance, Eph. vi, 18.
9. It must plead the promises, Psa. cxix, 49.

How to pray aright, Rom. viii, 26, 27.

Assurance of answer, Matt. xviii, 19; vi, 8, 25, 33.
1. As to spiritual blessing, John xiv, 13-18.
2. As to temporal blessing, Luke xviii, 38; Matt. vi, 25.

Examples, Dan. ix, 20; Acts x, 4; Luke xxiii, 42; David; Psa. xviii, 6; Jonah ii, 2, 10; Elisha; 2 Kings iv, 33-35; Solomon; 1 Kings iii, 9, 12.

Promises, Matt. vii, 7, 8; Jer. xxix, 12; Isa. lviii, 9.

CONDITIONS OF PREVAILING PRAYER.

Obedience, 1 John iii, 22: "Whatsover we ask, we receive of Him, because we keep His commandments, and do those things that are pleasing in His sight."

Faith, Matt. xxi, 22: "All things whatsoever ye shall ask in prayer, believing, ye shall receive."

Name of Christ, John xiv, 13: "Whatsover ye shall ask in My name, that will I do, that the Father may be glorified in the Son."

Abiding in Christ, John xv, 7: "If ye abide in Me, and My words abide in you, ye shall ask what ye will, and it shall be done unto you."

Conformity with God's will, 1 John v, 14: "This is the confidence that we have in Him, that, if we ask anything according to His will, He heareth us."

Help of the Spirit, Rom. viii, 26: "The Spirit also helpeth our infirmities; for we know not what we should pray for as we ought; but the Spirit itself maketh intercession for us with groanings which cannot be uttered."

H. E. BROWN.

HELPS TO PREVAILING PRAYER.

Earnestness. James v, 16: "The effectual fervent prayer of a righteous man availeth much."

Perseverance, Luke xviii, 4–8: "Shall not God avenge His own elect, which cry day and night unto Him, though He bear long with them?" "I tell you that He will avenge them speedily."

Union for one object, Matt. xviii, 19: "If two of you shall agree on earth as touching anything that they shall ask, it shall be done for them of My Father which is in heaven."

Fasting, Matt. xvii, 21: "This kind goeth not out but by prayer and fasting."

Large requests. Psa. lxxxi, 10: "Open thy mouth wide, and I will fill it."

Submission, Matt. xxvi, 39: "Nevertheless, not as I will, but as thou wilt."

H. E. BROWN.

ELEMENTS OF EFFECTUAL PRAYER.

1. To the Father, John xvi, 23, 24.
2. In the name of Jesus, John xiv, 13, 14: xvi, 23, 24.
3. In faith, James i, 6; Mark xi, 24; 1 Tim. ii, 8.
4. In communion, John xv, 7.
5. In obedience, 1 John iii, 22.
6. In submission, 1 John v, 14, 15; James iv, 7; Matt. xxvi, 39–42.
7. In perseverance, Col. iv, 2; Luke xviii, 1; Eph. vi, 18.
8. In humility, James iv, 10.
9. With a forgiving spirit, Matt. v, 23, 24 (1 Peter iii, 7); Mark xi, 25, 26; Eph. iv, 32.
10. With thanksgiving. Phil. iv, 6.
11. With fruitfulness, John xv, 16.
12. With belief that we have the petitions, Mark xi. 24, R. V.; 1 John v, 14, 15.

HOW TO MAKE PRAYER MEETINGS ATTRACTIVE.

1. Get all the people close together, Ezra iii, 1; Neh. viii, 1; Matt. xviii, 20; Acts xii. 12: Acts ii, 1.

2. The leader should occupy but little time. His work is simply to direct the minds of those present to something definite for prayer and meditation. All talks should be short, Ecc. v, 2: 1 Cor. ii, 1–5, etc.

3. All prayers should be short and to the point. without repetition, Matt. vi, 7–13. Short prayers the rule of the Bible. Some illustrations:
Moses — Deut. ix, 26–29.
Solomon — 1 Kings iii, 6–9.
Elisha — 2 Kings vi, 17, 18.
Hezekiah — 2 Kings xix, 15–19.
Jeremiah — xxxiii, 16–25, etc.
Paul — Eph. iii. 14–21.
Our Savior — Matt. xxvi, 39; John xvii.

4. We should have special prayer for special cases, Acts xii, 5. Christ encouraged specific prayer, Mark x, 46–51. Have requests, 1 Thess. v, 25; 2 Thess. iii, 1.

5. Have good singing with some point in it, Psa. lvii, 7–9; lix, 16; lxxxix, 1; ci, 1; civ, 33; 1 Cor. xiv, 15. Use an organ to lead, Psa. cl, 4; 2 Chron. xxx, 21; Psa. lxxxvii, 7. Avoid having formal prayers or addresses, if possible. They will kill a meeting. The Sermon on the Mount and the Lord's Prayer (for disciples)

will serve to illustrate the true Scriptural idea of informal directness in addresses and prayers.

7. Some hints as to how we should pray:
(a) In humility, Psa. ix. 12.
(b) In faith, Heb. xi, 6.
(c) In reliance on Holy Spirit for help, Rom. viii, 26.
(d) Fervently; earnestly, James v, 16.
(e) In accordance with God's will, Matt. xxiv, 39; 1 John v, 14.
(f) In a forgiving spirit, Mark xi, 25, 26.
(g) With confession, Dan. ix, 4, 5; 1 John i, 9.
(h) With thanksgiving, Phil. iv, 6.
(i) Ask in Christ's name, John xiv, 14. Let us be always in the Spirit of prayer, Eph. vi, 18.

JOHN H. ELLIOTT.

PRAYER.

What prayer is, Ex. xxxii, 9–11; 1 Sam. i. 13; Phil. iv, 6. Why we should pray, Isa. lv, 6; Matt. vii, 7; James v, 16; Luke xi, 9, 10. How we should pray:

1. *In faith*, Heb. xi, 6; Psa. lxii, 8; James i, 6; Mark xi, 24; John xv, 7; James v, 15; 1 John v, 14, 15.
2. *In sincerity*, 2 Chron. vii, 14; Ps. cxlv, 18; Deut. iv, 29; Jer. xxix, 13; James iv, 3.
3. *In the name of Jesus*, John xiv, 13; xv, 16; Heb. ii, 18; John xvi, 33; Eph. v, 20.
4. *With humility*, Ps. lxxxvi, 1; Luke xviii, 11–14; Ecc. v, 2; 2 Chron. vii, 14.
5. *With importunity*, Gen. xxxii, 26; Isa. lxii, 1; Eph. vi, 18; Luke xviii, 1–7.

When we should pray:
1. *Daily*, Ps. lxxxvi, 3. Ps. v, 3; Dan. vi, 10.
2. *In trouble*, Ps. l, 15; Ps. cvii, 6; Ps. xlvi, 1.
3. *In prosperity*, Deut. viii, 10.
4. *Always*, 1 Thess. v, 17; Luke xxi, 36.

Promises of answers, Job xxxiii, 26; Matt. vii, 7; John v, 7; Matt. xviii, 19; Jer. xxxiii. 3; Eph. iii, 30.

Power of, or answer to prayer, 2 Kings vi, 17, 18; Isa. xxxviii, 1–5; Luke xxiii, 42, 43; James v, 17, 18; Acts iv, 31.

P. A. WIETING.

PRAYER HELPS.

I. John xv, 7 — Abiding in Christ.
II. John xv, 7 — His Word abiding in us.
III. 1 John iii, 22 — Doing His commandments.
IV. Matt. xviii, 19 — Union.
V. Jer. xxix, 13 — Seeking with whole heart.
VI. Heb. xi, 6 — Praying with faith.
VII. 1 John v, 14 — According to His will.

A. M. WILSON.

THE LORD'S PRAYER.

I. *Our Father* — believers are children, John i, 12, 13; Gal, iii, 26; 1 John v, 1.
II. *Hallowed be Thy name* — believers are worshippers, John iv, 23; Phil. iii, 3.
III. *Thy kingdom come* — believers are subjects, Luke xii, 32; xxii, 29, 30; Heb. xi, 28.
IV. *Thy will be done* — believers are servants, John xii, 26; Rom. vi, 16; 1 Peter ii, 16.
V. *Give our needful food* — believers are beggars, Matt. vii. 7–11; John xiv, 13, 14.
VI. *Forgive us our debts* — believers are sinners, Rom. vii, 18; James iii, 2; 1 John i, 8, 9.
VII. *Deliver us from evil* — believers are saints, Rom. i. 7; Col. i, 12–14; 2 Tim. i, 9.

MEDITATION ON PRAYER.

Our Savior taught us to pray, "Our Father, which art in heaven," Rom. viii, 15; Jer. iii, iv. Because He is full of compassion, Psa. ciii, 13. And over all, Eph. iv, 6.

"Hallowed be thy name," Deut. xxviii, 58; Psa. cxi, 9. Because praise is acceptable to God, Psa. i, 23. "Thy kingdom come," Rev. ix, 15; xii, 18; Zech. xiv, 9. In the heart, Isa. xxvi, 13. Through the world, Psa. lxvii, 2-7; Isa. iii, 10. "Thy will be done on earth, as it is in heaven," Psa. ciii, 20, 21; cxliii, 10. Which teaches us acquiescence in the will of God, 1 Sam. iii, 18; Jud. x, 15. "Give us this day our daily bread"—including all spiritual and temporal wants,—Isa. xli, 17; Psa. cv, 40; Isa. xxxiii, 16. "Forgive us our debts, or trespasses," 1 John i, 9; Jer. iii, 12, 13; Mark ii, 7. "And lead us not into temptation," Matt. xxvi, 41; Psa. cxix, 117, 133. "But deliver us from evil," Psa. cxix, 10; xvii, 5, 8. "For thine is the kingdom," Rev. v, 12, 13. "The power," Matt. xxviii, 18; Isa. ix, 6, 7. "And the glory," Psa. cxlv, 11; 1 Tim. i, 17. "For ever." We have here a full and comprehensive prayer, containing all we need, for "our heavenly Father" knoweth what thing we have need of before we ask Him, Matt. vi, 32. His loving kindness is great, and His power is infinite, and He bids us come to Him with childlike love and confidence, and plead our Savior's merits, and the promise, "Whatsoever ye shall ask the Father in My name, He will give it to you." —*Y. M. C. A. Watchman.*

BIBLE INSTANCES OF EARNEST PRAYER.

Hannah—1 Sam. i, 13, 16.
Jabez—1 Chron. iv, 10.
Solomon—2 Chron. vi, 13, etc.
Manasseh—2 Chron. xxxiii, 13.
Ezra—Ezra ix, 5, 6.
Nehemiah—Neh. i, 4, etc.
Job—Job vi, 8; xxxi, 35.
David—Ps. xxviii, 1, 2; xlvii, 9; lxi. 1, 2.
Jeremiah—Lam. iii, 41.
Daniel—Dan. ix, 3-10.
Jonah—Jonah ii, 7.

Habakuk—Hab. iii, 2.
Prodigal Son—Luke xv, 21.
The publican—Luke xviii, 13.
Our Savior's prayer—John xi, 41, 42; xvii.
David's experience was: "This poor man cried, and the Lord heard him, and saved him out of all his troubles." From all the above examples we see that earnest prayer is an entreating, imploring call upon God, and saying in our hearts. "I will not let Thee go except Thou bless me." Such hearty prayer will bring down the blessing. If an earthly parent will attend to the earnest call and entreaties of his child, how much more will our heavenly Father!— *Y. M. C. A. Watchman.*

HEAVEN.

Read Rev. xxi, 1-7.
I. Heaven as a city, Rev. xxi, 10, 11.
1. "Many Mansions," John xiv, 2, 3.
2. "River of Life" there, Rev. xxii, 1.
3. Tree of Life, Rev. xxii, 2.
II. Who shall be there?
1. God, 1 Kings, viii, 26, 30.
2. Christ, Rev. xxii, 3.
3. Angels, Matt. xviii, 10.
4. Children, Matt. xix, 14.
5. Great company, Rev. v, 11.
6. Those kept by God, 1 Peter i, 3-5.
7. They that do, Rev. xxii, 14.
III. Who shall not be there? Rev. xxi, 8; 1 Cor. vi, 9, 10; Gal. v, 19, 21; Matt. iv, 1; Rev. xxii, 11 (first half).
What shall be there?
1. Song, Rev. v, 9, 10.
2. Worship, Rev. v, 11. 12.
3. Satisfaction, Psa. xvii, 15.
IV. What shall not be there ?
1. Curse, Rev. xxii, 3.
2. Night, Rev. xxi, 25; xxii, 5.
3. Tears, Death, Sorrow, Pain, Rev. xxi, 4.
4. Defilement, Rev. xxi, 27.

V. Possible not to enter:
Outer darkness, Matt. xxv, 30; **xxii,** 13.
Entrance depends:
1. On present life, Matt. xxv, 34–36, 41–43, 46.
2. On overcoming sin, Rev. ii, 7; iii, 5.

How shall we overcome?
1. Through Christ, Hebrews ix, 28.
2. He is the Way, John xiv, 6.
"*So shall we be ever with the Lord,*" 1 Thess. iv, 17.

J. E. BROWN.

SOME BETTER THINGS FOR US.

BY J. H. BROOKES.

Hebrews xi, 40.

THE Epistle itself explains in what respect Christians of the present dispensation have the advantage over saints who lived under the law. Hence we are not left to the wild conjectures in which so many indulge, when they read that God has "provided [margin, foreseen] some better thing for us." Many passages that at first seem perplexing and difficult would become plain to a diligent student of the Bible, if he would act upon the hint given by the inspired apostles: "Which things also we speak, not in the words which man's wisdom teacheth, but which the Holy Ghost teacheth comparing spiritual things with spiritual" (1 Cor. ii, 13). Comparing the statement, "some better thing for us" with other places in which the better thing is directly mentioned, the meaning of the languages will be easily understood.

First, "a better hope" (Heb. vii, 19). It is a hope described as rejoicing, saving, abounding, abiding, laid up for us in heaven, linked to glory and helmet, an anchor both sure and steadfast, living, purifying, fixed upon the speedy and certain coming of our Lord (Rom. v, 2–5; viii, 24; xii, 12; xv, 13; 1 Cor. xiii, 13; Col. i, 5–27; Heb. vi, 18–20; 1 Pet. i, 3; Tit. ii, 13; 1 John iii, 2, 3).

Second, "a better covenant" (Heb. vii, 22). Twenty times the word is rendered *covenant*, and thirteen times *testament*. It is well that it is thus doubly translated, for that which was at first a covenant becomes a testament by the death of Jesus, and doubly guarded in the fulfillment of its promises. It is a better covenant, therefore, not only because it involves higher blessings, but because the fulfillment of its provisions, passing over the ever recurring failures of man, depends upon the faithfulness of the Father, the Son and the Holy Ghost (Matt. xxvi, 28; Rom. xi, 27–29; Gal. iii, 17; iv, 24–26; Heb. xii, 24; xiii, 20; 1 Cor. i, 8, 9; 2 Cor. v, 5, 6; Rev. iii, 14).

Third, "better promises" (Heb. viii, 6). The old covenant was established upon the promise of the people, and was scarcely given before it was shamefully broken (Ex. xix, 5-8; xxiv, 3-8; xxxii, 1-8). But the new covenant was established upon the promise of Jesus that He would keep it, and it is needless to say that the promise was fulfilled in the minutest particular. One end to be attained by a salvation wholly of grace is declared to be that "the promise might be sure to all the seed" (Rom. iv, 16); for all the promises of God in Him are yea, and in Him amen, unto the glory of God by us (2 Cor. i, 20. Gal. iii, 16, 21, 22; iv, 28; Eph. i, 13; iii, 6; 1 Tim. iv, 8; 2 Tim. i, 1; Heb. x, 23; Isa. i, 12; 1 John ii, 25).

Fourth, "better sacrifices" (Heb. ix, 23). The superiority of Christ's atoning death over the sacrifices under the law is sufficiently indicated in the preceding part of the chapter, "Neither by the blood of goats and calves, but by His own blood He entered in once into the holy place, having obtained eternal redemption." If the blood of these poor beasts could cleanse from ceremonial defilement, "how much more shall the blood of Christ, who, through the eternal Spirit, offered Himself without spot to God, purge your conscience from dead works to serve the living God?" In the following chapter it is said that the law can never with those sacrifices, which they offered year by year continually, make the comers thereunto perfect." But Christ having once in the end of the world appeared to put away sin by the sacrifice of Himself, the blessed truth is announced. By one offering He hath perfected forever them that are sanctified" (Rom. v, 6-9; Gal. iii, 13: Eph. i, 7; ii, 13; Col. i, 12-14; Heb. ix, 28; 1 Pet. i, 18, 19; 1 John i, 7; Rev. i, 5, 6).

Fifth, "a better and enduring substance" (Heb. x, 34). The Hebrew Christians had taken even joyfully the spoiling of their goods for Christ's sake, knowing that they had for themselves in heaven a better substance. They had been taught that they were "partakers of the heavenly calling" (Heb. iii, 1); and having received "the promise of eternal inheritance" (Heb. ix, 15). The loss of earthly goods could not disturb their happiness for a moment. Israel corporately, or as a people, had the promise of earthly blessing, but the church has a better substance (Heb. xi, 16; Eph. i, 3; 2 Cor. v, 1; Phil. iii, 20; Col. i, 5; 1 Pet. i, 4; Rev. xxi, 1, 10).

Sixth, "a better resurrection" (Heb. xi, 35). The few who were raised out of death into life under the law (1 Kings xvii, 17-24; 2 Kings iv, 18-37; xiii, 21) returned to the grave; but under grace the believer is looking forward to a resurrection that death can never touch. The Lord Himself shall descend from heaven with a shout, and the dead in Christ shall rise first; then the righteous who are living shall be caught up together with them in clouds, to meet the Lord in the air. "Christ the first fruits; afterward, they that are Christ's at His coming." "Blessed and holy is he that hath part in the first resurrection." It is a resurrection out of, or from among the dead, and it is the peculiar privilege of those who, through faith have even now everlasting life (John v, 24, 29; xi, 25, 26; Acts iv, 2; Rom. vi, 5; 1 Cor. xv, 20, 23, 42, 43; Phil. iii, 10; ii, 21; Rev. xx, 5, 6).

Seventh, "the bood of sprinkling, that speaketh better things than that of Abel" (Heb. xii, 24). Here are mentioned seven great and precious privileges, to which believers are already come:

1. Mount Zion, or grace (Psa. cxxxii, 13, 14).
2. The heavenly Jerusalem (Gal. iv, 26).
3. The myriads which form the general assembly of God's angel host and church of the first born ones (Heb. i, 14; Rev. v, 9–11).
4. God the judge of all (Rom. vii, 33).
5. The spirits of just men (Heb. xi, 13).
6. Jesus, the mediator of the new covenant (Gal. iii, 20).
7. The blood of sprinkling that speaketh better things tnat Abel (Heb. ix, 22–28).

Surely God has foreseen some better things for us who are saved by grace.

ANOINTING FOR SERVICE.

BY D. L. MOODY.

THE subject before us is the gift of the Holy Spirit for service. This is quite different from His convincing or converting power. The churches are full of men whom God would use. He will use them as soon as they are ready to be used. Have you been used during the past year in the salvation of souls as much as God wanted to use you? God has put us here that we may give testimony. He desires that our testimony should be clear and convincing. But instead, it is often badly mixed, and is rejected. What you need is an anointing for service that shall enable you to give such testimony, and to give it in such a way that God can use it. Many never think to ask for this anointing for service. This anointing is beyond the question of being saved. Let us open our Bibles and see what God will show us concerning this anointing. Turn to the last chapter of Exodus, thirty-third and thirty-fourth verses: "So Moses finished the work * * * and the glory of God filled the Tabernacle." You see God filled it as soon as it was ready. 2 Chron. v, 13, 14: "The house was filled with a cloud, even the cloud of the Lord; so that the priest could not stand to minister by reason of the cloud." The moment the Temple was finished and dedicated to God, His glory filled it. So with us; are we ready at this moment to be filled with His glory?" John xiv, 17: "Ye know Him; dwelleth with you." The difference between a believer and an unbeliever is God's abiding presence. 1 Cor. vi, 19: "Know ye that your body is the temple of the Holy Ghost * * * and ye are not your own?" The believer is one called out from the world and specially fitted for God's service. It would have been impossible for to have stood up to preach before such an audience as this except for the abiding presence of the Holy Spirit. Surely, if God would abide in these bodies, we should take good care of them, and not defile them. You may be a son of God, and yet not have the power for service. The work of those who are not thus anointed will be as hay and stubble. All we do in mere human strength must be burned up. If you get into heaven, it will be as by the skin of your teeth (see 1 Cor. iii, 11, 15). The devil will deceive us at this point if possible. Matt. iii, 16: "He saw the Spirit of God descending like a dove, and lighting upon him." Jesus was anointed for His work, and went forth in a Divine strength. We can never overcome until filled with this power. How contrary to all this is the spirit of criticism in so many churches. The eloquence of Gabriel would do no good without the power of God. Your sermons are but sounding brass till God speaks through you. See in Luke iv, 18, how Christ spoke of the Spirit of God being upon Him, to anoint Him for His work of preaching to the poor. It was by the Divine anointing that Samson had such power; that Elijah was able to shut up the clouds and withhold the dew. Ahab laughed, but there was no dew or rain until God's anointed prophet prayed for them. Christ cast out devils by the Spirit of God (Matt. xii, 28), and so may we. If He needed this power, how much more do we need it? There are three kinds of Christians:

1. "Those who have life somewhere hidden away down in their souls, but there is no flow. They are so near dead, that you can hardly tell whether they are dead or alive. I suppose they will get to heaven, but they will have no stars in their crowns. They will receive no 'Well done, good and faithful servant.' 'But,' some one says, 'there are three degrees in heaven.' Oh, yes. 'I thought if a man got to heaven he would be perfectly happy.' So he will. His cup may be full, but it may be a very small cup. His capacity for enjoyment is very small.

2. "Some are like the Samaritan woman, who received the water of life, and bubbled up and ran over a little as she ran into the city to call her friends to see the wonderful man who had told her so much.

3. "But I want to be like those Christians who are described in

thirty-eighth verse of the seventh chapter of John: 'Out of whose belly shall flow rivers of living water.' A man said the other day : 'That man Moody must be a greedy man. See how God has blessed him, and still he is asking for more.' Yes, I do want more ; my heart is crying for more. But it is not more happiness that I want. No, no. I want a baptism for service — not to talk of self ; willing to be anything; only as I am ready for service. It is said — and I believe it — that God uses the vessel that is nearest. A false impression has gone out that there are certain men whom God can use to accomplish great things. He will use any and all of us if we are ready. We are to be willing to do great things or small. I believe the angel Gabriel would be willing to rule an empire or sweep a street, just as God desires. So should we be willing to serve just as God directs. 'If we are not filled with the Spirit,' we should use the Word rather than our own experience. The Word is 'the sword of the Spirit.' A well drilled army will put to rout a much larger company of raw recruits. There is scarcely a town in the country where more than a half a dozen efficient workers could be found to deal wisely with inquirers. They don't know how to wield 'the sword of the Spirit.' If I am 'filled with the Spirit,' I shall know how to use the Word of God. We are not to defend the Word, but to use it. If men attack the Bible, give them more Bible. It is sharp, and will surely cut if we know how to wield it. There is so much of self, flesh, that there is a want of Spirit. If we are filled with the Spirit, there is no room for strife, jealousy, or deceit. Heaven's measure is full, pressed down, and running over. If you have not enough grace to treat your neighbor right, you have not God's measure."

A brother in Chicago said one could find out who is thirsty if he went through the congregation with a pail full of good, cool water. Everybody that was thirsty would come to him for a drink. If our bucket is empty we cannot tell who is thirsty. The world is filled with people who are famishing with thirst. If you have water, they want to know where you got it, that they may drink, and be refreshed. My soul cries out for this fullness.

After Christ had risen, He breathed upon His disciples, saying : "Receive ye the Holy Ghost." They are already converted men, but needed a new baptism. As Christ was about to ascend, He bid His disciples "tarry at Jerusalem" untill they should be endued with power from on high. It was not enough that they had been converted, and had again received the spirit. He must come again, and with a mightier baptism than ever before.

"Is there power in your words? If not, you need another baptism. When the Holy Spirit had filled me years ago, I preached an old sermon that had been of no service. Many were led by that sermon to inquire the way of salvation. It is not new sermons, or new preachers, or new methods, but new power that we want. If we wait till we get it, He will not disappoint us. The Holy Spirit is here all the time, but we want Him in power.

"In Acts iv we find that the disciples were commanded by the rulers not to speak at all in the name of Jesus. They could not stand that, but had a prayer meeting, and asked for help; and again they were filled with the Holy Ghost, so that they could face all opposition, and speak the Word of God with boldness.

"People sometimes ask me, Have you got the second blessing? Though I had the thousandth blessing, I need a fresh one to-day. Last year's sap will not answer for this year. I know men that were filled, that have no power to-day. If God and I agree that I should have a new blessing, what is to hinder it? The eighth chapter of Acts shows that men sometimes receive the Holy Ghost after believing. The men at Ephesus had not so much as heard that there was any Holy Ghost. I fear some men, in these days, hardly know that there is any Holy Ghost. I saw some farms in California very green and fruitful, and others alongside dry and barren. I soon learned that the green were irrigated. So with Christians. Some are irrigated with the 'water of life,' and some are dying for the want of it. They number over their formal prayers, and goad themselves up to doing their duty, but have no spontaneous, loving life. I am not dissatisfied or complaining. God has given me a very sweet twenty years and a happy family; but I want Divine power. God wants to give this power to every man. When I went to England and began to talk of this anointing I saw a leading divine eyeing me closely, and after service go quickly out. He did not come back for several days. I thought he was offended. By and by he returned, with his face all aglow with joy. He saw his need, and sought and received the anointing. His church would not hold the people that came to hear him. Months after he told me he had not preached a sermon since the baptism without conversions. A man in Edinburgh was so feeble that he could not preach but once a week. He got full of the Spirit, and could preach every day, and got well in body. The oil of grace upon the machinery of the body makes it run easy. It is so easy to preach and to work, if we are first anointed.

"How the mother needs this filling that she may train her children right. A lady in Philadelphia said to me in great earnestness, 'Can I get it?' 'Yes.' A few days after she came, rejoicing over her servants converted, as well as eight scholars in her Sunday school class, and her husband greatly blessed. In another place seventy-nine persons dated their conversion from that woman. When the Lord would take Elijah up into heaven, Elijah said to

Elisha, 'Tarry here, I pray thee.' And Elisha said, 'I will not leave thee.' Again and again Elijah said, 'Tarry behind;' Elisha refused, till finally Elijah said to him, 'Ask what I shall do for thee;' and he answered, 'Let a double portion of thy Spirit be upon me.' Elijah answered that his request was a hard one, but it should be granted if he saw him when he was taken up. So Elisha followed close after Elijah, and refused to take his eyes off from him, and was rewarded with a double portion of his Spirit, so that he performed double the miracles that Elijah did. Let us, like Elisha, ask for great things, and refuse to be satisfied without them. Do you want more power? It is not me you need, but a fresh baptism for service. Eternity alone can tell the result of you fifty or a hundred here to-night, if you are filled with the Holy Ghost."

CHRISTIAN UNITY.

Promoted by Christ, John xvii, 21 (John x, 16): "That they all may be one; as Thou, Father, *art* in me, and I in Thee, that they also may be one in us."
Paul, 1 Cor. i, 10 (Phil. ii, 2): "I beseech you, brethren, by the name of our Lord Jesus Christ, that ye all speak the same thing, and *that* there be no divisions among you."
John, 1 John i, 7 (1 John iv, 7): "But if we walk in the light, as He is in the light, we have fellowship one with another."
Necessary to Christian Life, Rom. xii, 5 (1 Cor. xii, 21): "So we, *being* many, are one body in Christ, and every one members one of another.
Prosperity of the Church, 1 Cor. xii, 24–26 (2 Cor. xiii, 11): "God hath tempered the body together *** that there should be no schism in the body."
Glory of God, Rom. xii, 5, 6 (Rom. xv, 7): "That ye may with one mind *and* one mouth glorify God."
Its Progress begins with Conversion, 1 Cor. xii, 13 (Eph. ii, 19): "By one Spirit are we all baptized into one body."
Increases on Earth, 1 Thess. iii, 12 (1 Thess. iv, 9, 10): "And the Lord make you to increase and abound in love one toward another, and toward all."
Culminates in Heaven, Eph. i, 10 (Eph. v, 27): "That in the dispensation of the fullness of times He might gather together in one all things in Christ, both which are in heaven, and which are on earth."
H. E. BROWN.

THE UNITIES IN EPHESIANS.

I. Unity of the Family:
1. Husband and wife, v, 22, 25.
2. Father and child, vi, 1, 4.
3. Master and servant, vi, 5, 6.

II. Unity of the Church:
1. In the individual church, iv, 11–13.
2. In the church at large, iv, 3–7. The seven "ones."
3. Of Jew and Gentile, ii, 11–14; iii, 6.
4. In heaven and on earth, i, 10.

III. Expressions and Symbols of Unity:
1. "Together," ii, 5, 6.
2. "Bond of peace," iv, 3.
3. "Building," ii, 20–22.
4. "Body," i, 22, 23.
5. "Fellow citizens," ii, 19.
6. "Fellowship," iii, 9.
7. "Household," ii, 19. "Family," iii, 15. "Father," iv, 6.
J. E. BROWN.

THE MOON THE TYPE OF THE CHURCH.

I. It is ordained, Ps. viii, 3.
II. It gives light, Gen. i, 15, 16.
III. It puts forth precious things, Deut. xxxiii, 14.
IV. It is a faithful witness in heaven, Ps. lxxxix, 37.
V. It walks in brightness, Job xxxi, 26,
VI. It endures, Ps. lxxii, 5, 7.
VII. It shall be as the light of the sun, Isa. xxx, 26.

WHAT IS A CHRISTIAN?

First. In faith he is a believer in Jesus Christ. " God so loved the world that He gave His only begotten Son, that whosoever believeth in Him should have everlasting life. * * * He that believeth on Him is not condemned, but he that believeth not is condemned already, because he hath not believed in the name of the only begotten Son of God " (John iii, 16, 18). " He that believeth on the Son hath everlasting life, and he that believeth not the Son shall not see life; but the wrath of God abideth on him" (John iii, 36). "This is the work of God, that ye believe on Him whom He hath sent" (John vi, 29). "This is the will of Him that sent me, that every one which seeth the Son, and believeth on Him, may have everlasting life, and I will raise him up at the last day " (John vi, 40). See also John xi, 25; Acts x, 43; xiii, 39; xvi, 31; 1 John v, 13.

Second. In relationship he is a child of God. "As many as received Him, to them gave He power to become the sons of God, even to them that believe on His name, which were born not of blood, nor of the will of the flesh, nor of the will of man, but of God " (John i, 12, 13). " Ye are all the children of God by faith in Jesus Christ " (Gal. iii, 26). When the fullness of the time was come, God sent forth His Son, made of a woman, made under the law, to redeem those that were under the law, that we might receive the adoption of sons. And because ye are sons God hath sent forth the Spirit of His Son into your hearts, crying Abba, Father" (Gal. iv, 4–6). "Beloved, now are we the sons of God, and it doth not yet appear what we shall be, but we know that when He shall appear, we shall be like Him, for we shall see Him as He is " (1 John iii, 2). "Whosoever believeth that Jesus is the Christ is born of God " (1 John v, 1).

Third. In communion he is a friend of Christ.. "Henceforth I call you not servants, for the servant knoweth not what his lord doeth; but I have called you friends, for all things that I have heard of my Father I have made known unto you " (John xv, 15). "Go to my brethren and say unto them, I ascend unto my Father and your Father, and to my God and to your God" (John xx, 17). "Both He that sanctifieth and they who are sanctified are all of one, for which cause he is not ashamed to call them brethren. Forasmuch then as the children are partakers of flesh and blood, He also Himself likewise (the word likewise means "close by the side of") took part of the same, that through death He might destroy him that had the power of death, that is, the devil. * * * For verily he took not on Him the nature of angels; but He took on Him (the same word is translated *caught*, when Jesus caught Peter sinking in the waves) the seed of Abraham" (Heb. ii, 11–16). "Truly our fellowship is with the Father, and with His Son, Jesus Christ" (1 John i, 3). "And there is a friend that sticketh closer than a brother" (Prov. xviii, 24).

Fourth. In character he is a saint, or sanctified, or separated one. "To all that be in Rome, beloved of God, called to be saints" (Rom. i, 7). "Wherefore Jesus also, that He might sanctify the people with His own blood, suffered without the gate" (Heb. xiii, 12). "As He which hath called you holy, so be ye holy in all manner of conversation; because it is written, Be ye holy, for I am holy" (1 Pet. i, 14, 15). "We thus judge, that if one died for all * * * that they which evil should not henceforth live unto themselves, but unto Him which died for them and rose again" (2 Cor. v, 14, 15). "To me, to live is Christ" (Phil. i, 21). "And the very God of peace sanctify you wholly; and I pray God your whole Spirit and soul and body be preserved blameless unto the coming of our Lord Jesus Christ" (1 Thess. v, 23).

Fifth. In conflict he is a soldier. "Thou, therefore, endure hardness as a good soldier of Jesus Christ. No man that warreth entangleth himself with the affairs of this life, that he may please Him who hath chosen him to be a soldier (2 Tim. ii, 3, 4). "Fight the good fight of faith; lay hold on eternal life, whereunto thou art also called, and hast professed a good profession before many witnesses" (1 Tim. vi, 12). "Watch ye; stand fast in the faith; quit you like men; be strong" (1 Cor. xvi, 13). "Wherefore, take unto you the whole armor of God, that ye may be able to withstand in the evil day, and, having done all [margin, overcome], to stand" (Eph. vi, 13). "Be thou faithful unto death, and I will give thee the crown of life" (Rev. ii, 10).

Sixth. In the world he is a stranger and pilgrim. "Dearly beloved, I beseech you as strangers and pilgrims, abstain from fleshly lusts which war against the soul" (1 Pet. ii, 11). "For our conversation [or citizenship] is in heaven, from whence also we look for the Savior, the Lord Jesus Christ" (Phil. iii, 20). "They are not of the world, even as I am not of the world" (John xiv, 16). "Behold, what manner of love the Father hath bestowed upon us, that we should be called the sons of God; therefore the world knoweth us not, because it knew Him not" (1 John iii, 1). "God forbid that I should glory, save in the cross of our Lord Jesus Christ, by whom the world is crucified unto me, and I unto the world" (Gal. vi, 14).

Seventh. In expectation he is an heir. "If children, then heirs; heirs of God and joint heirs with Christ; if so be that we suffer with Him, that we may be also glorified together" (Rom. viii, 17). "If ye be Christ's, then are ye Abraham's seed, and heirs according to the promise" (Gal. iii, 29). "Wherefore thou art no more a servant, but a son; and if a son, then an heir of God through Christ" (Gal. iv, 7). "That, being justified by His grace, we should be made heirs according to the hope of eternal life" (Titus iii, 7). "Blessed be the God and Father of our Lord Jesus Christ, which, according to His abundant mercy, hath begotten us again unto a lively hope by the resurrection of Jesus Christ from the dead to an inheritance incorruptible and undefiled, and that fadeth not away, reserved in heaven for you" (1 Pet. i, 3, 4). — *The Truth.*

THE LORD'S JEWELS.

BY HENRY MOREHOUSE.

"They shall be mine, saith the Lord of hosts, in that day when I make up my jewels" (Mal. iii, 17).

Please take your Bible and turn to a few passages of Scripture in connection with a subject which, I trust God, the power of the Holy Spirit will make a blessing to every one of us. I want, in opening, to say that it may be that some of my friends may disagree with me as to the view I take; but if you do disagree, do not let us quarrel. If your view be better than mine, you have every right to keep it; but if mine be the more Scriptural, then you have every right to accept it. On matters of opinion every man has a right to his own view; but when it comes to "thus saith the Lord," neither your view nor mine is worth a penny. I wish, then, as to one of the sweetest truths I find in the Bible, to go to the Word of God, that we may learn what it says, and not what we think.

One of the sweetest subjects in the Bible is, "What we are to God." What God is to us is very precious; but it is wonderful to find what God says we are to Him. We sometimes say we could not live without Christ; neither could we. We say we could not be satisfied without Christ; and we could not. We say we could not be happy without Christ; and we could not. But on the other hand, remember Christ could not live without us, would not be satisfied without us, and would not be happy without us. He could not be all this without those for whom He died, that He might have them forever with Him in glory. First, turn to Matt. xiii, 45, and look at that sweet parable. In reading that parable, I used to think the Lord Jesus Christ was the pearl of great price, I was the merchantman, and the price which I paid was one sin and another which I gave up to accept Christ. Now, in reading this blessed Word, I can find no place in which the sinner is said to purchase Christ, or eternal life, or anything else. Certainly, in that beautiful chapter in Isaiah the sinner is invited to "come buy wine and milk;" but it is "without money and without price." If we are not to pay anything, then it is a gift which we receive, not a purchase which we make. Again it is said, "Buy the truth and sell it not;" but this is for the Christian, and not for the unsaved soul. The sinner cannot purchase salvation; Christ has purchased it. The Lord Jesus Christ has purchased His church; He was the purchaser, not the church. Remember, it makes all the difference in the world to make sure of this, because the buyer has a right to sell. If I had purchased Christ, then I could part with Him. But if He has purchased me, I cannot part with Him; I am His by right of purchase. Men do not buy with the intention of selling at a loss. So, when the Lord Jesus Christ purchased the church He paid a very high price for it, and He can never part with it until He gets a higher price; that He can never get. He laid down His own life for the church, and the church is safe until a higher price be offered. Eighteen hundred years ago Satan offered a price — "All these things will I give Thee if Thou wilt fall down and worship me." The price was too low. Christ was about to pay His life-blood for the church, and He would not sell it for these earthly things.

Turn to one or two passages to prove this point. In Acts xx, 28, there you get the merchantman, the pearl of great price, and the price paid. Again in Gal. ii, 20.

Once more, in 1 Cor. vi, 19, 20; vii, 23. If we had time I might read fifty passages to prove that it is Christ who purchased the church, and not the church which purchased Christ. Well, now look at the common sense view of it. Suppose I go into one of the grand jewelers' shops in London, and say: "Do you sell pearls?" "Yes." "Have you any fine ones?" He goes to a great safe and brings out a tray covered with chamois leather. "Here are some as fine as you will get in London." I look at them and see one above all the rest in beauty and purity, and I say: "What is the price of that?" "It is very expensive. Do you wish to buy it?" "Yes, I do." "Then it is £20,000." "Well, to-morrow I will come and buy that pearl." Next day, I drive up to the door of the grand shop in a covered wagon. I jump out, and go in and say: "I have come for that pearl." "Have you got the money?" "Well, not exactly the money." "What then?" "Oh, I have been to every part of London, and gathered all the refuse, and rubbish, and filth I could find, and have brought a whole load of it to pay for the pearl." The jeweler would think I was mad; and yet it is no more foolish than to think that my sins and iniquities will pay for "the pearl of great price." Only the Lord Jesus Christ could pay the price required for that pearl, and He died to purchase it. The pearl of great price is the church, the merchantman is Christ, and the price is His own precious life-blood, paid eighteen hundred years ago on the cross. Think now; He called us "pearls." What are pearls noted for? For purity. I suppose the purest thing upon earth is a pearl. The very moment it is found it is perfect and pure, needing neither polishing or grinding. So the church of God upon earth ought to be pure, "even as He is pure," because the Lord Jesus Christ calls us His pearls. He calls us so because He would have us pure. Do you know where the purest pearls are found? In the deepest depths. The pearl divers have to go to the bottom of the ocean for them, and the deeper they go, the purer are the pearls found. So the pearl of great price was down in the depths of sin and degradation, but the Lord Jesus Christ plunged from the very height of glory, until He cried out: "All thy waves and thy billows have gone over me," and there He found the pearl which He sought. When He came up again He had secured the pearl of great price — the church of God — which he had purchased with His own life blood. We are safe because He has purchased us, and has died for us; but He would have us to be pure and holy, and let our good works be seen by the world, that He may be glorified; and our heavenly Father praised.

Now turn to Mal. iii, 17, and here, in contrast to the pearls, we have the Lord's "jewels." Every one of us know that the church is one in the Lord Jesus Christ; therefore, it is not pearls in the plural number, but "the pearl," that is in the singular number. Here, however, it is my jewels; not my jewel. As individual saints, then, He calls us His jewels. What are jewels for? Ladies get them that they may be admired. So the Lord Jesus Christ gets jewels that He may be admired. How careful must we be that we so live, by His grace, that He may be admired in us. Now, a few passages as to jewels. Turn to Job xxviii. You find that the whole of the chapter is taken up with jewels. All the precious stones that we know of are mentioned here, and verse ten says: "His eye seeth every precious thing." What encouragement to us in seeking to win precious jewels for Him; in the roughest and vilest places His eye sees them! Search the Word, and see where the Lord found His jewels. Out of Moab He brought one bright jewel—Ruth. Another bright gem was found a harlot in Jericho. In that gloomy prison Paul and Silas found a lovely jewel—the Philippian jailor. So do we still find such jewels for the Master's crown, just where we least expect them. But when God sends us to look for them we must search diligently. Precious stones are found by the careful seeker. True, they are occasionally found, as it were, by accident; but generally it is by diligence in searching. Some little time ago a black fellow found a beautiful diamond on the diamond fields. Some one asked: "Why is it that the best stones are found by natives, and not by white men?" "Because we black fellows get down on our knees to look for them, and white men don't like to get dow in the dirt." So it is when we get on our knees, we find the beautiful jewels for our Master. As workers for Christ, we may meet with a great deal of disappointment and trial; but that is nothing to the joy of finding just one precious soul as a bright jewel to set in the crown of the Lord Jesus Christ. What is the trouble? He will repay it all. These friends (alluding to Mr. and Mrs. Scott, who were present, on the eve of their departure) are going from us to far off China. What for? To find precious jewels. It is a great undertaking; but it is well worth while. Yes, it is worth a thousand times that trouble, if only one jewel be found through their means—a soul saved by grace. Let us go on then, brothers and sisters, seeking for these precious jewels for the Lord. He sees where they are, and will guide us to them if we are seeking to serve Him. Sometimes He permits us to win many; but if it be only one, it is worth while. I believe, when we see Christ, our greatest joy in His presence will be that we found some of those jewels that deck His crown. Now turn to Exod. xii, 35, 36. Many people seem to think, when they read these words, that they must make some kind of apology for the Israelites. It needs no apology whatever. God commanded it, and what God does must be all right. He can make no mistake, and if God told them to spoil the Egyptians, they had got the right to do it; but what did they get? "Jewels." What did they do with them? When the Tabernacle was subsequently erected, there was a great deal of gold, and silver, and jewels employed. So Egypt's spoil became the material for the Tabernacle of God. Therefore, instead of being wrong to take the jewels from Egypt, it would have been wrong not to have taken them. So the Christian who goes to Canaan, without taking some precious jewels for the temple of God that is now being built is doing wrong. Souls are to be taken out of this Egypt to form the temple of God for ever and ever.

Now turn to 1 Chron. xxix, 2. Notice "glistening stones." There is a difference between a pearl and a diamond. The pearl is perfect and pure when found; the diamond is not. These stones glistened because they had been cut. That is what the Lord is doing with us here. He is cutting His precious jewels, that they may glisten in His holy temple. He chastens us that He may cause us to shine. Some murmur because they are chastened. They should rather murmur if they were not chastened. The jeweler does not cut and polish a pave-stone. No; it is the precious stone he cuts. It is then a sign that the Lord counts us worth cutting when He chastens us. He lets the world alone, but He chastens the church. The Lord Jesus Christ would have us to be glittering stones, and so He chastens us. The pearl is known for its purity; the diamond for its beauty. We should have both qualities, and if we are pure we shall be beautiful; no doubt about that. Now another thing about the diamond. I used to imagine that the diamond would give light in the darkest spot; but it does not. I had one given to me some time ago, and I found when I took it into a dark room, it ceased to sparkle. Take a diamond into the darkest mine, hold it before you, and it will shine no more than the paving-stone does; but let one gleam of light come from any part of the universe, and it will catch the ray. It is only a reflector — nothing else. So with us. When we get away from Christ, we give forth no light, not even a sparkle; but let a beam of His light enter our souls, and it will instantly shine, forth; we will reflect it. That is what the Christian, and each individual Christian is — a reflector. Our lustre in this dark, benighted world comes from Him alone. Now I will tell you how diamonds are cut. Some time ago I went with Major Whittle to the watch manufactory of which he was then the manager. After seeing other parts of the works, we went into the room where they cut jewels for the watches. I said to the man there, "Please tell me how you cut jewels." "How do you think!" "I suppose you use a good file." "The best file in the world would not graze the surface of a diamond." "How do you do it then?" "I just take one diamond to cut another." That is how the Lord does with His jewels. He uses one jewel to cut another. We talk about bad surroundings, a bad world, and bad people hurting us. I tell you, all the power of the world and the people in it, and the devil himself, cannot damage one of God's jewels. Satan cleverly uses one jewel to mar another, and both get injured in his hand. So, do we find that all the real danger to the church arises from within? So Satan manages to spoil our beauty. But in God's hand one of His jewels is used to cut and polish another, and there is no marring. Are we using our tongues or our lips to mar the beauty of a fellow Christian ? Shame on us to do the devil's work ! Never should we lend ourselves to his ends. May God help us to yield ourselves to no hand but that of our blessed Master, the Lord Jesus Christ.

Turn now to 2 Chron. iii, 4–6. In that temple there were a great many things that seemed useless. The foundation stones were useful ; the great beams were wanted ; but as for those jewels they appear to be useless. What are they for ? For ornament and beauty. They were to garnish the house and make it beautiful. So there are some of God's saints who seem to be useless.

I went lately to see an invalid, a Christian lady. I found her lying on a couch helpless. She could not move, and could only use one hand ; yet she seemed very happy. I asked : "How long have you been lying here ? " "I have been helpless for eighteen years." "Are you miserable ? " "No ; I am as happy as I can be." And so she seemed. She could do nothing but lie there and ornament the house. She glorified God in her helplessness. Paul, the great apostle, could do no more. No one can do more than glorify God in the place where He has set him. Glorify God by being satisfied to do or suffer His will, filling the place He would have us in thus ornamenting the house. For this we want grinding. In Lancaster we are having a very hard time at present. Mills are stopped and factories closed. One gentleman said the other day, that he feared the coming winter would be harder for the people than even the dark winter of the American war. Yet, friends, I tell you that many who formerly would not be known as Christians, are now, under this grinding, and cutting, and polishing, becoming bright ornaments of the church. Lately I visited a famous pottery. In one room I found a young lady painting a beautiful flower on a vase. I said : "You take a great deal of trouble with that." "Yes, it takes a long time to do it." But what is the use ? With my finger I could in a moment spoil the flower. "How do you manage to keep the painting on the vase ? " "When I have finished the vase, a man comes and takes the vase to the fire, and after it has passed through the fire, no power in the world can take it off." Ah, friends, we must pass through the fire. The Lord Jesus Christ would paint on us the likeness of the beautiful Rose of Sharon ; contact with the world takes it off ; but he puts us in the fire and burns it in ; then it will not rub off. The lessons learned in the fire of affliction are never forgotten. I suppose we all know that, and every Christian learns at length to thank God that he was afflicted and passed through the fire. And now I must close ; but turn to one more passage, the last chapter but one in the Bible. There we see the church, the great city, the holy Jerusalem, descending out of heaven from God, and it is likened unto a jewel. There it is, perfected at last in the beauty of holiness. Some time ago, I was staying with a scientific gentleman known to most of you. I was talking to him of diamonds, and he asked: "Do you know what a diamond is?" "No; I do not." "Nothing but carbon; that is, charcoal. I could reduce a diamond to a mere piece of carbon in a short while." "But can you make that carbon into a diamond?" "No one can do that." "Oh, yes, I know one who can." "What do you mean?" "The Lord Jesus Christ can. He takes the worthless carbon and transforms it into the precious diamond to shine in His crown."

May the Lord help us to be like the pearl and diamond; to be pure and beautiful, shining back the light of the sun of righteousness.

THE BELIEVER'S CONDITION.

WHAT I WAS.

"Shapen in iniquity, and in sin did my mother conceive me," Ps. li, 5.

"By nature the child of wrath, even as others," Eph. ii, 3.

"Have sinned, and come short of the glory of God" Rom. iii. 23.

"Having no hope, and without God in the world," Eph. ii, 12.
"Cursed is every one that continueth not in all things written in the book of the law to do them." Gal. iii, 10.
"My sins as scarlet." Isa. 1, 18.
"Dead in trespasses and sins," Eph. ii, 1.

"The soul that sinneth, it shall die," Ezek. xviii, 4.

"No soundness in my flesh because of thine anger; neither was there any peace in my bones because of my sin," Ps. xxxviii, 3.
"Condemned already," John iii, 18.
"Under sin." Gal. iii, 22.

"My sin was ever before me," Ps. li, 3.

"I knew not God," Gal. iv, 8.

WHAT I AM.

"Born again not of corruptible seed, but of incorruptible, by the Word of God, which liveth and abideth forever," 1 Peter i, 23.
"A child of God and if a child, then heir, heir of God and joint heir with Christ," Rom. viii, 16, 17. "Saved from wrath through Him," Rom. v, 9.
"The blood of Jesus Christ His Son has cleansed me from all sin," 1 John i, 7.
"Saved to the uttermost," Heb. vii, 25.
"Christ has redeemed me from the curse of the law, being made a curse for me," Gal. iii, 13.

"Whiter than snow," Ps. li, 7.
"Alive unto God through Jesus Christ our Lord," Rom. vi, 11. "Forgiven all trespasses," Col. ii, 13.
"He Himself bore my sins in His own body on the tree," 1 Peter ii, 24.
"Am passed from death unto life," John v, 14.
"Complete in Him," Col. ii, 10.
"He is my peace, Eph. ii, 14.

"I shall not come into condemnation," John v, 24.
"Thou hast cast all my sins behind thy back," Isa. xxxviii, 17.
"As far as the east from the west, so far hath He removed my transgressions from me," Ps. ciii, 12.
"I know that my Redeemer liveth," Job xix. 25.

"Through fear of death all my life-time subject to bondage," Heb. ii, 15.

"A heart deceitful above all things and desperately wicked," Jer. xvii, 9.

"Far off," Eph. ii, 13.

"An enemy of the cross of Christ," Phil. iii, 18.

"Was in unbelief," Rom. xi, 32.

"Of the devil," 1 John iii, 8.

"My end destruction," Phil. iii, 19.

"A fearful looking for of judgment." Heb. x, 27.

"Yea, though I walk through the valley of the shadow of death, I will fear no evil," Ps. xxiii, 4.

"In Christ Jesus a new creature," 2 Cor. v, 17.

"Made nigh by the blood of Christ," Eph. ii, 13.

"Accepted in the Beloved," Eph. i, 6.

"Meet to be partakers of the inheritance of the saints in light," Col. i, 12.

"I know whom I have believed, and am persuaded that He is able to keep that which I have committed unto Him against that day," 2 Tim. i, 12.

"Ye are Christ's, and Christ is God's," 1 Cor. iii, 23.

"My end everlasting life," Rom. vi, 22.

"When the Chief Shepherd shall appear, I shall receive a crown of glory that fadeth not away," 1 Peter v, 4.

GRACE.

"Only by the grace of God I am what I am," 1 Cor. xv, 10. "For by grace I was saved through faith and that not of myself; it was the gift of God," Eph. ii, 18. "For no man can come to me unless the Father draw him," John vi, 44. — *The Truth.*

CHRISTIAN POSITION.

Exodus xiv, 27–31.

When God's people, redeemed with the blood of a spotless lamb, saw the rush of the waters over the chariots, and the horsemen and all the host of Pharoah, they stood with Egypt behind them, the Red Sea between them and the land of bondage, Canaan before them, the wilderness around them, looking up for daily food and guidance across the trackless desert, believing the Lord and singing the song of victory. Such is still the position of all who have been redeemed "with the precious blood of Christ, as of a lamb without blemish and without spot," 1 Pet. i, 19. The world is behind them, for it has been crucified unto them, and they unto the world, Gal. vi, 14. The waters of death roll between them and their former bondage, Rom. vi, 2; vii, 4, 6; Gal. i, 4; Col. iii, 3. "The promised inheritance is before them," Eph. i, 13, 14; Heb. vi, 17–20; 1 Peter i, 3–5. "The wilderness is around them," John xvi, 33; xvii, 16; Acts xiv, 22; 1 Peter ii, 11. "They are looking up in entire dependence, but in confident hope," Matt. vi, 11; John xv, 5; Phil. iii, 20, 21; Titus ii, 13. "Their special characteristic, as distinguishing them from all the world, is faith," John iii, 16; Acts xvi, 31; Rom. iv. 5; 2 Cor. v, 7; Heb. xi, 6. "It is their privilege to be always singing the praises of redeeming love," Ps. cxxxviii, 5;

Acts xvi, 25; Eph. v, 19; Rev. v, 9, 10.

J. H. BROOKES, D.D.

THE BELIEVER'S POSITION.

1. *What we were,* 1 Peter ii. 10; Eph. ii, 12, 13; Rom. v, 8; vi, 6; Eph. ii, 3, 1.
2. *What we are,* Eph. ii, 13, 18; 1 John iii, 2; 1 Peter ii, 9, 10; Eph. iv, 30; 1 Cor. vi, 11; 1 Cor. iii, 23; Rom. vii, 14: Eph. ii, 20; 1 Peter i, 5.
3. *What we are not,* 1 Cor. vi, 10; Rom. vi. 14; Rom. viii, 9, 12.
4. *What we know,* Rom. vii, 18; 2 Tim. i, 12; 1 John iii, 14; Rom. viii, 28 (26); 2 Cor. v, 1; 1 John iii, 2.
5. *What we have,* Eph. i, 7; ii, 18; 1 John v, 13; ii, 1, 20; 2 Peter i, 19; Heb. vi, 19.
6. *What we shall be,* Col. iii, 4; 1 John iii, 2.

REV. GEO. F. PENTECOST.

DISCIPLES INDEED.

It must be clear to any diligent reader of the New Testament, that discipleship refers to progress in the Christian life, rather than to entrance upon that life ; to growth in grace, rather than to the beginning of grace. By faith, and faith alone, one is saved ; by obedience one is sanctified ; by believing one has life : by the doing the will of God, he has life more abundantly. When one asks : "What shall I do to be saved?" he is not told to take up his cross, or to bring forth the fruits of righteousness, or to exercise love to men. It would be legalism to give such answers. For these are good works ; and salvation is "not of works, lest any man should boast." It is purely of grace that we are saved ; therefore the sole condition of having life, is that we believe on the name of the Son of God.

But after birth cometh growth ; and growth is discipleship, or the continuing in the life of God, and the increasing in the knowledge of God. A child may be born, but may not grow up. And there are those in the church who are saved — so far as we can judge — but who are not growing. They present examples of arrested development. They have barely received the life of God, but by their lack of service and obedience, they seem to be dooming themselves to a stunted and dwarfed immortality. Now, Christ would have us be disciples, as well as saved ones.

With these thoughts in mind, let us note the conditions of discipleship which the Lord himself lays down :

1. Growth in knowledge. "If ye continue in My word, then are ye My disciples indeed," John viii. 31. Observe, that Christ said this to "those Jews which believed on Him." They were believers already, and therefore saved ones; now He would teach them how to go on to the higher stages of the Christian life. A disciple is a learner ; and the Master says, substantially : "Since you have now received the Word by faith, study it, and grow in the knowledge of it." Faith matriculates us into the school of Christ, but only by diligent continuance in learning can we advance from stage to stage in the knowledge of God.

2. Self denial. "And whosoever doth not bear his cross and come after Me, cannot be My disciple." Luke xiv, 27. We are saved by looking at the cross ; we are made disciples by lifting the cross. We "behold the Lamb of God, who taketh away the sins of the world," and by one believing glance receive eternal life ; we are sanctified by taking up the cross daily, and following our Lord. Christ bore the cross to save us, and in that fact alone we are to rest. But we are to bear the cross, following after Him, that we may be conformed to Him, and made like Him. Christ's cross for justification ; our cross for sanctification.

3. Fruitfulness. "Herein is My Father glorified, that ye bear much fruit; so shall ye be My disciples," John xv, 8. The branch is grafted into the true vine by regeneration. If it abides in the vine, it brings forth much fruit. Hence, to say "that ye bear much fruit," is equivalent to saying "that ye abide in living and constant communion with Christ. If one is in Christ he is justified; only as he abides in Christ is he being sanctified. Fruitfulness, then, is the proof of abiding, and continuance, and growth in grace. In others it is a condition of being a disciple indeed.

4. Brotherly Love. "By this shall all men know that ye are My disciples, if ye have love one to another," John xiii, 35. Just as abiding in Christ begets fruitfulness, so abiding in Him begets love. "He that dwelleth in love, dwelleth in God and God in him." "If a man say, I love God, and hateth his brother, he is a liar." Brotherly love, therefore, is the truest badge and credential of fellowship with Christ, and hence of discipleship. "Love is the gravitation of the soul." If the soul is resting in Christ, it must exhibit the fruits thereof in sincere love of the brethren.

5. Unworldliness. "Whosoever he be of you that forsaketh not all he hath, cannot be My disciple," Luke xiv, 33. Notice, that in the connection of this text, we have the same contrast between the beginning and the continuance of the Christian life. The parable of the unfinished tower illustrates this. "This man began to build, and was not able to finish." A disciple, indeed, is one who has counted all things but loss for the excellency of the knowledge of Christ Jesus the Lord. Such an one will not be forever studying how to "make the most of both worlds;" to get all the enjoyment and wealth and luxury which this life can afford, and yet have heaven also.

May the Lord teach us to be disciples indeed.

A. J. GORDON, D.D.

COST OF DISCIPLESHIP.

GIVE UP,

Property, Mark x, 21: "One thing thou lackest; go thy way, sell whatsoever thou hast, and give to the poor, and thou shalt have treasure in heaven; and come, take up the cross and follow Me."

Relations, Luke xiv, 26: "If any man come to Me, and hate not his father, and mother, and wife, and children, and brethren, and sisters, yea, and his own life also, he cannot be My disciple."

Worldly Pleasures, 1 John ii, 15, 16: "If any man love the world, the love of the Father is not in him."

ENDURE,

Chastisements, Hebrews xii, 6, 7: "When the Lord loveth he chasteneth, and scourgeth every son whom he receiveth."

Hatred, Matt. x, 22: "Ye shall be hated of all *men* for My name's sake."

Self denial, Matt. xvi, 24: "If any man will come after Me, let him deny himself, and take up his cross, and follow Me."

LABOR FOR

Personal Purity, 1 John iii, 3: "Every man that hath this hope in him purifieth himself, even as he is pure."

Salvation of Souls, Mark i, 17: "Come ye after Me, and I will make you to become fishers of men."

Glory of God, 1 Corinthians x, 31: "Whether therefore ye eat, or drink, or whatsoever ye do, do all to the glory of God."

H. E. BROWN.

SEVEN THINGS ABOUT THE BELIEVER'S LIFE.

I. Its source is God. as He is author of all life, Heb. xi, 3; Acts xvii, 24, 25, 28. So He is the giver of eternal life, Rom. vi, 23; 1 John v, 10–13. We are also told when His purpose was formed to give us this life, Eph. i, 4; 1 Peter i, 18–21. With all the boast of modern science, it cannot produce life even in its feeblest and lowest manifestation.

II. Its channel is Christ and Christ crucified, John i, 4; iii, 14–16; iv, 14; v, 24, 26, 29, 40; vi, 27, 33, 35, 40; xi, 25; xiv, 6; xvii, 1, 2. We are further taught that this life is obtained only through His death, Gen. iii, 21; iv, 4; Ex. xii, 13; Lev. i, 4, 5; xvi, 14; xvii, 11; Isa. liii, 5, 6; Matt. xxvi, 28; John x, 17, 18; xii, 24; 1 Cor. xv, 3; 2 Cor. v, 21; 1 Peter ii, 24; iii, 18; 1 John i, 7.

III. Its security is Christ risen, John xiv, 19; Rom. iv, 25; v, 8–10; viii, 33, 34; Col. iii, 1–3; Heb. ix, 24. This risen Christ is always with His believing people, and the continuance of His life is the proof and pledge that the life they have received through faith in His name can never be lost, Matt. xxviii, 20; John x, 27–29; Rom. viii, 35–39; Eph. i, 22, 23; ii, 4–7; v, 30; Col. ii, 10; Heb. xiii, 5, 6.

IV. Its power is the Holy Ghost, John iii, 5; vii, 38, 39; xiv, 16, 17, 26; xvi, 7–14; i, 8; iv, 31–33; vii, 55; viii, 18, 19; x, 43–48; Rom. viii, 9–17; xv, 13. It is most important to see that it is only as we are walking in unhindered communion with the Spirit the power of this life is maintained, and only thus can we understand the Word, or feel an interest in prayer, or honor God, 1 Cor. ii, 10–14; iii, 16, 17; vi, 11–20; Gal. v, 16–25; Eph. iv, 30; 1 Thess. v, 19.

V. Its manifestation is likeness to Christ, Matt. xi, 28–30; John xiii, 15; xv, 14; Acts iv, 13; Rom. viii, 29; 2 Cor. iii, 3, 18; 1 Peter ii, 21; 1 John iii, 1, 2. It is not only the privilege, but the duty, and it is not only the duty, but the privilege, of all who believe on His name to study His character and conduct as set forth in the Gospels, and to be conformed to His ways, 1 John ii, 4–6; 1 Peter iv, 1–4; Heb. xiii, 7–16; Tit. iii, 8; 1 Thess. iv, 1; Col. i, 10; Eph. v, 1, 2.

VI. Its sphere is heaven, Matt. vi, 20, 21; Luke x, 20; John xiv, 2, 3; Eph. i, 2; Phil. iii, 20, 21; Heb. iii, 1; x, 34; 1 Peter i, 4; Rev. xxi, 2, 10. The atmosphere of heaven will be a congenial element in which this life, unhindered by sin and untrammeled by self, can move in the testimony and of service of Christ with joy unspeakable and full of glory, Ps. xvi, 11; Luke xxiii, 43; 2 Cor. xii, 4; Rev. xxi, 4.

VII. Its duration is eternity.
1. The life is said to be eternal, Matt. xxv, 46.
2. The salvation is eternal, Heb. v, 9.
3. The redemption is eternal, Heb. ix, 12.
4. The inheritance is eternal, Heb. ix, 15.
5. The covenant is eternal, Heb. xiii, 20.
6. The glory is eternal, 1 Peter v, 10.
7. The crown is eternal, 1 Peter v, 4. Well, therefore, may every believer cherish the aim that animated the apostle Paul as expressed in 1 Cor. ix, 24–27; 2 Cor. v, 9, 14; Phil. i, 21.

JAMES H. BROOKES. D.D.

WORKING FOR GOD.

First. It must be distinctly understood that there is no such thing in the Bible as working for salvation. Indeed all work of any kind for salvation is positively forbidden. Thus on the great day of atonement God significantly declared, "Whatsoever soul it be that doeth any work in that same day, the same soul will I destroy from among his people," Lev. xxiii, 30. When it came to atonement, not a stroke of work was permitted, but God did it all. "To him that worketh not but believeth on Him that justifieth the ungodly, his faith is counted for righteousness," Rom. iv, 5. "For by grace are ye saved through faith; and that not of yourselves; it is the gift of God, not of works, lest any man should boast." Eph. ii, 8, 9. Such is still the plainly revealed and only way of salvation, and hence it is not intelligent to tell a sinner to keep on trying. It is Scriptural and sensible to tell him to quit trying and go to trusting, Luke vii. 50; John vi, 29, 47; Acts x, 43; xiii, 89; xvi, 31; Rom. iii, 24–26; xi, 6.

Second. But when we are the children of God by faith in Jesus Christ, then, and not before, the command comes: "Son, go work to-day in My vineyard," Matt. xxi, 28. Mark it; God does not say: "Slave, go work," for He does not want, and will not have a slave's work; but "Son." It is like another text which ignorant persons are continually addressing to the unregenerate: "My son, give me thine heart," Prov. xxiii, 26. But a sinner has to be a son by the quickening power of the Holy Ghost through faith in Christ, before he can give his heart; and the words should never be used except in an appeal to Christians. Yet faith is an active principle, for it "worketh by love," Gal. v, 6; and "we are His workmanship, created in Christ Jesus unto good works, which God hath before ordained that we should walk in them," Eph. ii, 10; Col. i, 10; 1 Thess. i, 3; 2 Thess. ii, 16, 17; Tit. iii, 8; 1 Cor. xv, 58; Rev. xiv, 13.

Third. That we ought to work for Him, and must work for Him, is clear enough from the fact that God is our Father, and that He bought us. He said to the mean Jews, nearly as mean and ungrateful as the Gentiles: "A son knoweth his father, and a servant his master; if I be a father, where is mine honor? and if I be a master, where is my fear?" Mal. i, 6. "What!" exclaimed the apostle in a grieved and indignant tone. "know ye not that your body is the temple of the Holy Ghost which is in you, which ye have of God, and ye are not your own? For ye are bought with a price," 1 Cor. vi, 19, 20. "Who gave Himself for us, that He might redeem us from all iniquity, and purify unto Himself a peculiar people [a people for His own possession], zealous of good works," Tit. ii, 14. Oh, what a price was paid for our redemption, and what a perfect Redeemer He is, for He is both the purchaser and the price, Acts xx, 28; Gal. ii, 20; Eph. i, 7; Col. i, 12–14; 1 Peter i, 19; ii, 9.

Fourth. In view of all this, there must be personal work. "For none of us liveth to himself, and no man dieth to himself. * * * So then every one of us shall give account of himself to God," Rom. xiv, 7, 12. "Let every one of you please his neighbor for his good to edification," Rom. xv, 2. When Jesus had called all the people unto Him, "He said unto them: Hearken unto me, every one of you," Mark vii, 14. "To every man his work * * * and what I say unto you, I say unto all, — watch," Mark xiii, 34, 37. "God is not unrighteous to forget your work and labor of love, which ye have showed toward His name, in that ye have ministered to the saints, and do minister; and we desire that every one of you do show the same diligence to the full assurance of hope to the end," Heb. vi, 10, 11.

Fifth. Nor should it be forgotten, in pondering the question of personal work, that the eye of the Lord is ever upon us. There is nothing more solemn and searching in all the inspired writings than the phrase, so often repeated in the prophetic sketch of the history of the church: "I know thy works," Rev. ii, 2, 9, 13, 19; iii, 1, 8, 15. He is with us all the days, even unto the end of the age, Matt. xxviii, 20; and what does He see on most of these days? After

His ascension, it is said, the disciples "went forth and preached everywhere, the Lord working with them," Mark xvi, 20; but the Lord cannot work with them unless they too are working. It is enough to make us bow our heads with shame to think of our sluggishness and stupidity, especially when we hear Him saying of a lazy, worldly church: "I will kill her children with death; and all the churches shall know that I am He which searcheth the reins and hearts; and I will give unto every one of you according to your works," Rev. ii, 23.

Sixth. Let us think for a moment of the motives that urge saved people to work. "Let your light so shine before men that they may see your good works, and glorify your Father which is in heaven," Matt. v, 16. That is a good motive. "The love of Christ constraineth us," 2 Cor. v, 14. That is a sweet motive. "Wherefore we labor that, whether present or absent, we may be approved of Him," 2 Cor. v, 9. That is a noble motive. "I must work the works of Him that sent me while it is day; the night cometh, when no man can work," John ix, 4. That is an urgent motive. "He that doeth the will of God abideth forever," 1 John ii, 17. That is a pleasing motive. "Whosoever gives only a cup of water to one who belongs to Christ, shall not lose his reward," Mark ix, 41. That is a stirring motive. "God hath chosen the weak things to confound the mighty," 1 Cor. i, 27. That is a comforting motive. "Let him know that he which converteth a sinner from the error of his way shall save a soul from death," Jas. v, 20. That is a mighty motive.

Seventh. A day of reckoning is rapidly approaching, when all the works of believers will pass in review before the judgment seat of Christ, and their station in eternity will be determined by the fidelity which they have manifested for His name and truth. Read carefully and prayerfully, Ecc. xii, 14; Dan. xii, 2, 3; Matt. xvi, 27; xxv, 14–30; Luke xix, 12–26; 1 Cor. iii, 13–15; 2 Cor. v, 16; Rev. xxii, 12. — *The Truth.*

CHRISTIAN WORK.

I. The Field, Matt. xiii, 38; Gal. vi, 10. Special field for each, just where God has located him. "Unto all," rich, poor, non-church goers, young men, children in your alleys. "As we have opportunity."

II. Condition of the Field, John iv, 35; Matt. ix, 37. "Say not four months." "White already to harvest." "Laborers few."

III. Who are to be the Laborers? 2 Cor. vi, 1; Matt. xx, 6, 7; Mark xiii, 34; Mark vi, 31, etc. Miracle of the feeding the 5,000. Every disciple to bring all he has, no matter how small, of time, talent, opportunity; thus consecrated to and blessed by the Master, a little one may feed a multitude, Matt. xxv, 14–40. The Talents and the judgment seat.

IV. How to Work, Eccl. ix, 10; John ix, 4; 1 Cor. xv, 58. This to be the Spirit of our whole life, not simply of special occasions

The Example of Jesus, Acts x, 38; Luke vi, 40; John xvii, 4.

The activity of the Son of God our pattern. "Finished the work which Thou gavest me to do." A Christian should be able to say this "finished" at the close of each day.

V. The Spirit of the Worker, Acts ix, 6; Isa. vi, 8. "What wilt Thou have me to do?" Characteristic of St. Paul. He confers not with flesh and blood. Does not allow prejudice or preference to govern him. What does God want of me? "Here am I." "Send me." Isaiah's lips first touched with the live coals from the altar. This our spirit if we allow the Holy Ghost to prepare and empower us for our work.

VI. Results of Work, Ps. cxxvi, 6; John iv, 35; Dan. xii, 3; Jas. v, 20.

"Bearing precious seed." The Word of God the sword of the Spirit.

VII. *Power for Work*, 2 Cor. ix, 8. Note the "alls." Isa. l, 7.—Mr. Moody's special text.

Rev. Geo. A. Hall.

THE CHRISTIAN WORKER'S HELPER.

I. The teacher of Divine truth must depend upon the power of the Spirit of truth, which is personal, Divine, and which is given to man on certain conditions, which conditions are laid down plainly in the Word of God.

II. *The Holy Spirit imparts the qualities needed by the teacher.*

1. He gives the appreciation of the truth: "That ye may approve things that are excellent," Phil. i, 10.

2. He gives a taste for truth: "Whatsoever things are true," Phil. iv, 8.

3. He gives a personal, experimental knowledge of the truth: "Hereby know we," etc., 1 John iv, 13.

4. He gives the spirit of fidelity to the truth, Luke xii, 11, 12; Mark xiii, 11.

5. He gives long suffering, patience and gentleness in teaching the truth, Gal. v, 22, 23.

6. He gives, by His constant indwelling as the Comforter, joy and delight in the truth, John xiv, 16, 17; Acts xiii, 52.

7. He gives intellectual quickening, thus enabling us to know the truth, John xvi, 13.

8. He gives enthusiasm in teaching the truth, Isa. lxi, 1.

9. He gives us access to the Father in prayer, thus increasing our Divine and supernatural power with men as the teachers of the truth, Rom. viii, 26; Eph. iii, 16.

III. *How may we secure the presence, the inspiration and power of the Holy Spirit?*

1. He proceeded from the Father, John xv, 26; and, therefore, we must look to the Father.

2. He is given through the intercession of the Son, John xiv, 16; therefore we must look to Jesus Christ.

3. He is given in connection with the truth, Acts x, 44; xi, 15; therefore we must look to the Word of God, and to the institutions of the church.

4. He is given in answer to prayer, Acts iv, 31; viii, 15; Eph. i, 16, 17; iii, 16; therefore we must look to the Father and to the Son in earnest, fervent, believing prayer.

5. He is given on condition of the entire surrender of ourselves to His indwelling, 1 Cor. vi, 19, 20; therefore we must yield our bodies and souls to Him.

6. He is given on condition of active devotion of all our powers to to Him in holy, obedient service, Acts v, 32; Eph. iv, 31.

J. H. Vincent, D.D.

THE WORKER'S MODEL.

The officers sent to arrest Jesus made the following excuse when they returned to the council without Him: "Never man spake like this man." This unintended tribute to the Lord Jesus Christ, as the peerless teacher, the teacher of the ages, we accept as true in its most literal and in its fullest sense.

I. *See His preparation:*

He possessed all knowledge, Col. ii, 3.

He was pure and sinless, Heb. vii, 26; 1 John iii, 5; 1 Pet. ii, 22.

He had experience as a man, Heb. ii, 18; iv, 15.

He was possessed by the Holy Ghost, Isa. lxi, 1; John i, 1; Phil. ii, 7; Col. ii, 9.

II. *See His Spirit:*

Unselfish, Luke ii, 49; xxii, 42; Rom. xv, 3.

He was full of sympathy, John xi, 5, 35; Luke xxiii, 28.

He was wholly absorbed in His one work, John iv, 31–34; ii, 17.

He was full of the Spirit of prayer, Mark i, 35; xiv, 32–36.

He was full of charity, patience and catholicity, Matt. xviii, 21, 22; Luke ix, 54–56; John iii, 16, 17; Mark xvi, 15.

III. See His matter:
The glad tidings of the kingdom, Mark i, 14, 15.

IV. See His manner:
Persuasive and authoritative, Matt. iv, 21, 22; xiii, 2; Mark i, 37, 38; ii, 1, 2, 13, 22, 27.

V. See His method:
A master of circumstances. An illustrative, interrogative, demonstrative teacher. A bold and plain-speaking teacher.

VI. See His perpetuated influence, Matt. xxviii, 18–20; Rev. i, 8, 12–18.

VII. See His success, Rev. vii, 9–17.

J. H. VINCENT, D.D

CHRIST AS AN EXAMPLE TO CHRISTIAN WORKERS.

We represent Christ, 2 Cor. v, 17–20. He is our example in all things, Phil. ii, 5; 1 John ii, 6. Let us look at His example in some of the points in the human side of His nature, which are most essential to us as His followers and representatives. Under each point a few passages are added which apply His example to us. He has set us an example.

I. In His faithful witnessing for God, Rev. i, 5; xix, 11; Luke xxiv, 48; Acts i. 8; ii, 32, etc.

II. In His devotion to His work, Luke ii, 49; John ix, 4; Luke iv, 10; x, 1; John xvii, 4; Eccl. ix, 10. In His holy life, Heb. vii, 26; iv, 15; 1 Peter ii, 21–23; 1 Peter i, 15, 16, 22.

(*a*) He was unworldly, xv, 18–20; 1 John ii, 15–17.

(*b*) Humble, John xiii, 4–17; Rom. xii, 3.

(*c*) Obedient, John iv, 34; vi, 38; viii, 29; Matt. xxvi, 39–44; John xv, 15.

IV. In His sympathy, Matt. ix, 28, 29; xv, 21, 22; Matt. x. 31; Luke vii, 13. One soul was audience enough for His greatest sermons; *e. g.,* Nicodemus, Woman of Samaria.

V. He was aided by the Holy Ghost.

(*a*) Anointed and sealed, John i, 32, 33; vi, 27; Acts x, 38; 2 Cor. i, 21, 22; 1 John ii, 27.

(*b*) Led, Matt. iv, 1; Luke iv, 1; Rom. viii, 14.

(*c*) Acted in His power, Luke iv, 14; Acts i, 8; vi, 5–8.

VI. He was a thorough student of God's Word. Take any one of the Gospels, and see how frequently He quotes from the Old Testament Scriptures, Matt. iv, 4; vii, 10 (all His replies to Satan taken from the book of Deuteronomy, now almost a sealed book to most Christians); v, 21, 27, 33, 38, 43; ix, 13; xi, 10; xii, 3, 4, 5; xiii, 14–16; xv, 7–9; xix, 4, 5; xxi, 13, 16, 42; xxii, 31, 32, 44; xxvii, 46; 2 Tim. 3, 16, 17; Josh. i, 8; 1 John ii, 24.

VII. He was pre-eminently a man of prayer. Look at His prayers recorded in a single Gospel — that of Luke, for example, which presents Him as the Son of Man, Luke iii, 21, 22; v, 15–17; vi, 12, 13; ix, 18–20, 28, 29; xi, 12, 13; xxii, 31, 32, 40–45; xxiii, 34; xxiv, 50, 51; Eph. vi, 18; Phil. iv, 6. In conclusion, Ps. cxxvi, 6; 1 John iii, 2. Taken away, Isa. vi, 7.

J. M. McCONAUGHY.

THE CHRISTIAN WORKER'S POWER FOR SERVICE.

BY HENRY MOORHOUSE.

WE are going to-night, just for a little while, to speak of our power. The power the Lord Jesus Christ has given us to win souls for Him; let us see where we get that power from. If you turn with me to the 5th chapter of John's Gospel, and read from the 31st verse, you will see where our power comes from. Now, my friends, you have noticed in reading these beautiful verses, that there are four witnesses given to the Lord Jesus Christ. First, given by Himself. "If I bear witness of myself," etc. Every word had to be established. It was not that the words He spake were not true, but the people were not bound to accept them unless there was another sent. Then came John the Baptist; then there were His own miracles, and then there was the witness His own Father bore to Him. Now the Lord Jesus Christ says, "If you will not believe my testimony, the testimony of John the Baptist, the testimony of the miracles, the testimony of my Father," etc., there is only one other, and that is the Scriptures. When "the Scriptures" are mentioned, the Old Testament Scriptures are meant, because the New Testament was not written. Do not be going to other books so much, but stick to the Book. The Old Testament Scriptures are just photographs of the Lord Jesus Christ from Genesis to Malachi, and He who gets the Old Testament Scriptures in his mind, is just on a rock that all the devils in hell cannot shake him from. There are 530 quotations in the New Testament from the Old. I suppose that nearly one-half of the New Testament consists of quotations from the first five books of Moses. The Lord Jesus Christ said, "Search the Scriptures." Sometimes a young man will come to me and say: "What books would you recommend me to read in order that I may better understand the Bible?" "What part of the Bible do you want to understand better?" "The New Testament." "Then study the Old. If the Old, then study the New" (2 Pet. i, 19). The best exposition of the New Testament is the Old; and of the Old the New.

In the eighteenth verse of this chapter we have a voice speaking; in the nineteenth, a more sure word of prophecy — something more sure than a voice. Now my friends, I think there is great honor set upon God's Word here by God's Holy Spirit. "A more sure word of prophecy." What is that? The Old Testament Scriptures. I tell you true rest, and true peace, and true assurance can never be got except by the Scriptures. God teaches me through His word, and in no other way. I met with a young man some time ago, looking the picture of misery; the next time I saw him he was quite changed, and had a bright, happy smile of his face. What was the cause of the change? He had got assurance of salvation. "How did you get it?" I said. "I went with a friend of mine over to hear Mr. Moody. This friend of mine, some time before, had a dream. He dreamed he saw the Lord Jesus Christ, and Christ said to him, 'Thy sins are forgiven thee.' After this I kept praying to the Lord, and asking Him to send me a dream, and I wondered why God did not hear me; but, thank God, I have got something better than a dream now; I have got His own Word." If I were to go out and look up into the sky, and see a finger pointing to these words, "Harry Moorhouse, your sins are forgiven you," why, that might be an optical illusion. I would sooner have the Word of the living God to trust to. In the 16th of Luke, in the parable of the rich man and Lazarus, we find the rich man wanting some one to go from the dead to warn his friends. But we read in verses 29–31: Back again to the Bible, back again to the Scriptures. How many of us, my friends, think if we could work some miracles people would believe in God; but God tells us — speaking to us through Abraham — that if they will not believe through the Scriptures, "neither will they * * * though one rose from the dead." When we preach, let us take care that we give them the Word of the living God, the Word of God, and that only. Everything else that we say is like putting pebbles in a garden — they never grow; but the truth is like putting seed which will grow up. I am sure no true servant will care to shine at the expense of his Master. We want the Master to be everything, and for us to be nothing.

We read in the fourth chapter of Luke how Christ overcame Satan by the Word of God.

You know in these three temptations of Satan, Christ conquered with the Scriptures. You know how He said: "It is written," and Satan did not dare to say it is not true. I tell you, my friends, Satan is not an infidel. Jesus was hungry, and Satan says: "Command that these stones be made bread." Why was this the first fierce attack that Satan made upon Christ? Where would have been the sin of making the bread? If the Lord Jesus Christ turned into bread every mountain, it would not be wrong ; and if He were to turn the river Thames into milk, where would be the sin ? Why would it have been sin then to turn the stones into bread ? It was to satisfy Himself, and what sin would there have been in that ? Will you turn to Matthew iii, 16, and read with me. Now we see where the sin was. Here was the Savior baptized — the Father speaks to Him from heaven — Satan comes to Him and said : "If Thou be the Son of God ; " it was as if he said : "Do not believe it because your Father said it, but believe it if you have power to work miracles." Is not this the way Satan tempts us now ? Do not believe it because God said it, but because of some wonderful feeling, some experience. My friends, I tell you to beware of the "ifs" of the devil. When God speaks, let us believe Him just because He says it ; just believe as a little child. Will you turn to 2 Timothy iii, 14, to the end. See how much we get in Scripture. When you get a house thoroughly furnished, anything else becomes lumber ; the Scripture tells us how we are to get our house full. Now, my friends, whatever you do, search the Scriptures. Get your mind throughly filled with the Word of God. The water cannot flow out of us if it is not in us. We must read the Bible ; we must search the Bible, and we cannot make mistakes so long as it is God's Word that we read, and God's Word that we tell. I want just to tell you a little incident. I went out to America some years ago, and I came in contact with a friend, a Christian man. He used to get up at seven in the morning and work till late at night ; most of his evenings were spent at some meeting. When he got home, he was tired out ; too tired to read the Bible. I used to say : "My friend, I never see you read the Bible." He used to preach on Sundays, and would just take his Bible on Saturday afternoon, and find a text, and then take all the books about the text, and read what was said on it (he had a fine library). "Now," I said, "just you lock up that book-case, and give the key to your wife, and tell her not to let you have it ; and just read your Bible alone." "What for?" "To understand it." " Oh, I shall understand it when I get to heaven." I left him, but met him again after a certain time. He had been reading the book of Jeremiah for two weeks ; he came out of the room with his face beaming, and to every one he met he would say : "Did you ever see this in Jeremiah ? " When I first met him he was fighting with a straw, but after this he had a sword to fight with. It is the weapon that makes all the difference. When you tell people your opinion, it is like beating the mountain with a feather. What we want is the Bible.

"Search the Scriptures," says the Lord Jesus Christ. How we ought to thank the Lord that we can get a Bible, from Genesis to the Revelation, for six pence. Carry one in your pocket, and whenever you have a minute, take it out and commit a verse to memory until you get your mind stored with it ; then go out and fight your Master's battles. May God bless you, my dear friends, for Jesus' sake !

THE WORK OF THE INQUIRY ROOM.

BY DWIGHT L. MOODY.

EVEN in the best sermon, something may be said which will be a remedy to one but poison to another. As no two persons are alike, so the same advice never suits two persons alike, and Christian experiences vary as much as characters do. The medicine that will do for one disease will not do for another, and two persons afflicted with the same spiritual malady cannot be given the same prescription. But when you go into the inquiry room, you must have all the remedies at hand. The Bible I consider the great medicine book for all spiritual troubles. You must never give your own experience; nor should you give vent to any of your own opinions.

Confine yourself closely to the Bible. There is not a difficulty put forward which the Bible does not answer. If you undertake to tell an inquirer how you felt when you were converted, the chances are he will look for a similar experience; and if he does not get it, he will give up in despair.

About the first persons that we have to deal with in the inquiry room are your nominal Christians; and right here I want to correct an impression that has got abroad, and into print, that I do not think a halting Christian will get to heaven. This is not so ; but I favor their getting a little joy on this earth, and not going hobbling to heaven on crutches when they can go on the wing. I would like to speak about nominal Christians, but must hurry on. Suffice it to say, I usually point out to them fifth chapter and thirteenth verse of the first Epistle of John. The second class are the backsliders — those who have once known Christ, but have left Him. These need a peculiar handling. There is a good deal in Jeremiah that applies to them ; as, for instance, "Thus saith the Lord ! what iniquity have you found in me ?" I hold them right down to that. There is no reason for their leaving Christ, unless they have found some iniquity in Him ; and then I try to have them find out if the iniquity may not have crept into themselves. Then, again, in the second chapter and ninth verse of Jeremiah : "I will yet plead with thee, saith the Lord, and with your children's children will I plead." God is pleading with them, and all they have to do is to come back. If they still hold out, I pass to the nineteenth verse: "Thine own wickedness shall correct thee, and thy backslidings shall reprove thee." I never knew a backslider in my life whose iniquity did not come back upon him by the ruin of his family. Then to console them, I just turn to the fourteenth chapter of Hosea: "O, Israel, return thou unto the Lord thy God; I will heal their backslidings; I will love them freely, for mine anger is turned away." A great deal better than all your exhortations is to them just what God says.

The third class are those who are slightly convinced. You don't want to deal with those in any other way than to show them they are under the law. They must find out they are miserable sinners before they can do anything else. You must just show them what they are. Oh, how tired I am of this superficial work! People who are seeking salvation must give up all this levity and curiosity, and vanity and worldliness. I think that the third chapter of Romans, and tenth verse, does very well to probe a man with: "And it is written, there none righteous; no, not one." If I cannot get them on any other sin, I am sure to hit them on the sin of unbelief, which is the mother of all sin. Adam fell right there. Do not mind how careless people seem in the inquiry room. The most seemingly indifferent person will probably come again to-morrow night. No matter how they take it, hold up the looking-glass and let people see themselves, and know how ugly they are. You will have done your duty then. But bear in mind that it always pays to sit down and talk with the oldest and most indifferent person you encounter, and tell them of the beauty and comfort of religion. Your work must be deep and thorough. I had rather have one hundred converts through and through, than have a thousand swept into churches who don't know whether they are changed or not. I would have every one come to this subject thoughtfully, with all their will about them.

I have continually urged ministers to be very careful who they receive into the churches, and not to administer baptism until they are sure the professions are more than words. The first chapter of the Epistle of John, and the second verse of the one hundred and forty-third Psalm, are very useful in the inquiry room. If a man has tact he can approach any one at all times on the subject of religion without giving offense. If he is fond of horses, talk about horses; if business, talk about business, or whatever else it may be; and just as soon as you turn the subject round, the first thing you know you will both be discussing the subject of religion. I long ago made a resolution not to let a day pass without speaking to some one about their soul. It is so long since I have been rebuffed that I can't remember it. Now I just make enough mistakes to keep me humble. The most people make one grand mistake, and that is, they refrain from doing anything, just for fear of making a few little ones.

The fourth class are those who are convinced they are sinners. For these I usually choose the first chapter and eighteenth verse of Isaiah: "Come now, and let us reason together," and so on; and then the forty-third chapter and twentieth verse. The third chapter and fifteenth verse of John is also valuable; but John v, 24, is my favorite text. You know it is a good thing to have a person converted on the rock of a scriptural text. Its good to see them see how it looks. Sometimes the printed Word has more force than the spoken. To me it is a beautiful thing to see an acknowledged sinner with God's Word in his hand, pondering over it on the eve of awakening to a realization of eternal joy. There is a good deal in Isaiah that is good to read to this class; also the tenth chapter and tenth verse of Romans. It is a great mistake to tell a person he is converted. That is something for them and God to settle. Another mistake is to count converts. All we can say is, so many have professed conversion. The only record of conversion there is, is kept in heaven. Last of all, and greatest of all, the best thing to do with inquirers is to kneel down and pray with them.

WORKERS PREPARED FOR SERVICE.

Isaiah vi.

I. God's holiness must be seen, Ex. iii, 5; xv, 11; Lev. xvi, 2; xx, 25, 26; Num. v, 2, 3; Hab. i, 13.

II. He must be seen in Christ, John i, 18; 1 Tim. vi, 16; Heb. i, 1-3; Phil. ii, 5-8; John xiv, 9.

III. He must know what man is by nature, Gen. vi, 5; Job xxv, 4; Ps. li, 5; Jer. xvii. 9; Isa. lxiv, 6; Rom. iii, 9-19; 1 John i, 8, 10.

IV. There must be personal confession, Judges vi, 22; xiii, 22; Job xl, 4; xlii, 5, 6; Dan. x, 5-8; Luke v, 8; Rev. i, 17, 18.

V. He must see that holiness is satisfied, Lev. ix. 24; i. 4, 5; Eph. v, i, 2; Heb. ix, 26-28; Rom. iii, 21-26; 2 Cor. v, 21.

VI. That sin is purged, Ps. ciii, 12; Isa. xxxviii. 17; xliv. 22; Jer. l, 20; Mic. vii, 19; Eph. i, 7; Col. ii, 13; Heb. x, 17.

VII. Then follows consecration, 1 Cor. vi, 19, 20; 2 Cor. v, 14, 15; Rom. xii, 1; xiv, 8; Gal. ii, 20; Phil. i, 21. — *The Truth.*

PERSONAL WORK.

I. Instances of, in the life of Jesus. He employed this method at the very beginning, John i, 38.

Other instances—Nicodemus, John, iii, 1-21; Samaritan woman, John iv, 7-26. Call of Matthew, Luke v, 27. Man blind from his birth, John ix, 35; Zaccheus, Luke xix, 5. He closed His life with personal work, Luke xxiii, 43. On the day of His resurrection, Luke xxiv, 13-31.

II. Same method employed in apostolic church. Philip and the eunuch, Acts viii, 26-39. Conversion of Saul, Acts ix, 3-6. Introduction of the Gospel to the Gentiles, Acts x. Conversion of jailer, Acts xvii, 29-31. Paul in Ephesus, Acts xx, 20. Paul in Rome, Acts xxviii, 30, 31.

III. These men carried enthusiasm into their work, Acts iv, 20; Acts xxvi, 24.

L. D. WISHARD.

WHAT TO DO.

Golden text, Paul's question, Acts ix, 6.

Question asked by the conscience:
(*a*) Of religionists, Luke xviii, 18; John vi, 28.
(*b*) Of men under alarm, Luke iii, 9, 10.
(*c*) Under conviction of sin, Acts xvi, 30.
(*d*) In true repentance, text.

How to get the right answer, or the true conscience keeper:
Emphatic words of text, "Lord," "thou," John xii, 48; John vi, 29.

The right answer:
1. In reference to God:
(*a*) Fear, Ps. xxv, 14; Ps. lxxxv, 9; Prov. xxiv, 26, 27.
(*b*) Seek, Deut. iv, 29; Heb. ii, 6; Jer. xxix, 13.
(*c*) Love, Jude 21; 1 Cor. viii, 3; Rom. viii, 28.
(*d*) Rejoice in, Phil. iv, 4.
(*e*) Serve, Heb. xii, 28; Rom. vi, 13; Rom. xii, 1.
The right means to this end, Rom. v, 1, 2; Rom. viii, 1; viii, 8; xii, 2.

2. In reference to ourselves.

(a) Walk by faith, Gal. ii, 20; Heb. x, 38; Eph. vi, 16.
(b) Watchfulness and prayer, Mark xiv, 38; 1 Cor. xvi, 13; Eph. vi, 18.
(c) Diligence, Heb. vi, 11, 12; Rom. xii, 11; 1 Cor. xv, 58.
(d) Thankfulness, Eph. v, 20; 2 Cor. vi, 10.
(e) Patience and perseverance, Heb. xii, 1; James v, 10.
(f) Entire sanctification, 2 Pet. i, 5, 6, 7; Eph. v, 9; 1 Thess. v, 23.

3. *In reference to others.*
Golden text, Luke vi. 31.
(a) Love, John xiii, 35; 1 John iii, 14, 18, 19; 2 Cor. xiii, 11; Eph. iv, 31, 32.
(b) Speech, Eph. iv, 25; Ps. xv, 1, 3.
(c) Conduct, Gal. vi, 10; Heb. xiii, 16; Heb. x, 24, 25; Phil. ii, 15, 16.

Summary:

1. To Christians, Phil. iv, 8; Gal. vi, 9.
2. To all, Ecc. xii, 13, 14.

REV. A. G. VERMILYE.

HINTS ON DEALING WITH INQUIRERS.

Deal with the inquirer alone if possible. Converse in a low tone of voice. Be careful to find out his spiritual condition, and then be ready to promptly suggest God's remedy for his trouble. Do not debate any point. Meet every difficulty with "Thus saith the Lord." Listen attentively to every statement he has to make. Pray while you listen and wait.

Do not depend on past success in dealing with the unsaved, nor on your own knowledge of "the Word of God," your Christian experience or tact in pursuasion or illustration; it is the Spirit that quickeneth, John vi, 63.

Constantly remember that your work in reaching and saving men is, under the Holy Spirit, to make known to them the finished work that God has wrought in Christ for their salvation. Present clearly the truths set forth in Isa. liii, 3-6.

If the inquirer is inclined to look at his doubts or difficulties, says he believes this or that, has this bad habit or that, has "tried" and failed, do not wait to "reform" or correct his errors, but hold up Christ as a personal, living, loving, helping Savior—remembering Heb. vii, 25.

A few appropriate passages are better than a large number. Too many texts may confuse and perplex the inquirer.

Carry *your own Bible* with you to the service, and let the inquirer read for himself such texts as you desire the Spirit to use with him.

Never advise an inquirer to go home and read his Bible, or pray or try to do better; this is losing the present opportunity with no promise of a future or better one. Seek to bring him to an immediate decision. God says *now.*

Ever bear in mind it is not repentance, prayer nor faith that saves: these are only ways of approach to Christ: He alone saves, John xiv, 6.

Avoid speaking false peace. Never tell an inquirer he is saved. God the Holy Spirit will show him that when he has believed on the Lord Jesus Christ.

SUGGESTIVE SCRIPTURES.

For those who lack assurance—Doubters, John v, 24; vi, 47; xx, 30, 31; 1 John iii, 2; 2 Tim. i, 12; 1 John v, 13.

For those who have grown cold—Backsliders, Jer. iii, 5, 13, 19; iii, 12, 13, 14, 22, 23; Hosea xiv, 1, 2, 4; Ps. xxxii, 5; 1 John i, 9, etc.

For those not deeply convicted of sin—Indifferent, Isa. i, 5, 6; Rom. iii, 10, 12, 22, 23; 1 John i, 8, 10, etc.

For those who think they are too great sinners—Penitent, Isa. 1, 18; liii, 4, 5; Luke xix, 10; 1 Peter ii, 24, etc.

For those who don't know how to come—Inquiring, John i, 12; iii, 15,

16, 18, 36; v, 24; Isa. xxvi, 3, 4; Rev. xxii, 17; Isa. xlv, 22; lv, 1, etc.

For those who hesitate and say there is time enough yet — Procrastinators, Luke xii, 19, 20; James iv, 13, 14; 2 Cor. vi, 2, etc.

For those who are afraid they wont hold out — Faithless, Jude 24; Rom. xiv, 4; 2 Tim. i, 12, etc.

With those who have just decided for Christ's use — Heb. ii, 17, 18; iv, 15, 16; 1 Cor. x, 13, etc.

Mark such passages as the Spirit opens to you, and be able wisely to apply and enforce them. Every worker should have stored in his mind a list of his own, and acquire the habit of grouping texts. Depend all through every conversation with inquirers on the Holy Spirit to convince, convict, and convert.

Arranged by JOHN H. ELLIOTT.

CHRISTIAN WORK.
2 Tim. iii, 16, 17.

Works:
1. Wicked works, Col. i, 21.
2. Dead works, Heb. ix, 14.
3. Good works, Titus ii, 7-14; iii, 8.

The Scriptures given for the one purpose of fitting the believer for *good works.*

I. *The Foundation for a Beginning* — Created in Christ Jesus unto, etc., Eph. ii, 8-10.

II. *The furnishing for:*
The Word of God, 2 Tim. iii, 16, 17. It follows then that this fitness is of God and not of man, 2 Cor. ix, 8.

III. *The Secret of Success:*
1. Through the Word, 2 Tim. ii, 15; Josh. i, 8.
2. Through the Holy Spirit, John xx, 21, 22; Acts i, 8; Acts xviii, 24-28; Acts xix, 1-6.

IV. *The Reward:*
1. Only the work that abides will be rewarded, 1 Cor. iii, 11-15.
2. But the reward will be beyond all we can ask or think, Dan. xii, 8.

JOHN H. ELLIOTT.

HINDRANCES TO WORK.
I. Ridicule, Neh. lv, 1-3.
II. Open enmity, Neh. iv, 7, 8.
III. Unbelieving brethren, Neh. iv, 10.
IV. Wordly brethren, Neh. v, 1-6.
V. Offer of worldly friendship, Neh. vi, 5-8.
VII. Temptation to cowardice, Neh. vi, 10-14.

MAN AS A SINNER.
1. God made him upright, Gen. i, 27; Ecc. vii, 29. 2. As a free agent, Josh. xxiv, 15; 1 Kings xviii, 21. 3. He had a knowledge of God's will, Gen. ii, 16, 17; iii, 2, 3; Rom. i, 19, 20. 4. His disobedience was voluntary, Gen. iii, 6; 1 Tim. ii, 4. 5. His nature was corrupted, Gen. vi, 5; Ps. liii, 2, 3; Mark vii. 21-23; Rom. iii, 9-18; viii, 7, 8; 1 Cor. ii, 14. 6. He was condemned by law, Rom. iii, 19; Gal. iii, 10. 7. He tried to dethrone God: (*a*) as creator, Ps. liii, 1; Rom. i, 21, 23, 28; (*b*) as law-giver, Rom. iii, 19; (*c*) as king and ruler, 1 Sam. viii, 7, 8; (*d*) as Father, Isa. i, 2-4; Mal. i, 6; (*e*) as instructor and guide, Isa. viii, 19, 20; (*f*) as deliverer, Isa. xxx, 1, 2; lxiii, 9, 10; (*g*) as Redeemer and Savior, Isa. liii, 1-4; John xv, 21-25; xix, 1-6. 8. Man shown as a sinner in rejecting grace, Matt. xi, 28, 29; John v, 40; Acts xiii, 38, 39, 46.

D. W. WHITTLE.

THE UNCONVERTED ARE
Without Christ, Eph. ii, 12.
Without hope, Eph. ii, 12.
Without God, Eph. ii, 12.
Without truth, 1 Tim. vi, 5.
Without the Spirit, Jude 19.
Without strength, Rom. v, 6.
Without excuse, Rom. i, 20.

THE CONSEQUENCES OF SIN.
1. In this life:
(*a*) On the physical life; labor,

Gen, iii, 17-19; trouble, Isa. lvii, 20, 21; sorrow, Psa. xxxii, 10; death, James i, 15.
(b) On the mental life; ignorance, Prov. v, 22, 23; Titus i, 15.
(c) On the social life; impure, Rom. i, 29-32.
(d) On the moral life; corrupt, 2 Tim. iii, 2.
(e) On the spiritual life; bondage, 2 Peter ii, 19; John viii, 34; hopeless, Eph. ii. 12; blind and deaf, Acts xxviii, 27; dead, Eph. ii, 1.

2. *In the life to come:*
Appear before the Great Judge, 2 Cor. v, 10. Sentenced:
To separation from God, Matthew xxv, 41; and exclusion from heaven, Gal. v, 19-21; Rev. xxi, 1-8.
To eternal punishment, Matt. xv, 46. Reap what has been sown, Gal. vi, 7. The sinner shall know that he brought these things upon himself, and they are eternal, Luke xvi, 19-31.

A. M. WILSON.

WHAT GOD'S WORD SAYS ABOUT THE HEART.

I. Its conditions by nature:
(a) Evil. Gen. vi, 5: viii, 21.
(b) Desperately wicked, Jer. xvii, 9.
(c) Full of wickedness, Mark vii, 21.
(d) Hard, Mark x, 5; Eze. iii, 7.

II. God's knowledge of it, Ps. xliv, 21.

(a) He searches, 1 Chron. xxviii, 9.
(b) He pondereth. Prov. xxi, 2; xxiv, 12.

III. What should be done with it?
(a) Prepared unto God, 1 Sam. vii, 3.
(b) Kept, Prov. iv, 23.
(c) We should believe with whole heart, Rom. x, 10.
(d) We should love God with whole heart, Matt. xxii, 37.
(e) We should trust God with whole heart. Prov. iii, 5.

IV. What it is by God's grace:
(a) Fixed on God, Ps. cxii, 7.
(b) Tender, 2 Sam. xxiv, 10.
(c) Obedient, Ps. cxix, 112; Rom. vi, 17.
(d) Word of God in it, Ps. cxix, 11;
(e) *He longs for God.* Ps. lxxxiv, 2; xl, 8.
(f) Full of good treasure, Matt. xii, 35.

FRED. S. GOODMAN.

THE DANGER OF UNBELIEF.

In whom are we asked to have faith?
1st. In God, Mark xi. 22.
2d. In Christ, John vi, 29; John xiv, 1.
3d. In God's Word, Luke xvi, 29, with John v, 46; 2 Chron. xx, 20; Mark i, 15; Rom. iv, 21. May we have faith in one and reject the others? God was in Christ (2 Cor. v, 19; John xiv, 10), and testified (2 Tim. iii, 16) of Christ in the Old Testament (Luke xxiv, 27-44), and by Him in the New Testament, Heb. i. 1, 2; John iii, 34. To disbelieve in one, then, involves the rejection of all, John v, 23; John viii, 42-47; 1 John v, 10. What are the results of unbelief?

1st. God will require the words of Christ of us (Deut. xviii, 19), and judge us by them, John xii. 47, 48.
2d. We shall not be established (Isa. vii, 9), having built upon a foundation of sand, Matt. vii, 26, 27.
3d. We harden our hearts (Heb. iii. 12, 13), sear or defile our consciences (Titus i, 15), and persisting in it, become self deceived and rendered almost incapable of faith, 1 Cor. i. 18, with 2 Cor. iv, 3, 4; Luke xvi, 31; for we resist the Holy Spirit, John xvi, 9, with Acts vii, 51.
4th. In Christians, it hinders Christ's work about us (Matt. xiii, 58; Mark vi, 5, 6), and quenches the Spirit's work in and through us, Matt. xvii, 19, 20; John vii, 38, 39.
5th. It affects the loss of our priv-

ileges in Christ, Acts xiii, 40–46, and Acts xviii, 6, with Rom. xi, 20, 30, 31.

6th. It prevents any act that will please God, Rom. xiv, 23; Heb. xi, 6. Therefore makes prayer ineffectual (James i, 6, 7), even in the greatest extremity, Prov. i, 24, 29.

7th. It places us, then, with no way of escape (Heb. i, 1, 2, with Heb. ii, 1–4, and Heb. xii, 25) under condemnation (John iii, 18), with the wrath of God abiding on us, John iii, 36; left to die in our sins, John viii, 24; damned, Mark xvi, 16; and at the last day, Rev. xxi, 8.

C. E. DYER.

FOR THE SELF RIGHTEOUS.

All have sinned, Ps. xiv, 3· 1 Kings viii, 46.

He whose sins are in danger, Eze. xviii, 20; Rom. vi, 23 (first clause).

No one who rejects Christ is doing the best he can, for he does not obey God, John vi, 29; 1 John v, 10. 11.

J. E. BROWN.

WORDS FOR MAN.

Adam, Heb., Ahdahm, from Ahdam, to be red, ruddy. Often used collectively (man).

Ish, an individual, man of high degree. Often used collectively (man).

Enosh, frail, mortal man, from Ahnash, incurable, mortal (man).

Anahshim, plural of Enosh, also frequently of Ish (man).

Geber, strong man, from Gahbar, to be strong (man).

Methim, few in number, or mortal. Only used in the plural (men).

THE PUNISHMENT OF THOSE WHO PERSEVERE IN SIN.

Text: Prov. xxix, 1.

"He that being often reproved hardeneth *his* neck shall suddenly be destroyed, and that without remedy."

Sure. "I will surely consume them, saith the Lord," Jer. viii, 12, 13. "How shall we escape if we neglect so great salvation," Heb. ii, 2, 3.

Sudden. "This iniquity shall be to you as a breach ready to fall, swelling out in a high wall, whose breaking cometh suddenly at an instant," Isa. xxx, 13. "Therefore shall evil come upon thee; thou shalt not know from whence it riseth; and mischief shall fall upon thee; thou shalt not be able to put it off; and desolation shall come upon thee suddenly, *which* thou shalt not know," Isa. xlvii, 11.

Fearful. The hail shall sweep away the refuge of lies, and the waters shall overflow the hiding place, and your covenant with death shall be disannulled, and your agreement with hell shall not stand," Isa. xxviii, 17, 18.

"*It is* a fearful thing to fall into the hands of the living God," Heb. x. 31.

No Remedy. "But they mocked the messengers of God, and despised His words, and misused His prophets, until the wrath of the Lord arose against His people, till *there was* no remedy," 2 Chron. xxxvi, 16.

"He that is unjust, let him be unjust still; and he which is filthy, let him be filthy still," Rev. xxii, 11.

H. E. BROWN.

DECEIVED AND PUNISHED.

WILLINGLY DECEIVED BY

A Wicked Heart. "The heart *is* deceitful above all *things*, and desperately wicked; who can know it?" Jer. xvii, 9. Obad. iii, 4; Rom. vii, 11.

False Teachers. "There shall arise false Christs, and false prophets, and shall show great signs and wonders; insomuch that, if *it were* possible, they shall deceive the very elect," Matt. xxiv, 24. Col. ii, 8; 2 Peter ii, 1, 2.

Satan. "Satan himself is transformed into an angel of light," 2

Cor. xi, 14. 1 Tim. iv, 1; 2 Thess. ii, 9.

TERRIBLY PUNISHED BY

Strong Delusion. "And for this cause God shall send them strong delusion, that they should believe a lie," 2 Thess. ii, 11. Ezek. xiv, 9; 1 Kings xxii, 20–22.

Complete Destruction. "He feedeth on ashes; a deceived heart hath turned him aside, that he cannot deliver his soul, nor say, *Is there* not a lie in my right hand?" Isa. xliv, 20. 2 Thess. ii, 12; Prov. ix, 18.

H. E. BROWN.

ABIDING IN CHRIST.

The words "in" and "abiding in," which occur so constantly in Scripture, refer to two very distinct doctrines and conditions. The first signifies our union with Christ; the second our communion with Christ. The one refers to our standing as those who are saved; the other to our walk, as those who are obedient. If one has been regenerated, he is certainly in the Lord, though by his lack of strict watchfulness and continued prayer, he may not be abiding in Him.

In brief, the two words refer, the one to our regeneration, the other to our practical Christian life; as for example: "If any man be in Christ, he is a new creature," 2 Cor. v, 17; and, "He that saith he abideth in Him ought himself also so to walk, even as He walked," 1 John ii, 6.

What, now, are the promises and blessings connected with abiding in Christ:

1. Fruitfulness. "He that abideth in Me and I in Him, the same bringeth forth much fruit," John xv, 5. How obvious is this conclusion. Just in proportion to the communication of sap from the tree to the branch, will be the vigor and health and fruitfulness of the branch. A Christian abounds in the graces of the Spirit to the degree in which he abides in the living Christ.

2. Power in Prayer. "If ye abide in Me, and My words abide in you, ye shall ask what ye will, and it shall be done unto you," John xv, 7. If we are in intimate communion with the Lord, we learn to know His will, and to interpret His mind, so that we do not mistake in our asking. We ask amiss, and receive not, because our desires are merely selfish. Communion with Christ dissolves carnal desires, as the going into a warm room melts the snow-flakes from our coat.

3. Restraint from Sin. "Whosoever abideth in Him sinneth not," 1 John iii, 6. Of course sin cannot flourish in the presence of the sinless one. Because we say no man is free from sin, we do not for a moment deny that we ought to be free from it. "If we say we have no sin, we deceive ourselves." "If we say that we have not sinned, we make Him a liar." Here is the two-edged lie with which every perfectionist is certain to commit suicide. But if one could be found who was abiding perfectly in Christ, he would be sinless, because he would be perfectly like Christ, who is sinless.

4. Christlikeness. "He that saith he abideth in Him, ought so to walk, even as He walked," 1 John ii, 6. The external conduct must be He the perfect measure of the internal life. The hands on the dial-plate will exactly represent the accuracy and perfection of the machinery within. If we are in perfect accord with Christ's Spirit, we shall be in exact accord with His example.

5. Assurance. "And now, little children, abide in Him, that, when He shall appear, we may have confidence, and not be ashamed before Him at His coming," 1 John ii, 28. The perfect face can never be ashamed of its own image. When we shall see "the King in His beauty," we shall be like Him, if we are found abiding in Him, and He will not despise His own likeness. Therefore have we confidence before Him at His coming, if we are abiding in Him. But if we have a name to live, and are abiding in the world, and in the lusts and pleasures thereof; how we shall shrink abashed before Him, and how will He be ashamed of us! "As a dream when one awakeneth, so, O Lord, when Thou awakest, Thou shalt despise their image." "As for me, I will behold Thy face in righteousness; I shall be satisfied when I awake with Thy likeness."

A. J. GORDON, D. D.

ABIGAIL; A BRIEF EXPOSITION.

1 Samuel xxv.

A beautiful illustration of a redeemed sinner:

1. Her Name. Gift of the father All His gift in the kingdom of grace. Jesus, gift of God to the world, John iii, 16. Spirit, gift of Christ to the Church, John xvi, 7. Church, gift of the Father to the Son, John xvii, 22, 24. Names express character, Gen. xxxii, 28; John i, 42; Eph. ii, 12, 19.

2. Her Beauty. Righteousness makes the saint "all fair," Cant. ii, 14; iv, 7; Col. i, 21, 22; Rev. xxi, 9, 11.

3. Her Knowledge. The secret of the Lord is with them that fear Him, Psa. xxv, 14; Amos iii, 7. God must be discerned by faith, 1 Cor. i, 21. The unction of knowledge, 1 John ii, 20, 27.

4. Her Friendliness. No sympathy from Nabal. His name meant folly. He saw nothing lovely in the rejected David. Christ Jesus, "a root out of dry ground" to many, Isa. liii, 2, 3. The world at enmity with true believers, 1 John xv, 19, 20; xvi, 2.

5. Her Faith. It reached beyond circumstances. David was in poverty and rejection, Matt. xvi, 15–17.

She discerned his future exaltation, verse 30. So did Paul, concerning the true David, 2 Cor. iv, 8–19; Phil. ii, 9–11.

6. Her Service. It was two-fold. God has both priests and Levites. She ministered to David, Luke viii, 3; 1 Peter iv, 10, 11. She interceded for Nabal, Mark vii, 25–29. In serving David she remembered his young men. "Ye did it unto me," Matt. xxv, 40. Prayer is mighty. Moses for Israel. Let me alone, Moses, that I may curse Israel, Deut. ix, 14, 15. The power of a pleading church, Cant. vi, 5; Acts xii, 5.

7. Her Request for Herself, verse 31. "Lord, remember me," Luke xxiii, 42. David's answer, "Peace." "I have accepted thy person," Eph. i, 6. Jesus' desire for His own, John xvii, 24.

8. David's Men a Protection to Nabal. The church salt. Light. A city, Matt. v, 13, 14. Vine-branches. Witnesses. Servants. Epistles, John xvi, 20; Acts i, 8; 2 Cor. iii, 3.

9. The Lost Opportunity. A drunken sleep. Sinners asleep now. Some will awake too late, Matt. xxv, 11, 12. Saints are asleep also, Jonah i, 6; Eph. v, 14.

10. Abigail's Reward. She followed David in his rejection, Matt. xix, 27–29. When Nabal died, she married him, Eph. v, 27. The law is cruel as Nabal. It no longer has dominion over us, for it is dead to us, and we are joined to Christ, Rom. vii, 4–6.

11. He was her Deliverer, 1 Sam. xxx, 18. When he was exalted she shared his glory, 1 John iii, 2; Rom. viii, 17; 2 Tim. ii, 12; Rev. xix, 7, 8. "The glory which Thou gavest me, I have given them," John xvii, 22.

MRS. GEO. C. NEEDHAM.

ADDITION.

It is very interesting and instructive to note the method of spiritual growth laid down in the New Testament, as indicated by the constant use of the word "addition." How does the development of the Church begin and progress? On what principle is the body of Christ edified or built up?

First. By the addition of believing souls to Christ. "And believers were the more added to the Lord," Acts v, 14. "And much people was added unto the Lord," Acts xi, 24. To begin a church by the union of one man with another, is an utterly false principle. To say that a church is the voluntary association of persons for worship and edification, is an equally false definition. It is of no use to attempt to add together ciphers. Unless Christ be the numeral to give value to these naughts, we can get no real values. And a company of individuals simply joined one to the other, will have little spiritual worth. There may be union and compactness, but no contents—like the staves of a barrel hooped firmly together around nothing, and depending for their union upon leaning closely upon each other. The true addition is that which puts Christ first and compacts the whole body together about Him. And so, when an addition of believing souls has been made to Christ, the first unit, a church has been begun. Then the development can go on.

Secondly. By the addition of believers to the church. "And the Lord added to the church daily such as should be saved," Acts ii, 47. "And the same day there were added unto them about three thousand souls," Acts ii, 41. Believer can be joined to believer when the first has been joined to Christ. When the Divine Unit, the "Alpha" and the "First," has been received, all other unions of believer to believer, of disciple to disciple, begin to have a value. Let believers be added to the church when the church has been begun by additions to Christ.

The church is edified in the third place, by the addition of graces to the believer. "Add to your faith, virtue; and to virtue, knowledge; and to knowledge, temperance; and to temperance, patience; and to patience, godliness; and to godliness, brotherly kindness; and to brotherly kindness, charity." 2 Pet. i, 5–7. As in the growth of a tree, there is a two-fold addition constantly going on, from within and from without, or by development and by accretion, so in the building up of the church. As believers are added from without, grace must be added from within. If either of these processes fail to go on, the body will be weakened and deformed. Let a church be intent only on increasing its membership, and how soon will it become top-heavy — more branches than root. Let a church be wholly absorbed in cultivating its spiritual graces, and how soon will it become barren, its testimony and activity lost. Both processes must go on together — the adding of believers by faith, and the adding of faith to the believers.

The church is edified finally by the addition of God's grace and favor to it. "Seek ye first the kingdom of God, and His righteousness; and all these things shall be added unto you," Matt. vi, 33. Outward prosperity is not forbidden to the church of God. She is always to be "a little flock," indeed. She is never to bring all the world into her fold. But while a little flock, often despised and hated, she is sometime to "have rest and be edified," as in the beginning, "walking in the fear of the Lord, and in the comfort of the Holy Ghost, and being multiplied." But this outward prosperity will not come by being sought as an end. "The kingdom of God and His righteousness" must be sought — first and supremely; and then, as by a perquisite and revenue of this seeking, will certainly come these outward blessings.

A. J. GORDON, D. D.

AMUSEMENTS.

I. *Warning against sinful amusements*, Job. xxi, 11-13; 1 Cor. xv, 33; Prov. xlv, 13; xxi, 17; 2 Peter ii, 13; Eccl. xi, 9; Ps. i, 1; Ps. cxix, 115; Prov. i, 10; iv, 14; xxix, 8; 2 Pet. iii, 17.

II. *Right pleasures*, Prov. xv, 13; xvii, 22; Luke xv, 23, 24; 1 Thess. v, 16; John xvi, 33.

REV. W. F. CRAFTS.

A FEW OF GOD'S "ALLS."

All have sinned, Rom. iii, 23.

And so death passed upon all men, for that all have sinned, Rom. v, 12.

Christ Jesus who gave Himself a ransom for all, 1 Tim. ii, 5, 6.

Come unto Me, all ye that labor and are heavy laden, and I will give you rest, Matt. xi, 28.

All things are now ready, Luke xiv, 17.

The righteousness of God, which is by faith of Jesus Christ unto all and upon all them that believe, Rom. iii, 22.

All that believe are justified from all things, Acts xiii, 39.

ALLS, THREE IMPORTANT.

1 Tim. ii.

"I exhort, therefore, that, first of all, supplications, prayers, intercessions and giving up of thanks be made for all men."

"Who will have all men to be saved, and to come unto the knowledge of the truth."

"Who gave Himself a ransom for all, to be testified in due time."

I. The duty of praying for all men is laid down. Narrow and selfish hearts may narrow the circle of intercession within the limits of kindred, or church, or family; but if we pray with the heart of Him who loves the world, we shall embrace all the world in our prayers.

II. We are to pray for all men because God will have all men to be saved. The will of God must always determine the bounds of our intercession. "If we ask anything according to His will, He heareth us."

III. Because God "will have all men to be saved." Christ, who came not to do His own will, but the will of His Father, "gave Himself a ransom for all" Thus we can pray for all men because God "will have all men to be saved;" and because Christ "gave Himself according the will of God," that He might be "the Savior of all men, specially of those that believe."

A. J. GORDON, D.D.

APPEARINGS, THE THREE.

I. "Once in the end of the world hath He appeared to put away sin by the sacrifice of Himself," verse 26.

II. "For Christ is entered * * * into heaven itself, now to appear in the presence of God for us," verse 24.

III. "And unto them that look for Him shall He appear the second time, without sin unto salvation," verse 28.

Question: Where shall the ungodly and the sinner appear? 1 Peter iv, 18.

A PLEASANT JOURNEY.

The Christian walks in wisdom's way. Her ways are ways of pleasantness, and all her paths are peace, Prov. iii, 17. The Christian's way is a pleasant way. What makes it so?

I. In a journey much depends upon what one goes for. The Christian goes for a promised rest, Heb. iv, 9. And likewise for an inheritance, 1 Peter i, 4.

II. Much depends upon our

strength. The Christian has strength for the whole journey, Ps. lxxi, 16; Phil. iv, 13.

III. Much depends on the guide we have. The Christian has a faithful guide, Ps. xxxii, 8; Isa. xxx, 21; Rom. viii, 14.

IV. The Christian shall walk in the light, cxix, 105; Isa. lx, 19; John viii, 12.

V. The Christian's steps are ordered and cared for, Ps. xxxvii, 23; Prov. xvi, 9. And best of all, we have Christ's steps to follow, 1 Peter ii, 21.

VI. The way of the Christian lies through green pastures, Ps. xxiii, 2. See Ex. xv, 27.

VII. When the Christian's journey is ended, he puts up at his Father's house, John xiv, 2.

S. M. SAGFORD.

ARKS OF SCRIPTURE.

I. Noah's Ark. Gen. vi, 13, 14.
II. Moses' Ark, Ex. ii, 3.
III. God's Ark, Ex. xxv, 10, 22.

1. Noah's Ark.

1. Was provided by God; was of divine planning; and typical of the Lord Jesus, 2 Sam. xiv, 14; Rom. xi, 26.
2. Was built to save men, Gal. iv, 4, 5.
3. Was the only way of escape, Acts iv, 12.
4. Saved but eight. Many called, few chosen, Matt. vii, 13, 14; 1 Peter iii, 20.
5. It was a long time building. From Adam down to the cross, salvation had been prefigured through a protracted series of types, Heb. ix, 9-14.
6. There was but one door into the ark; and one day God Himself closed that, Luke xiii, 25; Acts iv, 12; Rev. iii, 7.
7. There was but one window, and that only afforded a view of the heavens, Ps. lxi, 2-4; cxxi, 1.
8. Both clean and unclean animals were admitted, and as many women as men, Isa. i, 18; Matt. ix, 13; 1 Tim. ii, 14, 15. Saved through the bearing of the child; *i. e.*, Jesus.
9. The raven departed, but the dove returned, and abode in the ark, Matt. vii, 22, 23; 1 John ii, 19.

The Ark of Noah has a voice for us:

Come in. Bring others. Room for all. There is duty in coming. Death in delaying. Delight in obeying.

2. Moses' Ark. This little ark, as well as Noah's, was daubed with pitch. In both these instances we get the primary sense of atonement, which is to cover over, Ps. xxxii, 1. Sin must be hidden from the Divine eye by atonement. Hence the exposure and punishment of sin is expressed by something uncovered, 1 Sam. vi, 19; Ps. xc, 8; Matt. xxii, 12.

Moses' Ark afforded shelter from the wrath of the king. It required great faith to risk the precious burden to it. Have we committed our choicest treasures to God's keeping? Matt. iii, 17, 18; Heb. xi, 23.

Moses' ark teaches:
The courage of faith, Heb. xii, 2, 3.
The watch care of God, Ps. cxxi, 3-7.
The security of the better ark, Jesus.

3. God's Ark. It was composed of three articles forming one piece of furniture. A true symbol of the glorious Trinity, Heb. ix, 23.
1. This ark divided the Jordan, Josh. iv, 7.
2. It captured the Philistines, 1 Sam. iv, 3; vii, 1, 10.
3. It dethroned Dagon, 1 Sam. v, 3.
4. Fifty thousand and seventy people killed by it for removing the blood sprinkled cover, 1 Sam. vi, 19.
5. Uzzah died before it, 2 Sam. vi, 7.
6. Was transferred to the temple, 2 Chron. v, 6, 10.
7. The other vessels of the Temple

were captured, Jer. ii, 19. The prophets make no mention of the fate of the ark; but in the Apocrypha it is said that God has hidden it away in safety. The ark was seen only by the high priest, symbol of Jehovah, whom we only can behold in Christ, John i, 18; Heb. i, 2, 3.

MRS. GEORGE C. NEEDHAM.

BACKSLIDING.

I. What is it? Turning the heart from God, 1 Kings xi, 9. Leaving first love, Rev. ii, 4. Forsaking God, Jer. ii, 9–13. Rebellion, Isa. i, 2. Regarding iniquity in my heart, Ps. lxvi, 18.

II. How men get into it. By neglect of God's Word, Ps. cxix, 9, 11, 43, 44. Neglect of prayer. Spiritual pride, Rev. iii, 17. Self-confidence, Mark xiv, 27–31. Following afar off, Matt. xxvi, 58.

III. How to get out of it. Healing from God, Hosea xiv, 4. Come, let us reason, Isa. i, 18. Remember and return, Rev. ii, 5. Humble, pray and seek, 2 Chron. vii, 13, 14. Acknowledge, Jer. iii, 12, 13. Confess, 1 John i, 9. Arise, Luke xv, 17–20.

IV. How to keep out of it. By shunning worldly company, Ps. i, 1–3. By cultivating a fervent spirit, Rom. xii, 11. By occupation of the mind on Christ, Heb. xii, 1, 2; 2 Cor. iii, 18. By being in earnest, Luke xiii, 24; Rightly esteeming the Word, Job xxiii, 12. Feeding on the Word, 1 Pet. ii, 2. Hiding the Word in the heart, Ps. cxix, 11. Growing in grace, 2 Pet. iii, 18. If ye do these things ye shall never fall, 2 Pet. i, 2–11.—*Y. M. C. A. Watchman.*

BACKSLIDERS.

PROOF OF

Diminished Love. "I have somewhat against thee, because thou hast left thy first love," Rev. ii, 4.

Self Confidence. "Thou sayest, I am rich, and increased with goods, and have need of nothing," Rev. iii, 17.

Unanswered prayer. "Your iniquities have separated between you and your God, and your sins have hid *His* face from you, that He will not hear," Isa. lxix, 1, 2.

CONDITION OF

Back toward God. "They have turned *their* back unto Me, and not *their* face," Jer. ii, 27.

Robbers. "Will a man rob God? Yet ye have robbed Me. But ye say, Wherein have we robbed Thee? In tithes and offerings," Mal. iii, 8.

Going to destruction. "In his trespass that he hath trespassed, and in his sin that he hath sinned, in them shall he die," Ezek. xviii, 24.

INVITATION TO

Return. "O Israel, return unto the Lord thy God," Hos. xiv, 1.

Bring Tithes. "Bring ye all the tithes into the storehouse, that there may be meat in My house, and prove Me now herewith, saith the Lord of hosts," Mal. iii, 10.

Receive God's best Gifts. "I counsel thee to buy of Me gold tried in the fire, that thou mayest be rich; and white raiment, that thou mayest be clothed," Rev. iii, 18.

H. E. BROWN.

BE'S, AS COMMANDS IN THE BIBLE.

"Be thou in the fear of the Lord all the day long," Prov. xxiii, 17.

Be at peace among yourselves, 1 Thess. v, 13.

Be content with such things as ye have, Heb. xiii, 5.

Be careful for nothing, Phil. iv, 6.

Be very courageous, Josh. xxiii, 6.

Be ye all of one mind, 1 Pet. iii, 8.

Be pitiful, 1 Pet. iii, 8.

Be courteous, 1 Pet. iii, 8.

Be thou faithful unto death, Rev. ii, 10.

Be glad in the Lord, Ps. xxxii, 11.

Be of good cheer, Acts xxiii, 11.

Be ye holy, for I am holy, 1 Pet. i, 16.
Be ye kind one to another, Eph. iv, 32.
Be kindly affectionate one to another, Rom. xii, 10.
Be ye mindful always of His covenant, 1 Chron. xvi, 15.
Be ye merciful, as your Father is merciful, Luke vi, 36.
Be not afraid of sudden fear, Prov. iii, 25.
Be not deceived; God is not mocked, Gal. vi, 17.
Be not overcome of evil, Rom. xii, 21.
Be not righteous overmuch, Ecc. vii, 16.
Be not wise in thine own eyes, Prov. iii, 7.
Be not unequally yoked together with unbelievers, 2 Cor. vi, 14–17.
Be ye separate, 2 Cor. vi, 14–17.
Be patient unto the coming of the Lord, James v, 7.
Be ye perfect, Matt. v, 48.
Be ye ready, Luke xii, 40.
Be ye reconciled to God, 2 Cor. v, 20.
Be renewed in the spirit of your mind, Eph. iv, 23.
Be not conformed to this world, Rom. xii, 2.
Be still, and know that I am God, Psa. xlvi, 10.
Be sober, be vigilant, 1 Pet. v, 8.
Be of the same mind one toward another, Rom. xii, 16.
Be strong in the Lord, Eph. vi, 10.
Be thankful, Col. iii, 15.
Be ye doers of the Word, Jas. i, 22.
Be ye angry, and sin not, Eph. iv, 26.
Be watchful, Rev. iii, 2.
Be zealous, therefore, and repent, Rev. iii, 19.
Be steadfast, unmovable, 1 Cor. xv, 58.

BELIEVERS—THE PLACE OF REFUGE.

1. At Christ's Cross. The place of peace, Col. i, 20; Gal. vi, 14.
Here we find refuge from the curse of the law and the conscience.
2. Before His Face. The place of light, 2 Cor. iv, 6; Ps. lxvii, 1, 2.
The face is an expression or revelation of the whole man. Here we find refuge from the darkness of our natural state.
3. On His Shoulders. The place of strength, Exod. xxvii, 9–12; Luke xv, 2.
Here we find refuge from the weakness of our own characters.
4. On His Bosom. The place of love, John xiii, 23; John xxi, 20; Ex. xxvii, 29, 30.
Here we find refuge from the unsatisfied cravings of our own nature; relief from care, disappointment and reproach.
5. At His Feet. The place of instruction, Deut. xxxiii, 3; Luke x, 39; Col. i, 9.
Here we find refuge from our own ignorance, follies and mistakes.
6. By His Side. The place of service. Luke viii, 1–3; Col. iii, 23, 24.
Here we find refuge from the emptiness of our own life and the ignobleness of its purposes.
7. In His Steps. The place of holiness, 1 Peter i, 21; 1 John ii, 6.
Here we find refuge from the passions — habits of our own evil natures.

REV. W. H. MARQUISS.

BELIEVER'S RELATION TO GOD·

I. Justification, or a new standing before God, Rom. iii, 26–30; Gal. iii, 8.
II. Repentance, or a new mind about God, Acts xx, 21; Rom. ii, 4.
III. Regeneration, or a new nature from God, John iii, 3; 2 Peter i, 4.
IV. Conversion, or a new life for God, 1 Thess. i, 9, 10; 1 Cor. x, 31.
V. Adoption, or a new attitude toward God, Rom. viii, 15; Gal. iv, 4–7.
VI. Sanctification, or separation unto God, 2 Cor. vi, 16–18; 2 Cor. vii, 1.

VII. Glorification, or the eternal state with God, Rev. xxi, 3; xxii, 3–5.

BLESSING—PLACES OF.

1. At the cross, Exod. xxix, 42; Gal. iii, 10, 13; Luke xxiii, 42.
2. In prayer, Exod. xxx, 36; Rev. viii, 3, 4; Heb. iv, 16.
3. In communion, Exod. xxv, 22; Ps. xxxix, 3; 1 John i, 3, 7.
4. Meeting with saints, Matt. xviii, 18–20; John xx, 19–26; Heb. x, 25.
5. At work in the vineyard, Cant. vii, 12; Matt. xxv, 34–40.
6. Suffering for Christ's sake, Matt. vi, 10–12; 2 Cor. iv, 17; 1 Peter iv, 13–16.
7. Place of trial, 1 Peter i, 6,. 7; James i, 3–12. See Abraham and Peter.

REV. R. CAMERON, B. A.

BIBLE, THE SUPPERS OF.

I. Worldly pleasure, Mark vi, 21.
II. Grace, Luke xiv, 16.
III. Love for Christ, John xii, 2.
IV. Redemption, John xiii, 2.
V. Communion, Rev. iii, 20.
VI. Marriage. Rev. xix, 9.
VII. Wrath, Rev. xix, 17.

These are the only suppers mentioned in the New Testament, and the word nowhere occurs in the Old Testament.

JAMES H. BROOKES.

CHRISTIAN RACE, RULES FOR.

I. "I will run in the way of Thy commandments," Ps. cxix, 32.
II. "Run after Thee," S. S. i, 4.
III. "Run well," Gal. v, 7.
IV. "Run not uncertainly," 1 Cor. ix, 26.
V. "Run with patience," Heb. xi, 1.
VI. "Run and not be weary," Isa. xi, 31.
VII. "Not run in vain," Phil. ii, 16.

COMMERCIAL TRAVELERS' QUESTIONS.

What house? 2 Cor. v, 1.
What line of goods? Gal. v, 22, 23.
What price? Gal. v, 1.
What route? Jer. 1, 5 ; Matt. vii, 14.
What town for Sabbath rest? Rev. xxi, 10–13, 21–27.
What the news? Luke ii, 10, 11.

J. E. BROWN.

CHRIST IN THE SONG OF SOLOMON.

I. Listening to the beloved, ii, 8.
II. Called by the beloved, ii, 10.
III. Claiming the beloved, ii, 16.
IV. Opening to the beloved, v, 5.
V. Praising the beloved, v, 9–16.
VI. Leaning upon the beloved, viii, 5.
VII. Long for the beloved, viii, 14.

CONFESSION.

I. Its necessity:
1. God required, Lev. v, 3; Hos. v, 15.
2. Exhortation to, Josh. vii, 19; Jer. iii, 13.

II. Its accompaniments:
1. Submission to punishment, Lev. xxvi, 41; Neh. ix, 33.
2. Prayer for forgiveness, 2 Sam. xxiv, 10; Psa. xxv, 11; li, 1; Jer. xiv, 7–9, 11.
3. Self abasement, Isa. lxiv, 5, 6; Jer. iii, 25.
4. Godly sorrow, Psa. xxxviii, 18; Sam. i, 20.
5. Forsaking sin, Prov. xxviii, 13.
6. Restitution, Num. v, 6, 7.

III. Its character:
1. Unreserved, Ps. xxxii, 5; li, 3; cvi, 6.
2. Illustrated, Luke xv, 21; xviii, 13.

IV. Its rewards:
1. God regards, Job xliii, 27, 28; Dan. ix, 20.
2. Promise relative to, Lev. xxvi, 40–42; Prov. xxviii, 13.
3. Pardon, Ps. xxxii, 5; 1 John i, 9.

CONTRASTS.

GENESIS.	REVELATION.
Earth created, i, 1.	Passed away, xxi, 1.
Night, i, 5.	No night there, xxii, 5.
Seas, i, 10.	No more sea, xxi, 1.
Sun and moon, i, 16, 17.	No need of sun, xx, 23.
Garden home for man, ii, 8.	City home for nations, xxi, 10.
Marriage of first Adam, ii, 18–23.	Marriage of second Adam, xix, 9.
First appearance of Satan, iii, 1.	His final doom, xx, 10.
Sorrow and suffering, iii, 16, 17.	No more sorrow, xxi, 4.
Curse, iii, 17.	No more curse, xxii, 3.
Driven from the tree of life, iii, 27.	Welcome back, xxii, 2.

CONVERSATION.

UNBELIEVERS.	BELIEVERS.
Lusts of the flesh, Eph. ii, 3.	Simple and sincere, 2 Cor. i, 12.
The old man, Eph. iv, 32.	Without covetousness, Heb. xiii, 5.
Self righteousness, Gal. i, 13.	Good, James iii, 13; 1 Peter iii, 16.
Vain, 1 Peter i, 18.	Chaste, 1 Peter iii, 1, 2.
Filthy, 2 Peter ii, 7.	Honest, 1 Peter ii, 12.
	Holy, 1 Peter i, 15; 2 Peter iii, 11.
	Christ, Heb. xiii, 7.

DEATH, THOUGHTS ON.

1. A dying testimony is not so important as a living one, Rom. xii, 1.
2. "Blessed are the dead who die in the Lord," Rev. xiv, 13.
3. "Asleep in Jesus," 1 Thess. iv, 13–18.
4. Stephen's first martyr fell asleep, Acts vii, 60.
Illustrations — Lazarus, John xi, 11. The maid, Matt. ix, 24.
5. "We shall not all sleep," 1 Cor. xv, 51.
6. Whether we wake or sleep, we shall be His, 1 Thess. v, 10; Phil. i, 21.
7. The awakening, Dan. xii, 2, 3.
(a) We shall be satisfied, Ps. xvii, 15.
(b) We shall be like Him, 1 John iii, 12.
(c) We shall see face to face, 1 Cor. xiii, 12.

JOHN H. ELLIOTT.

DECISION.

Choose whom ye will serve. "Choose you this day whom ye will serve." Josh. xxiv, 15.
"How long halt ye between two opinions? if the Lord be God, follow Him; but if Baal, *then* follow him, 1 Kings xviii, 21.
Choose heartily. "Thou shalt love the Lord thy God with all thine heart, and with all thy soul, and with all thy might," Deut. vi, 5.
"Whatsoever ye do, do it heartily, as to the Lord, and not unto men," Col. iii, 23.
You can serve but one. "No servant can serve two masters," Luke xvi, 13.
"Ye adulterers and adulteresses. know ye not that the friendship of the world is enmity with God? whosoever therefore will be a friend of the world is the enemy of God," James iv, 4.

Serve faithfully. "Whether therefore ye eat, or drink, or whatsoever ye do, do all to the glory of God," 1 Cor. x, 31.

"Because thou art lukewarm, and neither cold nor hot, I will spew thee out of my mouth," Rev. iii, 15, 16.

Better choose God. "I beseech you therefore, brethren, by the mercies of God, that ye present your bodies a living sacrifice, holy, acceptable unto God, *which is* your reasonable service," Rom. xii, 1.

"Love not the world, neither the things *that are* in the world. If any man love the world, the love of the Father is not in him," 1 John ii, 15, 17.

Trust in your choice. "Go and cry unto the gods which ye have chosen; let them deliver you in the time of your tribulation," Jud. x, 13, 14.

"Who *is* among you that feareth the Lord, that obeyeth the voice of his servant, that walketh *in* darkness, and hath no light? let him trust in the name of the Lord, and stay upon his God," Isaiah l, 10.

H. E. BROWN.

DIVINE HEALING.

BY MRS. H. A. DODGE.

A CAREFUL study of the Scriptures will reveal the following facts, viz.: That physical life is communicated to each person from God: "For He is thy life, and the length of thy days" (Deut. xxx, 20, m. c.). "For in Him we live, and move, and have our being" (Acts xvii, 28, f. c.). Sickness, sometimes caused by disobedience, under both law and grace: "If thou wilt diligently hearken to the voice of the Lord thy God, and wilt do that which is right in His sight, and wilt give ear to His commandments and keep all His statutes, I will put none of these diseases upon thee which I have brought upon the Egyptians; for I am the Lord that healeth thee" (Ex. xv, 26). "Afterward Jesus findeth him in the temple, and said unto him, Behold, thou art made whole; sin no more, lest a worst thing come unto thee" (John v, 14). That forgiveness is sometimes joined with healing: "Who forgiveth all thine iniquities, who healeth all thy diseases" (Ps. ciii, 3). "When Jesus saw their faith, He said unto the sick of the palsy, Son, thy sins be forgiven thee" (Mark ii, 5). Sickness is not always caused by the individual's sin, or carelessness of walk. "And the Lord said unto Satan, Hast thou considered my servant Job, that there is none like him in the earth, a perfect and an upright man, one that feareth God, and escheweth evil? and still he holdeth fast his integrity, although thou movedst me against him to destroy him without a cause. * * * So Satan went forth from the presence of the Lord, and smote Job with sore boils from the sole of his foot unto his crown" (Job ii, 3, 7). "Jesus answered, Neither hath this man sinned, nor his parents; but that the works of God should be made manifest in him" (John ix, 3). "Therefore His sisters sent unto Him, saying, Lord, behold he whom Thou lovest is sick. When Jesus heard that, He said, This sickness is not unto death, but for the glory of God, that the Son of God might be glorified thereby" (John xi, 3, 4). Our Lord appears to have varied the means used in recovering the sick, according to the faith of the applicant. In healing the sick servant of the centurion, at his desire,

He spake "the Word only" (Matt. viii, 8, 13). In the case of one deaf and with an impediment in his speech, He put his "fingers in his ears, and he did spit, and touched his tongue, and looking up to heaven, he sighed, and saith unto him, Ephphatha; that is, Be opened" (Mark vii, 33, 34). In many cases it is recorded that the Lord "touched" the afflicted person; in one case of blindness He spat on the eyes and twice laid hands on them (Mark viii, 22–25); in another case He spat on the ground and made clay of the spittle, and anointed the eyes, and said: "Go wash in the pool at Siloam" (John ix, 6, 7). There seems, also, to have been a difference in the time of healing; some being healed "immediately," and some "as they went," or were obedient (Matt. viii, 3; Luke xvii, 14; John ix, 11). Promises, conditions and means of healing during this dispensation: "And these signs shall follow them that believe: In my name shall they cast out devils; they shall speak with new tongues; they shall take up serpents; and if they drink any deadly thing it shall not hurt them; they shall lay hands on the sick, and they shall recover" (Mark xvi, 17, 18). "Verily, verily, I say unto you, he that believeth on Me the works that I do shall he do also; and greater works than these shall he do, because I go unto My Father" (John xiv, 12). "Is any sick among you? Let him call for the elders of the church; and let them pray over him, anointing him in the name of the Lord; and the prayer of faith shall save the sick, and the Lord shall raise him up; and if he have committed sins they shall be forgiven him" (James v, 14, 15). It is to be observed that the laying on of hands and the prayer of faith are only the channels to bring the power. In the last passage it is expressly declared "the Lord shall raise him up;" and in Mark xvi, 20, it is recorded the apostles "went forth and preached everywhere, the Lord working with them, confirming the Word with signs following." There seems to be but one case recorded in the New Testament where an applicant for healing was not helped — the case of the apostle Paul in 2 Cor. xii, 7–11. Twice he besought the Lord; then it was shown him what good was wrought out by the continuance of his thorn in the flesh, and he no longer desired it to depart. "Most gladly will I rather glory in my infirmity, that the power of Christ may rest upon me."

EIGHT ETERNAL THINGS.

Eternal redemption, Heb. ix, 12.
Eternal salvation, Heb. v, 9.
Eternal life, John x, 28.

These three grand eternal things the believer has now; and he waits for an

Eternal inheritance, Heb. ix, 15.
And an

Eternal weight of glory, 2 Cor. iv, 17.

The unbeliever has awaiting him

Eternal judgment, Heb. vi, 2.
Eternal damnation, Mark iii, 29.
Eternal fire. Jude 7.

Dear readers, which of these eternal portions is thine?

ETERNAL LIFE — WHAT IS IT, HOW CAN I GET IT, AND CAN I LOSE IT?

I. NOT ETERNAL EXISTENCE.

1 John v, 20.

1 John i, 1–6 — Life of God.
2 Peter i, 4 — Partakes of Divine nature.
Life of God coming down through the Son of God.
Quickened in me by the Spirit of God going back to God in fellowship.

II. ETERNAL LIFE — HOW DO I GET IT?

1. *By Faith*, John iii, 14–18, 36; v, 24.
Rom. v, 23 — Gift of God.
John xvii, 3 — By knowing Christ.
2. *A Present Possession*, John iii, 15, 18, 36; 1 John v, 24.
3. *The Knowledge of It*, 1 John v, 13; John v, 24; 1 John v, 12.

"Testimony of Word" — "Witness of Spirit."

III. CAN I LOSE IT?

No, I cannot.
1. *The Nature of the Life* — "Eternal life."
2. *The Purpose of God*, Rom. viii, 30, 32.
3. *Testimony of the Word of God*. John xiv, 19; x, 28, 29; xvii; 1 Peter i, 5.
4. *Christ's Substitutionary Work*.
5. *What is Union with Christ?* Col. i, 3, 5.
6. *Power of Christ's Intercession*. Rom. v, 9, 12; Heb. vii, 25.
7. *The Earnest of the Spirit*, 2 Cor. i, 21; Eph. i, 13, 14.

IV. WHAT ARE THE EVIDENCES OF THE LIFE?

1. *Doth not Commit Sin*, 1 John iii, 9.
2. *Doth Righteousness*, 1 John iv, 7, 8.
3. *Communion and Life, Difference Between*, 1 John i.

W. H. W.

EVERY MORNING.

Manna given, Ex. xvi, 21.
Incense offered, Ex. xxx, 7.
Praise, 1 Chron. xxiii, 30.
Service rendered, 1 Chron. ix, 26.
Sacrifice presented, 2 Chron. xiii, 11.
God visits, Job vii, 18.
God their arm, Isa. xxxiii, 2.
His compassions new, Lam. iii, 23.
Judgment, Zeph. iii, 5.

EXPECTATION.

I. The expectation of the unbeliever.

1. Wrath. In the light of God's Word, no unbeliever has the right to expect anything but wrath, John iii, 36; Heb. x, 26, 27; Prov. xi, 23. But even in the face of this, some will still hold to the hope that somehow they will escape the wrath of God, but God says such an expectation

2. Shall perish, or be cut off. Prov. x, 28; xi, 17; Job viii, 11-15; cf. Matt. vii, 26.

II. The expectation of the believer.

1. Its source, Psa. lxii, 5; and in contrast of the unbeliever,

2. It shall not perish or be cut off, Prov. xxiii, 17, 18; Prov. xxiv, 13, 14: but it will have

3. A blessed consummation, Titus ii, 13; 2 Pet. iii, 13, 14: 1 John iii, 2.

J. H. ELLIOTT.

FIVE EXCUSES OF MOSES.

"Who am I," Ex. iii, 11.
"What shall I say?" Ex. iii, 13.
"They will not believe me," Ex. iv, 1.
"I am not eloquent," Ex. iv, 10.
"Send, I pray Thee, by the hand of him whom thou shouldst send," Ex. iv, 13.

GOD'S ANSWERS.

"Certainly I will be with thee," Exod. iii, 12.
"I AM hath sent me unto you," Exod. iii, 14.
"They will believe the voice of the latter sign," Exod. iv, 8.
"I will be with thy mouth and teach thee what thou shalt say," Ex. iv, 12.
"Aaron, the Levite, thy brother," Ex. iv, 13.

J. H. ELLIOTT.

FAITHFUL SAYINGS.

"Let not sin, therefore, reign in your mortal body, that ye should obey it" (Rom. vi, 12). The whole question is not whether sin tempts or not, but whether it reigns or not (Brownlow North). "Forgive us our trespasses as we forgive," etc. (Matt. vi, 12). He that cannot forgive others, breaks the bridge over which he must pass himself (George Herbert). "The life that I now live in the flesh I live by the faith of the Son of God" (Gal. ii, 20). The natural life which we have is poisoned and condemned, and is continually taking part in the murder of Christ, by seeking enjoyment in the flesh, and the world which crucified Him; and we are enclosed in, and brought into constant contact with, that very flesh and that very world. Now what is our resource? Why, just this: We have another life in Jesus — a pure, blessed, unassailable life, a life uncondemned and untainted — even that eternal life which is in the Father and was manifested in the Son. Yes, we have it; there is no doubt on this matter; for "this is the record, that God hath given us eternal life, and this life is in His Son." We have it; it is ours, although the source of it is not within our own persons, but in Christ, the head of the body (Thomas Erskine.)

"To keep himself unspotted from the world" (James i, 27). The whole complexion of a negro is less noticed than a single stain on the feature of a white countenance (Jay). "A man shall be as a hiding place from the wind and a cover from the tempest" (Isa. xxxii, 2). I creep under my Lord's wings in the great shower, and the waters cannot reach me. Let fools laugh the fool's laughter, and scorn Christ, and bid the weeping captives in Babylon "sing them one of the songs of Zion." We may sing, even in our winter's storm, in the expectation of a summer's sun at the turn of the year. No created powers in hell or out of hell can mar our Lord's work, or spoil our song of joy. Let us, then, be glad, and rejoice in the salvation of our Lord; for faith had never yet cause to have tearful eyes, or a saddened brow, or to droop or die (Rutherford's "Letters").

"We preach Christ crucified" (1 Cor. i, 23). One of the peculiarities and beauties of St. Paul's style may be traced as occurring here. Twelve times does he refer to Christ in thirteen verses — a fit model for all who would be successors in the Spirit of the apostles. It was the wise counsel of Philip Henry: "Preach a crucified Savior in a crucified style."

"Thanks be unto God for His unspeakable gift" (2 Cor. ix, 15). We may say of Christ as one said to Cæsar, when he had received a magnificent present from him, "This is too much for me to receive." To which the emperor answered, "But it is not too great for me to give."

"Sorrow shall be turned into joy" (John xvi, 20). Has it never occurred to us, when surrounded by sorrows, that they may be sent to us only for our instruction — as we darken the cages of birds when we wish to teach them to sing? (Richter.)

"Faith which worketh by love" (Gal. v, vi). Teaching men morals is as though I had a clock that would not go, and I turned round one of the cog-wheels. But faith takes the key and winds up the main-spring, and the whole thing runs on readily (Spurgeon).

"Add to your faith virtue" (2 Pet. i, 5). The Greek word that is here rendered *add* has a great emphasis in it; it is taken from dancing round. "Link them," says the apostle, "hand in hand." As in dancing, virgins take hands, so we must pin hand to hand in these holy measures and lead up the dance of graces (Thomas Brooks).

FAITHFULNESS.

I. As servants, Matt. xxiv, 45; xxv, 21-23; Heb. iii, 2, 5; Luke xix, 13, 17; John xiii, 16; xv, 20.
II. As stewards, Luke xii, 42; 1 Cor. iv, 2; Tit. i, 17; 1 Pet. iv, 10.
III. In the least, Luke xvi, 10; xix, 17; Matt. xix, 30; xx, 16; Mark ix, 41.
IV. To the Lord, Acts xvi, 15; 1 Cor. iv. 17; Eph. i, 1.
V. As brethren, Col. i, 2; iv, 9; 1 Tim. iv, 12; 1 Pet. v, 12.
VI. As children, Tit. i, 6; Eph, vi, 4.
VII. In all things, 1 Tim. iii, 11; 3 John 5.

FIGURES IN HOSEA.

Those that depart from God are like:
A backsliding heifer, iv, 16.
Heart like an oven; while they sleep it is heating, vii, 6.
A cake not turned, vii, 8.
A silly dove, vii, 11.
A deceitful bow, vii, 16.
Have sown the wind; shall reap whirlwind, viii, 7.
Corn without stalk — no meal, viii, 7.
Vessel wherein is no pleasure, viii, 8.
Glory fly away as a bird, ix, 11.
Root dried up, ix, 16.
Empty vine, x, 1.
Hemlock in the furrows of the field, x, 4.
Foam upon the face of the waters, x, 7.
Plowed wickedness, reaped iniquity, x, 13.
Tremble as a bird, xi, 11.
Feedeth on wind, followeth east wind, xii, 1.
Morning cloud. Early dew. Chaff driven away. Smoke out of the chimney, xiii, 3.
Yet see chapter xiv, as to God's offer in grace to restore such.

D. W. WHITTLE.

FIVE THINGS NOT FULLY REALIZED.

1. We do not fully realize that we need pardon, Psa. xiv, 3; 1 Kings viii, 46; Rom. iii, 10, 12, 23; 1 John i, 8, 10. Rejecting Christ in sin, John vi, 29; 1 John iii, 23; v, 10, 11.
2. We do not fully realize that he who sins is in danger, Eze. xviii, 20; Rom. vi, 23.
3. We do not fully realize what Christ has done for us, John iii, 16; Rom. vi, 23; 1 John v, 11. Left His glory, John xvii, 5.
4. We do not fully realize that it was and is for *us*, John v, 24; vi, 37; Acts ii, 21; Rom. x, 13; Rev. xxii, 17.
5. We do not fully realize what God's love prompts Him to do for us. Redeemed us, Col. i, 12-14. Keeps us, Jude, 24, 25. Gives us heaven, John xiv, 3.

J. E. BROWN.

GIFTS OF GOD.

1. All good gifts from God, 1 James i, 17.
2. All things because of Christ, Num. xiv, 18; Rom. viii, 32.

3. God gives forever, Rom. xi, 29.
4. Christ the chief, Isa. xlii, 6; Isa. lv, 4; John iii, 16; John iv, 10; John vi, 32, 33.
5. Holy Spirit, Luke xi, 13; John xiv, 15, 17; Acts ii. 1.
6. Gifts to the church, Psa. lxviii, 18; Eph. iv, 7, 11; Psa. lxxxiv, 11; James iv, 6; Prov. xi, 6; James i, 5; Eph. ii, 8; Phil. i, 29; Rom. v, 16, 17; Psa. lxviii, 35; Ezek. xi, 19; Psa. xxix, 11: John xiv, 27; Matt. xi, 28, 29; Rom. vi, 23; 2 Pet. i, 3.

HENRY MOORHOUSE

"GOOD WORKS" IN EPISTLE TO TITUS.

I. The wicked cannot perform them, xvi.
II. The Christian worker should be an example of, ii, 7.
III. Should be "zealous of," ii, 14.
IV. Should urge others to be "ready" to do good works, iii, 1: To "maintain," iii 8, 14.

FRED. S. GOODMAN.

HEAVEN.

I. *Heaven is our Father's House,* John iv, 2; Isa. lxiii, 15: first clause; 1 Kings 8, 30; Matt. xxiii, 9; vi, 9; vii. 11.

II. *The Home of Jesus.*
1. Whence He came, John iii, 13; vi, 38.
2. Whither He has returned, John xx, 17; Acts iii, 21; Heb. ix, 24.
3. Whence He shall come again, 1 Thess. i, 10; iv, 16.

III. *The place from which the Spirit proceeds,* John i, 32; Acts ii, 2; 1 Peter i, 12.

IV. *The source of all earthly good,* John iii, 27; Jas. i, 17.

V. *The future abode of all believers,* John xiv, 2, 3; 2 Cor. v, 1; Heb. xi, 10.

IV. *The blessedness of Heaven consists:*
1. In freedom from sin, Ps. xvii, 15; 1 John iii, 2; Rev. xxi, 27.
2. Freedom from pain and sorrow, Rev. vii, 15–17; xxi, 4.
3. In being with Jesus, John xii, 26; Phil. i, 23: 1 Thess. iv, 17.
4. Seeing His glory, John xvii, 24; Rev. xxii, 4.
5. Receiving His reward, Matt. v, 12.

This reward is represented as:
(*a*) An inheritance, Acts xxvi, 18; Col. i, 12; 1 Peter i, 4; Rev. xxi, 7.
(*b*) A prize, Phil. iii, 14.
(*c*) A rest, Heb. iv, 9; Rev. xiv, 18.
(*d*) A kingdom, Matt. xxv, 34; Luke xxii, 29–30.
(*e*) A crown, 1 Cor. ix, 25; James i, 12; Rev. ii, 10, last clause; 2 Tim. iv, 8; 1 Peter v, 4.
(*f*) Fullness of knowledge, 1 Cor. xiii, 12.
(*g*) Fullness of life, Matt. xxv, 46.
(*h*) Fullness of joy, Ps. xvi, 11.

1. *Christians should rejoice because their names are now written in heaven,* Luke x, 20; Heb. xii, 23.
2. Strive to lay up treasures there, Matt. vi, 19, 20; Luke xii. 33.

"HOW TO GET STRONG AND HOW TO STAY SO."

TO YOUNG MEN.

Strength of two kinds:
1. *Physical.*
2. *Spiritual.*

The law of spiritual development exactly corresponds to the law of physical development: (1) Life; (2) Growth; (3) Mature strength. This may be simply traced in the spiritual as "the beginning of strength."

I. *Life.*
Jesus said the words I speak, etc., John vii, 63. I am the way, the truth, etc., John xiv, 6. The record says life only in the Son, 1 John v, 11, 12.

II. *Growth.* "How to get strong."
The Word able to build up, Acts xx, 32. Means of growth, 1 Pet. ii, 2.

III. *Mature strength.* "How to stay strong."

Young men — Word abideth, 1 John ii, 14. This is the promise fulfilled, John xv, 7. Abiding, John xiv, 23.

JOHN H. ELLIOTT.

HIDDEN.
1. Hidden ones, Psa. lxxxiii, 3.
2. Hidden treasure, Prov. ii, 4.
3. Hidden riches, Isa. xlv, 3.
4. Hidden things, Isa. xlviii, 6.
5. Hidden wisdom, 1 Cor. ii, 7.
6. Hidden life, Col. ii, 3.
7. Hidden manna, Rev. ii, 17.

HOW WE ARE TO SERVE GOD.
1. "Serve the Lord with all thine heart," Deut. x, 12.
2. "Serve Him without fear," Luke i, 74.
3. "Serve the Lord with gladness," Ps. c, 2.
4. "Serve with a willing mind," 1 Chron. xxviii, 9.
5. "Serve with pure conscience," 2 Tim. i, 3.
6. "Serve God acceptably with reverence," Heb. xii, 28.
7. "Serve the Lord with all humility," Acts xx, 19.

"IS THE YOUNG MAN SAFE?"
Ecc. xi, 9; xii, 1.

I. His life. How will he use it?
1. A wrong use, Luke xii, 16–21.
2. A right use, Rom. xiv, 7–9; Phil. i, 21.

II. His Walk. Which way will he go?
1. The wrong way, Psa. xxxiv, 4; Prov. xiii, 15; xiv, 12; xii, 15, 26; vii, 8, 27.
2. The right way, Prov. iii, 17; v, 6; Prov. iv, 18; John xiv, 6; Heb. x, 20.

III. His judgment. How will he stand? John v, 24; Psa. i, 4–6, John iii, 18.

IV. His safeguard. How secured, Ecc. xii; Isa. lv, 6–11.

JOHN H. ELLIOTT.

"JUST LET."
Col. iii, 16.

Let — to permit, allow, suffer. "Just let," in contrast "to try to make."

1. Who are to "just let?" Col. iii, 16. You, saints, Col. i, 2; *i.e.*, Christians.

2. What are Christians to "just let?"
Col. iii, 16 — "Let word of Christ dwell," etc.
Phil. ii, 5 — "Let this mind be in you," etc.
Matt. v, 16 — "Let your light so shine before men."
Col. iii, 15 — "Let peace of God rule in your hearts."
Heb. xiii, 5 — "Let your conversation be," etc.
Col. iv, 6 — "Let your speech," etc.

3. Why are Christians to "just let?"
Matt. v, 16 — That they may see your good works.
Col. iii, 16 — That we may teach and admonish, etc.

4. Where are they to "just let?"
Matt. v, 16 — Let shine *before men.*
Col. iii, 16 — Let dwell *in you.*

5. When are they "to let?"
Col. iii, 16 — Let word of Christ *dwell,* stay and abide always in you.

6. How are we "to let?"
Matt. v, 16 — Let *so* shine.
Col. iii, 16 — Let dwell *richly.*

JOHN'S TESTIMONY TO JESUS.

I. That He is Lord, John i, 2, 3; xiii, 13; Acts x, 38; Rev. xix, 16.

II. That He is the Lamb of God, John i, 29; Acts viii, 32; 1 Pet. i, 19; Rev. v, 12.

III. That He is the Son of God, John i, 34; Matt. xviii, 5; Acts ix, 20; Rom. i, 4.

IV. That He is the bridegroom, John iii, 29; 2 Cor. xi, 2; Eph. v, 27–29; Rev. xix, 7.

V. That He is above all, John iii, 31; Rom. ix, 5; Eph. i, 22; Phil. ii, 9; Col. i, 18.

VI. That all things are given into His hands, John iii, 35; xiii, 3; xvii, 2; Heb. i, 3.

VII. That faith in Him receives everlasting life, John iii, 36; v, 24; vi, 47; xi, 25.

JUDGMENT OF MATTHEW XXV.

WHEN DOES THIS JUDGMENT TAKE PLACE?

When the SON OF MAN is *revealed*, verse 31. Note,—THE SON OF MAN—not "the bridegroom" coming to take His bride to Himself, as in John xiv, 3, or in Matt. xxv, 1 to 10 (the sheep and goats cannot be the virgins); nor as "the Lord" who gave the talents, as in Matt. xxv, 19 to 30; nor as the "Son of David" in Luke i, 32 and 33; neither as the "Son of God," as in John v, 25 — but as THE SON OF MAN. And those judged will have to meet Him AS MEN on the earth. He has reckoned with His church long before this, and with the Jews also.

I believe it will take place between the judgment of His saints in the air and the millennium. Perhaps just after the dreadful scenes referred to in Zechariah xiv, 3, and parallel passages. For we must give room for all Scripture, not yet fulfilled, to come in, such as Luke xix, 27.

"But those mine enemies which would not that I should reign over them, bring hither and slay them before me."

Also Matt. xiii, 41:

"The Son of Man shall send forth His angels and they shall gather out of His kingdom all things that offend, and them which do iniquity."

The Son of Man is not revealed to the nations until He comes to destroy the man of sin which Paul refers to in 2 Thess. ii, 8.

"Whom the Lord shall consume with the Spirit of His mouth, and destroy with the brightness of His coming."

WHERE WILL THIS JUDGMENT TAKE PLACE?

In the Holy Land, where He descends, as all the prophets testify. See Joel iii, 1 and 2.

"For, behold, in those days and in that time, when I shall bring again the captivity of Judah and Jerusalem, I will also gather all nations, and will bring them down into the valley of Jehoshaphat, and will plead with them there for My people and for My heritage, Israel, whom they have scattered among the nations, and parted My lands."

And verse 12 of the same chapter:

"Let the heathen be wakened, and come up to the valley of Jehoshaphat; for there will I sit to judge all the heathen round about."

In Psalm xcvi, 12 and 13, we read:

"Let the field be joyful, and all that is therein; then shall all the trees of the wood rejoice before the Lord; for He cometh, for He cometh to judge the earth; He shall judge the world with righteousness, and the people with truth."

These and many such passages, cannot refer to the judgment seat of Christ, or to the great white throne, in Rev. xx.

WHO ARE THE PEOPLE BEING JUDGED?

The nations who are living on the earth. The judge divides them into two classes — sheep and goats. Who are these sheep? Some affirm all the good that ever was or ever will be; but of this, Scripture gives us no proof. Some say they are the brethren, meaning the church. How can that be, seeing these will be in their *natural bodies and then living* on the earth after the church has met the Lord in the air, according to 1 Thess. iv, 7. Some say "the goats" are all the bad that ever were or ever will be. To prove this would be equally difficult. In order that we may understand this matter, we must see what Scripture says about sheep.

You will find there are three kinds of sheep spoken of. See John x, 3–5 and 14.

3. To Him the porter openeth; and the sheep hear His voice and He calleth His own sheep by name, and leadeth them out.

4. And when He putteth forth His own sheep, He goeth before them, and the sheep follow Him; for they know His voice.

5. And a stranger they will not follow, but will flee from him; for they know not the voice of strangers.

6. This parable spake Jesus unto them: but they understood not what things they were which He spake unto them.

7. Then Jesus said unto them again, Verily, verily, I say unto you, I am the door of the sheep.

8. All that ever came before Me are thieves and robbers; but the sheep did not hear them.

9. I am the door; by Me if any man enter in, he shall be saved, and shall go in and out, and find pasture.

10. The thief cometh not, but for to steal, and to kill, and to destroy; I am come that they might have life, and that they might have *it* more abundantly.

11. I am the Good Shepherd; the Good Shepherd giveth His life for the sheep.

12. But he that is a hireling, and not the shepherd, whose own the sheep are not, seeth the wolf coming, and leaveth the sheep, and fleeth; and the wolf catcheth them, and scattereth the sheep.

13. The hireling fleeth, because he is a hireling and careth not for the sheep.

14. I am the Good Shepherd, and know My *sheep*, and am known of Mine.

This must mean believers of this dispensation, but in the sixteenth verse we read:

16. And other sheep I have, which are not of this fold; them also I must bring, and they shall hear My voice; and there shall be one flock, and one Shepherd.

("Flock" it should be in this verse.) There must be some others, therefore, Jew or Gentile, who will be saved, but not form a part of the church. In Matt. ix, 36, we read:

"But when He saw the multitudes, He was moved with compassion on them, because they fainted, and were scattered abroad, as *sheep* having no shepherd."

Also the Jews are called sheep in chapter x, 5 and 6:

"These twelve Jesus sent forth, and commanded them, saying, Go not into the way of the *Gentiles*, and into any city of the Samaritans enter ye not; but go rather to the lost *sheep* of the *house of Israel*."

And in xv, 22 and 24, we read:

"Behold, a woman of Canaan came out of the same coasts, and cried unto Him, saying, Have mercy on me, O Lord, thou son of David; my daughter is grievously vexed with a devil. But He answered her not a word. And His disciples came and besought Him, saying, Send her away; for she crieth after us. But He answered and said, I am not sent but unto the *lost sheep* of the house of Israel."

But in John x, 26 and 27.

"Ye believe not, because *ye are not of My sheep*, as I said unto you. *My sheep* hear My voice, *and I know them*, and they follow Me."

The reader will readily perceive "the *sheep* of the church," and of Israel, in the above; and in John xxi, 15–17, the *sheep* and *lambs* referred to are the church during our Lord's absence.

And to prove that there are parties saved, not Jews, nor included in the church, see Rev. xxi, 24, and parallel passages, speaking of the heavenly Jerusalem:

"And the *nations* of them *which are saved* shall walk in the light of it; and the kings of the earth do bring their glory and honor into it."

Yes, a time will come when both Jew and Gentile will unite in singing the 100th Psalm! We know this must be future, for since the fall of man the world, or all the earth, has never praised the Lord; only a very few of the human family. But a time is near when all, both Jew and Gentile, shall praise God and say: "We are His people and the sheep of His pasture."

These sheep in Matt. xxv are not to be judged according to law, or as ever having heard Paul's Gospel, but according to how they had acted for or against those whom the Judge calls HIS BRETHREN.

MOTHER.

A mother's care, 1 Sam. ii, 19; 2 Kings iv, 19, 20; Ex. ii, 8.

A mother's influence, Eze. xvi, 44; for good, 2 Tim. i, 5; for evil, 1 Kings xxii, 52; Jezebel, 2 Chron. xxii, 3; Athaliah, Matt. xiv, 8; Herodias.

Mother, a comforter, Isa. lxvi, 13.

A mother receives a son raised to life, 1 Kings xvii, 23; 2 Kings iv, 36; Luke vii, 15.

A mother giving a son to God, 1 Sam. i, 27, 28.

A mother's Teaching, Prov. xxxi, 1.

A mother's memory, Luke ii, 51.

A mother obeyed, Prov. i, 8; vi, 20; Luke ii, 51.

A mother despised, Prov. xv, 20; xxiii, 22; xxx, 17.

A mother blessed, Prov. xxxi, 28.

A mother's ending love, John xix, 25.

J. E. BROWN.

MOUNTAINS.

BY L. W. MUNHALL.

MONUMENTS of God's power, wisdom and love! How a sight of them lifts the thoughts of one, in harmony with the Creator, above the groveling, selfish and sordid things of life, into reverent and profitable contemplation of God and His attributes! I shall never forget the inspiration received when, from the plain above Denver, I caught my first sight of the Rocky mountains, in their "upheaved vastness," crowned with eternal snow, and set against a clear and wondrously tinted evening sky. Instinctively I uncovered my head, and impulsively quoted: "What is man that thou art mindful of him" (Psa. viii, 4).

"He that sitteth upon the circle of the earth" (Isa. xl, 22) hath taught us many of the gracious lessons of His Word from mountain summit and slope. It will be profitable to visit some of them in thought, and receive a lesson from the sacred history of each Sinai. From its fire and smoke-crowned summit we hear a voice that speaks in thunder, trumpet-tones of law. Sin is a violation of the law. Death, in its three-fold character, is set over against sin (Rom. vi, 23). First, spiritual death (Gen. ii, 17). Second, physical death (Gen. iii, 19). Third, the second death (Rev. xxi, 8). We are all sinful by nature (Psa. li, 5; Eph. ii, 3; Rom. v, 12). We are all sinners by practice (1 John i, 8, 10; Ecc. vii, 20; Rom. iii, 23). "Oh, wretched man that I am! who shall deliver me from the body of this death?" (Rom. vii, 24.) Shall we look to the law? No; for "by the deeds of the law shall no flesh be justified" (Rom. iii, 20). To the good we may do? No; for "all our righteounesses are as filthy rags" (Isa. lxiv, 6). To man? No; "vain is the help of man" (Psa. lx, 11). Can we buy it? No; "ye were not redeemed with corruptible things, as silver and gold" (1 Pet. i, 18, 19). What shall we do, then, to escape from this dark mountain which to touch is death? (Heb. xii, 18–21.) Is there no salvation? Yes; follow our "pillar of cloud," the Holy Spirit (John xvi, 13), and we shall be guided out of this wilderness, into the land of promise, to Mount

Calvary. But here is death and darkness also! Yes, but here is life; for "except a corn of wheat fall into the ground and die, it abideth alone; but if it die, it bringeth forth much fruit" (John xii, 24); and we are come unto "Jesus, the Mediator of the new covenant, and to the blood of sprinkling that speaketh better things than that of Abel" (Heb. xii, 24). "For it is the blood that maketh an atonement for the soul" (Lev. xvii, 11). "Without shedding of blood is no remission" (Heb. ix, 22). "And the blood of Jesus Christ, His Son, cleanseth us from all sin" (1 John i, 7; Isa. liii; John iii, 16; Rom. v, 6-9; 1 Pet. iii, 18). Did He die for every man? Yes (John xii, 32; Rom. vii, 18; viii, 32; 2 Cor. v, 14, 15; 1 Tim. ii, 6, Heb. ii, 9). Yes; "He is the propitiation * * * for the sin of the whole world" (1 John ii, 2; John i, 29; iv, 42; 1 John iv, 14). Since this is so, why are not all saved? God requires something on our part. He says, "Come unto me all ye that labor," etc. (Matt. xi, 28-30.) But some will not come (John v, 40). He says, "Look unto Me, and be ye saved, all the ends of the earth" (Isa. xlv, 22). But some will not look (Matt. xiii, 14, 15). He says, "Believe on the Lord Jesus Christ, and thou shalt be saved" (Acts xvi, 31). But some will not believe (John iii, 18, 36). We must approach Calvary by the way of Mount Moriah — the mount of offering. Here Abraham offered Isaac (Gen. xxii, 1-18). On this mount the temple was built (2 Chron. iii, 1), to which all offerings made to the Lord were brought. These offerings did not take away sin (Heb. x, 4-11). Neither can our offerings (Titus iii, 5-7). God required the Jew to bring his offering to the temple. God requires that the sinner bring an offering to Him (Psa. li, 17; Isa. lxvi, 1, 2; Psa. xxxiv, 18; Matt. ix, 12; Acts iii, 19; 2 Cor. vii, 10). Thus it is, if we, in penitence and faith, accept the finished work of Jesus, are made partakers of the Divine nature (2 Pet. i, 4).

Now, as God's dear children, let us journey to the northward. But here we are in the wilderness, and here is another dark mountain (quarentana); I supposed I should never have any more trouble! "The servant is not greater than his Lord" (John xv, 20). This is the mount of temptation (Matt. iv, 8-11). He "was in all points, tempted like, as we are" (Heb. iv, 15), therefore, "He is able to succor them that are tempted" (Heb. ii, 18). "Fear thou not for I am with thee," etc. (Isa. xli, 10); yes, but Satan is here, also, I know; but "resist" Him "steadfast in the faith" (1 Pet. v, 6-9; James iv, 7). "My grace is sufficient for thee" (2 Cor. xii, 9; 1 Cor. x, 13; Isa. xliii, 1, 2; John x, 28).

Let us push forward to the mount of beatitudes and hear from the lips of the Great Teacher the lesson of how we ought to live. (Matt. v, vi, vii). We are not to tarry here long, however, as God requires that we be "doers of the Word and not hearers only" (Jas. ii, 22);

and so by what we do, show to the world that we have been with Christ and learned of Him (Matt. v, 16). We must descend to the plain, to the level of every-day experience. But right here before us, to the southward rises another mountain. This is Gilboa. Here is where God taught Israel a very important lesson (Jud. vii). We must learn it if we would accomplish much for the Master. Remember, "the battle is not yours, but God's" (2 Chron. xx, 15). That it is "not by might, nor by power, but by My Spirit, saith the Lord of hosts" (Zech. iv, 6). "Our sufficiency is of God" (2 Cor. iii, 4). "For it is God who worketh in you," etc. (Phil. ii, 13.) "I can do all things through Christ, which strengtheneth me" (Phil. iv, 13). Read 1 Cor. i, 26-29; Psa. viii, 2; 2 Chron. iv, 7. O, that God may open the eyes of the young man! (2 Kings vi, 16, 17.)

In this confidence we turn and address ourselves to the work. Right before us, to the northward is Mount Tabor — the mount of transfiguration (Matt. xvii, 1-13). Here we are assured that Jesus is the Divine Son of God, in the fact of His transfiguration and the testimony of the Father. "This is My Beloved Son in whom I am well pleased." Here we are also taught the resurrection of the dead; Moses was present, whom Michael, the archangel (Jude. 9), buried where "no man knoweth" (Deut. xxxiv, 5, 6) nearly fifteen hundred years before. Elijah was also present — he who was taken bodily into heaven over nine hundred years before (2 Kings ii, 11; 1 Cor. xv).

This is a delightful place and we would tarry; but "here we have no continuing city, but we seek one to come" (Heb. xiii, 14). What do we know of that city? Let us journey toward the south, cross the Jordon and come to Mount Nebo or Pisgah. Here Moses reviewed the promise land — the earthly Canaan. Our faith lifts us to a clear vision of the heavenly Canaan (John xiv, 1-3; 2 Cor. v, 1; Rev. xxi; vii, 9-17).

Let us go up to Jerusalem; here is the mount of Olives, from which our Savior ascended into heaven, "and while they looked steadfastly toward heaven, as He went up, behold, two men stood by them in white apparel; which also said: Ye men of Galilee, why stand ye gazing up into heaven? The same Jesus which is taken up from you into heaven, shall so come in like manner as ye have seen Him go into heaven" (Acts i, 10, 11). "And they returned to Jerusalem with great joy" (Luke xxiv, 62). Coming from a funeral "with great joy!" This "blessed hope" (Titus ii, 13), the assurance that He will come again, is our joy also (Dan. vii, 13; Matt. xxvi, 64; Rev. i, 7; 2 Thess. i, 7-12; iii, 5; Rev. xvi, 15). "Be ye therefore ready also; for the Son of Man cometh at an hour when ye think not" (Luke xii, 40). "Blessed is that servant, whom his Lord, when He cometh, shall find so doing" (Luke xii, 43).

ON GIVING.

1. Special command, Luke vi, 38; Eccl. xi, 1; Prov. iii, 27, 28; xxviii, 27; Ps. xxxviii, 3; Deut. xv, 11; Mal. iii, 10.
2. To whom, Deut. xv, 7, 10; Eccl. xi, 2; Matt. xxv, 40; Deut, xiv, 29; Gal. vi, 10.
3. How much, Deut. xiv, 28; Prov. iii, 9, 10; Prov. xi, 24, 25; Mal. iii, 10.
4. Manner, Matt. vi, 1–3; Is. lviii, 6, 7; 2 Cor, ix, 6, 7; Deut. xv, 8, 9.
5. When, Gal. vi, 10; Matt. xxv, 35, 36.

S. G. HARRIS.

ONE THING.

1. The test question, Matt. xxi, 24.
2. The great deficiency, Mark x, 21.
3. Another test question, Luke vi, 9.
4. One thing needful, Luke x, 42.
5. Certainty of one thing, John ix, 25.
6. Paul's one purpose, Phil. iii, 13.

REV. W. M. GRIMES.

OF WHAT WE ARE PARTAKERS.

I. Partakers of the heavenly calling, Heb. iii, 1.
II. Partakers of Christ, Heb. iii, 14.
III. Partakers of chastisement, Heb. xii, 8.
IV. Partakers of His holiness, Heb. xii, 10.
V. Partakers of Christ's suffering, 1 Pet. iv, 13.
VI. Partakers of the Divine nature, 2 Pet. i, 4.
VII. Partakers of the inheritance, Col. i, 12.

PRECIOUS PROMISES.

2 Pet. i, 4.

1. Promised Savior, Gen. iii, 15; Isa. liii, 4–6; Matt. i, 21.
2. Promised forgiveness, Isa. i, 18; lv, 7; xliii, 25; Acts x, 43; Eph. i, 7.
3. Promised help, Josh. i, 9; Ps. xxvii, 1, 14; lxxxiv, 11; xci, 14, 15, Heb. xiii, 5, 6.
4. Promised rest, Isa. xxvi, 3, 4; Matt. xi, 28; Heb. iv, 9.
5. Promised comforter, John xiv, 16, 17, 18, 26; xv, 26; xxi, 7.
6. Promised coming, Matt. xxiv, 30; John xiv, 3; Jas. v, 8; Acts i, 9–11; Rev. xxii, 12, 20.
7. Promised glory, Col. iii. 4; Ps. xvi, 11; 1 John iii, 2 (with Matt. xxiv, 30); 1 Pet. v, 4.

FRED. S. GOODMAN.

PRESENT PRIVILEGES OF BELIEVERS IN HEBREWS X.

I. No more conscience of sin, verse 2.
II. Sanctified, verse 10.
III. Perfected forever, verse 14.
IV. The witness of the spirit, verse 15.
V. The priesthood of Christ, verse 21.
VI. Full assurance of faith, verse 22.
VII. In heaven an enduring substance, verse 34.

PREPARATION FOR THE LORD'S SUPPER.

I. Reading the Scriptures carefully and with the aid of the Holy Spirit, read Ps. li; Isa. liii; John vi, 17-19; 1 Cor. xiii; Gal. v, 19-26; Heb. ix, 10.

II. Self-examination as to:
1. Knowledge.
2. Faith.
3. Repentance.
4. Love.
5. New obedience.

Use God's Word as the test; not the life of other Christians.

III. Prayer.
1. Thanking God for His continued blessings, for His Holy Spirit, His Son and His church.
2. Renewing consecration.
3. Asking for faith to feed on Christ.
4. For the continuance of the Holy Spirit in the heart.

REV. JOHN C. HILL.

PROTECTION.

I have *before me* Israel's Mighty Lord, Is. lii, 12.

He gives me this assurance in His word, Deut. xxxi, 8.

I have *behind me* all along the way, Ps. cxxxix, 5.

The God of Israel, and from day to day, Ps. lxxiii, 23.

He holds me firmly in His own right hand, Ps. lxxiii, 23.

He is my Rock — enables me to stand, Ps. xviii, 2.

Around, about me — Refuge in distress, Ps. xxxiv, 7; xlvi, 1.

He covers me with His own righteousness, Is. lxi, 10.

The Lord of Hosts *is with me;* gives me strength, Ps. lxxi, 16.

His love embraces height and depth and length, Eph. iii, 18.

Encompassed thus, His hand I clearly see, Ps. cxxxix, 7.

Yea, from His presence I can never flee, Ps. cxxxix, 7.

Within me, wondrous words, and true, John xvii, 23.

My *comforter* and guide, the journey through, John xiv, 26.

His counsels *calm me* in earth's rude alarms, Ps. lxxiii, 24.

Beneath me are the everlasting arms, Deut. xxxiii, 27.

Above, and *through*, and *in us* all He lives, Eph. iv, 6.

And this for every sinner who believes, John iii, 16.

SATAN, PERSONALITY OF

One who has written on this subject, says "*a* Lord" may mean "a man;" "*the* Lord" fixes the expression to Jehovah. "A" Savior may be *a man;* but "the" Savior is Jesus only. We seldom meet the word "devil" in Scripture without the article "*the*" before it.

From Genesis to Revelations there appears to be one Being or Person, and *only one* knows as *Satan*. The fact that we never get the word Satan spoken of in the plural, ought to settle the question that there is but one. We find the word "devils" in many passages, and sometimes *a* devil. The word here is "*Daimon*," or "*Daimonim;*" which may mean "a heathen God," or "evil spirit;" but when we get "*the Devil*" (as in such passages as Matt. iv, 1, 5, 8, 11; xiii, 39; xxv, 41), he is called "Diabolos," which means *the Devil himself.*

The following are a few passages which speak of Satan:

I. His personality, Gen. iii, 13; Job i, 6-12; Matt. iv, 1-11; xii, 26; Acts v, 1-3.

II. His power, Luke iv, 6-8; 1 Chron. xxi, 1; Zech. iii, 1, 2; Matt. iv, 1-11; Rev. xii-xx; Job ii, 4-7.

III. His work. Active, 1 Pet. v, 8. "Goeth about." Destruction, 2 Cor. xi, 13; Eph. vi, 11, 12; 2 Tim. ii, 16; Rev. xii, 7-12. Subtle, 2 Cor. ii. 11. Object, 2 Cor. iv, 3, 4; 1 Pet. v, 8. "Devour," etc.

IV. His end, Rom. xvi, 20; Heb. ii, 14; Rev. xx, 5-10

V. How to gain the victory over him, Isa. iv, 7, 8; 1 Pet. v, 9; Matt. iv. It is written.

W. H. W.

"SENT."
John ix, 7.

God send His Son to save world, John iii, 17, 34.
He witnessed to this Himself, John v, 36, 38; vii, 29; viii, 42.
The impulse of His work, John ix, 4.
His mission, Rom. viii, 3; Gal. iv, 4; 1 John iv, 9.
He in turn sends His disciples out, John xx, 21.

JOHN H. ELLIOTT.

SEVEN INDISPENSABLE THINGS.

I. Without shedding of blood is no remission, Heb. ix, 22.
II. Without faith it is impossible to please God, Heb. xi, 6.
III. Without works faith is dead, James ii, 26.
IV. Without holiness no man shall see the Lord, Heb. xii, 14.
V. Without love I am nothing, 1 Cor. xiii, 1, 3.
VI. Without chastisement ye are not sons, Heb. xii, 8.
VII. Without Me (Jesus Christ), ye can do nothing, John xv, 5.

SEVEN TIMES SEVEN WONDERFUL THINGS.

I. God's love.

God's love for sinners, John iii, 16.
The manifestation of God's love, 1 John iv, 9.
God loved us when we did not love Him, 1 John iv, 10.
God loved us when we were as a loathsome corpse, Eph. ii, 4, 5.
God's commendation of His love, Rom. v, 8.
God's love leads Him to dwell with the man who loves His Son, John xiv, 23.
God's love is everlasting, Jer. xxxi, 3.

II. Christ's love.

The greatness of Christ's love, John xv, 13.
Christ's love for the church, Eph. v, 2.
Christ's personal love, Gal. ii, 20.
Christ's love unchangable, John xiii, 1.
Christ's love constraining, 2 Cor. v, 14, 15.

III. Christ's death.

Christ died for our sins, 1 Cor. xv, 3.
Christ bare our sins, 1 Pet. ii, 24.
Christ suffered for sins, 1 Pet, iii, 18.
Christ died for, in place of, instead of, sinners, Rom. v, 6.
Christ died for His enemies, Rom. v, 10.
Christ's death reaches in its atoning efficacy to the root of sin in the flesh, or in our ruined nature, Rom. viii, 3.
Christ's death lays a foundation broad enough for a lost world to stand upon, Heb. ii, 9.

IV. Faith in Christ.

Faith obtains salvation, Acts xvi, 31.
Faith secures everlasting life, John vi, 47.
Faith makes us partakers of the Divine nature, or children of God, 1 John v, 1.
Faith relieves us of any fear of the judgment as to our sins, John v, 24.
Faith introduces the sinner into the presence of God completely justified, Acts xiii, 39.
Faith, before any works of any kind are done, receives a righteousness which is accepted in the high court of heaven, Rom. iv, 5.
Faith, which excludes all merit of our own, renders our salvation perfectly secure, Rom. iv, 16.

V. The Believer's Sins.

They are removed from him, Psa. ciii, 12.
They are cast behind God's back, Isa. xxxviii, 17.
They are blotted out, Isa. xliv, 22.
They are cast into the depths of the sea, Mic. vii, 19.
They are thoroughly forgiven, past, present and future; for they

were all future when Christ died upon the cross, Col. ii, 13.

They are washed away, as if a stain disappeared and was lost to view under the cleansing hand of God Himself, 1 John i, 7.

They are not even remembered, Heb. x, 17.

VI. *The Holy Spirit.*

The Spirit quickens, or makes alive the dead soul, John vi, 63.

The Spirit abides forever with the believer, John xiv, 16, 17.

The Spirit dwells in the believer, 1 Cor. vi, 19.

The Spirit testifies of Christ, John xv, 26.

The Spirit is the only source of power in our testimony and service for the Lord Jesus, Acts i, 8.

The Spirit is at once the seal, marking us as God's own, and the earnest giving us the enjoyment of God's love, 2 Cor. i, 22.

The Spirit takes hold of our infirmities, and enables us to bear them, Rom. viii, 26.

VII. *The Word of God.*

The Word of God is the agency the Spirit uses to effect the new birth in the believer, 1 Peter i, 23.

The Word of God cleanses us from our defilements, John xv, 3.

The Word of God builds up and strengthens the believer, Acts xx, 32.

The Word of God lays bare what is in man, and shows him in his true light, Heb. iv, 12.

The Word of God, and the whole of it, is divinely inspired, 2 Tim. iii, 16, 17.

The Word of God alone is of any avail in efforts to save lost men, Jer. xxiii, 28, 29.

The Word of God will judge the unbeliever in the last great day, John xii, 48. — *The Truth.*

SEVEN MYSTERIES — A BIBLE READING.

BY A. J. GORDON, D. D.

The term *mystery* is constantly appearing in Scripture, and with just as definite and fixed significance as any word which can be mentioned. It is not simply a vague expression for whatever is hidden and obscure. Quite the contrary. It marks something which has been clearly revealed, and yet something which, from its very nature, is not generally apprehended. It is something that can be known and ought to be known by God's people; and yet something that is not known and would not be comprehended by those who are not His people. "It is given unto you to know the mysteries of the kingdom of heaven," says Jesus, "but to them it is not given." It may be said that the mysteries are the confidential secrets of the Lord — the revelations which He makes to His own, for their comfort and joy; and yet, secrets so subtle and spiritual and Divine, that only such as have been renewed and enlightened by the Holy Ghost can comprehend them. "The secret of the Lord is with them that fear Him, and He will show them His covenant" (Psa. xxv, 14). Let us glance briefly at some of the mysteries named in the New Testament.

I. The Mystery of the Incarnation. "Great is the mystery of godliness; God was manifest in the flesh, justified in the Spirit, seen of angels, preached unto the Gentiles, believed on in the world, received up into glory" (1 Tim. iii, 16). This is the starting point of redemption — the incarnation. It is a fact so clearly revealed that no disciple can, for a moment, be ignorant of it; and yet a fact so mysterious and incredible that the wisdom of this world has never ceased from the beginning to discredit and contradict it. "The Word was made flesh and dwelt among us" (John i, 14). "Who, being in the form of God * * * took upon Him the form of a servant, and was made in the likeness of man" (Phil. ii, 6, 7). These are distinct declarations of this great truth. It is at once a mystery and a manifestation — that in which God so hides His glory that the undevout and proud no longer recognize Him, while at the same time He so reveals His glory that the humble and the obedient exclaim, "We beheld His glory, the glory as of the only begotten of the Father." It is so great a manifestation, that a great thinker like Vinet says of it, that it is a "revelation which has as many sides as the sun has beams." "And yet so great a mystery," he adds, "that so far from attempting to explain it, we should rather a thousand times exclaim, with our foreheads in the dust, 'Even so Father, for so it hath seemed good in Thy sight.'"

II. The Mystery of the Divine Indwelling. "This mystery among the Gentiles, which is Christ in you, the hope of glory" (Col. i, 27). This mystery is supplementary to the other. By the incarnation God takes upon Himself our human nature; by regeneration we are made "partakers of the Divine nature." Through the birth of Christ God came in to inhabit our nature; by our new birth through the Spirit He comes in to inhabit our individual persons. "If a man love Me, he will keep My words; and My Father will love him, and we will come unto him and make our abode with him" (John xiv, 23). This is the second mystery: God dwelling in the believer through the Spirit — so great a wonder that Thomas Erskine says, "The church is God manifest in the flesh."

III. The Mystery of the Church. "The mystery of Christ, which in other ages was not made known to the sons of men, as it is now revealed unto His holy apostles and prophets by the Spirit, that the Gentiles should be fellow heirs, and of the same body, and partakers of His promise in Christ by the Gospel" (Eph. iii, 4–6). Nothing could seem more incredible to a Jew than that the middle wall of partition should be broken down, and the Gentiles be brought into the blessing of God's covenant. This is the mystery of this age, the gathering out from both Jew and Gentile "one new man," the church, which is the body and bride of Christ. It was this great secret which the apostle to the Gentiles carried abroad. "That I should preach among the Gentiles, and to make all men see what is the fellowship of the mystery," etc. We cannot wonder at the enthusiasm of Paul, sent forth, as he was, to bear such a glorious and inspiring secret. It was the office of spreading abroad this secret which he so magnified and gloried in, in Col. i, 25–27; iv, 3. This third mystery is closely related to the second. For, taking out this new body from Jew and Gentile, "making in Himself of twain one new man," He unites them to Himself by the Spirit, and thus this twain became one flesh." The church is a member of Christ's body, "of His flesh and of His bones." "This is a great mystery, but I speak concerning Christ and the church" (Eph. v, 32).

IV. The Mystery of Iniquity. "For the mystery of iniquity doth already work; only he who now letteth will let until he be taken out of the way. And then shall that wicked be revealed," etc. (2 Thess. ii, 7, 8.) The mystery of the true church has just been considered; this is the mystery of the false church. The one is "the bride, the Lamb's wife; the other is the great whore, the mother of harlots and abominations." It would seem utterly impossible that out of the pure, primitive church should be developed such a shameless apostacy as that which is here predicted, and that which we have already witnessed, filling the earth with its idolatries and abominations. But the apostles understood it perfectly. It was a painful secret, but they did not shut their eyes to it. It is needful that we should know the evil as well as the good, in order that we may not be dismayed and confounded when we witness apostacies and departures from the faith. Let us be sure that we heed and ponder all that the Lord has told us about "the mystery of iniquity" (1 John iv, 3; 2 John 7; Rev. xvii, 1–7). "And the angel said unto me," Wherefore didst thou marvel? I will tell thee the mystery of the woman. * * * The seven heads are seven mountains, on which the woman sitteth. * * * And the woman which thou sawest is that great city which reigneth over the kings of the earth" (Rev. xvii, 7, 9, 18).

V. The Mystery of Translation. "Behold, I show you a mystery; we shall not all sleep, but we shall all be changed, in a moment, in the twinkling of an eye, at the last trump" (1 Cor. xv, 51). There is no promise of Scripture which better illustrates the character of a mystery than this. It is a declaration that all men will not die. The generation of Christians that shall be living when Christ comes the second time, will not taste death, but will be translated in glorified bodies, to meet the Lord in the air, and be forever with Him. And yet, though this promise is written plainly on the pages of Scripture, how few know anything of it. What ought to be an open secret is rather a hidden mystery. Christians who ought to be instructed in this revelation, join with the world in its accepted maxim that "one thing is certain, that all men must die;" when one thing is certain that "we shall not all die." And even those who are appointed "stewards of the mysteries of God" are found unfaithful, and have forgotten the secret that was intrusted to them. Our hope is life, not death; glory, not the grave. Looking ever for the coming of the Lord from heaven, we are looking thereby for the translation and the transfiguration of our bodies.

VI. The Mystery of Israel. "For I would not, brethren, that ye should be ignorant of this mystery, lest ye should be wise in your own conceits, that blindness in part is happened to Israel, until the fullness of the Gentiles be come in. And so all Israel shall be saved" (Rom. xi, 25). How utterly hidden from the great mass of Christians is this truth — that the present blindness and hardness of heart which has come upon Israel is only temporary, to be followed by their national recovery, when the full number of the Gentiles shall have been gathered in. "I say, then, hath God cast away His people?" asks Paul. And, also, how many are so little in the secret of God's purposes that they are ready to say, "Yea, He hath?" God's Word is very explicit, however, and it cannot fail. When the mystery of translation shall have been accomplished, then this glorious one will begin to unfold. The nation that has been scattered and peeled shall once more be restored to God's favor; "the veil shall be taken from their faces;" they shall "look upon Him whom they have pierced, and mourn because of Him;" and they shall say at last, "Blessed is he who cometh in the name of the Lord" (2 Cor. iii, 16; Zech. xii, 10; Matt. xxiii, 38; Ezek. xxxv, 12–31).

VII. The Mystery of the Restitution of All Things. "Having made known unto us the mystery of His will, according to His good pleasure which He hath purposed in Himself; that in the dispensation of the fullness of times He might gather together in one all things in Christ, both which are in heaven and on earth; even in Him" (Eph. i, 9, 10). This mystery is so profound that it lies so beyond the limits of the present dispensation, that it is most difficult to explain it. It is a revelation in regard to the consummation of all things — the declaration of God's purpose to reunite all things as one harmonious whole under Jesus Christ. For a clear discussion of the passage and a presentation of all the different explanations of it, the reader is referred to Dr. Hodge's Commentary on Ephesians. It is enough that we see in it the final triumph of God's holy law, and the final harmony of the warring and discordant elements over which His kingdom extends. Let us cherish these holy secrets of the Lord; let us study more and more to fathom them until "the mystery of God shall be finished, as He hath declared to His servants the prophets."

SLIPPERY PLACES TO BE AVOIDED.

Prov. iv, 14–27.
I. *The Figure.*
II. *Some of the Places.*
1. Places of evil influences, verses 14, 15.
2. Association with evil men, vers. 14, 16–19.
3. Failure to heed good advice, vers. 20–22.
4. Failure to keep the heart right, ver. 23.
5. Idle words. ver. 24.

III. *How to Avoid.*
1. Ponder and be established, ver. 26; Psa. xi, 1–4; Psa. xxxvii, 23, 24; 2 Chron. xx, 20; Isa. vii, 9.
2. Turn not to the right hand or the left.
Fixedness of purpose, ver. 27.
John H. Elliott.

SOLDIERS—THE CHRISTIAN.
Eph. vi, 10–20.

His motto, 1 Cor. xvi, 13.
His armor, girdle, breast-plate, shoes, shield and helmet, sword— for marching; for defence; for assault.

GENERAL ORDERS.
1. Put none but Christians on guard, 2 Tim. ii, 2.
2. Watch the picket lines, ver. 18; 1 Peter v, 8.
3. Draw on headquarters for help, ver. 10; Rom. viii, 31.
4. Keep your sword bright, Col. iii, 16.
5. No dress parades in this service, 2 Cor. x; 17; Phil. ii, 3.
6. Fight it out on this line, 2 Tim. iv, 2; 2 Peter iii, 17.
7. No marching without orders, Psa. lxii, 5; lxxxv, 8.
8. Not called to high places but to *stand*, ver. 13.
9. Not to put out the fire, but pull men out, Jude 23.
10. No vacation or furlough given, Col. i, 23.
11. Not out until mustered out, 1 Peter i, 13.
If these orders are fully obeyed, one shall chase a thousand, and two put ten thousand to flight, Josh. xxiii, 10.
W. G. Carr.

TEMPERANCE.

A bstain from all appearance of evil, 1 Thess. v, 22.
B e not among wine bibbers, Prov. xxiii, 20.
S trong drink is raging, and whosoever is deceived thereby is not wise, Prov. xx, 1.
T he priests and the prophets have erred through strong drink, Isaiah xxviii, 7.
A t the last it biteth like a serpent; and stingeth like an adder, Prov. xxiii, 22.
I t is good neither to eat flesh, or drink wine, nor anything whereby thy brother stumbleth, or is offended, or is made weak, Rom. xiv, 21.
N o drunkard shall inherit the kingdom of God, 1 Cor. vi, 10.

THE ROCK OF THE BIBLE.

BY REV. CHARLES M. JONES, GOLDEN, COLORADO.

COLORADO greatly resembles Palestine, and a home among the Rocky mountains is continually expressing the mighty figures used in the Word of God. Abraham and David, Elijah and John the Baptist lived amid the lifted grandeur of the rock-laid hills. No wonder that the holy men of God should have found in the rocks of Judea the most forcible illustrations of the Gospel truths.

I. The Rock of the Divine Nature. "He is the rock; His work is perfect, for all His ways are judgment. A God of truth and without iniquity, just and right is He" (Deut. xxxii, 4). We do not enough appreciate that everything depends on just views of God. False religions, from Homer to Frothingham, have erred in giving man a deficient deity. They lack the power to draw men to a true life. "He that cometh to God must believe that He is" such a being as the Bible reveals Him to be — an active, holy, loving personality. If men conceive of a merely amiable being, careless of justice, they will consider it unnecessary to "come" to Him in the Scripture way of repentance and faith. If men conceive of Him as being moved only by burning wrath, they will be repelled, and the desire to come be paralyzed. The only conception which wins the heart and invites a cordial confidence is the God of the Bible, whose justice and mercy unite in Jesus, who can and does "draw all men." It is this God, the rock, who so loved the world that He gave His only begotten Son, and so we find:

II. The Rock of Salvation. "I will make a joyful noise to the rock of my salvation" (Psa. xcv, 1). "He hath set my feet upon a rock." How blessed is that conviction of salvation which we call assurance. Not rash confidence which claims a grace it never has appreciated, but that deep-founded joy which eighteen hundred years ago, declared: "That we may have boldness in the day of judgment, because as He is, so are we in this world;" and a hundred years ago blossomed into song: "Rock of Ages, Cleft for Me." But though salvation is assured, yet great weakness threatens unless we mount to :

III. The Rock of Divine Grace. "Lead me to the rock that is higher than I" (Psa. lxi, 2). When the Hebrews wished to express God's help in sustaining the soul, they exclaimed : "God is the rock of my heart." "O God, my rock and my Redeemer." And the translators, thinking the figure more vigorous and elegant, put "strength" in place of "rock." In Isa. xxvi, 4, the prophet wrote : "In the Lord Jehovah is the Rock of Ages," which they toned down to "everlasting strength." This is what made the religious life of the Hebrew people so vital. They grasped intensely at the necessity and privilege of Jehovah's help, which Jesus emphasized : "Without me ye can do nothing ;" and Paul professed : "I can do all things through Christ which strengtheneth me." But with salvation belongs not only a privilege, but a duty.

IV. The Rock of Confession. "Upon this rock I will build my church" (Matt. xvi, 18). It would be useless to dogmatize as to the precise meaning of a word upon which there is no general consent. All agree there was here a notable confession ; that a profession is of profound importance to the welfare of the individual Christian, and to the progress of Christianity. Peter was, ere long, no longer the ridiculous braggart, but became the unflinching witness. What a hopeful, almost irresistible day, when the Word of God shall be "sounded out" from every believer's mouth ! But not all believe the Gospel. The reason is found, with solemn meaning, in two rocks which we look at together.

V. The Rocks of Assent and Assurance. "Some seed fell upon a rock" (Luke viii, 6). "A wise man built his house upon a rock" (Matt. vii, 24). A rock is good to build upon, but not to sow upon ; makes a fine foundation for a dwelling, but a miserable harvest field. For the latter the rock assented readily, and grimly smiled at the seed's attempt to develop itself on its unrepentant bosom, and saw the gracious verdure perish without regret. Christ is a "rock of offense" only to those whose own hearts are hard as the nether millstone, but to those who receive Him He is as "the shadow of a great rock in a weary land." With Paul we can declare : "That rock was Christ," and with the poet exult :

"On Christ, the solid rock, I stand."

THE SEVEN WITNESSES.

It is noteworthy that, in the Gospel according to John, there are seven witnesses testifying to this one truth: "Jesus is the Christ, the Son of God, and all believing have life in His name," John xx, 31.

1. The Old Testament. "Ye search the Scriptures because ye think that in them ye have eternal life; and these are they which bare witness of Me; and ye will not come to Me, that ye may have eternal life," John v, 39, 40.

2. John, the Baptist. "Ye have sent unto John, and he hath borne witness unto the truth," v, 33; i, 15, 26, 27, 29, 32–36; iii, 26.

3. The Works of Jesus. "But the witness which I have is greater than that of John; for the works which the Father hath given Me to accomplish, the very works that I do, bear witness of Me that the Father hath sent Me," v, 36; iii, 2; x, 25; xv, 24; xiv, 11.

4. The Father. "And the Father which sent Me, He hath borne witness of Me," v, 37. And this was done by voice three times unto Jesus, the Son of God, as prophet, priest and king, Matt. iii, 17; John xii, 27, 28; Matt. xvii, 5.

5. Jesus Himself. "Even if I bear witness of Myself, My witness is true; for I know whence I came and whither I go," John viii, 14. On this occasion Jesus speaks from the depths of Divine self-consciousness, while in John v, 31, He waived that sort of testimony, and would appeal only to testimony "not from man," v, 32, 34; viii, 15; and setting even Himself aside, would have the Father justify Him.

6. The Holy Spirit. "The Spirit of truth, which proceedeth from the Father, He shall bear witness of Me," John xv, 26; 1 John v, 6.

7. The Believers. "And ye also bear witness," John xv, 27; 1 John v, 10, 13; Acts i, 8; 2 Tim. i, 8. The English word *martyr* is one who holds the testimony of Jesus, even unto death, Rev. ii, 13; xvii, 6. Jesus is Himself called "the faithful witness," Rev. i, 5; iii, 14; "who before Pontius Pilate witnessed the good confession," 1 Tim. vi, 13.

Looking back over these seven witnesses, how important it appears for Christians to be faithful and true witnesses. The world first considers them. They should know assuredly that they have eternal life, according to John v, 13, and so, not by hearsay, or at second hand, know and testify. Only from a personal knowledge of salvation and a holy life, will their testimony have weight. The Gospel of John testifies of life in the Son of God; the Epistle of John, of life in the sons of God, John xx, 31; 1 John x, 13.

W. J. ERDMAN.

THE "SHALL NOTS" OF JOHN'S GOSPEL.

THE BELIEVER.

Shall not come into condemnation, v, 24.

Shall not walk in darkness, viii, 12.

Shall never hunger, vi, 35.
Shall never thirst, iv, 14.
Shall not be plucked out of Christ's hand, x, 28.
Shall not perish, John iii, 15.
Shall never die, xi, 26.

THE THREE ENEMIES — HOW CONQUERED.

The world. "This is the victory that overcometh the world, even our faith," 1 John v, 4.
The flesh. "Walk in the Spirit, and ye shall not fulfill the lust of the flesh," Gal. v, 16.
The devil. "Resist the devil and he will flee from you," James iv, 7. — *Watchword.*

THE SOLDIER OF THE CROSS.

I. The enrollment, Joshua xxiv, 14, 15; Matt. vi, 24; Num. i, ii.
II. The captain, Isa. lv, 4; Josh. v, 13–15; Heb. ii, 10.
III. The armor, Eph. vi, 13–18; 2 Cor. x, 4.
IV. The orders, Josh. i, 9; 2 Tim. ii, 3, 4; 1 Tim. vi, 12; Deut. xx, 1.
V. The enemies, Eph. vi, 11, 12; Matt. x, 36.
VI. The signal for action, 2 Sam. v, 24.
VII. The battle-field, 2 Kings vi, 16, 17; Zech. x, 5.
VIII. The result, 2 Tim. iv, 7, 8; Ps. xviii, 37; Rev. ii, 10.
E. A. HOLDREDGE.

THINGS TO HOLD FAST.

I. That which is good, 1 Thess. v, 21.
II. The form of sound words, 2 Tim. i, 13.
III. The confidence and rejoicing of the hope, Heb. iii, 6.
IV. Our confession of Christ, Heb. iv, 14.
V. That which we have, Rev. ii, 25.
VI. What we have heard, Rev. iii, 23.
VII. Steadfastness in view of a crown, Rev. iii, 1.

THE "I WILLS" OF JESUS.

SPOKEN TO THE BELIEVER.

"I *will* not leave you comfortless."
"I *will* come to you," John xiv, 18.
"I *will* give you rest," Matt. xi, 28.
"I *will* in no wise cast out," John vi, 37.
"I *will* raise Him up at the last day," John vi, 40.
"I *will* love Him, and will manifest myself to Him," John xiv, 21.
"I *will* have mercy, and sacrifice," Matt. ix, 13.
"I *will* confess also before My Father," Matt. x, 32.
"I *will* come again and receive you with Myself," John xix, 37.

THE FOUR STEPS OF THE PRODIGAL'S RETURN.

I. *Conviction.* "Came to himself," Luke xv, 17.
II. *Contrition.* "No more worthy," Luke xv, 19.
III. *Confession.* "I have sinned," Luke xv, 18.
IV. *Conversion.* "He arose and came," Luke xv, 20.

THE BELIEVER'S WALK.

. Walk *after* God. OBEDIENCE, eut. xiii, 4.
2. Walk *before* God. PERFECTION, Gen. xvii, 1.
3. Walk *with* God. COMMUNION. Gen. v, 22.

WAITING ON THE LORD.

"Stayed," Isa. xxvi, 3, 4.

I. *What for?*
1. Mercy, pardon, Ps. cxxiii, 2; xxxix, 7, 8.
2. Guidance, Psa. xxv, 5.
3. Protection, Psa. lix, 9.
4. Fulfillment of God's Word, Heb. ii, 3.
5. Fulfillment of promises, Acts i, 4.

II. *How?*
1. Patiently, Psa. xxxvii, 7; xl, 1.

2. Earnestly, Psa. cxxx, 6.
3. Hope in the Word, Psa. cxxx, 5.
4. Resignedly, Lam. iii, 26.
5. In confident expectancy, Mic. vii, 7-9; Luke xii, 36.
III. When?
1. When weak, Isa. xl, 31.
2. When discouraged, Isa. l, 6-10.
3. In adversity, Ps. lix, 1-9.
4. All the day, Psa. xxv, 5.
5. Continually, Hosea xii, 6.
IV. Results.
1. Shall be saved, Prov. xx, 22; Isa. xxv, 9.
2. God hears, Ps. xl, 1.
3. God blesses, Isa. xxx, 18; Dan. xii, 12.
4. Experience His goodness, Lam. iii. 25.
5. Receive things prepared, Isa. lxiv, 4.   J. H. ELLIOTT.

WHAT THE LORD DOES FOR HIS PEOPLE.
Genesis.
Withhold nothing, Gen. xxii, 16.
1. The Lord appoints, Gen. xxiv, 44.
2. The Lord leads, Gen. xxiv, 48.
3. The Lord protects, Gen. xxiv, 50.
4. The Lord prospers, Gen. xxiv, 56.
5. The Lord blesses, Gen. xxv, 11.
6. The Lord directs, Gen. xxvi, 2.
7. The Lord multiplies, Gen. xxvi, 4.   FRANK G. PERKINS.

WHAT WE FIND WHEN WE FIND JESUS.
1. Rest, Isa. lvii, 20; Matt xi, 28. Rest from sin in service. Sing No. 309.
2. Peace, Isa. lvii, 21; John xiv, 27; xvi, 33. Permanent peace; the peace of rest. Sing No. 200.
3. Life, 1 John v, 12; Prov. viii, 35; John xii, 25. A life of rest and peace. Sing second and third verses, No. 46.
4. Home, John xiv, 1-3. Home for the life of rest and peace.
   J. HOWARD SEAL.

WHAT WE SHOULD DO FOR ONE ANOTHER.
"Love one another," John xv, 17.
"Serve one another," Gal. v, 13.
"Receive one another," Rom. xv, 7.
"Bear ye one another's burdens," Gal. vi, 2.
"Forbearing one another," Eph. iv, 32.
"Exhort one another," Heb. iii, 13.
"Confess to one another," Jas. v, 16.
"Consider one another," Heb. x, 24.
"Submit to one another," Eph. v, 21.
"Be kind to one another," Eph. iv, 32.
"Abound in love to one another," 1 Thess. iii, 12.
"Comfort one another," 1 Thess. iv, 18.
"Pray for one another," Jas. v, 16.

WHO ARE THE BRETHREN?
When the Lord separates the sheep from the goats, these brethren must be standing with Him. He could not say to the sheep, "Inasmuch as ye did it to one another," but He could point to a third party and say, "Inasmuch as ye have done it to one of these My brethren." In order to understand the term "brethren," see Matt. xii, 46-50; Acts vii, 22-25; Rom. ix, 3; Heb. ii, 12. By these Scriptures we find out that there are three different classes to whom the definition "brethren" is given.

1. Those related by natural birth to each other.

2. Those who are allied by bonds of nationality, and

3. Those who are believers in the Lord Jesus Christ, and occupy with Him resurrection ground.

We believe the brethren of Matt. xxv are Jews, who have been scattered during the last great struggle spoken of in Jer. xxx, 4-7; xxxi, 10,

7, 17, 20, and Gen. xii, 3; and that the nations are judged on the ground of their treatment of those whom Christ calls His brethren. And now notice the contrasts of the judgment of Matt. xxv and Rev. xx; nothing could be more opposite than they are.

CONTRASTS BETWEEN JUDGMENTS OF MATTHEW XXV AND REVELATION XX.

As in Matt. xxv, 31, to end.

1. A kingdom spoken of in Matt. xxv, 34.
2. No resurrection of the dead.
3. No dead judged.
4. Nations gathered, verse 32.
5. No destruction of the earth by fire.
6. No "books" opened.

Did these sheep know anything of Luke x, 20?

"Rejoice not that the Spirits are subject unto you, but rather rejoice because your names are written in heaven."

7. Death not destroyed here.

8. Here the Son of Man takes the kingdom, See Matt. xiii, 41–43.

"The Son of Man shall send forth His angels, and they shall gather out of His kingdom all things that offend, and them which do iniquity, and shall cast them into a furnace of fire; there shall be wailing and gnashing of teeth. Then shall the righteous shine forth as the sun in the kingdom of their Father. Who hath ears to hear, let him hear."

9. Satan not cast into eternal fire, but shut up for a thousand years, Rev. xx, 2, 3.

"And He laid hold on the dragon, that old serpent which is the devil and Satan, and bound him a thousand years, and shut him up, and set a seal upon him that he should deceive the nations no more till the thousand years should be fulfilled, and after that he should be loosed for a little season."

As in Rev. xx, 11, to end.

1. Nothing about a kingdom in Rev. xx.
2. The dead are raised, verses 5, 12, 13.
3. No living judged.
4. No nations mentioned.
5. Here it is destroyed, verses 9, 11.
6. Here are books, and the "Book of Life."

7. But it is at the Great White Throne, verse 14.

"The last enemy that shall be destroyed is death," 1 Cor. xv, 26.

8. Here He gives it up. See 1 Cor. xv. 24.

"Then cometh the end, when He shall have delivered up the kingdom to God, even the Father; when He shall have to put down all rule and all authority and power. For He must reign till He hath put all enemies under His feet."

9. Here He is cast where the beast and the false prophets were a thousand years before. See Rev. xix, 20, and xx, 10.

And the devil that deceived them was cast into the lake of fire and brimstone, where the beasts and false prophet are and shall be tormented day and night for ever and ever.

10. No new heavens and earth, but the kingdom prepared "from the foundation of the world. The church enters into glory prepared from BEFORE the foundation of the world."

10. At the final judgment the old pass away and the new appear, Rev. xxi, 1; 2 Pet. iii, 13.

11. sheep are not judged by, John xii, 48.

11. But John xii, 47, 48, is brought to bear in Rev. xx.

12. Those in Matt. xxv are judged without law, Rom. ii, 12. Never have heard the Gospel of Rom. ii, 16.

12. These are judged by the law, Rom. ii, 12.

13. This judgment turns entirely on the ground of works, nothing being said about faith.

13. The ground of this judgment is altogether different; we are not saved or lost because we do this or that, but according as we accept or reject Christ.

"He that heareth My Word and believeth on Him that sent Me hath everlasting life, and shall not come into condemnation, but is passed from death unto life," John v, 24.   W. H. W.

WEIGHTS AND MEASURES' ACT.

Just weight, just balance * * * shall ye have, Lev. xix, 36.

Ye shall have just balances, Ezek. xlv, 10.

Thou shalt not have in thy bags divers weights, a great and a small. Thou shalt not have in thy house divers measures, a great and a small. * * * Thou shalt have a perfect and just weight; a perfect and just measure shalt thou have, Deut. xxv, 13-15.

A just weight and balance are the Lord's, Prov. xvi, 11.

A false balance is an abomination to the Lord. A just weight is His delight, Prov. xi, 1.

Divers weights and divers measures are both alike abominations to the Lord, Prov. xx, 10.

Divers weights are an abomination unto the Lord, and a false balance is not good, Prov. xx, 23.

The scant measure is abominable, Micah vi, 10.

Making the ephah small and the shekel great, and falsifying the balance by deceit, Amos viii, 5.

Will a man rob God? Mal. iii, 8.

The Lord is a God of knowledge, and by Him actions are weighed, 1 Sam. ii, 3.

Thou art weighed in the balances, and art found wanting, Daniel v, 27
— *Words and Work.*

ANALYTICAL INDEX OF SUBJECTS.

A.

Abel, 65.
Abel's Blood, 204.
Abel, a Type, 53.
Abiding in Christ, 198, 222, 16.
Abigail, 240.
Ability of Christ, 98.
Abram's Faith, 163.
Abram's Seed, 113.
Acceptance, 24.
Activity, Christian, 34, 26.
Adam, a Type, 65, 53.
Adam and Eve, 65.
Addition, 240.
Adoption, 170, 168, 245.
Advents, two, 40.
Advent, Pre-millenial, 26.
Advocacy, 90.
Advocate, 97.
Advocate, meaning of, 90.
Advocate, object of, 92.
Altar of Burnt Offering, 48.
Altar of Incense, 49.
Alls, three important, 249.
Amusements, 242.
Anger, what is it? 144.
Anti-Christ, 114, 116, 112.
Anointing, 81.
Anointed for Service, 204.
Anointed by Holy Ghost, 56.
Appearings, three, 242, 39.
Apocalypse, 40.
Apostacy, 45, 40, 26.
Arks of Scripture, 243.
Ark of the Covenant, 49.
Assurance, basis of, 24, 10.
Assurance, 69, 24, 171, 235, 176, 274, 221, 239.
Assurance and Sonship, 112.
Atonement. 67, 70, 86, 49, 51, 166, 68, 69, 149.
Atonement, need of, 66.
Atonement and Reconciliation, 51.
Attributes of the Spirit, 128.
Attention and Study, 33.
Authority of Christ as Teacher, 116.
Authority of Word of God over Opinions and of Conduct, 32.

B.

Backsliding, 143, 232, 34, 244, 231.
Baptism, 24.
Beast, mark of, 76.
Believers, 210.
Believer's Life, 222.
Believer's Relationship with God, 245.
Believers, Priests, 89.
Believer's Position, 93.
Believer's Place of Refuge, 245.
Behavior, 172.
Bible, Reading the, 27.
Bible Reading, Topical, 9.
Bible Reading and Studying, 32, 5.
Bible Reading, Christ's Method of, 7.
Bible Words, 9.
Bible, How to Study, 9, 17, 33.
Bible for Plain People, 18, 12.
Bible Marking, 22, 21.
Bible, Knowledge of, 22.
Bible Study and Gospel Work, 27.
Bible in Inquiry Room, 235.
Bible, Books of, 34.
Bible, How to Understand, 228.
Bible and Human Opinion, 230.
Bible Needed Now, 74.
Bible, Searching the, 230.
Bible, Doctrines of, 152.
Bible in the Inquiry Room, 231.
Bible and Newspaper, 73.
Bible Study for Individual Growth, 28.

Bible, Interest in, 6.
Bible and Commentaries, 17.
Bible Suppers, the, 246.
Blessed Hope, Ground of, 110.
Blessing, the Place of, 246.
Blood of Christ, What it Secures, 68.
Blood of Christ, Value of, 71.
Blood of Christ, Sprinkling of, 72.
Blood of Christ Shelters, 69.
Blood of Christ Delivers, 69.
Blood of Christ and Abel, 204.
Brotherly Love, 222.
Burnt Offering, 40, 45.

C.

Calling, Christian, What is it? 25, 182, 181.
Calling, Results of, 182.
Calvary, 202.
Candlestick, Golden, 48.
Cares, 149.
Chastisement, 222, 216, 35.
Character of God, 42.
Cherubim and Mercy Seats, 67.
Child of God, 230.
Child, Little, 239.
Christ and Anti-Christ, 109.
    Appropriated, 66.
    Accessible, 93.
    Ascension, 63.
    And Believer, 61.
    And Church, 65, 66.
    And Redeemed, 76.
    Acceptance in Him, 62.
    Appropriated, 68.
    Abiding in, 239.
    Blood of, 95.
    Confession of, 146.
    Conception of, 56.
    Coming with and for Saints, 111, 112.
    Coming How? 115.
    Coming Where? 115.
    Coming, Hope of Church, 101.
    Coming, not Death, 111.
    Coming, Personal, 111.
    Completeness in Him, 103.
    Death of, 266, 65, 179.
    Divinity of, 64.
    Example of, 121, 122.
    Expecting, 94.
    Everything, 123.

    Exaltation of, 93.
    Friendship, 106, 107.
    Gifts to His People, 120.
    Glorified, 92.
    Gospels, four, 33, 35, 36.
    Healer, 118,
    Humiliation of, 120, 63.
    Hiding Place, 121.
    High Priest, 98, 96.
    Humanity of, 95, 34.
    Intercession of, 98, 41.
    Joy of, 148.
    Looking to, 123.
    Likeness of, 112.
    Life, 146.
    Love of, 106, 266.
    Mind of, 120.
    Old Testament, 65, 45, 51.
    Offerings in, 55.
    Prescence of, 119.
    Peter, And, 118.
    Power of, 73.
    Person of, 24.
    Rejected, 117, 62.
    Redeemer, 118.
    Resurrection, 63.
    Superiority of, 95, 96.
    Second Coming of, 114, 154, 63 87, 13.
    Subject of Scripture, 15, 25 61.
    Sufferings of, 87, 63, 214.
    Sympathy of, 96.
    Stone, the, 118.
    Son of God, 64, 95, 10.
    Song, Solomon, 246.
    Teacher, 116, 226.
    Truth and Life, 122.
    Union with, 121, 190.
    Victory of, 93.
    Waiting, 96.
    Work finished, 92.
    What we Have in Him, 120.
Christian Conflict, 192, 188.
    Contrast, 220.
    Courage, 184.
    Experience, 34.
    Growth, 28, 221.
    Hated by World, 78.
    Life, What is it? 190.
    Normal, What is a? 231.
    Possession, 221.
    Position, 40, 35, 221, 182, 147, 220.
    Race, 246.

World, and a, 193.
Christianity and Judaism, 37
Church, Mystery of the, 38, 269.
Church, What is it? 25, 85.
Church, Dear to Christ, 213.
Church, Prosperity, 241.
Cleansing. 68, 69, 95.
Comfort in Affliction, 112.
Come, 152.
Commentaries, the best, 9.
Communion, 210, 223, 16, 154, 55, 241.
Commercial Traveler, 246.
Condemnation, 162.
Confession and Restoration, 30.
Confession, 196, 274, 246.
Conflict, 184, 191.
Consecration, 184, 72, 234, 73, 112.
Conversation, Christian, 183, 247.
Conversation, Unbelievers, 247.
Conversion Through Word, 60.
Conversion, 245.
Conviction, 125, 235, 134, 232.
Converts, Young, 84.
Covenant, better, 202.
Cross, The, 254.
Crowns of Scripture, 111.

D.

Daily Duties, 192.
Dates and Signs, 19.
Daysman, 90.
Death, 85, 149.
Death of Christ, Value of. 189.
Death, Shadow of, 80.
Death and Sin, 261.
Death, Spiritual, 23.
Death Not Coming of the Lord, 13.
Death, Thoughts on, 247.
Decision, 247.
Deliverance, 78.
Delusion, 239.
Departing, 24.
Destruction, 239.
Destruction of Jerusalem Not Lord's Coming, 13.
Diamond, What is a? 218.
Diamond Cutting, 216.
Discipleship, 222, 221.
Dispensations, Old and New, 34.
Disembodied State, 26.
Divine Nature, 176, 273.
Divine Healing, 249.
Divine Life, 40.

Divine Indwelling, 269.
Divinity of Christ, 40, 63.
Divinity of Holy Spirit, 128, 125.
Drink Offering, 57.

E.

Earnest of Spirit, 41.
Edification, 241.
Endure, 184.
Endurance. 184.
Enemies, Three, 276.
Enoch, a Type, 53, 65.
Epistles to Saints, 30.
Estrangement, 61.
Eternal, 223.
Eternal Life, 162, 223, 156.
Eternal Life, What is it? 251.
Eternal Life, How do I get it? 251.
Eternal Life, Can I loose it? 251.
Eternal Life, Evidences of, 251.
Eternal Things, 251.
Evangelistic and Pastoral Work, 39.
Examination, Self, 265.
Excuse Making, 143, 148, 252.
Experience, Christian, 83.
Expectation of Believers, 252.
Expectation of Unbelievers, 252.

F.

Failures, 149.
Faith, 140, 155, 166, 197, 266.
Faith, What it is, 150, 151, 163.
    Necessity of, 150, 151.
    Object of, 24, 69, 150, 152, 163.
    Exercise of, 151.
    Power of, 150, 151.
    Simplicity of, 150.
    Examples of, 151.
    Triumphs of, 162.
    Results of, 24.
    Walk, and, 152, 163.
    Word of, 152.
    Bible, and, 33.
    Works, and, 151, 152, 163.
    Forgiveness, and, 163.
    Healing, 249.
Faithfulness, 255,-112.
Faithful Sayings, 254.
Fellowship, 37, 79.
Fellowship and Life, 11.
Flesh, What is it? 103, 187, 191.
    Cannot be improved, 104, 187.
    No good thing in, 192.

Still in Believer, 108, 192.
Mortified, 105.
Reckoned dead, 192.
Spirit, and, 187, 191.
Works of, 104, 187.
Following Christ, 82.
Food, Spiritual, 81.
Forgiveness, 118, 163, 165, 166, 229
    Ground of, 165, 166.
    Completeness, 165, 167.
    Consequences of, 166.
    Conditions of, 165.
    Righteousness, 11
Four Gospels, 58.
Freedom, 148.
Friend, Characteristics of, 107.
Fruitfulness, 183, 222, 239.

G.

Galatians, Epistle of, 188.
General Resurrection, 100.
Gentiles, 35.
Genesis and Revelation, Contrasts, 247.
Giving, 264.
Glory of God, 222.
Glorified God, 217.
Glorified, 96, 246.
God, Attributes of, 42.
    Counsels of, 38.
    Gifts of, 255.
    Holiness of, 67, 234.
    Love of, 62, 63, 266.
    Righteousness of, 37.
    Salvation of, 38.
    Titles of, 41.
Godhead, 128.
Good Shepherd, 86.
Good Works, 35.
Grace of God, 145, 220, 237, 274.
Grace and Law, 145.
Grace, Falling from, 145.
Grace and Government, 68, 145.
Grace, Blessings of, 145.
Graces, Christian, 241.
Gracious Mercy, 67.
Growth, 256.
Great Tribulation, 112.
Gospel, 37, 139, 142.
    Authority of, 145.
    In Names, 148.
    Invitation of, 147.
    Railroad, 148.

Grace of God, 147.
Gospels and Epistles, Relation of, 36.

H.

Head and Body, 39.
Helps to Bible Study, 27, 32.
Healing, Divine, 249, 250.
Healing and Anointing, 250.
Healing, Methods of, 250.
Health, 148.
Heaven, 179, 200, 256.
    How gained, 77.
    Who shall be there, 200.
    Who shall not be there, 200.
    What we have there, 60.
Hell, Testimony of Word concerning, 60.
Holy Spirit Abiding, 25, 136, 189.
    Anointing, 134.
    Attributes of, 123, 125.
    Christ, and, 56, 128.
    Convincing, 204.
    Church, in, 135, 136.
    Church, and, 135, 137.
    Conviction of, 127.
    Divinity of, 25, 124.
    Emblems of, 125.
    History of, 133.
    Hindrances to, 134.
    How given, 226.
    Indwelling of, 124, 127.
    Inspiring, 123, 133.
    Intercessor, 41.
    Ministry, and, 135, 137.
    Names of, 128, 129, 138.
    Need of, 134.
    Personality of, 25.
    Presence of, 123, 124, 127, 189.
    Power of, 119.
    Power of Guidance, 136.
    Power of Life, 136.
    Power of Knowledge, 136.
    Power of Testimony, 136.
    Power of Service, 136.
    Power of Prayer, 136.
    Promise of, 134, 138, 207, 226.
    Seal and Earnest, 41, 124.
    Sonship, 134.
    Service for, 205, 207.
    Symbols of, 138.
    Teacher, 15, 16, 17, 32, 137, 226.
    Types of, 530.

Work of, 124, 126, 129, 130, 132, 133, 134.
Holiness, Necessity of, 11, 179.
　Source of, 11, 106.
　Progressive, 179.
Holy Life, 146.
Holy Place and Most Holy, 48.
Hold Fast, 276.
Hope of the Gospel, 185.
Hope, Blessed, the, 26.
Hope, Better, 202.
Hosea, Figures of, 235.
Humanity of Christ, 56.
How to Study Bible, 52.
Hypocrisy, 148.
Hyssop, 62.
Hidden, 257.

I.

Ignorance, 14.
Incarnation, 18.
Iniquity, Mystery of, 269.
Imputation, 149.
Imprecatory Psalms, 52.
Image of Daniel, 115.
Inspiration, 13, 14, 17, 23, 59, 60.
Intercession, 41, 90, 97, 167.
Inquirers, Advice in regard to, 140, 235.
Inquiry Meeting, 139.
Inquiry Room, 142, 231.
Isaac, a Type, 53.
Israel, Deliverance of, 100.
　History of, 63, 113.
　Present condition of, 113.
　Restoration of, 26, 113.
　Repentance of, 114.
　God's Centre, 115.
Interval of the Church, 114.

J.

Jehovah, 43.
Jesus Worshipped, 64.
Jesus, Name of, 64.
Jerusalem. Seat of Government, 115.
Jewish History, 113.
Jewels, the Lord's, 212, 214.
Joseph, a Type, 53, 54.
Journey, A Pleasant, 242.
Joy, Christian, 18.
Joy and Sonship, 11.
Joy, Source of, 11.

Joy marred, 11.
Joy in Philippians, 181.
Joy in Creation, 119.
Joy in Redemption, 119.
Judgment, 68, 101, 156.
Judgment of Believer's Sins, 57, 110.
Judgment Seat of Christ, 110.
Judgment of Believer, 112.
Judgment of Service, 110.
Judgment and Reward, 111.
Judgment, Final, 26.
Judgment, Where will it take place? 258.
Judgment, Pre-millennial, 258.
Judgment of Nations, 258.
Judaism and Christianity, 37.
Justification, 68, 69, 90, 95, 121, 245.
Justification, What is it? 169.
Justification, Need of, 168.
Justification, Source of, 168, 169.
Justification, by Law, 169.
Justification by Faith, 169.
Justification of Life, 170.
Justification, Result of, 168.

K.

Kingdom, 34.
Kingdom, Type of, 34.
Kingdom of God, 115.
Knowledge, 221.

L.

Lamb of God, 70, 74, 76.
Last Days, 35, 154.
Laver of Brass, 48, 67.
Law, Demands of, 176.
Law and Gospel, 66.
Law, Redeemed from, 172.
Led by Spirit, 126.
Let Just, 257.
Life, 205, 256.
Life, Christian, 36, 121, 222, 249.
Life, Source of, 223.
Life Manifested, 223.
Life in the Spirit, 126.
Life and Unity, 209.
Life and Fellowship, 11.
Light Needed, 216.
Liberty, 162.
Lord's Supper, 264.
Love of God, 62.
Lot, A Warning, 53.

M.

Man, 238.
   Fallen, 155.
   Failure of, 113.
   First and Second, 66.
   History of, 104.
   Hiding from God, 62.
   Lost, 146.
   Natural state of, 23, 72, 219.
   Nature of, —.
   Original Creation, 23.
   Ruling, 66.
   What is he? 236.
Manna, 67, 68.
Meat Offering, 56.
Mediator, 89, 97, 147.
Meekness, 183.
Melchizedek, 97.
Members of Christ, 232.
Memorial Feast, 68.
Mercy and Law, 67.
Mercy Seat, 67.
Mercy Rejected, 67.
Message from God, 146.
Methods of Bible Study, 32.
Millennium, 100, 101.
   How introduced, 26.
   Offerings, 57.
   Priesthood, 89.
   Type of, 53.
Ministry, What is it? 51.
   Of the Word, 60.
   Human and Divine, 7.
Morality, 24, 148.
Mountains, 261.
Moon, a Type, 209.
Moriah, 262.
Moses, a Type, 54.
Murderer, What is a? 144.
Mysteries, Seven, 268.
Mystery, The Church a, 38.

N.

Names and Titles of God, 61.
Name of the Father, 76.
   What is expressed by? 41, 44.
Natures, The two, 191.
Nations, Gathered, 115.
   Conversion of, 115.
   Judgment of, 114.
   Position of, 115.
Nearness, 68, 69.

New Creation, 61.
New Birth, 66, 161, 162.
New Testament, Blood of, 68.
Nourishment, 156.
Nobility, True, 12.
Novel Reading, 18.
Noah, A Type, 53, 265.

O.

Obedience, 197.
   Communion, and, 16.
Object of Faith, 150.
Offerings, Christ in, 45, 72.
Olives, Mount of, 263.
Old Testament, 275.
   Christ in the, 15, 51.
Oneness of Father and Son, 117.
   Christ and Believers, 211.
Oracles of God, 59.

P.

Passover, 66, 71.
Pastoral Instruction, 35.
Patience, 112, 184.
Patient Teacher, 116.
Partakers, 264.
Pardon, 148.
Peace, Author of, 180.
   Characteristics of, 180.
   Secured, 180.
   Source of, 180.
   Promise of, 181.
   Of God, 180.
   How to get, 181.
   God of, 181.
   Offering, 55.
Pearl of Great Price, 214.
Perfection, 56, 179.
Perseverance, 286.
Power, Meaning of, 119.
   Christ, of, 64, 65, 119.
   Manifested. 86, 119.
   Of Elijah, 208.
   For work, 225, 227, 235.
Prayer, 197, 265.
   Effectual, 198.
   Acceptable, 196.
   Conditions of, 197.
   Prevailing, 64.
   Necessity of, 64.
   Power of, 239.
   Helpers to, 199.

The Lord's, 199.
Instances of, 200.
When to, 196.
What is, 195.
Why all should, 195.
Study, and, 33.
For what, 196.
Meditation and, 199.
Meetings, 198.
Praise, 186.
Preach, What to, 66.
Preach, How to, 60.
Preparation for Work, 236.
Priesthood, object of, 89.
   Qualifications for, 97.
   Where carried on, 97.
   Results of, —.
   God and, 98.
   Characteristics of, 98.
   Believer and, 98.
   Scene of, 96.
   And Advocacy, 89.
   Necessity of, 179.
   Nature of, 90.
Priest, Work of, 55.
Promises, Better, 202.
   To whom made, 66.
Progress, 81.
Propitiation, 62.
Prophecy, 14.
   Study of, 18, 19, 20.
   Three things in, 114.
   Interpretation of, 14.
Prophetic Outlines, 113.
Propitiation, 5, 51, 121.
Promises, To whom made, 30, 264.
Purchase, 95.
Progressive Revelation, 52.
Protection, 265.
Privileges of Believers, 264.
Purposes, Divine, 34.
Purity of Christ, 24, 66, 222.
Punishment, 238.

Q.

Quickening, 123.

R.

Rationalism, 39.
Ransom Money, 149.
Regeneration, 125, 245.
   Necessity of, 24, 159, 161.

What is it? 191, 159, 160, 161, 162, 188.
   Power of, 160.
   Instrumentality of, 159.
   Author of, 159.
Redemption and Purchase, 176.
   Applied, 174.
   Consummated, 24, 34, 35, 69, 95, 172, 173, 175, 220.
Redeemed, 68.
Repentance, 164, 166, 245.
   Need of, 158.
   What is it? 157, 158, 164, 165.
   How produced, 158.
   Importance of, 165.
   A gift, 165.
   False, 165.
   Examples of, 165.
   True, 157, 165.
   Time of, 165.
   Motives to, 164.
   And Forgiveness, 57.
Reconciliation, 61, 62.
Refuge of Believer, 245.
Rest of Christ, 93.
Rest, 79.
Rest of Soul, 41.
Resurrection, in Old Testament, 99.
   The first, 100.
   Spiritual, 100.
Resurrections, two, 13, 41.
Resurrection, hope, 99.
   of Christ, fruits of, 99, 156.
   And Millenniums, 100, 148.
   Better, 203.
Restitution of all Things, 56, 271.
Restoration of Soul, 79.
   Israel, 112.
Revelation, Divine, 61.
Revival, 61.
Reward, 39, 256.
Righteousness and Grace, 62.
Rocks, 273.
Rod and Staff, 80.

S.

Saint, 2, 11.
Saints, position of, 66.
Sacrifice of Christ, 145, 146.
Sacrifices, —.
Safety, 156, 257.

Salvation, 176, 178, 273.
   Need of, 40, 177.
Salvation and Holy Spirit, 177.
Salvation through Christ, 176.
Salvation, present, 177.
Salvation, possession of, 38.
   Benefits of, 178.
   Evidenced, 178.
   Secured, 146.
   Conflict of, 177.
   Final, 38, 146.
   Three-fold, 178.
Sanctification, 39, 40, 59, 68, 78, 79, 121, 128, 245.
Satan, Personality of, 73, 265.
Satan's Work, 238, 265.
Satan, Power of, 83, 265.
Satisfaction, 79, 118, 154.
Scepticism and Word of God, 29.
Science and Bible, 17.
Scriptures, What they are, 59.
Scripture, Perversion of, 30.
   Misapplied, 30.
   Studying, 12, 32, 33.
   For all, 15, 25.
   Subject of, 14, 60.
Second Advent, 85, 39, 101, 111, 114.
Second Coming of Christ, not the Destruction of Jerusalem, 20.
Sealing, 178.
Self Deception, 238.
Self Denial, 221.
Separation, 69, 152, 154, 222.
Service, Power for, 228.
Service, 248, 257.
   Preparation for, 234.
Seventy Weeks of Daniel, 114.
Shepherd, 79.
   Signification of, 78, 85.
   Christ, the, 77, 79.
   Christ, 79, 88.
   Seeking Sheep, 84.
Sheep, Christ's, 88.
   of Christ, Marks of, 81.
   Three kinds of, 259.
Shew Bread, Table, 49.
Sin, Born in, 144.
   What is it? 147, 166.
   And God's Character, 5.
   God's Testimony about, 60.
   Consequence of, 145, 236.
   Punished, 147, 238.
   And Death, 261.

Put away, 96, 164, 179.
   Forgiven, 95, 266.
Sickness and Healing, 249.
Sinai, 261.
Soldiers, 211, 272, 276.
Sonship, 170, 230.
   And Service, 224.
   And Joy, 11.
Sovereign Grace, 155.
Spirit Given, 70.
   Earnest of, 126.
   Quenching, 126.
   Sealing, 125.
   Striving, 124.
   teaches, 12, 135.
   Walk in, 189.
   Witness of, 125.
Strangers and Pilgrims, 211.
Strength, 256.
Stewardship, 193.
Substitution, 51, 61.
Suffering and Glory, 52.
Suffering, 179.
Suppers, Bible, 246
Supplication, 196.
Submission, 197.

T.

Tabernacle, The, 54.
   A Type, 45, 65.
   Coverings of, 48.
Tabor, 263.
Tact, 232.
Teaching, 116.
Teaching of Christ, 117.
Teacher, Faithful, 46, 226.
Teachers, False, 238.
Temple, 205.
Temptation, 11, 73, 179, 229.
Temperance, 272.
Temple, Stones of, 217.
Temple, Believer's Body, 205.
Testimony, 11, 148.
   to Christ, 228.
Thanksgiving, 185, 196.
Titles of God, 44.
Transfiguration, 117.
Trespass Offering, 56.
Tribulation, 114.
Trinity, 42, 23.
Two Nations, 103, 105.
Typology, 52.
Type of Church, 65.

U.

Unbelief, 150, 237.
   the Ground of Condemnation, 144.
Unconverted, 152.
Unity, 209.
Union, 35, 37, 38, 189, 209, 241.

V.

Vail, The, 48.
Victory, 69, 188.
Views and Scripture, 212.
Visible Coming, 114.

W.

Walk, Christian, 53, 182, 189.
   Results of, 183.
   and Warfare, 38.
Warfare and Victory, 34.
Watchfulness, 112, 193, 194, 195.
Weakness, 149.
Weight and Measures, 279.
Witnesses, Seven, 275.
Witness, Two-fold, 10.
World, Conversion of, 26.
   End of the, 100.
   History of, 115.
   Power of, 84.
   What it cannot do, 34.
Word of God, —.
   Anxious inquirer, 29, 233.
   Appeal to, 12.
   Basis of faith, 10, 16.
   Experience and, 29.
   Feelings and, 16.
   How to use it, 205.
   Ministering, the, 60.
   New birth, and, 59.
   Object of, 59.
   Plain book, 13.
   Power of, 29, 59, 60, 229.
   Reward and, 61.
   Sanctifying, 61.
   Scepticism, and, 29.
   Spiritualized, 13.
   Study of, 20.
   Testimony to God, 60.
   Testimony to Heaven, 60.
   Tradition, and, 10.
   To all, 12, 32.
Work, Christian, 224, 225, 234, 239.
   Devotion in, 227.
   Hindrances to, 236.
   How to, 182.
   Manner of, 225, 227.
   Methods of, 227, 234.
   Model of, 225, 226.
   Personal, 28, 224, 234.
   Power for, 226.
   Preparation for, 226, 227.
   Reward of, 236.
   Success in, 236.
Worker, Christian, 223, 226, 234.
   Christian, example of, 227.
Works good, 256.

INDEX TO BIBLE READINGS.

A.

Abiding in Christ, 239.
Acceptable Prayer, 196.
Adam and Eve, 65.
Adoption, 168.
Advantages of Bible Reading, 6.
Advocacy, 91.
Alls, 242.
A Message from God, 146.
Amusements, 242.
Anointing for Service, 204.
A Pleasant Journey, 242.
Appearings Three, 242.
Arks of Scripture, 243.
Assurance, 170, 181.

B.

Backsliding, 244.
Be's, as Commands, 244.
Believer's Life, 222.
Believer's Place of Refuge, 245.
Believer's Position, 221.
Believer's Walk, 276.
Believer's Relation to God, 245.
Better Things, 202.
Bible Marking, 21.
Bible Readings, 8.
Bible Suppers, 246.
Blessing, Places of, 246.
Books of Bible, 34.
Books of New Testament, 36.
Burnt Offering, 54.

C.

Christ, 120.
Christ and Anti-Christ, 109.
Christ Everything, 123.
Christ in the Old Testament, 51.
Christ in Song of Solomon, 246.
Christ's Gifts to His People, 120.
Christ's Method of Teaching, 116.
Christ our Example, 122.
Christ Glorified, 92.
Christ our Hiding Place, 121.
Christ, Looking to, 120.
Christ our Life, 121.
Christ, Mind of, 120.
Christian's Place of Refuge, 121.
Christ Rejected, 117.
Christ's Work, 49.
Christian and the World, 193.
Christian Calling, 181.
Christian Conflict, 192.
Christian Position, 220.
Christian Race, 246.
Christian Unity, 209.
Christian Work, 225, 236.
Christian Worker, 226.
Commercial Travelers, 246.
Completeness in Christ, 103.
Confession, 246.
Consecration, 184.
Contrasts, 247.
Conversation, 247.
Courage, 184.

D.

Danger of Unbelief, 237.
Dealing with Inquirers, 235.
Death, 247.
Decision, 247.
Disciples, 221, 222.
Divine Healing, 249.
Divine Reconcilliation, 61.
Divine Titles, 41.
Divinity of Spirit, 124.
Double Truths of Scripture, 40.
Drink Offering, The, 57.

E.

Effectual Prayer, 198.
Endurance, 184.
Eight Eternal Things, 251.
Eternal Life, What is it? 251.
Every Morning, 251.
Excuses, 148.
Expectation, 252.

F.

Faith, Exposition of, 150.
Faith, Importance of, 150.
Faith in Christ, 69.
Faith, Object of, 152.
Faith, What it is and what it does, 151.
Faithful Sayings, 253.
Faithfulness, 255.
Forgiveness, 167.
Five Excuses of Moses, 252.
Friendship with Christ, 106.

G.

General Orders, 272.
God Loves Thee, 63.
God's Word the Means of Revival, 60.
Good Tidings, 148.
Good Works, 256.
Gospel of Grace of God, 147
Gospel Invitation, 147.
Gospel in the Inquiry Room, 139.
Gospel Railroad, 148.
Grace, 145, 220.

H.

Heaven, 256, 200.
Helps to Prayer, 198.
Hidden, 257.
Hindrances to Work, 236.
Holiness, 179.
Holy Spirit, 123, 124, 127, 133.
Holy Spirit, Attributes of, 128.
Holy Spirit and the Church, 135, 137.
Holy Spirit and Godhead, 128.
Holy Spirit and Ministry, 138.
Holy Spirit, Power of, 129, 134, 136.
How to Serve God, 257.
How to Study the Bible, 33.
How God Forgives Sin, 166.

I.

Is the Young Man Safe? 257.
Israel, 113.

J.

Jehovah, Titles of God, 61.
Jesus Himself, 63.
Jesus, Name of, 64.
Joy in Phillipians, 181.
Judgment Seat of Christ, 110.
Justification, 168, 169.
Just Let, 257.
John's Testimony to Jesus, 257.

L.

Lamb of God, 70, 71.
Looking to Christ, 120.
Love of Christ, 106.
Love of God, 62.

M.

Manna, 67.
Man as a Sinner, 236.
Man and His Salvation, 176.
Meat Offering, The, 56.
Meekness, 183.
Mercy Seat, 67.
Millenial Reign, 114.
Mind of Christ, 120.
Ministry of the Word, 60.
Misapplied Scripture, 30.
Mountains, 261.

O.

On Giving, 264.
One Thing, 264.
Of What We are Partakers, 264.
Our Great High Priest, 89, 95, 97.
Our Sonship, 170.

P.

Passover, 66.
Peace Offering, 55.
Peace, 181.
Peace Left and Peace Given, 181.
Peace of God, 180.
Perfection, 179.
Personality of Christ, 123.
Personal Bible Study, 26.
Power of Christ upon Believer, 119.
Power for Service, 228.
Praise to God, 186.
Prayer, 197, 199.
Prayer Meetings, 198.

Precious Promises, 264.
Preparation for Lord's Supper, 264.
Preparation for Service, 234.
Priesthood, 98.
Priesthood of Christ, 88, 96.
Principles of Interpretation, 12.
Privileges of Believers, 264.
Prodigal Son, 276.
Prophetic Outlines, 113.
Promises, 69.
Propitiation, 50.
Protection, 265.
Punishment of Sin, 238.

R.

Ransom Money, 140.
Reconcilliation, 50–61.
Redemption, 172, 175.
Redemption and Purchase, 176.
Regeneration; 159.
Repentance, 164, 165.
Repentance and Forgiveness, 157.
Resurrecton, The, 99.
Rocks of the Bible, 273

S.

Sacrifices of the Old Testament, 45.
Salvation, 176.
Salvation Three-fold, 178.
Sanctification, 178, 179.
Satan, Personality of, 265.
Sealing, 178.
Sent, 266.
Seven Mysteries, 268.
Seven Times Seven, 266.
Seven Indispensable Things, 260.
Seven Things About the Flesh, 192.
Seven Witnesses, 275.
Shall Nots of John's Gospel, 275.
Shepherd, The Good, 77, 88.
Sin and Forgiveness, 166.
Sin Offering, The, 57.
Slippery Places, 272.
Soldiers, The Christian, 272.
Strong, How to Get, 256.
Study of the Bible, 17.
Substitution, 51.

T.

Tabernacle Types, 46.
Temperance, 272.
Thanksgiving, 185.

That Sweet Word, Come, 153.
The Blessed Hope, 101, 110.
The Blood of Christ, 95.
The Christian's Joy, 181.
The Christian's Walk, 182.
The Coming of the Lord, 115.
The Condition of the Heart, 237.
Three Enemies and How Conquered, 276.
The Flesh and Spirit, 187.
The Forgiveness of Sins, 165.
The Lord's Jewels, 212.
The Lord's Prayer, 199.
The Inquiry Room, 231.
The Joy of Christ, 119.
The Just, 170.
The New Nature, 191.
The New Birth, 161, 162.
The Old Man and the New, 191.
The Second Coming of Christ, 101.
The Soldier of the Cross, 276.
The Stone, 118.
The Transfiguration, 117.
Things to Hold Fast, 276.
The Unconverted, 236.
Trespass Offering, The, 56.
The Way, Truth and Life, 122.

U.

Unbelief, 70.

W.

Walking with God, 182.
Waiting on God, 276.
Watch, 193.
Watchfulness, 193.
Watchwords, 195.
Weights and Measures Act, 260.
What Christ is to Us, 121.
What God Saith, 60.
What I Was and What I Am. 219.
What is a Christian, 210.
What We Have in Christ, 118.
What the Lord Does for His People, 277.
What We Should Do for One Another, 217.
Why Written, 9.
Work of Holy Spirit, 126.
Workers Example, The, 226.
Worker's Model, 226.
Working for God, 223.

ERRATA.—Page 37, line 6, read "Chapters i to viii." Line 8, read "Chapters viii to xii." Line 9, read "Chapters xiii to xx." Page 191, Title, for "The New Natures," read "The Two Natures." Page 36, line 7, for "defects," read "effects."

www.ingramcontent.com/pod-product-compliance
Lightning Source LLC
Chambersburg PA
CBHW032056220426
43664CB00008B/1017